# Corporate Defense and the Value Preservation Imperative

## Bulletproof Your
## Corporate Defense Program

T0359119

# Internal Audit and IT Audit

Series Editor: Dan Swanson

# Corporate Defense and the Value Preservation Imperative

## Bulletproof Your Corporate Defense Program

### Sean Lyons

**CRC Press**
Taylor & Francis Group
Boca Raton  London  New York

CRC Press is an imprint of the
Taylor & Francis Group, an **informa** business

AN AUERBACH BOOK

First published 2017 by Auerbach Publisher

Published 2019 by CRC Press
Taylor & Francis Group
6000 Broken Sound Parkway NW, Suite 300
Boca Raton, FL 33487-2742

First issued in paperback 2020

© 2017 by Taylor & Francis Group, LLC
CRC Press is an imprint of Taylor & Francis Group, an Informa business

No claim to original U.S. Government works

ISBN 13: 978-1-4987-4228-3 (hbk)
ISBN 13: 978-0-367-56793-4 (pbk)

---

**Library of Congress Cataloging-in-Publication Data**

Names: Lyons, Sean (Sean Gilbert), 1966- author.
Title: Corporate defense and the value preservation imperative : bulletproof your corporate defense program / Sean Lyons.
Description: Boca Raton, FL : CRC Press, 2017. | Series: Internal audit and IT audit series | Includes bibliographical references and index.
Identifiers: LCCN 2016013712 | ISBN 9781498742283 (alk. paper)
Subjects: LCSH: Corporate image. | Corporate culture. | Corporations--Public relations. | Corporations--Investor relations. | Corporations--Valuation.
Classification: LCC HD59.2 .L96 2017 | DDC 659.2--dc23
LC record available at https://lccn.loc.gov/2016013712

---

Visit the Taylor & Francis Web site at
http://www.taylorandfrancis.com

and the CRC Press Web site at
http://www.crcpress.com

# Contents

# SECTION II    A Tactical Perspective

# SECTION III    *An Operational Perspective*

## SECTION IV   An Integrated Perspective

# Preface

## VALUE PRESERVATION AND CORPORATE DEFENSE

Stakeholders naturally expect successful organizations to deliver sustainable value over the long term. In the aftermath of the financial crisis and ongoing corporate scandals, many stakeholder groups are now questioning the adequacy of the measures currently being undertaken by organizations to safeguard and preserve stakeholder value. Not surprisingly it is common for postmortem investigations into the causes of corporate scandals to typically identify deficiencies and weaknesses in the corporate defense program of the organization(s) concerned. These deficiencies and weaknesses can begin with the nonexistence of a corporate defense program; however, individual corporate defense issues can also vary considerably. Typically, examples of these issues can include failures in corporate governance, poor risk management, compliance failures, unreliable intelligence, inadequate security, insufficient resilience, ineffective controls, and the failures by assurance providers. The existence of more than one of these issues in any given organization tends to exacerbate the initial problem and can eventually result in exponential collateral damage to stakeholder value. When these types of issues become systemic within an industry or business sector, it will very often result in some form of a broader crisis within that industry or sector, and, in some cases, this will spill over into the broader economy.

Logically, if deficiencies and weaknesses in corporate defense programs tend to result in corporate losses and failures, then improved corporate defense programs will help better safeguard against the occurrence of such scenarios. What is needed is effective corporate defense rather than corporate defense theater. This requires the design and implementation of more robust corporate defense programs that will help to not only safeguard stakeholder interests but also to optimize stakeholder value.

## ABOUT THIS BOOK

This is the first book on the market to finally address the umbrella term *corporate defense*, and to explain how an integrated corporate defense program can help address an organization's value preservation imperative. For the first time, the reader is provided with a complete picture of how corporate defense operates all the way from the boardroom to the frontlines. It provides comprehensive guidance on how to implement an integrated corporate defense program by addressing this challenge from strategic, tactical, and operational perspectives. This arrangement provides readers with a holistic view of corporate defense. It enables readers to fully understand and appreciate an organization's value preservation imperative and the resulting requirement to deliver a robust corporate defense program. It addresses the corporate defense requirement from various perspectives and helps readers to understand the critical interconnections and interdependencies that exist at strategic, tactical, and operational levels. It facilitates the reader in comprehending the importance of appropriately prioritizing corporate defense at a strategic level, while also educating the reader in the importance of managing corporate defense at a tactical level, and executing corporate defense activities at an operational level.

## THE PURPOSE OF THIS BOOK

With the above in mind, the purpose of this book is therefore threefold. First, the focus of this book is on recognizing that delivering long-term sustainably requires both a focus on value creation and a focus on value preservation. Second, this book is intended to help to clarify the ongoing obligation on organizations to take adequate measures to preserve stakeholder value and to be able to demonstrate that they are taking appropriate actions to safeguard stakeholder interests. Third, this book is designed to help provide a comprehensive roadmap or blueprint for readers on how best to deliver a world-class corporate defense program in order to successfully achieve the value preservation imperative. This includes preserving existing value and preventing unnecessary losses.

## THE BOOK LAYOUT

This book is divided into four sections and is designed to provide the reader with a comprehensive understanding of corporate defense from top to bottom. Certain sections may however be of a greater interest to readers with relevant experience in that particular area.

> *Section I—A Strategic Perspective*: The strategic section will initially be of utmost interest to readers who are on board level or in executive management positions. From a strategic perspective, this section addresses the requirement for an organization to consider a balance between both short-term value creation and long-term value preservation as part of its business strategy. At a strategic level, this requires a corporate defense strategy that is in alignment with the overall business strategy.
>
> *Section II—A Tactical Perspective*: The tactical section will initially be of utmost interest to readers who are in C-suite or middle-management positions. From a tactical perspective, it addresses the organization's need to design a comprehensive corporate defense framework that enables the alignment, integration, and management of the organization's corporate defense-related activities (i.e., governance, risk, compliance, intelligence, security, resilience, controls, and assurance). This section also considers the specific aspects of the individual corporate defense-related activities in some detail.
>
> *Section III—An Operational Perspective*: The operational section will initially be of utmost interest to the readers who are in business line management positions or to those who are directly involved in the execution of corporate defense-related activities. From an operational perspective, it addresses the management and execution of the corporate defense program and considers the main challenges facing the implementation of such a program. It also considers the requirement to continuously monitor and report on the status of its ongoing progress.
>
> *Section IV—An Integrated Perspective*: The integrated section should be of interest to all readers irrespective of their position, experience, or background. From an integrated perspective, it addresses the value proposition associated with an effective corporate defense program. This section helps to outline the business case for such an effective corporate defense program by addressing its potential positive contribution at strategic, tactical, and operational levels.

Although certain sections may stimulate individual readers more than others depending on their background knowledge and experience, it is ultimately envisaged that the book will help each reader to develop a more rounded and holistic view of corporate defense and will provide them with a comprehensive understanding of the workings of corporate defense at all levels.

**Sean Lyons**

## ACKNOWLEDGMENTS

I thank Dan Swanson for encouraging me to write this book in the first instance and for his support and insightful feedback on the original manuscript. I also acknowledge Igor Lamser of the RiskCenter, David Honour of the Business Continuity and Resilience Journal, and Matteo Tonello of the Conference Board for being supportive of my work on corporate defense at its early stages and for helping to bring it to the attention of a wider audience. I would also like to acknowledge the following organizations for their invitations to speak to their members on corporate defense at different stages over the past 10 years: the Asian Confederation of Institute of Internal Auditors (ACIIA), the Professional Risk Managers' International Association (PRMIA), the Society of Actuaries (SOA), the Business Continuity Institute (BCI), ASIS International, the Intangible Asset Finance Society (IAFS), and the MIT Club of Portugal.

I especially acknowledge the input of Ross Coakley in helping to develop a visual representation of the corporate defense management (CDM) framework, in creating many of the images for this book, and for modeling the YouTube video entitled "Corporate Defense Management (CDM): A Multi-dimensional Framework." On a personal level, Ross was my very first friend and has remained a lifelong friend over the past five decades. His incredible scientific mind and his generous and helpful nature mean that his presence and company is always a very rewarding experience. Ross's positive attitude, bravery, and courage in dealing with his recent motor neuron disease (MND) diagnosis are an inspiration to all who know him. Thank you for all your help and I wish you well my dear friend.

I thank my mother Eileen and all my family and friends for their encouragement and support on this journey. Last but by no means least, I would like to dedicate this book to my late father, Michael Lyons.

# Author

**Sean Lyons** is globally recognized as a corporate defense thought leader and strategist. He is acknowledged as the pioneer responsible for proposing the umbrella term *corporate defense* to represent an organization's collective program for self-defense, and also for being the first to propose the extended *five lines of defense* oversight model that is currently receiving increasing levels of regulatory attention. Sean has published internationally, and has spoken as a subject matter expert at lectures, seminars, and conferences in Europe, North America, and Asia. These speaking engagements include topics such as corporate governance, enterprise risk management (ERM), compliance, security, business continuity, internal controls, assurance, and governance, risk and compliance (GRC). His work on corporate defense has been cited in a number of books and a multitude of other publications on the above topics. As the architect of the cross-functional discipline of CDM, he is widely regarded as the foremost authority in this emerging field. With more than 20 years of experience in corporate defense activities, he is a firm advocate of the requirement for corporate defense to play a more prominent role in corporate strategy. In an effort to help achieve this objective, Sean has been an active contributor to public consultations in many of the above topics.

In 2015, Sean was a member of the Editorial Advisory Board of the inaugural publication of the *Journal of Enterprise Risk Management*, the first academic journal to focus solely on enterprise risk management. In 2013, he was the invited keynote speaker at the Asian Confederation of Institute of Internal Auditors (ACIIA) Chief Audit Executive Leadership Forum in Mumbai, for their two-day conference entitled, "Enterprise Defense Management: Internal Auditors to the Fore" (a theme that was based on his CDM framework). In 2011, he was an invited member of the taskforce of the International Corporate Governance Network (ICGN) on promoting the ICGN *Corporate Risk Oversight Guidelines*. In 2010, the conference board published his influential paper entitled, "Security as a Critical Component of Corporate Defense" that was sponsored by the U.S. Department of Homeland Security (DHS) as part of their ongoing project to assess security risk exposure and business preparedness in the private sector. Sean was shortlisted as a finalist in the GRC MVP 2009 Awards run by the U.S.-based GRC Group (SOX Institute), which was cochaired by Senator Paul Sarbanes and Congressman Michael Oxley. These awards recognized individual achievements and professional contributions in governance, risk management, and compliance, and honored professionals who demonstrated excellence in this field. For a number of years, Sean was also the resident contributor in the field of corporate defense for the RiskCenter, a New York financial risk management media company (then based on the Wall Street).

Selected publications of his work are presently available for download online at http://ssrn.com/author=904765.

# Section I

## A Strategic Perspective

# 1 Business Strategy and Value Preservation

> The superior man, when resting in safety, does not forget that danger may come.[*]
>
> **Confucius**

## 1.1 CORPORATE STRATEGY IN AN ERA SEEKING SUSTAINABLE SUCCESS

So far the twenty-first century has already seen a litany of corporate failures and financial scandals that have had a significant impact on the reputation of the corporate world, and perhaps more tellingly on broader society. The early part of this century highlighted the dangers of excessive optimism with the boom and bust of the dotcom bubble, and it also identified continued weaknesses and deficiencies in corporate behavior resulting in the demise of corporate giants such as WorldCom, Enron, and Arthur Anderson. At the time such events were heralded as valuable lessons and served as warnings for future generations. Less than a decade later, the dangers of excessive optimism were again highlighted, this time by the occurrence of what is now commonly referred to as the great financial crisis that affected the planet on a global scale and its impact is still being felt in many geographic regions (UNCTAD 2010).

These events have clearly shaped how society, in general, now views the corporate world and indeed how it views the working of capitalism and the capitalist system. As a consequence, stakeholders all over the world are now placing increased pressure on organizations to focus on their stakeholder obligations, with a view to delivering sustainable value to stakeholders in the long term. This has resulted in more and more organizations recognizing their obligations in this regard, and

---

[*] Per *The Best Confucius Quotes*, April 2015, James Alexander, Crombie Jardine Publishing Ltd, Bath, UK.

many are now duly focusing their attention on the concept of sustainability and the delivery of long-term stakeholder value.

There now appears to be an increasing recognition that any such long-term obligation can only be delivered once the concept of sustainability in its broadest sense has been successfully incorporated into how the organization does its business. This means that long-term sustainability must be embedded into the organization's vision and become a common feature of consideration at strategic, tactical, and operational levels within the organization itself. It means addressing it within the corporate strategy.

Traditionally, the concept of corporate strategy was considered to be concerned with helping to ensure that the organization was capable of providing sustainable above average industry performance, thereby allowing it to perpetually deliver superior returns and help create wealth for its shareholders. The global financial crisis however clearly exposed systemic weaknesses in the prevailing corporate strategy on an international scale. The subsequent fallout from this seismic event has resulted in the reputation of the corporate world being severely tarnished in the eyes of many stakeholders. The resulting negative impact has been felt not only by shareholders but also by management, staff, clients, business partners, suppliers, regulators, local communities, and indeed society in general, who all have eventually suffered as a consequence of flawed corporate strategies.

The corporate world now faces multiple pressures to reform the manner in which business is conducted and how individual organizations are managed. Stakeholders are now demanding higher standards of corporate citizenship in terms of integrity, ethics, and accountability. They are also demanding an improved strategic direction in order to provide them with greater protection and assurance going forward. Increasing pressure in the form of proxy advisor demands and pressure from stakeholder activist groups have prompted a rigorous search for an improved approach to corporate strategy, one that is aimed at helping organizations to foster an age of long-term sustainability.

### 1.1.1   CORPORATE STRATEGY: A HIGH-LEVEL PERSPECTIVE

Corporate strategy is typically concerned with the overall scope and direction of an organization's strategic activities. It is concerned with the *big picture*, the complete strategic scope of the enterprise, and how its various business activities operate together in order to help achieve particular strategic goals and objectives. Corporate strategy is commonly used to help develop a long-term plan for a company's success, the main purpose being to help ensure that the business can outlast the competition over the long term, regardless of the type of internal or external conditions that may present themselves. It is regarded as the roadmap to be followed by the organization and can also impact on its culture and be a driver of corporate behavior.

#### 1.1.1.1   The Strategic Agenda

Corporate strategy will be dictated by the organization's strategic agenda. Typically, the board of directors set an organization's strategic agenda after giving due consideration to the relevant organizational conditions. The strategic agenda should be set to address the organization's aspirations in relation to issues such as growth, performance, and change. The board, in association with the executive management, should provide the vision and leadership required to determine the appropriate path that they consider will best deliver on the organization's aspirations over time.

An organization's aspirations should represent a reflection of its culture and the expectations of the organization as a whole. Corporate culture is commonly referred to as *the smell of the place* or *how things are done around here*. An organization's culture reflects the common shared values and ideals that are embedded within the organization. Values include the beliefs that are shared throughout the organization. They drive culture and strongly influence the behaviors, actions, and decisions of the board, management, and staff. The organization's aspirations are reflected in its sense of *raison d'être*, its aim, its reason for being. Its aspirations reflect the purpose of the organization, its ambitions, and the planned journey ahead. This journey ahead is best understood and described in the organization's vision and mission statements.

### 1.1.1.2 Vision and Mission Statement

The requirement for a vision and mission statement is aptly described in the following words by the late Warren Bennis, an influential authority on leadership, when he said: "To choose a direction, an executive must have developed a mental image of the possible and desirable future state of the organization. This image, which we call a vision, may be as vague as a dream or as precise as a goal or a mission statement" (Hindle 2008).

*The vision*: Ideally the corporate vision should help to immediately visualize the *big picture* by providing a description of the organization's desired future state. It represents a broad, forward-thinking image that the organization should have for its purpose and intentions before it sets out to achieve its goals and objectives. Typically a corporate vision should be short and succinct, and represent an inspiring image of its mindset and aspirations. It should describe where the organization wishes to go and what it is trying to create and develop. Ultimately it should describe what it intends to achieve in the future and should represent a source of motivation for the workforce.

*Mission statement*: A mission statement should typically be more detailed than the corporate vision and represent a statement of rationale regarding the fundamental purpose of the organization. It should help guide the decisions and actions of the organization and it is therefore important that it is stated clearly so that it is understood by all, and can serve as a constant reminder to its stakeholders of the purpose of the organization's existence. It can be used as a reference point to evaluate the current activities or to help resolve trade-offs or disputes between different stakeholders. The mission statement should broadly outline the aims of the organization and what unique contribution the organization provides to its stakeholders. The lack of a clear mission statement diminishes the organization's ability to verify that it is progressing on its intended course.

The vision and mission statements help provide a background to the organization's strategic objectives for the future, without specifying the measures that need to be taken to help achieve the desired goals. In this way, they help to provide a context within which the organization's strategy can be formulated.

### 1.1.1.3 Managing Corporate Strategy

The clearer the organization's vision and mission statement, the easier it is for the strategic management of the organization to clearly oversee the setting and implementation of its corporate strategy. The corporate strategy represents a statement of strategic intent for the organization by way of strategic objectives. The strategy itself should be based on the principal findings of the strategic assessment conducted by the organization's strategic management. It should clearly outline the strategic choices that have been made and the rationale supporting these choices. Corporate strategy refers to the highest business strategy of the organization. It should address the mix of markets the organization intends to compete in and the way in which the strategic network should be coordinated and integrated.

The board of directors and the executive management team are expected to bring considerable professional experience and diversified business insight to their contribution on the organization's corporate strategy. Their sound judgment, specialist knowledge, and leadership qualities will be of particular benefit when deciding on which services, products, and markets to compete, and in which geographic regions to operate. Management of the corporate strategy process typically involves a number of basic phases.

*Strategy formulation*: The corporate strategy is in effect the path that has been chosen in order to arrive at the end vision. It therefore represents the roadmap by which the organization intends to complete its mission. A clear formulation of the corporate strategy should help the board and executive management to connect the ideas, assumptions, and decisions that are driving the organization's strategic agenda. It should help to provide a definite plan of action going forward to achieve this end. In determining corporate strategy, due consideration should be given to matching the organization's strategic activities to the organization's environment, its available resources (e.g., people, processes, and technology), and the extent of its capabilities. Due consideration should also be given to the values the organization wishes to espouse and the expectations to be set for its various stakeholders. The strategy formulation process should help set the organization's strategic objectives and help to identify and select an appropriate business model. It should clearly state the organization's strategic goals and outline the strategic measures and initiatives required to achieve these objectives. These strategic goals should be tangible and achievable in order to be helpful in guiding all of the organization's business activities going forward.

*Strategic planning*: Corporate strategy is typically implemented via a strategic plan; however, there are many examples of organizations whose failure was attributed to its inability to successfully execute its strategy in practice. Successful strategy implementation requires a carefully planned approach, a very high level of discipline, and involves the effective implementation of critical business activities in order to make it work. It is unreasonable to expect the attainment of strategic goals without the adherence to a carefully planned approach and the implementation of the required tasks. The strategic planning process should consider the corporate culture, the resources available to the organization, and the projected timescales required to achieve the stated strategic objectives. The strategic plan should guide and direct the subsequent tactical and operational planning exercises, in order to help ensure that these plans are in alignment with the organization's strategic objectives. The resulting plans should identify tasks that are specific and measureable and will noticeably contribute toward the achievement of the strategic objectives. Many strategies fail due to poor or inadequate planning, and the quality of the final plans is generally a reflection of the quality of the planning process.

*Strategy execution*: Once a clear strategic plan has been formulated, the executive management is then responsible for ensuring the effective and efficient implementation of that corporate plan. Execution of the corporate strategy via implementation of the strategic plan is critical to success and should never be underestimated as it is never guaranteed. Indeed, many strategic commentators suggest that execution is the key to competitive success, as making the plan work can be an even bigger challenge than formulating strategy, or creating a strategic plan. There are many factors that can hinder successful execution, including internal politics, resistance to change, and the occurrence of hazard events. Execution involves putting the plan into action by translating planned tasks and activities into the completion of verifiable actions. It involves the effective performance of the necessary tasks outlined in the plans and this requires considerable organization, and employing resource management and change management practices. This is perhaps best achieved using a top-down approach that incorporates the full chain of command so that the required action steps are performed at strategic, tactical, and operational levels. The executive management team needs to collaborate with the line management to help ensure timely, effective, and efficient performance of the required tasks.

*Strategy review*: Once a strategy is executed according to the plan, there is a reasonable expectation that it will prove to be successful; however, a successful outcome can never be assumed or taken for granted as there is *many a slip between the cup and lip*. The strategy needs to be a living breathing concept that needs to be continuously monitored and assessed. The success or failure of a corporate strategy cannot be adequately assessed without a process to review how well the strategy is performing in practice. This should involve comparing the actual results against the benchmark of intended milestones and outcomes. A strategy review process represents an evaluation of the corporate strategy and substrategies, and an appraisal of the execution of the strategic plan. The process of strategy review is equally as important as the processes of strategy formulation, strategy planning, and strategy execution as it evaluates the logic and rationale of the original strategy and appraises the effectiveness and efficiency of the implementation of this strategy. It enables the organization to focus on the appropriateness of the current strategy and to question the soundness of previous assumptions, which may no longer stand up to scrutiny due to changing circumstances and the dynamic environment of the twenty-first century. It allows an organization to re-evaluate the validity of the previous strategic choices and the extent to which ongoing performance has helped achieve the desired results. It also allows an organization to measure the variance that exists between the original desired results and the organization's actual results.

In certain cases, a strategy may prove to be successful from the very beginning, and the organization may be prepared to ratify it and endorse it going forward. In other cases, it may be determined that there is a considerable room for improvement and that the existing strategy needs to be modified or adjusted accordingly. The extent of this modification will need to be considered on the back of the results of the strategy review. In certain scenarios, the results may indicate that a serious corrective action is required. In such cases, the existing strategy may be rejected as a failure, and it may be determined that a new strategy is required and needs to be formulated.

## 1.1.2  SHORT-, MEDIUM-, AND LONG-TERM ORIENTATIONS

An old Chinese proverb states that *a journey of a thousand miles begins with a single step* and so it is with corporate strategy. When considering the topic of corporate strategy, it is important to bear in mind that although an organization's vision may reside in the distant future, the corporate strategy should present a roadmap that will guide the organization toward the achievement of this long-term vision. This involves not only clearly identifying the organization's long-term strategic objectives, but also setting achievable strategic goals in the medium and short terms. Ideally short- and medium-term goals should be aligned to long-term strategic objectives so that the achievement of short- and medium-term goals act as stepping stones to the accomplishment of the longer-term strategic objectives, and in the process, fulfilling the organization's mission statement and ultimately realizing its corporate vision.

### 1.1.2.1  Short- or Long-Term View: A Sprint or a Marathon?

Although the adoption of a long-term focus in order to realize the corporate vision is indeed a worthy ambition, in the modern world it has to be acknowledged that a short-term focus is necessary in order to ensure immediate day-to-day survival. Short-term gains are required in order to achieve a long-term growth; however, excessive short-terms gains can sometimes lead to the detriment of the long-term growth and stability. It must, however, be accepted that to be successful in the long term, an organization also needs to have a certain degree of short-term success.

In the wake of the great financial crisis, many economic commentators are of the opinion that the world's financial markets are somewhat addicted to the short-term view, which in turn leads to an unhealthy obsession with the achievement of monthly revenue targets and quarterly earnings. In this light, short-sighted remuneration and compensation structures also often intensify this obsession. In fact, there is a prevailing notion that during the build-up to the global financial crisis, the business world in general became preoccupied with the pursuit of short-term gains and lost sight of the long-term bigger picture. This resulted in the development of what are often referred to as *strategic blind spots* that were later to negatively impact on wider society, both economically and socially.

### 1.1.2.2  The Way Forward

What is required is a balanced view whereby the organization has a clear understanding that there is no disconnect between an organization's present and future, so that they are intrinsically connected and do not exist in a vacuum. First, however, there needs to be an acknowledgment that short-term gains can indeed result in a long-term gain; however, excessive short-term gains can in fact result in a long-term pain. It must also be acknowledged that, in some cases, short-term pain is required in order to achieve a long-term gain; however, excessive short-term pain can in and of itself also lead to a long-term pain.

This acknowledgment can help an organization appreciate that what is required is a blended approach, where one eye is focused on the medium to long-term horizon and the other eye is focused on addressing short-term issues that need to be handled in the present. Although sustainability is generally associated with the long term, its achievement requires focusing on the short-, medium-, and long-term horizons, and an appreciation that there are times when short-term instant gratification is required to be sacrificed in order to help ensure longer-term gratification.

## 1.2 CORPORATE STRATEGY AND VALUE CREATION

Although one organization's vision and mission statement may differ considerably from that of another, generally speaking, the vision and mission statements are concerned with contributing value to the organization's primary stakeholders. Corporate strategy is subsequently concerned with actually delivering this value to these stakeholders over the short, medium, and long terms.

### 1.2.1 THE VALUE CONCEPT IN CORPORATE STRATEGY

The concept of value is an inherent aspect of the twenty-first century capitalism. The promise of value is therefore an integral part of any corporate strategy, and addressing this value proposition is an essential element of corporate strategy. Developing a value proposition is based on a review and analysis of the benefits that can be delivered by the organization to its stakeholders, less the associated costs. The residual balance represents the value proposition to its stakeholders. In order to address the value proposition, it is important to clearly understand the concept of value.

It is said that value is like beauty, as it is *in the eye of the beholder*, and it is often equated with a sense of worth that in turn can act as an incentive to take a desired action. The notion of value is increasingly being measured in both quantitative and qualitative terms in order to reflect both its tangible and intangible nature. Value may have different meanings in different contexts and to different stakeholders in terms of intrinsic as well as extrinsic value. In the final analysis, an organization's understanding of stakeholder value is best determined through engagement with its stakeholders.

#### 1.2.1.1 Business Value as a Strategic Concept

In the realms of strategic management, the term business value is perhaps a somewhat informal concept, without any agreed consensus. The term is generally used to include various forms of value that can help determine the corporate health of an organization. More recently, the term business value is being expanded beyond the traditional, financial, and economic value to also encompass numerous other forms of perceived value. Although historically the notion of value was predominantly associated with monetary contribution, not all forms of value are directly measured in pure monetary terms and a broader notion is now emerging.

As well as value that may be quantified in financial terms, value may also manifest itself in what is described as utility value. Utility value represents the qualitative aspect of value, and it reflects value as perceived in the minds of stakeholders such as consumers and users through its capacity to meet individual human needs. Utility value is therefore recognizable by its demand and in business it is realized through its consumption.

Value in the broader sense is therefore increasingly based on its worth to the stakeholder and the stakeholder's assessment of its worth. Stakeholder value may not necessarily be assessed from a single source such as its monetary benefit, but may also be assessed in terms of what it can provide to the stakeholder and how it can help the stakeholder to achieve their various objectives. Value may therefore be measured in terms of physical, emotional, and intellectual stimulation. Consequently, the value of a product or service and the price of a product or service are not necessarily one and the same thing. In the famous words of Warren Buffett, "Price is what you pay. Value is what you get."

Business value therefore can embrace both tangible and intangible assets such as the organization's balance sheet value and the value associated with its business model and other intellectual capital. Indeed, the concept of business value can also embrace the theory that an organization's value can best be viewed as a network of relationships with stakeholders who are both internal and external to the organization itself. In this context, business value is concerned with the value embedded in these relationships over time.

### 1.2.1.2 Value Delivery and Realization

In business, value needs to be considered in terms of the value delivered to the various stakeholders of the organization. Value delivery refers to how the organization provides benefits to its stakeholders in the short, medium, and long terms. Organizations are concerned with questions such as *what benefits are we providing, how are we providing these benefits, and who are we providing these benefits to?* Follow-on questions may include *how can we improve on our delivery of value?* Value delivery can therefore be considered to be a source of potential competitive advantage.

Value realization on the other hand can refer to the organization's own return on its investment (financial or otherwise). Value realization involves putting in place the appropriate set of activities that are required to help ensure the expected delivery of value. The objective is to ensure that the full projected value is attained within the expected timescales. Hence the realization of value is a critical element of any successful corporate strategy. For example, once value realization starts to occur in the form of increases in cash flows, profitability, net worth, and so on, additional strategic options may begin to present themselves. Such options can include the opportunity of further growth through acquisitions, newfound interests from potential capital partners, additional strategic alliance opportunities, and enhanced exit strategies. Each organization must clearly establish its own value realization metrics in order to monitor the process effectively.

From a shareholder perspective, value may be realized through annual dividend income, or via an attractive sale or other liquidity event that provides the opportunity to transform equity into cash or other valuable liquid assets. This may involve taking-up options, or the sale of stock or other assets in the organization, whether in whole or in part, at a value that is determined by the market, which may be in excess of the shareholders' initial investment, and thereby yielding a healthy return on that investment. Other stakeholders may realize value in nonfinancial ways such as through corporate social responsibility and environmental initiatives. Over time, the organization's capacity to realize sustainable value for its stakeholders is a function of the organization's ability to create and preserve value on an ongoing basis.

### 1.2.2 THE VALUE CREATION FOCUS

What does the term value creation mean? The International Integrated Reporting Council (IIRC) describes the value creation process as follows: "Value is created through an organization's business model, which takes inputs from the capitals and transforms them through business activities and interactions to produce outputs and outcomes that, over the short, medium and long term, create or destroy value for the organization, its stakeholders, society and the environment" (IIRC 2013a). An organization can therefore create value over time through conducting a wide range of business activities that in turn produce outputs. These activities can occur within the many different environments in which the organization operates, both internal and external to the organization itself. This involves developing and managing relationships with its key stakeholders* with whom it interacts, and on whom it depends for its survival. Value can be maximized by fulfilling the needs of these key stakeholders while also considering the interests of society in general and the impact on the environment. The extent to which these needs and interests are addressed will determine the type of value that is created.

---

* The nature of the stakeholder relationship is addressed in Chapter 3, Section 3.3.3.

#### 1.2.2.1   The Business Model

An organization's business model describes how the organization intends to go about creating value for its stakeholders. The business model lies at the core of an organization, and its long-term success will be determined by the resilience of its business model over time. An organization's chosen business model represents its business approach and the fundamentals of its business processes and key business activities. It reflects its system of inputs and outputs that in turn lead to outcomes that create value and help the organization to achieve its goals and objectives, and help to fulfill its mission statement in the longer term.

Organizations that operate in a number of different market segments may employ more than one business model; however, due consideration needs to be applied to appreciating the level of interconnectivity that exists between these business models and their business activities. The business model typically includes addressing a number of issues.

*Key business activities*: The business model should clearly identify and outline the key business activities that the organization intends to operate. Generally an organization's key business activities involve the processes by which the organization intends to convert its inputs to outputs. These outputs generally take the form of either products or services that can provide value to the organization's key stakeholders. When considering its business model, the organization should clarify how it intends to differentiate itself in the marketplace in terms of such issues as its unique selling point (USP) (e.g., product differentiation, market segmentation, supply chain, and distribution channels) to be used to deliver its products or services to its stakeholders. It should focus on how the organization intends to convey its message to its key stakeholders and how it intends to communicate with them on an ongoing basis.

*The inputs*: The essence of the business model is the conversion of inputs into outputs in order to create value. The business model should clearly identify and outline the key inputs required by the organization, which when applied through the business process will convert into value-added outputs. These key inputs represent those ingredients that the organization depends on in order to deliver value. The performance of its business activities provides the organization with its source of differentiation by converting its key inputs from raw materials into its finished end product. Key inputs are derived from various types of capital whereby business activities draw on many types of capital in one form or another as inputs into the value creation process. The key inputs and how they relate to the various capitals from which they are derived represent a critical aspect of the organization's business model. How the corporate strategy links key inputs to capitals, opportunities, risk, and financial performance is critical to the success of the strategy.

*The capitals*: The business model should clearly identify and outline the types of capitals the organization depends on for its success. Organizations typically depend on different types of capital whether they are considered tangible or intangible capitals. There is no currently universal agreement on the different types of capitals, and they may be classified in different ways by different organizations. One example is the six types of capitals identified by the IIRC as follows: *financial capital, manufactured capital, intellectual capital, human capital, social and relationship capital, and natural capital* (IIRC 2013b). These capitals represent stores of values in various forms that become inputs into the organization's business model. Such capitals can be used to release value in the form of producing outputs and outcomes when they interact and are combined, transformed, and leveraged through an organization's business process. Value is therefore created by the resulting increase, decrease, or transformation of the capitals.

The overall stock of the value stores, which is provided by the capitals, is not fixed over time, but rather they are in a continuous state of flux as they are increased, decreased, or transformed through the activities and outputs of the organization. Consequently such interactions can in fact enhance, modify, or otherwise affect the overall capital stock. Although in theory the organization's aim is to create value in its capitals, in practice this may also involve the depletion or destruction of the value stored in some capitals while at the same time increasing it in others. In general, this can result in an overall net increase or decrease in the overall stock of the capitals.

Ultimately whether the net effect is perceived as either an increase or decrease may well depend on the perspective of the stakeholder concerned. In many instances, returns in financial capital may be dependent on interrelationships among other forms of capital in which stakeholders have different interests, for example, society and the environment. Also, not all of the capitals required by the organization are necessarily owned by that organization. Certain capitals may be the property of the organization, whereas certain others may be owned, belong to, or be an entitlement of various other stakeholder groups who in turn share in both the value created and their associated costs.

As noted earlier, there are different types of capital that organizations typically depend on for their success; however, not all organizations are equally dependent on the same capitals; therefore, different capitals will have different relevance to different organizations. Although it is likely that most organizations will interact with all of the capitals mentioned earlier, to a certain degree, some of these interactions may be considered immaterial in terms of the organization's business model.

Whether certain capitals are increasing or decreasing can affect the availability, quality, and affordability of those capitals. This is a particular issue of concern for capitals of which there is a limited supply, and capitals that are not possible to be renewed. It is important to bear in mind that the availability and supply of certain capitals can be seriously impacted by the extent to which organizations, both collectively and individually, interact with these capitals. Ultimately, such issues can in turn have a serious impact on the long-term viability of an organization's business model.

*Innovation*: The business model should clearly identify and outline the organization's USP over that of its competition. An organization's long-term success or failure may well be determined by how the organization addresses the age-old requirement to be innovative. The business model should clearly address the organization's attitude to innovation and its approach to responding to change. The flexibility of its strategy, the agility of the business model, and the organization's capacity and capability in adapting to change can have a profound impact on the organization's long-term viability. This may be of particular relevance when faced with sourcing inputs and capitals, and adapting business activities. Logically, the key to a long-term success lies in the extent to which the organization can foster an innovative mindset throughout the enterprise so that it becomes embedded in the corporate culture and is continually present in day-to-day activities.

### 1.2.2.2  The Value Creation Process

The concept of value creation lies at the very heart of corporate strategy and the business model. The value creation process itself involves initially taking the business inputs and putting them through the business model in order to eventually produce desired benefits in the form of business outputs and outcomes at the other end of the process. This process can involve applying the organization's business processes in order to combine or transform the organization's capitals, thus producing both positive and negative effects on these capitals with the intended result of the creation of value for the organization and its key stakeholders. The nature of those effects will determine the extent of the value created and the outcomes for the different stakeholder groups.

Generally speaking, value can be created over short-, medium-, and long-term time horizons, and it can be created through the use of different capitals and created for different stakeholder groups. Creating value will often involve a trade-off between the effect on different capitals, some positive and some negative. Such a trade-off should consider the effects both individually and collectively. Assessing the nature of the value created involves considering the nature of the interdependences that exist between the capitals and their relationships with the various stakeholder groups. It is doubtful that long-term sustainable value can be created by solely focusing on increasing one individual capital at the expense of all of the other capitals. The value creation process is typically concerned with a number of issues.

*Value drivers*: The value creation process is concerned with determining the organization's value drivers. Typically it is the organization's value drivers that distinguish it from its competitors as they have a critical role to play in the organization's ability to create value over the short, medium, and long terms. Value drivers can vary by types of business; they can be generic, industry specific, or organizational specific and their range can vary from one organization to another. They reflect certain key elements, characteristics, or attributes that make an organization attractive to its stakeholders. Such elements consist of those unique activities, capabilities, and core competencies that enable an organization to provide a perceived competitive advantage in the perception of its stakeholders.

Value drivers may be tangible or intangible as both can contribute to the creation of value by an organization. They may reflect tangible assets owned by the organization or intangible assets that help to increase the overall desirability of the organization in the eyes of its stakeholders. In the twenty-first century, intangible assets are now increasingly being perceived as primary value drivers. Value drivers reflect those factors that are identified as having the most significant impact on the future value of the organization and those factors that can be most effectively managed and controlled. Therefore identifying and managing value drivers can help an organization to focus its attention on the key activities that are most likely to help in achieving its short-, medium-, and long-term goals and objectives.

*Outputs and outcomes*: The value creation process is concerned with determining the organization's required outputs and preferred outcomes. From a value creation perspective, there is a subtle but important distinction between an *output* and an *outcome*. The organization's business model represents a series of processes and activities that convert inputs to outputs. As outputs tend to be process driven, they therefore refer to planned deliverables whereby the end product typically tends to be tangible in nature and therefore can be accurately anticipated in advance, and precisely and objectively measured in quantitative terms on completion.

Outcomes, on the other hand, refer to the impact that the outputs may have on the stakeholders, both internal and external. Stakeholder reaction is typically reflected by its impact on the organization's capitals. Outcomes therefore relate to the ultimate payoff, the value added to the stakeholder as a direct or indirect result of the outputs. Therefore outputs have an impact on outcomes, but it is important to appreciate that they are not the same thing. As outcomes tend to be reaction driven, they are by their very nature less predictable than outputs and hence more difficult to anticipate as they can take place over multiple time frames.

Although an outcome may be less predictable, it is still measureable in terms of its impact (financial and nonfinancial) on the organization's capitals. This measurement may be more subjective and qualitative when dealing with nonfinancial capitals. Although outcomes can result in the anticipated, planned, or intended consequence of an output, it must also be understood that it can also result in an unanticipated, unplanned, or unintended consequence. As an outcome represents the occurrence of a change in circumstance for a stakeholder, which is a result of targeted outputs, it is important to understand that such a change can have either positive or negative consequences, which means that an outcome can present either a potential upside or a potential downside for the stakeholder and in turn the organization itself.

Although the traditional corporate strategy and the setting of strategic objectives have been primarily concerned with focusing the potential upside and intended positive outcomes, an emerging contemporary view focuses on an appreciation that corporate strategy must also include a sufficient focus on the potential downside and unintended negative outcomes. A balanced corporate strategy should therefore incorporate a degree of both value creation and value preservation.

## 1.3 DEFENSE OF THE REALM: THE VALUE PRESERVATION IMPERATIVE

In business as in many other aspects of life, the reality is that the nature of uncertainty means that an organization's activities can either have a positive or a negative impact on the value it delivers to its stakeholders. Over a prolonged period of time, this value experience may include numerous fluctuations as a result of both positive impacts and negative impacts. Successful organizations however depend on their ability to both create and sustain value over the short, medium, and long terms. Over the long term, value is compounded by both creating and preserving value.

Once an organization has succeeded in creating value, it then faces the dual challenge of continuing to create value on an ongoing basis while simultaneously ensuring that it can also preserve the value that is created. Therefore, a focus on value creation alone is not considered to be sufficient, it must be accompanied by a focus on value preservation. In any event, successful organizations learn to continuously monitor the dynamics between value creation and value preservation. Unfortunately in many unsuccessful organizations, although value creation quite rightly received due consideration in corporate strategy, there is far less evidence to suggest that value preservation received a similar consideration. In general, it would appear that the requirement to preserve value is much less appreciated and therefore is often neglected.

### 1.3.1 THE CONCEPT OF VALUE PRESERVATION

What precisely is meant by the concept of value preservation? If on the one hand value creation is primarily concerned with delivering a potential upside, then on the other hand value preservation is primarily concerned with protecting against a potential downside. Indeed, there are some who would argue that *a dollar of value preserved is indeed a dollar of value created*. Logically organizations that exhibit an ability to preserve the value they have created over an extended period of time tend to be successful, whereas organizations that are unable to preserve their value tend to fall by the wayside. An inability to successfully preserve value will inevitably result in a decline in, or destruction of, value. The value preservation concept therefore lies at the heart of lasting sustainability.

The value preservation imperative represents an organization's obligation to its stakeholders to take adequate steps to preserve value. It represents the measures (formal or otherwise) taken by an organization to defend itself and the interests of its stakeholders from a multitude of potential hazards (i.e., risks, threats, and vulnerabilities), the occurrence of which could be detrimental to the achievement of the organization's objectives. To successfully deliver on this obligation, an organization requires an appropriate program for self-defense.

#### 1.3.1.1   The Threat of Value Reduction and Destruction

In business, organizations are constantly faced with the threat of value reduction, and often it is the extent of any value reduction that can determine the organization's ultimate fate. The existence of such a threat is simply the reality of doing business. The root cause of such threats can vary considerably, as can their timing and scale. Ultimately there are an unlimited number of events or series of events that can occur over the short, medium, and long term, which can result in the reduction or destruction of stakeholder value. Protecting and defending against the loss of stakeholder value is the kernel of the value preservation imperative. This includes an obligation to take adequate steps to anticipate, prevent, detect, and react to hazard events in order to avoid, mitigate, and manage any potential exposure in a timely manner. Although the extent to which an organization was expected to fulfill this obligation may once have been perceived as somewhat optional, this is no longer the case as it is now considered a business imperative whereby stakeholders expect and demand increasingly higher levels of due diligence in this regard.

#### 1.3.1.2   Value Erosion, Depletion, and Decline

Organizations need to be wary that value can decline in a number of ways, ranging from its sudden depletion as a result of an unexpected liability, its gradual erosion over time due to an outdated or inflexible business model, or its complete destruction due to flawed strategic assumptions. Without taking adequate steps to help preserve value, stakeholders of the organization may find their value being eroded and the organization may find its value declining year on year. Such a decline in value can be witnessed in many different ways, all of which can result in a negative impact for stakeholders either directly or indirectly. For example, it can be witnessed in decreasing market shares, decreasing revenues, increasing costs, decreasing assets, increasing liabilities, lower profits, higher losses, lower share prices, and lower market capitalization.

### 1.3.2   The Corporate Defense Necessity[*]

In order to help preserve value, organizations are now expected to take steps to protect stakeholder value, and the protection of stakeholder value is synonymous with corporate defense-related practices such as corporate governance, risk management, and compliance activities. Such practices are considered necessary to help defend stakeholder value against the vagaries of any potential threats that could result in value reduction or destruction. In the eyes of an increasing number of stakeholders, once value has been created, it then needs to be protected and defended.

The cost associated with defending stakeholder value was traditionally considered to be part of the inherent costs of doing business; however, more enlightened organizations are no longer regarding this as a cost but rather as an investment in the organization's own long-term sustainability. This suggests that corporate defense-related practices can also represent an opportunity for the organization to create a competitive advantage in the form of security over stakeholder value. It is anticipated by some that such stakeholder value security will in time attract a premium that will be factored into future stakeholder value calculations.

#### 1.3.2.1   Defending and Safeguarding Stakeholder Interests

The calculation of stakeholder value involves an assessment of the extent to which stakeholder value is being optimized, and this can include the extent to which stakeholder interests are being

---

[*] Failure by an organization to recognize this necessity will be seen by many stakeholders as representing a strategic "Red Flag".

safeguarded. In other words, there is an expectation that organizations are not only working toward adding to, or increasing stakeholder value, but also taking measures to protect the existing stakeholder value from decline. For example, shareholders expect the organization to take measures to help protect the organization's share price and its market capitalization.

In the twenty-first century, stakeholders are now demanding at least reasonable levels of due diligence in this regard and are increasingly prepared to hold the organization to account should they be considered negligent in their efforts. At a minimum, there is now an expectation that the organization will take all appropriate measures to ensure that it has adequate corporate defense initiatives in place. Organizations are expected to at least be able to provide reasonable comfort that stakeholder value will not be diminished.

### 1.3.2.2   The Necessity for Improved Corporate Defense Measures

In the build-up to the financial crisis, there were clear signs that stakeholder interests were not being adequately defended (Lyons 2006a), and the subsequent fallout from the related global economic recession has highlighted common weaknesses and deficiencies in relation to organizations' corporate defense activities. Ongoing events continually expose how so many organizations in various business sectors all over the world have failed to adequately defend the interests of their multiple stakeholders. This has resulted in the reputation of the corporate sector being severely tarnished in the eyes of many stakeholders.

Numerous national and international reviews have clearly highlighted the general failure to fully appreciate and consider the potential threat to stakeholder value as a core issue. Many of these reviews identified weaknesses and deficiencies in corporate defense-related activities as having a significant contribution to the occurrence of this economic downturn and have particularly identified areas such as failures in corporate governance and the management of risk and compliance as major contributory factors: "We conclude that dramatic failures of corporate governance and risk management at many systematically important financial institutions were a key cause of this crisis" (FCIC 2011). As a result, numerous stakeholder groups are now demanding improvements in the corporate defense-related measures employed by their organizations to defend their interests. These improvements need to start at a strategic level, beginning with looking at how the value preservation imperative is addressed when setting the corporate strategy.

### 1.3.3   Reimagining Corporate Strategy

Historically, when setting strategy, business organizations have tended to treat the critical issues of value creation and value preservation as separate issues. In retrospect, given the nature of their symbiotic relationship, this has proven to be both an artificial and dangerous segregation. Although, in general, corporate strategy does tend to formally address the issue of how the organization intends to create its value, the equally important issue of how the organization intends to preserve its value generally does not form part of corporate strategy. A similar observation very often applies to the foundations of the organization's business model. The result has been a clear distinction between the overall corporate strategy and a corporate defense substrategy, as generally speaking the strategic echelons of the organization tend to consider the issue of corporate defense as somewhat peripheral to corporate strategy and the business model. Consequently the board and executive management tend to approach corporate defense-related matters with extreme caution because they do not understand how corporate defense fits with corporate strategy. In fact, corporate defense matters can tend to become relegated so far down the strategic priority list that their relevance becomes difficult to establish. In extreme situations, those involved in corporate defense activities can feel as if they are regarded as almost like second-class citizens within the organization. In such circumstances, corporate defense practices can become disengaged from core business activities, and can very often exist in silo-type environments, whereby they operate as an afterthought to core business activities. This type of attitude simply cannot be allowed to continue;

things have to change, and going forward the corporate defense strategy needs to be considered as an essential element of the overall corporate strategy.

### 1.3.3.1   Re-Examine the Way We Do Business

In many organizations, what is now required is a fundamental re-examination of how their business is conducted. This will involve a serious reframing of how they currently view the creation and preservation of value in the context of their corporate strategy and business model. They will need to redefine not only how their corporate strategy but also how the foundations of their business model address the corporate defense conundrum. Their business fundamentals need to formally incorporate the requirement for an adequate corporate defense strategy in order to help ensure value preservation and facilitate the build-up of business value over time.

Logically it is much more difficult to build-up significant business value over time if while creating new value, existing value is being depleted or destroyed at the same time. It is important that going forward when an organization addresses the challenge of defending stakeholder value within its corporate strategy and that this is clearly stated in terms of strategic objectives and clearly identified as a strategic activity within its business model. Indeed, prudence would suggest that a sustainable corporate strategy and business model should balance the organization's desire to increase its value over time, with the stakeholder desire to defend the value that has already been realized. Long-term sustainable success requires the two to go hand-in-hand, a concept that needs to be embedded throughout the organization, and across all of its business activities. An appreciation of how an organization needs to address defending its stakeholder value has far reaching implications at strategic, tactical, and operational levels and presents interesting challenges for the organization itself.

### 1.3.3.2   Corporate Defense Is No Longer Considered Optional

To establish a sustainable strategy and business model, an organization needs to actively and systematically embed corporate defense-related practices at the strategic, tactical, and operational levels. Embedding the corporate defense concept into an organization's DNA requires a basic acknowledgment from the very top to the very bottom of the organization that good corporate defense represents a business imperative, rather than some sort of prerogative or optional add-on. Redefining strategy and the business model to incorporate the appropriate mix between the focus on increasing value and defending value will have significant implications for the organization and all of its stakeholders.

## 1.4   STRIKING A BALANCE BETWEEN OFFENSE AND DEFENSE

Military to civilian transition.

An old sporting aphorism states that *offense wins games, defense wins championships*. In business speak, offense refers to the focus on bringing the dollar in through the front door, whereas defense refers to the focus on preventing the dollar from leaving through the back door (Lyons 2014). In other words, in the corporate world, offensive activities are associated with the organization's focus on upside rewards, whereas defensive activities are associated with the organization's focus on the prevention of downside loss. What is essential is finding the correct balance between taking larger risks and reaping larger rewards. If organizations in the twenty-first century are to deliver long-term sustainable value, they must learn to achieve a healthy balance between their focus on offense and their focus on defense. Getting this balance right can help provide better opportunities for delivering long-term sustainable value.

A commonly held view of economic theory is that the Western capitalist model is primarily driven by the motivating factors of greed and fear. The former is the motivation to extend ourselves in search of even greater rewards, whereas the latter is the motivation to protect what has already been achieved lest it should be taken from us. Progress no doubt requires both, whereas prudence and common sense would suggest that long-term sustainability requires a healthy blending of the two.

Unfortunately the search for balance, or the middle path, is not a new concept and is one that goes back thousands of years. In the Western philosophy, especially that of the Greek philosopher Aristotle, the *golden mean* represented the desirable middle between two extremes, one of excess, the other of deficiency. Another famous Greek philosopher Socrates taught that man "must know how to choose the mean and avoid the extremes on either side, as far as possible." The search for balance continues to this day.

### 1.4.1 THE TAO OF CORPORATE DEFENSE

In the Eastern philosophy, the Taoist tradition places great emphasis on the search for harmony between opposing extremes or forces. Taoism refers to the concept of the *yin* and *yang,* which is used to describe how seemingly opposing forces are inherently interconnected and interdependent in the natural world. Each of these forces is present within the other and in turn gives rise to the other. There are many examples of natural dualities such as dark and light, night and day, female and male, wet and dry, and action and inaction that are cast as yin and yang in the Taoist thought. In the corporate context, perhaps the duality of offense and defense can best be understood and appreciated when viewed in this context.

#### 1.4.1.1 Offense and Defense Viewed as Yin and Yang

Viewing offense and defense in terms of the Taoist duality can help provide a higher level of insight into this complex relationship. Offense (yin) and defense (yang) are considered to be antagonistic yet complementary principles that fit together seamlessly. They represent opposites that are bound together and intertwined, and are capable of working together in a perfect harmony. Offense and defense are considered to be the two halves within a greater whole and together they complete a unifying circle. Their relationship is not static as every aspect of business has both offense and defense aspects, and these continuously interact and never exist in a stationary state as the balance ebbs and flows. It is therefore impossible to talk about offense or defense without a reference to the opposite, as offense and defense are rooted together and one cannot survive without the other. It is therefore important that they are not separated or addressed in isolation.

In essence, offense and defense actually transform each another, as each contains a portion of the other within it. Offense contains within it the potential for defense, and defense contains within it the potential for offense. They are finely balanced in a dynamic equilibrium, whereby a deficiency in one can unbalance their relationship, and if one disappears the other is very likely to follow. In short, when either offensive or defensive activities become the subordinate, the whole is likely to suffer eventually.

Unfortunately, in the business world, this is rarely immediately apparent because offense elements are clear and obvious, whereas defense elements are more hidden and subtle. Therefore extremes in offense are far more regular than extremes in defense, although this can also occur. Ultimately, however, extremes in either offense or defense can result in the development of an organization that is putting its long-term sustainability in jeopardy.

### 1.4.2 The Current Strategic Imbalance

Unfortunately, the financial crisis and indeed more recent corporate scandals continue to clearly highlight the imbalance that currently exists between offense and defense in the corporate mind-set. Recent events indicate that short-termism tends to focus disproportionately on the former, often neglecting the latter. Such a mind-set has resulted in excessive risk taking in search of short-term rewards at the expense of longer-term sustainability.

There were many reasons for the financial crisis, and the following strategic, tactical, and operational issues have strongly contributed to the unhealthy imbalance referred to earlier (Lyons 2012a):

- An overly narrow focus on pure financial metrics while ignoring important nonfinancial issues
- A focus on short-term interests at the expense of broader, long-term stakeholder interests
- The lack of board-level appreciation of the necessity of having a formal, systematic *corporate defense program* in place within their organization to help ensure that their stakeholder interests are adequately safeguarded
- The lack of a seat at the C-suite table for a *defense champion* to challenge, scrutinize, and add a degree of balance to the formulation of corporate strategy and policies
- The resulting lack of transparency and responsibility for corporate defense where accountability is fragmented and diluted at the executive management level
- The lack of coherent coordination of defense-related activities at a functional level, leading to the development of silo-type structures that are not in alignment with one another but rather operate in isolation, resulting in both ineffectiveness and inefficiency

Although a great deal of work has been undertaken since the financial crisis to improve corporate behavior, there is sufficient evidence available to suggest that many of these issues still need to be addressed as weaknesses and deficiencies in corporate defense activities remain commonplace. Examples include the rogue trader Jerome Kerviel at Societe Generale, the cyber theft at SONY, the health and safety issues in the clothing industry in Bangladesh, and more recently the Volkswagen emissions scandal, to name but a few. This will require a notable correction to the current imbalance in order to create a natural harmony between offense and defense.

#### 1.4.2.1 Achieving a Healthy Balance

The challenge facing organizations is wide ranging; however, restoring a natural equilibrium between offense and defense in the corporate mind-set will go a long way toward improving the situation going forward. This requires joined-up thinking and perhaps can best be achieved by a degree of tweaking and joining of the existing dots, rather than by a complete overhaul of the entire system.

Correction of this current imbalance requires a broader stakeholder (shareholders, clients, staff, business partners, local communities, and society) focus and a more holistic view of how best to safeguard these stakeholder interests in the long term. Ensuring that there is a sufficient focus on long-term sustainability (i.e., survival) will require a subtle shift in corporate consciousness. Such a shift will necessitate a change of attitude in relation to the fundamentals of corporate health and a clear appreciation of corporate health requirements in the short, medium, and long terms. This will involve further educating the corporate world so that defensive behavior can be seen in a positive light and as being necessary for the achievement of long-term sustainability, rather than being seen as a necessary evil. Corporate defense is not about business prevention; it is about doing the right business in the right way.

In far too many organizations there is a defense deficit. Corporate defense is more likely to be implied in corporate strategy rather than being considered a core element of business strategy, and more often than not there is an absence of any formal corporate defense strategy. Corporate strategy must therefore incorporate a balance between offense and defense in order to arrive at a natural equilibrium. This will require a subtle blending of these antagonistic yet complementary principles that are inherently intertwined and mutually interdependent within a dynamic system. In essence, the principles of offense and defense represent two sides of the same coin, and therefore cannot and should not be addressed in isolation from one another.

# 2 The Corporate Defense Landscape

In the business world, the rearview mirror is always clearer than the windshield.[*]

**Warren Buffett**

## 2.1 SETTING THE SCENE FOR CORPORATE DEFENSE

Chapter 1 outlined the requirement for organizations to ensure that the dual imperatives of value creation and value preservation are adequately addressed within corporate strategy and the business model. It addressed how an organization needs to consider its value creation and value preservation obligations in terms of offense and defense, and how these two imperatives are best addressed in an integrated manner rather than in isolation, in order to ensure that a healthy balance is achieved between offense and defense. The concept of the value preservation imperative was identified as an organization's obligation to its stakeholders to defend the stakeholder value and to ensure that appropriate measures are taken to help defend against the value reduction and destruction. Addressing the value preservation imperative involves ensuring that the organization has adequate and robust corporate defense measures put in place at strategic, tactical, and operational levels.

### 2.1.1 A HIGH-LEVEL OVERVIEW

When an organization is initially considering the value preservation imperative and its corporate defense requirements, it is important that it should begin with a high-level overview of the organization's situation and circumstances. This should involve due consideration of its circumstances

---

[*] Per *The Tao of Warren Buffett*, 2006, Mary Buffet and David Clarke, SCRIBNER, New York, NY.

viewed from a macroperspective in terms of general issues external to the organization itself, and from a microperspective in terms of the specific internal issues within the organization.

### 2.1.1.1  Unique Circumstances

Every organization is unique and therefore each organization will find itself in a unique situation facing its own unique set of circumstances and its own unique conditions. Because of this, each organization must be aware that although the general principles may be the same, it will in all likelihood have slightly different requirements to other similar organizations. Each organization will face its own unique challenges, and these are likely to be influenced by its own unique corporate culture, its precise geographic location, the business sector in which it operates, and the internal operations of its business units, divisions, departments, and functions. This is further reinforced by the uniqueness of the organization's people, processes, and systems. Although each organization's own challenges may be somewhat unique, there are certain common challenges that are faced by many organizations and that can only be successfully addressed by a common approach.

### 2.1.1.2  The Restoration of Stakeholder Trust

One common challenge facing many organizations is the challenge of restoring stakeholder trust. In the aftermath of the financial crisis, anecdotal evidence and numerous surveys suggest that trust in business has declined, yet trust is vital to a business activity (ACCA 2014). This decline in trust by stakeholders has been stimulated by an increasing perception of a lack of ethical behavior in business, which is accompanied by a perceived lack of accountability for this behavior. Corporate failures at multiple stakeholder levels contributed to the financial crisis, whereas subsequent economic austerity measures have disproportionately impacted on the lives of the ordinary people. This chain of events has certainly damaged stakeholder trust and resulted in stakeholder trust in the entire capitalist system now being at an all time low. Such dissatisfaction has resulted in increased support for the emerging concepts such as *corporate social responsibility*, *inclusive capitalism*, and the *shared value* concept.

Many regard these corporate failures as an exposure of either shocking incompetence or gross negligence on behalf of many stakeholder groups (i.e., boards, external auditors, rating agencies, regulators, etc.). It has highlighted how these groups clearly failed to exercise due to diligence in the performance of their duties. In many instances, there is a perception that these stakeholder groups do not appear to have been held to account for their failures. In fact, there is a perception that they have actually been rewarded for the actions. Indeed, in many cases the general public has been asked to trust these same stakeholder groups to lead them out of the mess that they themselves helped to create. Not surprisingly, many have expressed doubts that those who have already been proven to have failed them in the past should now be trusted to do a competent job in the future.

A similar decline is evident in the general public's trust in the structure of our society in general. A seemingly increasing number of commentators and conspiracy theorists suggest that there was in fact an element of collusion between those at the very top of the food chain (i.e., captains of industry, bankers, lawyers, academics, political leaders, etc.).* The perceived lack of being held to account among the elite has created a perception of impunity, and highlights the perceived double standards in law enforcement between the white- and blue-collar crimes. The resulting sense of injustice among the general public helped give birth to the *Occupy* campaign amid the growing sense of inequity between the elite 1% and the remaining 99% of the population. This increasing lack of trust has heightened social tensions and increased the feeling of discrimination among many minority groups. Going forward, both business and society need to urgently address this sense of betrayal

---

* U.S. Democratic senator from Massachusetts, Elizabeth Warren, has famously championed the theme that "The game is rigged!" and that it favors those who wield power in money and politics. She raised this topic in a prime-time speech to the Democratic National Convention in September 2012 and addressed it in her book entitled *A Fighting Chance* published by Metropolitan Books in 2014. This is a theme which US Democratic Presidential candidate Bernie Sanders has echoed in his campaign.

of trust. In order to help rebuild an atmosphere of mutual trust between the relevant stakeholder groups, what is needed is to start by restoring a sense of justice and fairness.* Although this is no doubt a wider macrochallenge, every organization has an important role to play in maintaining trust among its own stakeholder groups.

## 2.2 THE EVOLVING CORPORATE LANDSCAPE OF THE TWENTY-FIRST CENTURY

Over the past century, the unprecedented changes that have occurred in the global landscape are also reflected in the ever-changing corporate landscape. During this time, the corporate environment has undergone a considerable change, and this has certainly affected the manner in which an organization conducts its business. Commercial evolution and progression has meant that the corporate environment has been dramatically transformed, and this transformation is continuing at an ever increasing rate. Suffice it to say that the corporate environment of the twenty-first century bears little resemblance to the environment in which previous generations conducted their business, and it is reasonable to expect that the corporate environment will continue to evolve. Perhaps the only uncertainty remaining is the manner of this evolution and the subsequent impact it will have on the corporate world.

### 2.2.1 Extraordinary Times and Extraordinary Challenges

The twenty-first century is already proving to be one of the most interesting periods in the development of human civilization. Although the twentieth century may have represented a unique period in our history, the twenty-first century has already seen such a progress that it is next to impossible to predict what the world will look like by the end of this century. It is therefore not an exaggeration to state that we are currently living in extraordinary times as we are witness to extraordinary changes occurring both globally and locally. These extraordinary changes in turn mean that we are also facing extraordinary challenges, and although certain challenges remain constant, it is likely that the challenges of tomorrow will be very different from those of yesterday and today. It is therefore important to realize that the extent of these challenges will need to be fully appreciated in order that they can be met and overcome.

#### 2.2.1.1 An Accelerating Rate of Change

It is said that nothing is more inevitable than change. The former U.S. President John F. Kennedy once stated that "Change is the law of life. And those who look only to the past or present are certain to miss the future" (U.S. Government Printing Office 1964). With change, of course, comes progress, and with progress comes responsibility. Of course, all former periods of time have had to deal with the challenges associated with an inevitable change; however, it is fair to say that the twenty-first century is perhaps faced with an unprecedented level of change. Modern organizations are faced with an escalating and ever-accelerating change, and the pace at which this change is occurring is constantly increasing and reaching exponential rates. As the velocity of change continues to accelerate at an alarming rate, this has already resulted in the need for increasingly complex challenges to be addressed in much tighter time frames. It is the speed at which change is occurring that may yet prove to be the greatest challenge to corporate survival. A number of issues have specifically contributed to this speed of change.

*Technological innovation*: One major source of change has been technological innovation. In a digital age, a tech-savvy generation has overseen dramatic advances in the technology, and organizations have been impacted by the advent of the Internet, mobile technology,

---

* South Africa's King Code of Corporate Governance published by the Institute of Directors in South Africa in 2009 already places an inclusive stakeholder approach at the centre of its corporate governance framework.

cloud computing, and so on. Technological innovation has seen the business world witness dynamic changes to business practices by enabling more efficient utilization of resources and the development of new products, processes, and systems. Although technology has certainly helped facilitate economic growth, it is also associated with negative social and environmental issues, particularly in relation to energy consumption and the depletion of natural resources. That said, technology has become increasingly pervasive so much so that rapidly changing technology can have a significant impact, positive or negative, on every aspect of the business. Many consider information technology and the knowledge economy to be the primary driver of the accelerating rate of change in the twenty-first century. Whether it is the primary driver or not in the business world is open to debate; however, there are very few who would disagree that it has become the primary business enabler.

*Globalization*: Technological innovation has certainly contributed to and enabled the accelerated development of the phenomenon of globalization. The move toward a global village has to all intents and purposes shrunk the world and reshaped how business is done as more and more organizations are now required to operate on a 24/7 basis. Although it has certainly helped to generate a sustained economic growth for a generation, it has also resulted in a far more interconnected and interdependent world. The emergence of global markets and global players has opened up incredible business opportunities; however, it has also resulted in new and advanced threats that threaten the very existence of many organizations. It is argued by some that although globalization has facilitated economic growth, expansion, and development, it has also increasingly exposed local, national, and international organizations to heightened levels of vulnerability via the occurrence of global economic recessions and depressions. This in itself presents its own set of challenges.

*Complex systems*: Although globalization and technological innovation have many positive attributes, they have also contributed to an increase in business complexity, particularly in relation to the complexity of information technology and the use of technological models. By opening up new markets and developing new ways to produce and deliver products and services, what has resulted is an increasingly interconnected system composed of multidimensional complex relationships between the many parts of this system. These complex networks are increasingly interrelated, interlinked, interconnected, and interdependent, and this in itself puts many new issues on the business agenda. This level of complexity can make it increasingly difficult to comprehend the nonlinear dynamics of the interconnected components and the extent and nature of the interdependences that exist between the components within such a complex system. This in turn presents complex challenges for organizations in terms of finding effective ways of managing increasingly complex systems.

### 2.2.1.2  An Uncertain and Unpredictable World

These complex systems increase an organization's level of uncertainty, as certainty depends on complete knowledge, which becomes increasingly difficult to possess when dealing with nonlinear complex systems, and the exponential variations of the possible interactions. Without complete knowledge, certainty cannot be ascertained particularly if there is the possibility of more than one future outcome. The greater the number of possible outcomes, the more unpredictable the situation, and although it may be possible to qualify the level of uncertainty, this too is dependent on the level of the unknown. It is therefore somewhat ironic that in the *information age* of the twenty-first century, many organizations appear less confident in predicting and dealing with future events. Indeed, given their new-found access to much greater levels of information, if anything, many organizations now appear to have become less certain about the future outcomes, which can lead to a degree of decision paralysis. A number of issues appear to have given rise to this increased level of uncertainty and a greater sense of instability.

*The Information conundrum*: Given that more and more emphasis is now being placed on the information processes, a major challenge for organizations is to transform the raw data into accurate and meaningful intelligence in a timely manner. More data can now be obtained faster than ever before, but this is not necessarily resulting in better or more accurate data. Although there is an increasing abundance of available data, very often this is simply resulting in data overload adding no positive value, rather than filling the knowledge gap. Often the integrity of information received can be suspect as a result of being invalid, incomplete, or inaccurate. It may also be considered irrelevant or obsolete if not delivered in a timely manner, as decisions can no longer be made based on yesterday's news. Information also remains imperfect when it is rendered provisional, temporary, or subject to change at any point in time. Given the ever increasing rate of change previously referred to, this is no time for complacency, as the information reported yesterday or even this morning may no longer be valid given the possible changes in the parameters that can occur in an instant.

The requirement for real-time information has never been greater, yet it may no longer be sufficient to receive real-time information; there has already been a change in emphasis and a requirement for the anticipative information. It is hoped that this anticipative information can be delivered via the use of sophisticated predictive modeling and analytics in an attempt to address this requirement. The financial crisis however has clearly highlighted the dangers associated with relying on results produced using the predictive models unless one clearly understands the constraints related to the lack of perfect information. Regardless of the sophistication of the model used, the quality of the output is dependent on the quality of the input.

*Turbulent times*: The new millennium has certainly seen a high degree of turbulence, and organizations must be prepared to operate under turbulent and unstable conditions for the foreseeable future. During times of such significant changes and dynamic developments, there will always be evolving challenges for organizations to overcome. These challenges may arise as the result of volatile financial markets, economic storms, military wars, natural disasters, or other less catastrophic business events, which can also negatively impact on the stakeholder value. There will always be circumstances which arise that put stress on organizations achieving their objectives as such is the nature of turbulence. The world is a turbulent place and a rapidly changing world can be an even more turbulent place. The corporate world should not be considered immune from such turbulence and the challenges it poses.

## 2.2.2 Global and Corporate Implications

The impact of these constantly changing circumstances will have far-reaching implications at a global level, which will in turn have an impact on the corporate world in general, on business sectors, and on individual organizations. Obviously, the specific impact may vary on a case by the case basis depending on individual circumstances as each organization is faced with its own unique set of challenges. These new challenges can be regarded as idiosyncratic, as they can represent either a threat or an opportunity to the various organizations concerned. Seen in this light, new challenges can present both positive and negative implications, and each organization's success or failure will be dependent on how it addresses these challenges.

### 2.2.2.1 Global Concerns

Certain issues are now being generally recognized as representing potentially significant threats to the health of the global economy, and are increasingly being considered the subject of a major global concern. As these are global issues, they will need to be addressed at a global level; however, they still have the potential to have a positive or negative impact on individual organizations. Organizations therefore need to consider the potential impact of these issues for themselves and determine whether the organization should view them as either threats or opportunities.

*Global issues*: Given the increasing level of globalization and the resulting high degrees of impact, interconnectedness, and interdependences, the knock on the ramifications of negative incidents occurring on one corner of the globe can have profound implications all over the world. These issues no longer respect national boundaries as local issues can now become national, international, and global overnight. Conversely, international issues can also become a subject of concern at the national and local levels. Given the relationship between the global economy and the corporate world, organizations need to fully understand, appreciate, plan, and prepare for the potential ramification of global issues. The World Economic Forum (WEF) has an ongoing initiative that identifies the potential global issues of concern. These issues are reported in its WEF Global Risks report each year, and the 2015 report (WEF 2015) categorizes them as follows:

- *Economic risks*: Includes issues such as high structural unemployment or underemployment, fiscal crises in key economies, and asset bubble in a major economy
- *Environmental risks*: Includes issues such as extreme weather events (e.g., floods and storms), failure of climate-change adaption, and major natural catastrophes (e.g., earthquake, tsunami, volcanic eruption, and geomagnetic storms)
- *Geopolitical risks*: Includes such issues as an interstate conflict with regional consequences, state collapse, or crisis (e.g., civil conflict, military coup, and failed states), and weapons of mass destruction
- *Societal risks*: Includes such issues as water crises, profound social instability, and rapid and massive spread of infectious diseases
- *Technological risks*: Includes such issues as large-scale cyber attacks, massive incident of data fraud or theft, and massive and widespread misuse of technologies (e.g., 3D printing, artificial intelligence, geo-engineering, and synthetic biology)

Organizations need to be cognizant of how global issues can impact them and their stakeholders, and keep abreast of changing global circumstances on an ongoing basis.

### 2.2.2.2  Evolving and Mutating Hazards

An analysis of global issues can certainly lead to a perception that the corporate world is now operating in an environment with a heightened threat level, as since the turn of the century the dangers facing the corporate world appear to have transformed dramatically. Potential hazards now appear to exist all around, both from within the organization itself and also from the external world. An environment of dynamic change is also a breathing ground for the dynamic hazards, and as a result, with each passing day, organizations are faced with new and more sophisticated hazards and threats to their very existence. There is little doubt that rapidly evolving technologies can also present increasingly complex challenges, and, as a result, the potential for hazards is continuously evolving, morphing, and mutating. This means that the nature of risks, threats, and vulnerabilities is also constantly evolving, morphing, and mutating. In the real world, it would appear that such mutation is constantly keeping one step ahead of mitigation measures, and constantly looking for ways to exploit as yet unknown vulnerabilities. As previously stated, each organization is unique and as such the types of hazards to which an organization is exposed can vary between organizations. Each organization is however required to be aware of its own unique circumstances and to be vigilant and robust in its defense against the occurrence of its own unique hazard scenarios. There are however certain hazard events that many organizations will have in common.

*Hazard\* events*: Failure by an organization to put sufficiently robust defense measures in place can result in the occurrence of hazard events that can be damaging to the organization and potentially reduce or destroy the stakeholder value. The occurrence of hazard events can negatively impact on the organization and severely damage it both financially and nonfinancially. They can also result in the significant damage to the reputation of the organization, which in turn can spark a series of additional hazard events. The level of potential damage can vary depending on the type of hazard events or a series of events; however, the implementation of sufficiently robust corporate defense measures can help the organization to avoid or mitigate the direct impact of these events, and also help minimize any subsequent collateral damage.

Examples of the potential issues that can result in the occurrence of hazard events and that are typically facing organizations are listed in Table 2.1.

Organizations need to be mindful that these types of hazard events regularly occur to organizations around the world, and they need to be cognizant of their own exposure to the occurrence of such hazard events and vigilant in their efforts to prevent their occurrence.

### 2.2.2.3 The Corporate Damage

The twenty-first century has already seen more than its fair share of corporate casualties, and this has done considerable damage to the stakeholder confidence and the reputation of the corporate world. It has also resulted in damage to the stakeholder perceptions of corporate integrity and corporate competency, and resulted in demands for the improved business practices. In addition to the damage caused by the fallout of global financial crisis, there have been examples of numerous high-profile scandals, perhaps on an unprecedented scale, and these have included some spectacular examples of large blue-chip organizations whose vulnerability to serious threats to their very survival has been exposed, sometimes with the catastrophic results. Recent examples include money laundering and tax scandals at HSBC, the *London Whale* trading loss at JPMorgan Chase, and the BP Deepwater Horizon accident and the fallout. Subsequent investigations into high-profile scandals typically only serve to highlight the fact that the vulnerabilities exposed by these scandals were the result of weaknesses in the defense-related practices of the organizations concerned, and deficiencies in their systems of checks and balances. These investigations invariably highlighted the fact that the organizations concerned could have and should have addressed these vulnerabilities in

**TABLE 2.1**
**Potential Hazard Events**

| Macroperspective | Microperspective |
| --- | --- |
| Economic slowdown or slow recovery | Damage to reputation or brand |
| Political risk and uncertainties | Failure to attract or retain top talent |
| Natural disasters/extreme weather | Failure to innovate or meet client needs |
| Regulatory or legislative changes | Cyber terrorism and cyber threats |
| Increasing competition | Internal and external fraud |
| Attitudes to white-collar crime | Business interruption |
| Increases in organized crime | Insolvency and bankruptcy |
| Unstable financial markets | Cash flow and liquidity problems |
| Tax and financial reporting | Corruption and money laundering |
| Nation–state cyber espionage | Complex transaction loss |

---

\* Traditionally, the term *hazard* may have been used interchangeably with the term *risk*. In recent times, however, many risk practitioners now prefer to refer to risk as the possibility for *upside risk* and *downside risk*. In order to avoid any possible confusion, the author has chosen to use the term *hazard* to represent the occurrence of an event that has a negative impact on the organization's achievement of its objectives.

a more effective manner. By being unable to adequately defend their stakeholder interests, many of these organizations have faced considerable stakeholder backlash, not to mention damage to their reputations. As a result, public attention has firmly focused on corporate practices, whereas the issue of corporate ethics has also been subject to increased scrutiny.

In addition, in the post-Enron era, buoyed by the sheer magnitude of the financial impact of the global financial crisis and the subsequent economic turmoil, international regulators have been prompted into action. In an attempt to help restore public confidence, international regulators have been busy investigating these events and uncovering their root causes. Consequently, we have seen the introduction of a litany of compliance-related issues, including a multitude of legislation, regulations, codes of practice, and other best practice guidelines. The goal is to help prevent these scenarios repeating themselves again in the future; however, these initiatives also create their own practical challenges for organizations in terms of ensuring they are in conformance. Some fear that because many of these initiatives were seen as knee-jerk reactions aimed at addressing yesterday's risk rather than a more holistic approach that they may well also produce their own set of unintended consequences at some future point. Organizations also need to bear this in mind rather than blindly following these new protocols.

## 2.3  ANALYSIS OF YOUR STRATEGIC ENVIRONMENT

Faced with this evolving global landscape where ongoing developments are having an unprecedented impact on the corporate world, organizations must themselves ascertain the possible extent to which these developments are impacting, and could potentially impact, on the achievement of their own objectives. In order to identify opportunities, remain competitive, and help ensure survival, it is crucial for organizations to clearly understand the environment in which they operate. This process needs to start with an honest self-examination, and by the performance of a strategic analysis of their environment in order to first obtain a strategic assessment of their own circumstances. Given that many successful organizations have grown from local to regional to national to international to intercontinental over time, this can prove to be a complex undertaking. Global multinational organizations have an abundance of cross-border and transnational issues that need to be considered in the equation; however, such matters represent an even greater necessity to perform a strategic analysis.

### 2.3.1  A STRATEGIC VIEW

Obtaining a strategic view involves taking a step back in order to be in a position to see the bigger picture. Every organization needs to have a clear strategic perspective of its circumstances in order to determine its current situation, and to form a view in relation to the possible future opportunities and threats. This is, of course, an ongoing process that will help inform the success of the corporate strategy, and the extent to which the corporate strategy may need to be adapted in order to account for possible future events. A strategic view involves an element of self-examination in the context of the organization's vision, mission statement, corporate strategy, and business model.

#### 2.3.1.1  A Crow's Nest Approach Required to See the Forest from the Trees

A high-level strategic view is best obtained by adopting what is commonly referred to as a helicopter view or crow's nest approach. This involves crucial decision makers looking at the entire landscape in terms of space and time, and specifically considering the positive or negative possibilities in terms of the short-, medium-, and long-term implications. The adoption of such a high-level view can help allow the organization to consider the business from a broader perspective, and allow it to put what it has experienced in the past and what it considers it is likely to encounter in the future in the proper context. Very often, a strategic view enables the organization to take a step back and actually see *the forest from the trees*. This is particularly important where a clear formal strategy may have been lacking in the past. A clear strategic view can help an organization assess the extent to which matters such as the vision, its mission statement, and corporate strategy are considered to be up-to-date or require revision.

## 2.3.2 Viewing in a Macrocontext

Assessing the strategic environment involves evaluating the impact of certain macroevents that may be outside the organization's sphere of influence and considering their possible implications for the organization. Organizations are now far more aware that recent systemic crises such as the global financial crisis have highlighted that both governments and societies are less able to cope with the global challenges than was previously expected. In addition, given that the levels of interconnectivity and interdependence between businesses, markets, people, and nations have greatly increased, the prospect of rapid contagion through increasingly interconnected systems has heightened concerns over global economic resilience. Organizations therefore cannot afford to view themselves within a cocoon, and must acknowledge and appreciate the potential indirect impact that macroevents may have on the organization's objectives and its business activities.

### 2.3.2.1 Critical Examination of Macroissues

A strategic analysis means that organizations must be aware of breaking issues and emerging trends, and continuously examine how these matters may impact on their activities. This includes assessing macroevents and critically examining how these events could possibly represent opportunities or threats to the organization and its stakeholders. The following are simple examples of the type of issues that the organization needs to consider.

*Economic issues*: The organization should consider the possible implications of economic issues of the day on the organization's ability to continue to achieve its objectives. Examples of typical questions include
- What possible implications could an energy price shock to the global economy have on our own business?
- What are the possible consequences of unmanageable inflation for our business?

*Environmental issues*: The organization should consider the possible implications of environmental issues of the day on the organization's ability to continue to achieve its objectives. Examples of typical questions include
- What are the possible implications of the occurrence of a major biodiversity loss and ecosystem collapse for our business?
- What man-made environmental catastrophes (e.g., oil spill and radioactive contamination) would have the greatest impact on our business activities?

*Geopolitical issues*: The organization should consider the possible implications of geopolitical issues of the day on the organization's ability to continue to achieve its objectives. Examples of typical questions include
- What impact could the failure of national governance (e.g., corruption, illicit trade, organized crime, impunity, and political deadlock) have on our business activities?
- What are the possible consequences of large-scale terrorist attacks for our business?

*Societal issues*: The organization should consider the possible implications of societal issues of the day on the organization's ability to continue to achieve its objectives. Examples of typical questions include
- What possible implications could the development of food crises have on our own business?
- What possible impact could large-scale involuntary migration have on our business activities?

*Technological issues*: The organization should consider the possible implications of technological issues of the day on the organization's ability to continue to achieve its objectives. Examples of typical questions include
- What are the possible consequences of a breakdown of critical information infrastructure and networks for our business?
- What are the possible threats of a disruptive technology to our industry?

### 2.3.3   Viewing in a Microcontext

Assessing the strategic environment also involves evaluating the impact of certain microevents that may be within the organization's sphere of influence and considering their possible implications for the organization. The organization needs to assess and evaluate all issues that are likely to directly impact on its business. Changes that occur to various aspects of the business sector are also likely to impact on the organization; therefore, the organization needs to consider the implications of any possible changes. A strategic analysis involves considering a number of specific microissues.

#### 2.3.3.1   Critical Examination of Microissues

The organization needs to consider different aspects of the business that it has chosen to operate. It must understand the workings and be aware of emerging trends and any specific breaking issues in each of these areas. The organization must continuously monitor and analyze activities within these areas and constantly assess and evaluate how issues in these areas could impact on its business. This includes assessing different events and critically examining how these events could possibly represent opportunities or threats to the organization and its stakeholders. Examples of the areas of concern and the type of issues that the organization needs to consider, including some simple examples of generic questions to be considered, are listed in Table 2.2.

---

**TABLE 2.2**
**Examples of Areas of Concern and Types of Issues**

| | **The Business Sector** |
|---|---|
| Products: | What possible implications could the launch of an innovative new product by one of our competitors have on our current sales projections? |
| Services: | What are the possible consequences for our business if a competitor were able to deliver a faster and cheaper service due to the use of new technology? |

| | **The Market** |
|---|---|
| Market size: | What possible implications could a long-term stagnation of the market size have on our own business? |
| Market share: | What are the main threats to our strategy to increase our current market share over the next 5 years? |
| Competition: | How vulnerable is our unique selling point to being copied or plagiarized by our competition? |

| | **Financials** |
|---|---|
| Turnover: | How vulnerable is our business to significant failure to achieve our target turnover volumes in a given calendar year? |
| Cash-flow: | What impact could sustained reductions in our projected cash-flows have on our liquidity position? |
| Operating costs: | What would be the possible implications for our business should our operating costs increase substantially in the short term? |
| Profitability: | What are the potential consequences to the business should the organization incur a significant unexpected loss in a given year? |

| | **Business Trends** |
|---|---|
| Global: | What potential impact could changes in global business trends have on our business? |
| Regional: | What potential impact could changes in regional business trends have on our business? |
| National: | What potential impact could changes in national business trends have on our business? |
| Local: | What potential impact could changes in local business trends have on our business? |

| | **Environmental Analysis** |
|---|---|
| Natural: | What impact could radical changes to the natural environment have on our stakeholders? |
| Business: | What possible impact could radical changes to consumer behavior have on our business? |
| Economic: | What are the possible implications for our business to radical changes to the current level of economic prosperity? |
| Organization: | What changes to our working environment could result in positive or negative outcomes for our workforce? |

## 2.4 RECOGNITION OF POTENTIAL HAZARDS

Hazards represent the occurrence of events that negatively impact on the achievement of business objectives. The Australian and New Zealand Standards define it as follows: *Hazard: a source of potential harm* (AS/NZS 2004). Typically, hazard events occur as a result of the existence and extent of three business elements: risks, threats, and vulnerabilities. The interaction of these three elements will invariably determine the type and degree of the hazard experienced. One of the most important aspects of corporate defense is the ability, capacity, and capability to anticipate potential hazards before they materialize. Once a potential hazard has been identified, measures can be taken to address the associated risks, threats, and vulnerabilities. Risks can be mitigated, threats can be countered, and vulnerabilities can be reduced. Although the occurrence of a hazard may not always be prevented, measures can be taken to alleviate the potential damage associated with the occurrence of such a hazard.

### 2.4.1 HINDSIGHT, INSIGHT, AND FORESIGHT

Hindsight allows us to learn from mistakes of the past; however, in business, to be able to correctly anticipate an event in advance ideally requires a degree of both insight and foresight. A degree of insight is required in order to have the ability to appreciate the true nature of the event in question and to intuitively recognize the inner workings of such an event. Insight represents the ability to acutely observe the occurrence of an event and to fully understand the relationships in play, and the specific cause and effect within the context of the event in question. Without sufficient insight into a given subject matter, it is unreasonable to expect an organization to be able to accurately predict the occurrence of a hazard event. Foresight, on the other hand, is concerned with the organization's ability to imagine or predict and thus plan for events that are likely to occur in the future. In order to act in a prudent manner, an organization must possess sufficient foresight within its ranks. Again without the presence of sufficient foresight, it is unreasonable to expect an organization to accurately predict the occurrence of a hazard event.

#### 2.4.1.1 Adding Insight

An organization can take certain measures to help and ensure that it has sufficient insight in its particular chosen business. In order to ensure it has a deep understanding of the industry, the organization must ensure that it has employed an appropriate level of suitably qualified individuals with sufficient experience and expertise in their related fields. Typically, where there is a lack of adequate insight, this may manifest itself in hidden cracks whereby the organization is not aware of its deficit in this regard until after a hazard has occurred. Where a deficit is identified, this can often be addressed by specialist education and training initiatives.

#### 2.4.1.2 Addressing Foresight

An organization can also take certain measures to address any perceived lack of foresight by ensuring it engages in the appropriate activities that can help to predict and anticipate future hazards. Such activities could include scenario analysis, simulation exercises, and so on. The objective is to uncover any potential blind spots that have remained under the covers and are not in plain view. Diversity can also help to remove blinkers, introduce peripheral vision, and help the organization to better see around the corners. Brainstorming by a group with diverse backgrounds can help improve the organization's ability to foretell the occurrence of events and to more accurately forecast the possible outcomes. An organization should therefore ensure that there is a sufficient diversity of thought, qualification, experience, and expertise in place at all levels within the organization, beginning at the boardroom.

### 2.4.2    PREDICTABILITY AND RANDOMNESS

Although possessing a certain degree of insight and foresight can certainy help an organization to better anticipate and predict future events, without complete knowledge there is no crystal ball to prophesize the future with absolute certainty. Given the growing level of interconnectivity in the increasingly complex world in which we live, organizations rarely if ever possess complete knowledge of the facts, and, as a result, there is always an element of uncertainty present.

Randomness presents itself as a measure of the uncertainty of an outcome and implies the concept of chance. The notion of the occurrence of random events refers to a perceived lack of predictability in the occurrence of an event. A random event is perceived to have no intelligible order or may not follow a predictable pattern or sequence. In certain cases, although there may be an element of predictability in relation to the frequency of the occurrence of a series of events, the actual occurrence of the individual event within the series may remain random and unpredictable.

As a consequence, when an organization is assessing the potential occurrence of hazard events, there is an element of uncertainty regarding the timing of such an occurrence given a lack of complete knowledge of how the event may manifest itself. Although it may be possible to determine the likelihood that an event will occur within a given time frame, it may not be possible to determine precisely when it may occur within that given time frame. For example, a once in a 100-year event may occur tomorrow morning, it may not occur until 100 years from now, or it may occur at any point within that time period. However, there is also the possibility that it may never occur within the predicted 100-year time frame.

Similarly, because of interconnectedness, there is a degree of uncertainty surrounding the actual outcome of a particular hazard event as the effect of contagion is also difficult to accurately predict. Contagion involves the possible knock-on effect in the other related areas as a result of the initial hazard event. In other words, one hazard event can cause a ripple effect and result in a number of other hazard events. Therefore, although it may be possible to determine the magnitude of the initial impact, it may prove far more difficult to determine the magnitude of the subsequent collateral damage as a result of contagion.

#### 2.4.2.1    Uncertainty and Risk

There is an old business expression that states *no risk, no reward*. Success in business requires taking risks and typically the level of potential reward is commensurate with the level of risk involved, although this is not always the case. In business, there is clearly a degree of uncertainty present in all decision making. Risk and uncertainty go hand-in-hand. Although the concept of uncertainty to a large extent is focused on the predictability of an event, the concept of risk is traditionally focused on the probability of occurrence and the projected impact. To aid in decision making, significant technological innovations have resulted in the development of sophisticated risk models and predictive analytics. When used correctly, there is no doubt that these tools can help decision makers to make better, more informed, decisions; however, their limitations need to be understood. The projections from these tools are only as reliable as the data the projections are based on. Unfortunately, if there are incomplete data, the projections then become less reliable. In reality, access to complete data is a rarity. As a consequence, although certain events can be predicted with a certain level of confidence, other events cannot be predicted in advance with any great accuracy or confidence.

In the business world, it is unreasonable to expect that all hazard events will be predicted in advance. Due to the unpredictable nature of hazards, some events will be expected, whereas others will unexpectedly occur without sufficient prior warning. In order to prepare for both the expected and the unexpected, organizations need to put certain minimum safeguards in place to help mitigate and minimize the impact of hazard events. This is the business of corporate defense.

## 2.4.2.2   Black Swans and Perfect Storms

A *black swan* is a term coined to describe the occurrence of a rare event that can be potentially devastating to an organization (Taleb 2007). A black swan event typically defies probability as it does not fit into the familiar distribution patterns and is closely associated with the concept of *unknown unknowns,*[*] a term coined to describe an extreme level of ignorance on a particular topic, whereby an organization does not even know that which it does not know. Therefore, the occurrence of a black swan event cannot reasonably be expected to be predicted in advance. In such situations, the organization may not have appropriate safeguards in place and thus be particularly vulnerable to its impact.

A *perfect storm* is a term used to describe the occurrence of an event that is aggravated by the simultaneous occurrence of a combination of unlikely minor events, or a rare set of circumstances that can result in an impact of extreme magnitude. Perfect storms are generally considered to be outside the range of conventional forecast. In some cases, a perfect storm condition may be required to trigger for the occurrence of a black swan event.

It is however common to hear the spokesperson for a particular organization that was clearly unprepared for the occurrence of a particular hazard event to state in the media that the event was considered to be a black swan or a perfect storm. The reality however is often different, given that the occurrence of such an event should have been expected, and adequate safeguards should have been put in place in advance. Genuine perfect storms and black swans are rare events that could not be reasonably predicted.

## 2.4.3   Understanding Hazards

Apart from black swans and perfect storms, generally speaking, hazards can be anticipated in advance and are reasonably predictable. Anticipation allows for adequate preparation to put measures in place in order to safeguard and defend against its occurrence. When considering hazard events, it is important to appreciate and understand the circumstances that allow hazards to prevail.

## 2.4.3.1   Hazard Elements

When dealing with the occurrence of hazard events, certain issues need to be considered, which will have a bearing on the extent to which the hazard needs to be addressed.

*Risk, probability, and impact*: A very important aspect to consider is the risk associated with the occurrence of the hazard event. Risk is generally assessed in terms of the probability of the occurrence of the event and the potential severity of impact of the event should it occur. A formal risk assessment process allows for the prioritization of work when preparing to safeguard against the occurrence of a hazard event, and to take steps to mitigate its potential impact

*Threats and threat levels*: Another important aspect to consider is the specific threats, that may accelerate the possibility of the occurrence of the hazard event. A threat may be represented by the intention of an individual or group to engage in the coercive action that is intended to inflict damage on the organization. Threat vectors can materialize from either inside or outside of an organization, and these may be the result of a particular grievance or simply a perceived opportunity to benefit in some way from the damage caused. The threat level needs to be evaluated and factored into the hazard assessment. When contemplating hazard safeguards and mitigation, the threat level needs to be considered in terms of space and time dimensions with regard to where and when particular action needs to be taken.

---

[*] A term made famous after remarks made by the former U.S. Defense Secretary Donald Rumsfeld during a Department of Defense (DOD) news briefing on February 12, 2002 during the early stages of the conflict in Iraq.

*Vulnerability*: Having considered the risk and threat elements of hazard event preparation, the organization must also consider its vulnerability to the occurrence of a hazard event. Vulnerability refers to the organization's inability to prevent the occurrence of a hazard event and its inability to withstand the effects of the hazard event. Vulnerability to specific threats should be carefully evaluated. Vulnerability can typically be a result of a lack of preparedness for a particular event. It can however also arise as a result of internal incompetence or a deliberate act of corruption or sabotage by an employee.

All of the aforementioned elements need to be appropriately addressed when considering the organization's exposure to potential hazards and in determining the appropriate course of action to follow.

### 2.4.3.2  Hazard Conditions

Organizations need to be aware of certain conditions that increase or decrease the likelihood of a hazard event occurring, and increase or decrease the likely impact of such an event should it occur. Examples of these conditions include the following:

*Frailty*: In the business world, the concept of frailty is associated with a state of weakness or deficiency in a particular area(s) that can result in increased organizational vulnerability to stress situations and lead to higher levels of risk exposure. An example would be the existence of a frail system of internal controls whereby the organization either did not have the right internal controls in place, or the internal controls in place are not being implemented in the right manner, thereby exposing the organization to increased levels of risk.

*Fragility*: In the business world, an organization may be regarded as fragile if it is considered that it does not have strong, sturdy, or robust structures in place. An example would be, that by failing to recruit at the required talent level for critical positions within the organization it is likely that this will result in poor performance, and leave the organization vulnerable to poor results, which could easily damage the organization's continued existence.

*Robustness*: In the business context, the term robustness is associated with the organization's strength and toughness in the face of hazard events. It is associated with its ability to resist the impact of a hazard event and reflects the healthiness of the organization in that capacity. The higher the organization's standard of robustness, the greater the probability that it will be able to achieve sustainability.

*Resilience*[*]: In the business context, the term resilience refers to the organization's capacity to withstand, rebound, or recover from the direct and indirect consequences of a shock, disturbance, or disruption. It reflects the ability to survive the occurrence of a hazard event. Long-term sustainability requires heightened levels of resilience.

*Antifragility*: In the business context, antifragility is a relatively new concept that refers to an organization that when exposed to a hazard event has systems in place to help to increase its capability levels and thereby become immune to a similar hazard event in the future. In effect, the organization learns from the experience, improves, adapts, and evolves to become a more robust organization than it was before the occurrence of the hazard event. The concept was developed by Nassim Nicholas Taleb who states that "Antifragility is beyond resilience or robustness. The resilient resists shocks and stays the same; the antifragile gets better" (Taleb 2012).

Every organization needs to be aware of its current condition in order to appreciate the level of preparation required in order to be in the best position to deal with the occurrence of hazard events. From a corporate defense perspective, the concepts of both frailty and fragility are considered in a

---

[*] The concept of *resilience* is addressed in more detail in Chapter 10.

negative light as they unnecessarily expose the organization to heightened levels of risk. Typically, organizations should focus developing and improving their levels of robustness, resilience, and antifragility.

### 2.4.4 INTERCONNECTIVITY, CONTAGION, AND THE CASCADE OF CONSEQUENCES

Recent technological innovations have resulted in a higher level of interconnectivity than at any other point in human history. With the development of mobile phones, social media, and the Internet, the world has become much more interconnected and this interconnectivity is even more evident in the business world. When dealing with hazards, it is important for organizations to fully appreciate the phenomenon of interconnectivity and the resulting cascade of consequences that can result from contagion, leaving organizations more vulnerable than ever before.

#### 2.4.4.1 The Interconnectivity of Hazard Events

Doing business in an interconnected world means that organizations need to appreciate that just as individuals and businesses are more closely connected, so too are the hazards facing organizations. Hazards are much more interconnected today than in the past and appear to be connected by a complex web whose links are yet to be fully understood. Hazards are by their very nature pervasive, insomuch as they are capable of occurring everywhere. Twenty-first century hazards have also become more fluid and volatile so much so that a hazard event in the United States can now disrupt international markets in an instant. The collapse of Lehman Brothers and the global impact of the financial crisis that followed served to raise universal awareness of hazard interconnectivity and help to focus attention on a better understanding of how hazards interconnect. This includes developing an improved understanding of the complex systems of interrelationships and interdependencies that create hazard events as well as the context in which the hazard occurs.

The study of hazard interconnectivity is concerned with identifying a correlation or causation link between the different hazard events and hazard elements. Although some links may appear obvious and easy to identify, others are much less obvious as there may be no direct causal links but are rather indirectly linked through mutual or common connections. In some cases, the precise combination and mix present may actually create new unknown or unexpected hazard events. Such hazards can be very difficult to anticipate and prepare for, and require extremely robust scenario planning. It can also be extremely challenging to predict how such events will impact on the organization either directly or indirectly.

#### 2.4.4.2 The Butterfly Effect and the Cascade of Consequences

Hazard contagion not only occurs through direct links in the hazard landscape but also through indirect links as a result of the complex interaction of multiple events on a multidimensional level. The risk of contagion means that it is no longer sufficient to understand the workings of an individual hazard event in isolation as its interlinkages create the possibility of additional hazard events. These events may occur within the organization itself or indeed external to the organization impacting on other stakeholders in the process.

Organizations must now appreciate that actions taken in one part of the world can have ripple effects thousands of miles away and that these effects can occur hours, days, weeks, months, and even years after the original actions were taken. Seemingly small incidents with hidden connections can result in unexpected consequences. The knock-on impact can often be similar to the domino effect and can spiral out of control very quickly. Seemingly insignificant events can trigger larger events, and it is the collateral damage that can have catastrophic consequences. A series of hazard events is therefore one of those issues that can creep up through the organization, starting as a low-level hazard event that can later manifest itself into much higher-level issues that can impact on reputation and create strategic risks, where the potential financial impact can grow exponentially as the cascade of consequences materializes.

Hazard assessment is therefore not only concerned with the direct first-order consequence to the hazard itself but must also focus on how a first-order hazard event can quickly escalate. It must consider the potential knock-on effect of indirect second- and third-order consequences that can manifest themselves further down the line. Due to the increasing complexity and interdependency of enterprise operations, a hazard event can not only result in damage to, or the unavailability of, an asset, but it can also impact on the organization's business capability resulting in operational downtime that can have a subsequent negative impact on performance and productivity. Hazard events can not only facilitate the perpetration of serious crimes but can also lead to the increased risk of a compliance breach that can result in fines, penalties, and even criminal prosecutions. Such activities can not only create a competitive disadvantage but can also have a negative impact on an organization's reputation and brand image, leading to customer dissatisfaction, decreased sales and market share, and ultimately a fall in share price and market value. The following example may help illustrate how the cascade of consequences can occur and how it can impact on an organization.

### BP DEEPWATER HORIZON OIL SPILL

The BP Deepwater Horizon oil spill at the Macondo oil well in the Gulf of Mexico in April 2010 is an extreme example of hazard contagion and the potential cascade of consequences playing out in practice. An operational issue led to an explosion on the oil rig that resulted in the death of 11 people and an additional 17 injuries. The resulting oil spill lasted 87 days in what was considered to be the largest accidental oil spill in the history of the petroleum industry. The oil spill caused significant damage to the environment and adversely impacted on marine and wildlife habitats, and the fishing and tourism industries, with clean-up operations taking years to address. In October 2010, as a result of public sentiment, BP's CEO Tony Hayward was replaced. In 2012, BP pleaded guilty to numerous criminal charges that included 11 counts of felony manslaughter with the U.S. Department of Justice. In July 2015, BP agreed to pay $18.7 billion to settle all federal and state claims arising from the spill, the largest corporate settlement in the U.S. history. It is estimated that BP incurred costs of in excess of $50 billion in legal and clean-up costs. Ultimately, the BP organization has also suffered untold damage to its reputation.

Defending against the occurrence of potential hazards therefore requires a clear appreciation of the potential negative impact the occurrence of a single hazardous event can have and the potential for this event to mutate at an exponential rate unless the appropriate measures are in place to anticipate, prevent, detect, and react. Organizations must therefore get a firm grasp of the *how and why* a hazard occurs and a clear understanding of the dynamic interactions that result in the occurrence of the hazard event. Rather than treating hazard assessment as an exercise involving discrete events, it must now be viewed in a more holistic manner.

# 3 Value Preservation and the Corporate Defense Initiative

Value preservation is considered to be very important to our organization, unfortunately we don't have time for it right now as we are just too busy.*

**Anonymous**

## 3.1 VALUE PRESERVATION IMPERATIVE CONSIDERED

The occurrence of an individual hazard event or a series of connected hazard events can inflict serious damage on the value created by an organization. The preservation of value represents one of the dual strategic obligations of any organization; therefore, it is imperative that an organization takes appropriate steps to actively defend the organization from the damage of potential hazards, and in the process safeguard stakeholder interests and preserve stakeholder value.

### 3.1.1 CORPORATE DEFENSE: AN IMPLICATION OF DOING BUSINESS

As addressed in the previous chapter, the business world is a trade-off between taking risks and reaping rewards. The potential occurrence of hazard events is therefore a by-product of doing business, and this is a certainty that every organization must accept when it enters into business. Given that value preservation is an organizational imperative and corporate defense represents the measures taken to help preserve value, from an organization's perspective, corporate defense must be considered an implication of doing business and an obligation to its stakeholders.

---

* An off the record comment to the author by a CEO.

### 3.1.1.1 Corporate Defense Obligation

Doing business automatically imposes certain obligations on an organization that are expected to be fulfilled. Socially, ethically, and morally an organization has a duty of care to conduct its business to a reasonable standard so as not to do harm to the interests of its stakeholders. This means that the organization must be able to demonstrate that due care was taken in the performance of its duties.

Given its position of trust, an organization also has a legal and fiduciary duty to act for the benefit and in the best interests of its shareholders. This duty of care could also reasonably be expected to be extended to take reasonable measures to safeguard the interests of its stakeholders. This means that the organization should be able to demonstrate that it has taken appropriate steps to preserve value and defend against the negative impact of hazard events over the short-, medium-, and long-term time horizons. It could therefore be argued that such appropriate steps should start with ensuring that a robust corporate defense program has been put in place in order to help preserve stakeholder value. The term *corporate defense* in this context represents an umbrella term used to describe the organization's collective efforts at self-defense.

### 3.1.1.2 Acceptance of the Challenge

The value preservation imperative presents an organization with a fundamental challenge that demands proper attention at the highest levels of the organization. It is debatable as to whether it should receive the exact same strategic level of attention as the value creation imperative; however, it is clearly an issue that requires the due attention of the board and executive management. As guardians of the organization and stakeholder interests, the board and executive management have a duty of care to accept responsibility for addressing the value preservation challenge. This means that they are responsible for overseeing the organization's corporate defense initiative, whatever that may be. An organization's corporate defense initiative represents ongoing efforts to address corporate defense-related matters, whether these efforts are formal or informal. Obviously, the greater the level of formality, the easier it is to demonstrate the efforts made by the organization to fulfill its value preservation obligation. Corporate defense should be considered to be like the concept of justice, *not only must it be practiced but it must be seen to be practiced.*

### 3.1.2 Manner of the Corporate Defense Initiative

Each organization must determine for itself if it is adequately addressing its corporate defense obligation, and whether or not it can demonstrate that it has taken adequate steps in this regard. This means examining and assessing the development of its corporate defense initiative to date, and evaluating the extent to which this initiative requires improvement in order to be confident that it is discharging its duties in a reasonable manner, and in a manner that is likely to instill confidence in its stakeholders.

Every organization will have some form of corporate defense initiative in operation, and there will be at least certain corporate defense measures already in place, whether by chance or by design. Examples of typical corporate defense measures are outlined in Table 3.1.

**TABLE 3.1**
**Typical Corporate Defense Measures**

| | |
|---|---|
| Corporate governance activities | Security operations |
| Risk management activities | Business continuity planning |
| Compliance activities | Internal controls |
| Information systems | Internal audit function |

In the minds of an increasing number of stakeholders, it is the extent to which an organization has adopted a formal structured approach to its corporate defense initiative that best demonstrates the extent to which reasonable care has been exercised or not as the case may be.

### 3.1.2.1   A Guide to Corporate Defense Priorities

The corporate defense initiative in place can act as a guide as to what the organization considers to be its priorities in relation to corporate defense-related matters. These will include certain corporate defense measures taken by the organization to defend itself from the occurrence of hazards focusing on addressing risks, threats, and vulnerabilities. In some organizations, the corporate defense initiative will consist of various individual initiatives set-up by the organization over time as a reaction to certain matters that have been prioritized from time to time, be they specific to the organization itself or to the business sector in which it operates in. This type of reactive approach generally results in situations whereby these initiatives tend to be set-up on a stand-alone basis to address the immediate priority rather than being part of an elaborate plan to improve corporate defense measures in the organization in general. In this way the corporate defense initiative is a reflection of the priorities of the past rather than a reflection of the future challenges facing the organization.

### 3.1.2.2   Assessing the Current Approach to Corporate Defense

In order to establish a clear picture of the extent of the organization's corporate defense initiative and where its priorities currently lie, it is necessary to assess its current approach. An examination of the current approach can help determine the organization's level of commitment to fulfilling its corporate defense obligations. This can include assessing the extent to which corporate defense activities are performed on a day-to-day basis or on a periodic basis. It can include assessing whether these activities are managed in a silo-type approach or whether they are managed in a more coordinated and integrated approach. Such an assessment can also include the form corporate defense activities take within the organization. It can include whether they are performed in a piecemeal manner and considered as additional responsibilities that are allocated to business staff, or whether they are driven by centralized corporate defense-related functions with specialist expertise in these areas.

This type of assessment can include the resources made available to corporate defense activities in the performance of their duties and responsibilities, and the financial means allocated to these activities as a percentage of the overall budget. It can include assessing how corporate defense activities are arranged and structured within the organization and the associated policies, practices, and procedures in place to address corporate defense activities. An organization's level of commitment to corporate defense can be determined by the number of personnel dedicated to its corporate defense-related activities, and its levels of experience, qualifications, and expertise. It can also be determined by expressing this number as a percentage of total personnel.

## 3.2   UNDERSTANDING CORPORATE DEFENSE FOCUS

It is important to not only establish the level of the organization's focus on, and commitment to, corporate defense activities but also to understand the rationale behind this focus. In reality the nature and extent of the organization's focus on corporate defense will have a critical impact on the effectiveness of the corporate defense initiative. In order to be in a position to gain an understanding of the organization's focus and to be able to form an intelligent assessment, it is first necessary to have a clear appreciation of the concept of defense, how it can be interpreted in different contexts, and how it can be viewed from different perspectives.

### 3.2.1   THE SCIENCE AND ART OF DEFENSE

Effective defense can involve known and unknown threats, expected and unexpected occurrences, controllable and uncontrollable situations, and intended and unintended outcomes. Therefore, effective defense needs to be considered as both a science and an art. The theory underpinning what is required to be done under different sets of circumstances is the science of defense, while how these circumstances are actually managed in practice is the art of defense.

The science of defense represents the body of knowledge behind the various defense disciplines. It refers to theories and principles, and also the use of scientific equipment and practices such as the use of mathematical models and statistical data. It applies to principles and studies that can be applied universally and the establishment of cause and effect relationships. In the corporate world however science has its limitations as it is not possible to repeat experimentation under the exact same conditions given that the corporate world is in a continuous state of flux.

The art of defense represents the practical application of theory in the real world. It refers to the requirement to possess a competent level of practical knowledge, personal skills, and creativity in order to effectively manage and execute in practice. This requires continuous repetition and practice, and it requires a degree of creativity and innovation in order to adapt to changing circumstances and to get the best out of every situation. It involves utilizing resources and above all dealing with human beings whose behavior can be inconsistent, irrational, and unpredictable.

In order to deliver effective defense, organizations are required to achieve a necessary collaboration of science and art in order to ensure that there is the appropriate level of theoretical knowledge and practical know-how present. When dealing with defense matters, science and art really do go hand-in-hand.

### 3.2.1.1   Lessons Need to Be Learned from Previous Failures

For corporate defense to develop and evolve, lessons need to be learned from previous failures. The financial crisis provided a clear example of how many organizations failed in their value preservation imperative and illustrated how they failed to put adequate corporate defense measures in place to safeguard stakeholder interests and preserve their stakeholder value. This would indicate that either these organizations did not fully appreciate their corporate defense obligation and therefore did not pay sufficient attention to it, or that they did not fully understand the science and art of corporate defense and were therefore unable to design and execute their plans effectively in practice. Lessons need to be learned from these failings in order to ensure that the required improvements are made and that organizations are adequately insulated against financial, physical, and reputational damage going forward.

### 3.2.1.2   The Concept of Defense

Any improvements must start with the requirement for a clear appreciation of the concept of defense. The verb to defend is generally defined as to take measures to make or keep safe from danger, attack, or harm, and implies the actions of protecting, safeguarding, shielding, supporting, or preserving. The requirement to defend can be associated with an individual, group, place, or thing, and can be associated with honor, reputation, territory, assets, and allies (Lyons 2009a). Organizations need to begin by considering the concept of defense and how it applies in different contexts.

### 3.2.2   THE DEFENSE CONCEPT IN DIFFERENT CONTEXTS

The concept of defense can mean different things to different people, and its precise objectives may therefore vary from one situation or a set of circumstances to another. In order to get a clear appreciation of the concept of defense, it is necessary to understand how the notion of defense is applied under different circumstances and in different contextual settings.

### 3.2.2.1   Defense in the National Context

In most developed economies governments consider it their duty to defend their citizens as a fundamental duty, and consequently the responsibility for national defense is held in high regard. The post of *Minister* or *Secretary of Defense* is generally considered to be a senior cabinet position, reporting to the Prime Minister or President. The Minister or Secretary of Defense has a responsibility for managing the Ministry or Department of Defense. The Ministry or Department of Defense in turn generally has ultimate responsibility for formulating defense strategy and policy, and for integrating policies and plans in order to achieve defense objectives. All defense-related activities, including Army, Navy, and Air Force, ultimately report to this Department or Ministry while still retaining responsibility for tactical planning and for on the ground operation, implementation, and execution. This allows for the strategic alignment of all defense-related activities while also (if competently applied) facilitating the tactical co-ordination and operational integration of these activities.

### 3.2.2.2  Defense in the Sporting Context

In team sports in particular there is a real appreciation of the requirement to focus on defensive strategies and tactics in order to ensure that these are successfully implemented in the field of play. There is a clear understanding of the relationships that exist between the interaction of both offensive and defensive personnel, and how collectively as a team there is a requirement to have an appropriate balance between these two interdependent disciplines. Coaches are aware that in order to be successful on the field of play, the game-plan must include the team's ability to be able to both attack and defend as required, and be capable of turning defense into offense and vice versa as the occasion demands. Many teams have specialist defensive coaches who are dedicated to helping to develop the diverse skills required in order to execute their strategies and tactics effectively. These coaches are very much aware that the defensive unit as a whole is made up of individual special-ist positions that need to be filled by players of suitable character and ability. Developing the unit begins with recruiting the required squad of individuals and by coaching these individuals on the necessary technical skills required. The selection of the starting line-up is based on the players best suited to address the team's defensive requirements. These selected players must then be coached on how to play as a cohesive defensive unit. This unit must learn to play and interact with the offensive unit as a team so that all the players involved are contributing to the greater common goal. Finally, the team must learn to continually develop both its individual and collective skills in order to con-stantly improve, and in order to reach the increasingly higher levels of performance required if it is to achieve sustainable success.

### 3.2.2.3  Defense in the Corporate Context

Although the term *corporate defense* has been in use for many years and is perhaps intuitively understood, its specific meaning can differ from person to person and indeed from organization to organization. Its precise definition can also vary depending on the circumstances in which it is applied. Typically, it is addressed only as a reactive response to a legal compliance issue, pending litigation, or to defend against a hostile takeover (i.e., poison pill, etc.). At other times it is only addressed in a very narrow focus such as a security or resilience issue. As a result, the very objec-tive of defending the organization appears not to be fully understood or indeed its requirement fully appreciated. Many defense-related activities are however employed by organizations to help to safeguard against, and to mitigate, risks, threats, and hazards. These activities do share a common high-level objective, that of helping to defend the organization, and therefore it could be said that they represent multiple layers of defense. Corporate defense therefore in its broadest sense could be said to represent an organization's collective program for self-defense. The traditional lines of defense in the corporate world are represented by the board having responsibility for corporate governance, executive management having responsibility for the control environment, with over-sight committees and various defense-related functions (i.e., compliance and risk management, etc.) having responsibility for providing supplementary support and assurance. Additionally internal audit has responsibility for auditing the previously mentioned aspects, and external audit for provid-ing independent assurance in relation to the preparation of accounts, and so on. Unfortunately, all too commonly defense-related activities are very often not managed in a coordinated manner and are therefore not operating in unison toward common goals and objectives. Frequently, they actually operate independently and in isolation of one another in silo-type structures.

### 3.2.3   Differing Corporate Defense Perspectives

Corporate defense as a concept is not new; however, it is an evolving concept. Given the continuing glut of corporate scandals, it is fair to say that as a concept it is still in its infancy as it appears that it is still not fully understood or appreciated. This gives rise to the fact that there continues to be a number of different perspectives on the purpose, function, and requirement for corporate defense.

#### 3.2.3.1   Perspectives on Self-Defense

The concept of defense originated from the notion of self-defense, and throughout history the notion of self-defense has been viewed from many different perspectives. To this end, self-defense also appears to be intrinsically linked with offense and often times it becomes difficult to separate the two.

When discussing the topic with psychologists, some may view offense and defense as intertwined and choose to discuss self-defense from the perspective of one of our most basic instincts, the fight or flight response to a threat, which we are told dates back to the earliest human beings. Such a response to a direct or perceived threat may also be discussed in terms of the human condition and its motivation to seek out pleasure and to avoid pain. In terms of self-defense, the fight instinct is often associated with a desire to stand our ground and risk injury or death in order to protect and retain our material possessions. The flight instinct on the other hand is associated with fleeing the scene in order to avoid a conflict and preserve our lives, but in the process abandon our material possessions that are often considered to be replaceable.

Some scientists may choose to discuss the origins and developments of self-defense in terms of human adaptation during times where the *law of the jungle* prevailed. They may discuss how actual survival was predominantly based upon the notion of the *survival of the fittest*. They may choose to describe this survival as a function of where human beings featured in the food chain. They may choose to discuss the important role of the alpha male in advancing human genetics. They may discuss how the development of various forms of self-defense also led to the development of enhanced fighting skills, which were also used in order to obtain an advantage over rivals.

Military historians may choose to view self-defense as how humans have developed weaponry, originally to protect themselves, their families, their villages, and later their nations from their enemies. They may make reference to how earliest human beings began by using sticks and stones and how they developed sharp wood and rocks as weapons for both self-defense and attack. They may refer to how humans later progressed to the use of knives, arrows, spears, swords, and shields. They may refer to how generations of human beings continually developed more sophisticated weaponry in the shape of guns and canons. They may eventually point to how our most recent generations have developed machine guns and bombs and how this ongoing development has finally resulted in weapons of mass destruction such as chemical and biological warfare and ultimately nuclear weaponry.

#### 3.2.3.2   A Traditional Corporate Defense Perspective

In the past conversations between senior executives regarding the topic of corporate defense were based on the premise that it was regarded as a necessary evil with associated overheads and costs. Quite often these conversations were restricted to discussing either the impact of security or litigation on the organization. This is referred to as the traditional view.

Unfortunately, this view represents a very narrow perspective and a somewhat restricted focus, as corporate defense has the potential for a far more comprehensive brief. This traditional mind-set is generally one of a reactionary nature, where corporate defense issues only appear on the radar after a serious incident has occurred and which has more than likely already attracted stakeholder attention. Indeed, in this type of environment priorities can tend to fluctuate on an almost daily basis, in a direct response to the most recent incidents, and for some this can present a very frustrating working environment.

In an organization with a traditional view of corporate defense, many defense-related activities tend to operate in silo-type structures. This means that they are not in alignment with one another, but rather they operate in isolation. There tends to be little or no interaction, sharing of information, or indeed collaboration. Frequently, there is also very little cross-functional support among these activities, but rather they can very often be the subject of internal power struggles. As a consequence of this type of traditional mindset, an organization can be subject to typically negative results. Generally speaking this type of attitude can result in an organization operating in a crisis management mode, whereby it finds itself continuously fire-fighting on a day-to-day basis.

Very often in such cases the overall responsibility and accountability for corporate defense is dispersed or fragmented, and can also be found to be diluted or ambiguous. In fact, in certain scenarios it can sometimes appear to be nonexistent. This can obviously result in dangerous omissions or gaps, and these in turn can create vulnerabilities that can later be exploited, rendering many other corporate defense-related efforts ineffective in the process. All of the intersection, duplication, and overlap of activities that can occur in the silo-type environment can also result in considerable inefficiencies and unnecessary redundancies from an operational perspective. Finally, the power struggles that can occur in silo-type structures can actually develop into full-scale turf wars, and this can have a very negative impact on the organization, and can ultimately be extremely detrimental to the organization's health.

### 3.2.3.3 An Emerging Corporate Defense Perspective

There is however a growing recognition that a more comprehensive, progressive, and proactive approach is now required in order to defend the organization, and indeed the interests of all the stakeholders. This contemporary view of corporate defense (Lyons 2006b) suggests that, in the modern era, organizations now have to accept that the corporate world is faced with unique challenges, including an ever-accelerating rate of change. The knock-on implications mean that knowledge must now be considered to be at best provisional, imperfect, or obsolete, as it is subject to change at any point of time. An increasing number of visionaries, thought leaders, and commentators are suggesting that organizations now find themselves in a corporate world that is facing everchanging and more sophisticated threats. The result being that the level of unpredictability in this world now appears also to be increasing as do the associated levels of uncertainty and danger. The contemporary view therefore suggests that, under such circumstances, the traditional approach to corporate defense is no longer considered to be adequate and that, in such an environment, it is considered that a reactive approach is clearly no longer sustainable. Organizations now have to appreciate that defending itself and its stakeholders includes not only safeguarding and protecting, but also valuing the interests of all of its stakeholders. This suggests that organizations need to increasingly adopt a stakeholder perspective in order to establish what the concept of corporate defense means to its stakeholders.

## 3.3 CORPORATE DEFENSE CONDITIONS

The success or failure of the organization's corporate defense efforts and activities can be very much influenced by the prevailing conditions present within the organization itself. These conditions include issues such as the state of the organization's health and the type of culture present in the organization, both of which can have a significant impact on how corporate defense is perceived and how corporate defense-related activities are performed.

### 3.3.1 CORPORATE HEALTH

An assessment of the health of an organization involves not only considering tangible matters such as its financial and economic health but also less tangible health matters such as its integrity, ethics, and morals. While the monitoring of performance and productivity is obviously very important and can be an indication of the organization's health condition, other health aspects such as its levels of robustness and resilience also require monitoring. Organizational health can also include assessing the health and safety, and welfare and wellbeing of its management, staff, and other stakeholders. From a corporate defense perspective, an organization's health can be viewed in terms of human health, and its health plan should ideally include value preservation routines and exercises in order to demonstrate a defensible standard of care.

### 3.3.1.1 Corporate Health and Human Health

Organizational health can be considered to be similar to human health (e.g., physical, emotional, mental, and material) in the fact that it can respond when treated and it can deteriorate if neglected. "Just as people may seem reasonably well today but may not have the physical condition for the rigors of a long and active life, so too companies that are profitable in the short term may not have what it takes to perform well year after year" (Dobbs et al. 2005). An organization must achieve a certain level of health and remain healthy over time in order to achieve long-term sustainability, as an unhealthy organization is limited in its potential to grow and develop over an expanded period of time. Regular health checks are therefore advisable, and these should be performed by suitably qualified individuals or groups so that any unhealthy symptoms can be diagnosed and remedied as early as possible.

In human health there is recognition that *prevention is better than cure*, and this begins with the adoption of a healthy attitude. A strong emphasis is placed on living a healthy lifestyle, on developing a healthy regime, and on the adherence to healthy behavior. A healthy lifestyle incorporates a healthy balance between exercise, diet, and rest, and maintaining a healthy regime requires a certain level of discipline and involves restraint in the short term in order to reap the benefits over the longer term. Healthy behavior also involves the avoidance of extremely high-risk activities and the elimination dysfunctional behavior. Certain conditions are required in order to help improve health levels, and health screens can focus on matters such as weight and cardio levels, and can involve monitoring such issues as heart rate, cholesterol, and body fat.

A healthy robust organization is capable of achieving higher levels of performance and increased levels of productivity while also being more resistant to shocks and disruptions. Corporate defense activities therefore have a vital role to play in nurturing organizational health, and helping ensure the organization remains healthy over time. In this regard, corporate defense activities can provide the organization with periodic health screening and ongoing fitness checks.

### 3.3.1.2 The Human Factor

Any organization that is attempting to address its corporate health issues need to consider the human factor and its possible impact on the organization. When dealing with human beings, additional care needs to be taken and the challenge presented by the human factor should never be underestimated. As noted earlier, human beings can be inconsistent, irrational, and unpredictable in their behavior and therefore human behavior introduces the concept of behavior risk as a unique risk that requires appropriate consideration.

Human beings play some role in every organization and although their precise influence may vary, human behavior is intertwined with organizational behavior and it is an issue that requires due attention. The development of human relationships can impact on all interaction and communication with the stakeholders of the organization, and these relationships will define the level of trust present in each case. The success or failure of any initiative that requires any form of human interaction be it in the form of daily co-operation with other departments and functions in the performance of day-to-day duties, or group collaboration on a particular project, is all dependent on the human relationships involved and on healthy human behavior. From a corporate defense perspective, in order for healthy human behavior to evolve an appropriate culture needs to be fostered and appropriate conditions put in place such as ensuring the right mix of information, motivation, and incentives.

### 3.3.2 Organization Culture and Subcultures

It has been widely suggested that an unhealthy corporate culture (overly focused on the short term) was at the heart of much of what went wrong in the lead-up to the financial crisis. To understand an organization's culture, one must also understand the prevailing corporate culture and indeed the culture of the society. Corporate culture should not be viewed in a vacuum as it is heavily influenced by, and is a reflection of, the culture of the society in which it operates.

Organizational culture is often referred to as *how things get done around here*. Organizational culture is a somewhat intangible concept as it is said to represent the collective ethos, morals, and values of the members of the organization. Culture develops over time and is a product of the organization's history, traditions, and experiences, which in turn foster the ethics, attitudes, and habits that tend to prevail within the organization. Organizational culture can permeate throughout the entire organization and guides what happens in the organization, and how its members think and feel about various issues as well as how they themselves identify with the organization. It is derived from the organization's vision, strategy, and management style, and is reflected in the shared assumptions and beliefs that define what is considered to be appropriate behavior, and therefore determines how the organization operates on a day-to-day basis. An organization's culture is therefore a reflection of the behaviors, choices, and decisions made by the organization.

Organizational behavior is substantially influenced by the culture of the organization itself and influences how its members interact with one another and with its stakeholders. The extent to which human behavior is influenced by the culture of the organization will be influenced by the degree to which the culture is embraced at different levels within the organization. Where the primary organizational culture is not embraced, separate subcultures may develop with differing attitudes, beliefs, and philosophies. The extent to which the primary culture is integrated into the organization or whether disparate and conflicting subcultures develop may be determined by the extent to which the different business units, departments, and functions are integrated within the organization.

The type of culture present in the organization will have a big impact on how corporate defense is perceived and attitudes toward it. Collective attitudes to issues such as integrity, morality, honesty, trust, and transparency almost certainly impact on decisionmaking at all levels of the organization. Human beings are guided by their own set of values. In the twenty-first century, however, there is perhaps greater diversity of values than at any point in our history. While diversity introduces many different views and perspectives that can help form a more complete picture, it can also result in greater difficulty in getting agreement or arriving at a consensus on a common set of values. The presence of values or indeed the absence of values, often expressed in codes of business conduct or codes of ethics, can play a major role in guiding behavior and determining the manner in which the organization creates value and preserves value.

### 3.3.2.1 Tone at the Top

An organization's culture and health can be very much influenced by the tone set at the top of the organization. "Corporate culture refers to the company's core values and objectives, as expressed through the attitudes and behavior of the board and senior management" (Harner 2013). Tone at the top is about organizational leadership and reflects the attitude of the organization's senior leaders toward a variety of issues, situations, and circumstances. It sets the tone for the organization, particularly in relation to issues such as ethics and integrity. The ethical leadership provided by the organization's hierarchy sets the standard by which the rest of the organization takes its direction. This is particularly important in relation to issues such as the organization's attitude to misconduct, malfeasance, and creating an antifraud environment.

Many commentators believe that the tone at the top filters down the chain of command and sets the culture for the organization. The same could also be said of the culture of broader society. The cult of celebrity has no doubt had a significant influence on twenty-first century society, and this has manifested itself in the tone set by many of today's leaders. If our leaders and influencers in society (i.e., captains of industry and political leaders, etc.) and in business (board members and CEOs, etc.) do not set the appropriate moral tone and ethical values, it is unlikely that a healthy culture will evolve by itself. The organization's leadership team has a dual role, that of *talking the talk* and that of *walking the walk*. This means setting, promoting, communicating, and supporting the implementation of various codes of conduct and, equally as important, complying with these codes themselves in the performance of their own duties. It is by their own actions that the leadership message will be interpreted and therefore leaders need to demonstrate their commitment through their action and the performance of their duties. As it is often said, *actions speak louder than words* and it is the actions of leaders that give a true indication of their commitment to integrity and ethical behavior, and this can have a trickle-down effect throughout the organization. A modus operandi of *do as I say and not as I do* is highly unlikely to have a positive impact on an organization's health, culture, and behavior. At the end of the day, a poor tone at the top can make it extremely difficult for corporate defense activities to operate effectively.

### 3.3.2.2 Corporate Defense Culture

A corporate defense culture should be regarded as a component of organizational culture and specifically refers to the organization's attitude to its corporate defense activities. It refers to the atmosphere within which corporate defense activities are conducted and the environment in which corporate defense practitioners operate their daily duties. An organization's corporate defense culture refers to the values, beliefs, and behaviors of the management and staff in relation to corporate defense activities and the meaning attached to such behaviors. Like corporate culture, a corporate defense culture develops over time, and it can be influenced from the top-down (i.e., tone at the top) or from the bottom-up (i.e., tone at the bottom), as well as being influenced by middle management (i.e., tone at the middle).

An organization needs to be aware of whether it has a common attitude toward all its corporate defense activities, or whether it has a different attitude to individual corporate defense activities. For example, how do management and staff view the role of the risk management and internal audit functions and how does it value the importance of risk management and internal audit activities? What about compliance or security activities and so on? It is important to realize that there may in fact be different subcultures in operation each reflecting different attitudes and beliefs in relation to different corporate defense activities. This can be the result of an inconsistent tone at the top or perhaps the result of individual bias within the chain of command.

For best results, it is important that the corporate defense culture is in congruence with the overall culture of the organization as any incongruence will only hamper the effectiveness of the corporate defense initiative. The overall corporate defense culture of the organization reflects the extent to which the organization respects and supports its obligation to preserve stakeholder value and safeguard stakeholder interests. Ideally, there will be a consistency across all corporate defense activities; however, this is not guaranteed and it is not uncommon to find different levels of commitment to each of the different corporate defense components. Unfortunately, differing attitudes to individual corporate defense activities can result in weaknesses or deficiencies in that component, which in turn can lead to the creation of a particular vulnerability.

### 3.3.3 NATURE OF THE STAKEHOLDER RELATIONSHIP

The relationship that exists among stakeholders can have a significant influence on the effectiveness of an organization's activities. Positive relationships can create a positive environment in which to perform day-to-day activities, whereas negative relationships can create a negative environment that can actually frustrate its efforts. This also applies to the corporate defense initiative and the nature of its stakeholder relationship. South Africa's King III Corporate Governance code seeks to emphasize the inclusive stakeholder approach. "In the case of the 'stakeholder inclusive' approach, the board of directors considers the legitimate interests and expectations of stakeholders on the basis that this is in the best interests of the company, and not merely as an instrument to serve the interests of the shareholder" (IOD SA 2009).

### 3.3.3.1 A Stakeholder View

Each organization needs to be acutely aware of its stakeholders and their individual interests. Addressing stakeholder relations involves identifying all relevant stakeholders and engaging with these stakeholders in order to identify potential conflicts of interest, and how best to address these conflicts of interest. Constructive engagement is a critical aspect of developing positive stakeholder relations as the organization's stakeholders need to feel like valued partners. This can also help the organization to better understand and appreciate potential stakeholder expectations and help in the setting of realistic expectations. At the end of the day, stakeholders need to feel that their interests are being taken seriously and are being appropriately addressed by their organization.

In its broadest sense, the term *stakeholder* can be used to refer to all parties with a vested interest in the activities of the organization. Table 3.2 lists examples of typical stakeholder groups that all organizations need to be aware of and mindful of their interests.

If an organization thinks in terms of the broader stakeholder interests, then it may begin to realize that yes there has to be an economic and monetary focus, but it also needs to recognize that it is not all about numbers, quarter-end figures, and bottom-line financials; these issues do not necessarily resonate with all of its stakeholders. To get the required top-down and equally important bottom-up buy in, an organization has to look beyond this; it needs to ensure that it is selling the organization's message to all of its stakeholders, including line management and of course its staff, a stakeholder quite often neglected. It has to realize that stakeholders are not only concerned with financial incentives but are also concerned with their health and safety, and their welfare and well-being. Developments in different aspects of corporate responsibility have helped organizations to slowly realize that they have entered into an unwritten social contract that confers certain duties and obligations on them, and these obligations need to be adequately addressed. The corporate social responsibility (CSR) movement in particular has served to highlight how stakeholder expectations are changing in relation to corporate obligations on matters such as social issues, sustainability issues, and environmental issues.

### 3.3.3.2 Safeguarding Stakeholder Interests

Organizations have a legal and moral duty of care to take appropriate measures to shield stakeholders from potential hazard events. The value preservation imperative obliges an organization to carefully consider the interests of its stakeholders and to take appropriate measures to help preserve stakeholder value.

From the perspective of the corporate defense initiative within the organization, there are specific stakeholders that need to be considered. Examples include the board, executive management, business line management and staff, business support services, and the management and staff of

---

**TABLE 3.2**

**Examples of Stakeholder Groups**

| | |
|---|---|
| Clients | Business partners and suppliers[a] |
| Shareholders | Regulators |
| Management | Local communities |
| Workforce (staff, employees, workers) | Society |

[a] This includes creditors, debtors, and other supply chain partners.

the individual corporate defense functions themselves (e.g., risk management and compliance). The corporate defense initiative needs to focus on these stakeholders as people, not just numbers or bottom-line financials. It needs to take on a stakeholder perspective, where each individual stakeholder is considered to be a human being, with human needs and human expectations. It needs to value the importance of human beings, and help ensure that their health, safety, welfare, and wellbeing are appropriately prioritized. It is only by adopting a *hearts and minds* approach that an organization can hope to foster the necessary foundation of trust vital to the establishment of the essential top-down, bottom-up culture required. Obviously from the human perspective, corporate defense is therefore an extremely responsible station.

Safeguarding stakeholder interests requires identifying and understanding what it is that stakeholders actually value. Organizations need to be conscious that in the real world value is determined by the recipient rather than the creator, and therefore they also need to clearly identify the intended recipients. They need to be clear as to not only what it is that their stakeholders place value on but also be clear as to what this value actually looks like, how it can be created, and what measures are needed to help preserve it. They need to be clear on how their stakeholders measure this value and whether any perceived value is of a tangible or intangible nature. Obviously, different stakeholders may have different ideas about what constitutes value to them, and it is quite probable that there will be stakeholders with conflicting interests. For example, certain shareholders may be primarily concerned with financial value and matters such as revenues, profits, and share price, whereas other stakeholder groups may be more concerned with the organization's social contributions, its charitable support, or its ecological footprint.

## 3.4 ASSESSING THE EXISTING CORPORATE DEFENSE POSTURE

In order to determine if stakeholder expectations are being adequately addressed, an organization needs to assess its current posture in relation to value preservation. This should involve considering how the value preservation imperative currently fits into the organization's strategy and the extent to which the organization's stated objectives incorporate its value preservation obligations. It means considering the value preservation stance the organization has taken to date and its existing outlook concerning its corporate defense activities. It involves considering the positioning of its corporate defense activities and the priorities associated with these activities at strategic, tactical, and operational levels.

### 3.4.1 THE ATTITUDE TO CORPORATE DEFENSE

Establishing the organization's current attitude to corporate defense is the first step to being able to determine where it needs to go from here. In reality an organization's attitude to corporate defense activities establishes the legitimacy of the corporate defense agenda and the extent to which corporate defense objectives are genuinely integrated into the business. The promotion of a positive attitude to corporate defense can positively influence the organization's mind-set and how people think about corporate defense. It can also influence people's point of view and their behavior toward corporate defense activities throughout the organization. If the attitude to date has been less than positive, then certain measures may need to be taken to remedy this situation.

#### 3.4.1.1 Meaning of Corporate Defense in Your Organization

Each organization needs to have a clear understanding of what corporate defense means to that organization and to its stakeholders. It needs to be clear as to the precise purpose being served by the existence of its current corporate defense activities and the extent to which this purpose is generally understood throughout the organization. It needs to be aware of the corporate defense reference points within the organization and the extent to which corporate defense activities are being organized and conducted in a structured or unstructured manner. It needs to establish the extent to which the organization as a whole has a clear understanding of the point of having corporate defense activities in operation. Examples of basic stakeholder questions include

- What is it that needs to be defended?
- What does the organization need to defend against?
- What defensive measures does the organization need to put in place?

### 3.4.1.2  The Corporate Defense Mind-Set

An organization's attitude to corporate defense is a reflection of its mind-set, and vice versa. Each organization needs to be aware of its prevailing mind-set when it comes to the topic of corporate defense. The mind-set in place will have a profound impact on how corporate defense activities are prioritized within the organization. For example, certain organizations may view corporate defense activities in a somewhat negative light and consider them to be costly overheads, whereas other organizations may view them in a more positive light and consider them an essential aspect of delivering long-term sustainable value. Certain organizations may view them as a hindrance to business activities or a business disabler, whereas others may view them as a necessary component of business activities or a business enabler. Some organizations may adopt a passive or reactive outlook to corporate defense activities and only focus on them when a serious issue arises, whereas others may adopt a more assertive or proactive outlook by trying to keep abreast of emerging best practices and putting measures in place as early as possible. In some organizations, all corporate defense activities may be viewed separately or individually with very little consistency, whereas in other organizations they may be viewed in a more unified or collective manner. It is important that each organization examines its own relationship with its corporate defense obligation and with its individual corporate defense-related activities in order to obtain a clear picture of its existing mind-set.

### 3.4.1.3  The Historical Context

Viewing its corporate defense initiative in a historical context can help an organization to form a clearer view of its current status quo. This can help to clarify the extent to which corporate defense and corporate defense activities have already been considered by the organization and the extent to which corporate defense issues are already being addressed. Examples of stakeholder questions include

- Does your organization already have a structured corporate defense program in place?
- Does your organization have a corporate defense vision and/or mission statement?
- Does your organization already have a formal corporate defense strategy in place?
- Does your organization have a formal corporate defense framework in place?
- Does your organization have a formal corporate defense plan in place?

### 3.4.1.4  The Message Transmitted

Each organization needs to consider and reflect on the corporate defense message that the organization has transmitted up until this point. This message can provide good insights into, and is a good indication of, how corporate defense is viewed within the organization. Clearly establishing the type of corporate defense message that has been transmitted to date can be determined by looking at the current status, influence, and authority, associated with corporate defense responsibilities within the organization. This includes considering the extent to which corporate defense practitioners have an influence on decision making at the highest levels of the organization. Whether or not a corporate defense champion has a seat at the top table will also provide a good indication in this regard. Examples of stakeholder questions include

- Where does the overall responsibility for corporate defense lie in your organization?
- Which individual has responsibility for corporate defense at the board level?

- What individual has responsibility for corporate defense at the executive management level?
- Who is the most senior corporate defense officer in your organization?

Due consideration should also be given to the organization's current level of commitment to its corporate defense activities. This will help determine the existing corporate defense capacity and capability, and may also help in the assessment of the extent of improvements required. Examples of stakeholder questions include

- What corporate defense resources has the organization already invested in?
- What is the total annual budget for corporate defense activities?
- How much is this budget when expressed as a percentage of the overall annual budget?

### 3.4.2 ELEVATING THE CORPORATE DEFENSE AGENDA

The emerging contemporary opinion suggests that the topic of corporate defense needs to occupy a more prominent position on the corporate agenda than has previously been the case. Having given due consideration to the organization's current attitude to corporate defense, it has to be determined if in fact corporate defense is currently being appropriately prioritized or whether it needs to be elevated up the corporate agenda. If it is decided that the corporate defense agenda does indeed need to be elevated to a more prominent position, then it is likely that certain issues must first be addressed.

#### 3.4.2.1 A Change in Mind-Set

First, there needs to be a recognition and acceptance at the top of the organization that an adequate corporate defense program is essential to the achievement of the long-term objectives of the organization. This may require a change in mind-set in certain organizations whereby corporate defense needs to be viewed in a more positive light. Corporate defense can no longer be viewed as a black art or some form of witchcraft as is sometimes suggested, even if this is merely said in jest. Rather than being viewed as a necessary evil, it needs to be viewed as an essential part of the business aimed at safeguarding the interests of the stakeholders and providing stakeholders with a sense of security, comfort, and confidence. It needs to be viewed as a business enabler rather than a disabler whereby corporate defense helps the organization to engage in prudent business activities, which will benefit the stakeholders in the long term, and to avoid engaging in business activities, which may be to the detriment of the stakeholders. Corporate defense needs to be viewed as an essential element of sound business practices and should be addressed as part of day-to-day business decision making rather than being addressed in isolation of the business. From the organization's perspective, it needs to be recognized that offense and defense are two sides of the same coin and therefore cannot and should not be addressed in isolation.

Any change in mind-set must begin at the top of the organization. The board must realize that it has the ultimate responsibility for corporate defense oversight, and it needs to accept that it has a duty to ensure that there is appropriate oversight of the organization's corporate defense initiative in place at strategic, tactical, and operational levels. In order to successfully alter an existing mind-set, this change needs to be driven by the board and executive management.

#### 3.4.2.2 A Seat at the Top Table

There is an old business expression that states that *if you don't have a seat at the table then you are not on the agenda*. This applies as much to the issues of corporate defense as it does to any other topic of interest. A seat at the top table provides corporate defense with a voice, and if corporate scandals have taught us anything, it is that organizations need to have a voice representing corporate defense at the top table. This voice should be similar to the Minister or Secretary of Defense in the National context and can offer a necessary counterbalance to the prioritization of short-term interests at the expense of long-term sustainability. Such a voice could help ensure that corporate defense implications will be integrated into strategic discussions and strategic decision making. This will help the board and executive management to ensure that due consideration is given to possible corporate defense implications in advance of major decisions being made and that corporate defense matters become integrated into the board reporting process.

A corporate defense representative or sponsor would be expected to be the champion of corporate defense within the organization and to provide leadership in this regard. This would involve communicating the corporate defense vision and mission statement throughout the organization and helping to raise the stature of the corporate defense functions where required. The corporate defense sponsor would be expected to provide counsel to the board and executive management in corporate defense-related matters and to provide input in relation to possible implications for the business. The position would include being considered a trusted advisor on such matters and offering an available and respected sounding board. It would also involve the mentoring and coaching of the corporate defense management team.

The corporate defense sponsor would be expected to liaise with other members of the C-suite and to help ensure that appropriate attention and consideration are given to corporate defense issues and their potential implications. It would also help to provide a necessary countermeasure when and if required, and help to ensure that there is sufficient and robust challenge to, and appropriate scrutiny of, issues that could potentially have a negative impact on the organization. It is essential that a healthy level of necessary tension exists throughout the organization in order to ensure that appropriate checks and balances are in place and are operating effectively.

### 3.4.2.3 A Cultural Shift Required

What is required is a cultural shift in how organizations view corporate defense activities. Organizations need to start viewing corporate defense activities as necessary and valuable assets. They need to better understand the intangible nature of these assets. They need to stop viewing these activities as an additional cost that it is required to endure, but rather as activities that can help provide essential value to the organization and the achievement of its objectives. Therefore, corporate defense activities must be viewed as investments, as providers of value in themselves, and there needs to be a clear understanding and appreciation of the nature of this value.

In order to obtain value for money from the existing investment into these activities, an organization needs to clearly understand the potential added value that these activities can provide to the organization and its activities, and establish requirements that are aligned to the organization's vision, mission statement, and strategy. Corporate defense activities need to be incorporated into the business model to not only make it easier for the organization to do the right things but also to help ensure that the right things are being done in the right way, by the right people, in the right places, at the right times. By embedding corporate defense into day-to-day business activities, it helps to ensure that it forms part of the organization's DNA and helps to ensure that everyday decisions are based on a balanced view with the objectives of the organization at heart.

### 3.4.2.4 A Change in Orientation

Such a change will also require those involved in corporate defense activities to also change the way in which they approach their activities. In order to help ensure alignment with the organization's vision, mission statement, and strategy, corporate defense practitioners will need to initially adopt a more strategic focus and need to replace their traditional *control-centric* or *risk-centric* orientation with a more *vision-centric, mission-centric, strategy-centric,* and *objective-centric* orientation. This means that their primary focus should first and foremost be on helping in the achievement of the organization's strategic objectives and ensuring that these objectives are set with the best long-term interests of the stakeholders in mind. It also means ensuring that the organization is taking the necessary steps to preserve value and to safeguard stakeholder interests. Such a strategic focus will help align corporate defense activities with the rest of the organization.

For some organizations, this will involve a change in focus from what can go wrong or what can be controlled, to a focus on what needs to go right and how it can best ensure that these things do go right without disruption. This means that rather than focusing on the effect of a hazard event and searching for a remedy that there is a sharper focus on addressing the cause of such an event and trying to prevent its occurrence in the first instance. As in human health, in everyday business, it is generally recognized that *prevention is better than cure*.

### 3.4.3 A PROGRAM FOR CHANGE

The extent of change required by any organization will be determined by its appraisal of its current situation, its satisfaction with this appraisal, and where the organization would like to see itself at different points in the future (i.e., short, medium, and long term). It is unlikely that any radical change in attitude and approach to corporate defense can be achieved overnight, and it will not be without its distinct challenges and difficulties. In order to achieve best results what is required is a dedicated program for change that incorporates a formal structured approach to addressing corporate defense at strategic, tactical, and operational levels. This program should ideally be demanded by stakeholders, initiated by the board of directors, and supported by executive management in order to shape the corporate defense agenda, and to help ensure that corporate defense activities are appropriately prioritized.

#### 3.4.3.1 Organizational Change

A program for change in corporate defense will need to factor in certain requirements for organizational change and be cognizant of the challenges that this can present to an organization. These can include challenges relating to internal politics, structural changes, and system changes. The application of change management techniques, processes, and practices can help smooth this transition. In addition, lessons learned by the organization from past experiences can also help to ensure that the required changes are addressed in the optimum manner and that unnecessary issues are avoided. The extent of these challenges can vary from one organization to another and need to be carefully managed in all cases.

#### 3.4.3.2 Behavioral Change

Any required changes in attitudes and mind-sets will need to take account of the human factor, which, as previously discussed, can be somewhat unpredictable, and any required changes to human behavior are likely to meet with some form of resistance due to alienation or resentment and so on. Therefore, the organization needs to be sensitive to the possible reactions it may receive. The extent of any resistance is likely to be influenced by the state of health of the organization's stakeholder relations, including the prevailing levels of trust and support present. It is also likely to be influenced by the culture of the organization and any subcultures that exist. In order to receive the requisite level of buy-in from its stakeholders, the organization needs to ensure that its sales pitch adequately addresses its stakeholder interests and that they feel sufficiently motivated to embrace any proposed changes. When setting the corporate defense agenda, the potential impact on stakeholders needs to receive due consideration.

#### 3.4.3.3 Shaping the Corporate Defense Agenda

In order to help shape the corporate defense agenda, an organization needs to consider the case for change, including the business case for a corporate defense program. The business case should focus on the value proposition and address benefits associated with an improved corporate defense initiative as well as the potential costs of inaction to the organization and its stakeholders. The corporate defense agenda should focus on achieving an appropriate balance between value creation and value preservation activities and promoting better decision-making at strategic, tactical, and operational levels. For best results the corporate defense agenda should be in alignment with the organization's business agenda and should also contribute to the setting of the business agenda.

# 4 The Corporate Defense Program and Strategy

Every battle is won before it is fought*

**Sun Tzu**

## 4.1 REQUIREMENT FOR A CORPORATE DEFENSE PROGRAM

When considering an organization's corporate defense program and what is involved, it may be helpful to consider it from a similar perspective to the Department or Ministry of Defense when it is considering a program for national defense (MOD 2010). A similar formal structured approach can help to ensure that all the major issues are identified and receive due consideration in the process. Obviously, the issues that need to be addressed are very different, but applying a similar formal methodology will be beneficial.

As previously mentioned, the delivery of long-term value and sustainable business success requires concentrated efforts by the organization in both value creation and value preservation. An organization's corporate defense program needs to address how it intends to deliver on the value preservation imperative and help ensure the preservation of stakeholder value in the short, medium, and long terms.

In order to help create the required cultural shift discussed in Chapter 3 and to help elevate corporate defense on the corporate agenda, there needs to be a carefully planned corporate defense program, which needs to be vigilantly managed. This is best achieved by designing a formal structured program that is specifically tailored to address the corporate defense challenges facing the organization at strategic, tactical, and operational levels.

---

* Per *Sun Tzu's The Art of War: Bilingual Edition with Complete Chinese and English Text*, 2008, Lionel Giles, Tuttle Publishing, Hong Kong.

Ideally, a corporate defense program should first and foremost have a strategic focus, which in turn provides direction at tactical and operational levels. Unfortunately, in many organizations, the individual defense-related programs (i.e., governance, compliance, assurance, etc.) can be tactically or operationally driven rather than being strategically driven, and this can result in a disjointed and uncoordinated approach to the value preservation obligation. Framing an effective approach to corporate defense should preferably involve an overarching program that assimilates all of these defense-related programs into a single coherent strategic approach.

A corporate defense program represents an organization's collective efforts to preserve stakeholder value and reflects how an organization is organized to safeguard its stakeholder interests. It reflects the collective measures taken by an organization to defend itself against the many hazards that can potentially damage stakeholder value. It basically represents the umbrella term used to describe the organization's collective program for self-defense.

### 4.1.1 Determining Your Corporate Defense Program Requirements

Corporate defense by its very nature is an interdisciplinary subject as it involves managing a number of interrelated disciplines, all of which have an important role to play in safeguarding the organization and its stakeholder interests. In order to maximize the effectiveness of an organization's corporate defense efforts, all defense-related activities need to be managed in a coordinated and integrated manner. In order to ensure that the organization's corporate defense program addresses the organization's requirements, the organization must first determine its precise requirements.

#### 4.1.1.1 Level of Formality and Structure

The organization of corporate defense programs can vary considerably from organization to organization. Typically, corporate defense programs can vary from being either a formal structured program or an informal unstructured program relying on ad-hoc efforts. They can vary from systems where all defense-related activities operate as integrated functions, or where they operate as standalone silo functions within the organization. They can vary from proactive programs requiring discipline, diligence, and vigilance, to reactive programs based on day-to-day fire-fighting, troubleshooting, emergency operations, and crisis management. While each organization must determine for itself the degree of formality and structure that best suits its circumstances, prudence would suggest that effective corporate defense requires a formal structured program.

#### 4.1.1.2 Assessment of Existing Capability

The organization must evaluate its own capabilities in relation to corporate defense. This should involve paying particular attention to its existing skills, qualifications, and expertise in relation to the individual critical corporate defense components. This will help to evaluate the consistency of current levels across different defense components, and help to identify the requirement to retain external expertise in specified areas. It will also help to identify required education and training initiatives in certain areas. Such an assessment will also help evaluate the level of delegation of oversight in areas that may be considered to be highly technical in nature (e.g., compliance and cyber security). The assessment of existing capability is an important early step in identifying corporate defense program requirements.

### 4.1.2 Designing a Formal Corporate Defense Program

Designing a robust corporate defense program requires the same high level of preparation and planning as is required for the organization's business (offense) program. The business program requires a vision, a mission statement, a strategy, and a business model in order to successfully integrate, coordinate, and manage the organization's efforts in relation to areas such as sales and marketing, advertising and promotion, research and development, product production, service distribution and delivery, logistics, and so on. Similarly, a comprehensive defense program requires a vision, a mission statement, a strategy, and a framework or model.

#### 4.1.2.1 Ambitions and Expectations

Corporate defense is concerned with the safeguarding of stakeholders' interests and therefore a formal approach to corporate defense should reflect the expectations of stakeholders. A formal program can help the organization to assess these expectations and to address them accordingly. The corporate defense program should address the ambitions of the business and support the achievement of the organization's business objectives. Such a program should be tailored to complement the fulfillment of the organization's business ambitions and be used to set corporate defense ambitions and expectations. This should include determining the nature of corporate defense activities and the scale and tempo of corporate defense operations.

#### 4.1.2.2 Formal Strategy and Planning

The corporate defense and other capabilities (including business capabilities) required to meet corporate defense ambitions and expectations are derived as part of the strategy and planning process. This process includes formally addressing the requirement for a corporate defense vision, mission statement, strategy, and framework. It involves clearly identifying the value that a corporate defense program is expected to deliver to the organization and its stakeholders. It also involves deciding on the key corporate defense activities and identifying expected issues such as the necessary inputs, capitals affected, innovation required, value drivers, expected outputs, and predicted outcomes. All of these issues need to form part of the strategy and planning process in order to ensure that they are appropriately considered as part of the program.

### 4.1.3 Identifying the Critical Components of Self-Defense

Every organization will have to put certain corporate defense-related activities in place within their organizational structure, and these may be present in different capacities at strategic, tactical, and operational levels. A corporate defense program ideally needs to incorporate all of these various corporate defense-related activities within its scope to help ensure that all defense activities are in alignment with one another, and to ensure that they are all in alignment with the business. Regardless of the scope of the program, it should at a minimum address what have been identified as the critical components of an organization's program for self-defense (see Figure 4.1). These components represent the fundamental cogs in the corporate defense wheel. For best results, all these components need to operate effectively.

---

*Governance*: How the organization is directed, managed, and controlled all the way from the boardroom to the frontlines.

*Risk*: How the organization identifies, measures, and manages the risks it is exposed to.

*Compliance*: How the organization ensures that its activities are in conformance with all relevant mandatory and voluntary requirements.

*Intelligence*: How the organization ensures that it gets the right information, for the right purpose, and in the right format, to the right person, in the right place and at the right time.

*Security*: How the organization ensures that it protects its critical assets from threats and danger, its people, information, technology, and facilities.

*Resilience*: How the organization ensures that it has the capacity to withstand, rebound, or recover from the direct and indirect consequences of a shock, disturbance, or disruption.

*Controls*: How the organization ensures that it has taken appropriate actions in order to address risks and to help ensure that the organization's objectives will be achieved.

*Assurance*: The system in place to provide a degree of confidence or a level of comfort to the stakeholders that everything is operating in a satisfactory manner (Lyons 2012b).

---

**FIGURE 4.1** Critical corporate defense components. (Each of these critical components are individually addressed in more detail in Chapters 9 and 10.)

#### 4.1.3.1  Outline of Critical Components

The fundamental corporate defense cogs refer to the eight critical components that are considered essential for an effective corporate defense program. Figure 4.1 provides a brief description of these eight critical components.

#### 4.1.3.2  Individual Subprograms

Effective corporate defense requires that each of these critical components is operating effectively throughout the organization. For best results, each of these critical components should also have its own individual subprogram that is in alignment with the overall corporate defense program. These are necessary in order to determine how best each of these components can help contribute to the corporate defense program, and how these components are expected to help achieve the corporate defense objectives. These subprograms can help ensure that each component is appropriately managed at strategic, tactical, and operational levels. A formal structured corporate defense program makes it far easier to ensure that all these components are in alignment, particularly if they are co-coordinated within the overall corporate defense structure.

#### 4.1.4  CORPORATE DEFENSE PROGRAM: STAKEHOLDER QUESTIONS

Stakeholders need to be prepared to put certain questions to their organization in relation to their organization's current corporate defense program. Organizations, in turn, need to be prepared to address these questions in an open and transparent manner. The following are examples of basic questions that stakeholders might be expected to ask:

- Does the organization currently have a formal corporate defense program in place?
- Has the corporate defense program been formally approved by the board?
- Does the organization have formal subprograms in place for each of the critical corporate defense components?

#### 4.1.5  CRITICAL COMPONENT DEFICIENCIES

It is common for postmortem investigations into the causes of large-scale corporate failures or scandals to typically identify deficiencies in a number of the different critical corporate defense components in the organization(s) concerned as being a significant contributing factor. The very fact that deficiencies exist in a number of these components can often exacerbate the initial impact and the subsequent collateral damage. The following example may help to illustrate this point.

---

**AIG FINANCIAL PRODUCTS—COLLATERALIZED DEBT OBLIGATIONS PORTFOLIO**

In September 2008, the U.S. Government rescued the AIG Group, at that time the world's largest insurance organization. The Congressional Oversight Panel Report (COP 2010) highlighted numerous issues on how the collateralized debt obligations (CDO) portfolio of AIG Financial Products (FP) contributed to the AIG Group rescue. Examples of the highlighted corporate defense issues include the following:

*Governance*: From a governance perspective, it stated that AIG had become so large that when Hank Greenberg, its chairman and CEO, stepped down in 2005, its leadership did not understand the vast web of interrelationships that existed within the group. It also stated that there had been lax oversight of AIG FP where the CDO portfolio resided.

---

*(Continued)*

*Risk*: From a risk perspective, it stated that management failed to understand the build up of risks in AIG FP and in particular in the CDO portfolio. It also stated that there was a lack of a sophisticated risk-management structure in place within AIG and noted that it failed to perform prudent risk versus reward analysis as potential risks far exceeded any potential rewards.

*Intelligence*: From an intelligence perspective, it stated that overall the CDO portfolio represented a complex structure involving cross-holdings and cross subsidizations across the entire AIG Group, which required multilevel communication. It noted that there was quite clearly ineffective information sharing between AIG and AIG FP and that systemic technology issues prevented aggregated measurement across the AIG Group.

*Resilience*: From a resilience perspective, it noted AIG had failed to put sufficient capital buffers in place to meet its collateral calls and it noted that the CDO model was insufficiently robust to anticipate the impact of the market meltdown.

*Controls*: From a controls perspective, it simply stated that AIG had inadequate valuation and risk controls in place.

*Assurance*: From an assurance perspective, it noted that a red flag raised by the external auditors PWC in 2007, noting a material weakness of the valuation of the AIG FP credit default swaps (CDS) portfolio did not receive sufficient attention.

These examples and other corporate defense deficiencies taken together resulted in an $85 billion taxpayer rescue package and serve as interesting examples of how individual deficiencies in a number of different defense components can collectively result in a potentially devastating situation.

## 4.2 CORPORATE DEFENSE VISION AND MISSION STATEMENT

As is the case with the overall corporate vision and mission statement, the defense vision and mission statement can help to set the strategic corporate defense agenda by helping to visualize the big picture. They can also help in focusing the organizational mind-set and providing a source of inspiration and motivation for those involved in corporate defense activities. Ideally, the corporate defense vision and mission statement should be in close alignment with the organization's overall vision and mission statement.

### 4.2.1 CORPORATE DEFENSE VISION

The corporate defense vision provides the organization with a degree of clarity in relation to the long-term aim of corporate defense within the organization. The long-term aim in turn provides the organization with a sense of direction, and the delivery of the long-term aim instills a sense of purpose for those involved in corporate defense activities. The organization's corporate defense vision is achieved by all defense-related activities working together to ensure that the corporate defense initiative is fit to address today's challenges, prepared to address the challenges of tomorrow, and capable of supporting the organization in building a better future.

#### 4.2.1.1 Drafting the Vision Statement

The vision statement should provide a clear description of the desired future state of corporate defense in the organization and help the organization to visualize the precise purpose of corporate defense and what it intends to achieve now and in the future. The vision statement should be short, clear, and succinct, and it should be tailored to the organization in question. The best vision statements are considered to be inspirational, memorable, and concise.

### 4.2.1.2 Corporate Defense Vision Statement: Examples

Basic examples of corporate defense vision statements include the following: Our corporate defense vision is to

- safeguard stakeholder interests and optimize stakeholder value
- support sustainable stakeholder value
- deliver a world class corporate defense program
- play our part in delivering long term stakeholder value by addressing our organization's value preservation imperative
- help to create a sustainable business

### 4.2.1.3 Corporate Defense Vision Statement: Stakeholder Questions

The following are examples of basic questions that stakeholders might be expected to ask in relation to the organization's corporate defense vision statement:

- Does the organization have a corporate defense vision?
- Does the organization have its corporate defense vision formally documented?
- How does this vision statement complement the organization's business vision?

## 4.2.2 THE CORPORATE DEFENSE MISSION STATEMENT

A corporate defense mission statement should provide a clear rationale as to how the corporate defense vision will be achieved and should help to clearly define the long-term corporate defense mission.

### 4.2.2.1 Drafting the Mission Statement

In drafting the mission statement, care should be taken to ensure that it clearly describes the fundamental purpose of the corporate defense program to the organization, and perhaps more importantly to its stakeholders. The mission statement should provide a clear statement of intent with regard to the corporate defense program's long-term mission, and act as a reference point in order to help in guiding future corporate defense decisions and actions. It should broadly outline the strategic aims of the corporate defense program in order to help clarify the corporate defense assignment, and help in setting achievable objectives and in setting realistic stakeholder expectations. The mission statement should also provide a clear understanding of how the organization views the role of corporate defense in the context of overall business strategy, thereby providing assistance in the formulation of the corporate defense strategy. As with the vision statement, the mission statement should be carefully tailored toward the circumstances of the organization in question.

### 4.2.2.2 Corporate Defense Mission Statement: Example

A basic example of a corporate defense mission statement is as follows:

> The corporate defense mission is to help ensure the long-term sustainability of the organization by helping to support its value creation efforts and by working to ensure that adequate and appropriate value preservation measures are in place and operating effectively. This will involve ensuring that all corporate defense activities are strategically aligned, tactically integrated, and operating in unison towards the common objectives of the organization.

### 4.2.2.3 Corporate Defense Mission Statement: Stakeholder Questions

The following are examples of basic questions that stakeholders might be expected to ask in relation to the organization's corporate defense mission statement:

- Has the organization determined its long-term corporate defense mission?
- Does the organization have a formally documented corporate defense mission statement?
- How does the mission statement complement the corporate defense vision?

### 4.2.3 CRITICAL COMPONENT VISION AND MISSION STATEMENTS

Each of the critical components of a corporate defense program should also have its own individual vision and mission statements that are in alignment with the overall corporate defense vision and mission statements. For example, there should be a risk management vision, a security vision, and so on, and there should be a governance mission statement, an intelligence mission statement, and so on. This will help provide clarity and direction in each of the critical corporate defense components.

## 4.3 THE CORPORATE DEFENSE STRATEGY

Once an organization has first established a clear corporate defense vision and an equally clear mission statement, it is then in a position to address its corporate defense strategy. Ideally, the corporate defense strategy needs to form part of the overall business strategy so that defense activities become integrated into all aspects of the business and operate throughout the organization. Without a defense strategy, corporate defense activities can become inconsistent, erratic, misaligned, and ineffective. The approach to preparing the corporate defense strategy should ideally mirror the organization's approach to preparing its business strategy as such a process will be familiar to the organization. This means that a certain degree of formality is required, and it is not acceptable for an organization to claim or take comfort in the fact that while no formal defense strategy exists, the corporate defense strategy is implied by virtue of the existence of its corporate defense activities. Such an approach is fraught with danger and is similar to *the tail wagging the dog* and while hazards may have been avoided in the past, it is highly unlikely to be an effective approach in the medium to long term.

Many organizations may not have a formal corporate defense strategy in place, which therefore reduces the likelihood that its corporate defense activities are being managed in an effective and efficient manner, and are in alignment with business strategy. This can lead to a dysfunctional organization with many internal conflicts as a result of a lack of clarity and conflicting objectives. Given the complexity of the prevailing corporate defense landscape (as addressed in Chapter 2), this places a premium on the requirement for a good defense strategy. In such circumstances, a corporate defense strategy needs to be both comprehensive and flexible, and focused on delivering on its mission statement and in the achievement of its corporate defense objectives.

### 4.3.1 FORMULATING THE CORPORATE DEFENSE STRATEGY

The corporate defense vision and mission statement should be in clear alignment with the organization's vision and mission statement, and likewise the corporate defense strategy should be in clear alignment with the corporate defense vision and mission statement. When formulating a corporate defense strategy, it is essential that it should outline at a strategic level the measures required by the organization in order to help achieve these long-term aims.

#### 4.3.1.1 Alignment with Business Strategy

The organization's business strategy should ideally outline the organization's approach to creating value for stakeholders, and therefore the corporate defense strategy should outline how it is intended to preserve this value over time. In the ideal scenario, the corporate defense strategy should be seen as an element of the overall business strategy that simply addresses the value preservation aspects of business strategy. In order to positively contribute to business strategy, the corporate defense strategy should mirror it at all times, and represent an upfront element of business strategy, rather than being seen as some sort of shadow strategy that remains forever lurking in the shadows.

### 4.3.1.2  Setting Strategic Objectives

Developing a corporate defense strategy that can be successfully executed in practice can represent a considerable challenge. It is important that the strategy is relevant and understandable, and this begins with the setting of the strategic objectives that are considered to be one of the fundamental building blocks of the organization's strategic plan. Corporate defense strategic objectives should be closely aligned to the corporate defense vision and mission statement as their purpose is to help convert the vision and mission statement into tangible actions, which in turn can help to achieve the required results. Objective setting should be from the top-down, and strategic objectives should help to guide tactical and operational objectives. They should help to determine where the organization's efforts are to be directed and differ from other objectives in that they tend to be long term in nature and can be broken down into broad categories. In many instances, strategic objectives may not be easily measured as they tend to be continuous and ongoing. Strategic objectives are required in relation to each of the key areas to be addressed by the corporate defense program.

### 4.3.1.3  Corporate Defense Strategic Objectives: Examples

Basic examples of corporate defense strategic objectives include the following:

- *Strategy*: To help influence a healthy balanced corporate strategy
- *Business model*: To add value to, and to positively contribute to, the business model
- *Value*: To help ensure the preservation of long-term sustainable value
- *Stakeholders*: To help increase stakeholder confidence and trust in the organization
- *Assets*: To help safeguard the organization's tangible and intangible assets
- *People, processes, and systems*: To manage all corporate defense-related activities (including people, processes, and systems) in a coordinated and integrated manner

### 4.3.1.4  Corporate Defense Strategy: Stakeholder Questions

The following are examples of basic questions that stakeholders might be expected to ask in relation to the organization's corporate defense strategy:

- Has the organization formulated a formal corporate defense strategy?
- Has the organization clearly set its corporate defense strategic objectives?
- Are the corporate defense objectives in alignment with the business objectives?

### 4.3.2  Critical Component Strategies

Each of the critical components should also formulate its own individual substrategies and set its own strategic objectives in its area of expertise. These substrategies should take their direction from the overall corporate defense strategy in order to ensure that they too are in alignment with the overall business strategy. Once these substrategies are in alignment with the overall corporate defense strategy, it is likely that they will also be in alignment with one another, although it would be prudent to cross-reference each of these substrategies and associated objectives with one another. For example, the risk management strategy should complement and be consistent with the internal controls strategy, compliance strategy, and so on. Where inconsistencies are identified, these need to be resolved judiciously.

## 4.4  CORPORATE DEFENSE FRAMEWORK

In order to help ensure that the corporate defense strategy is implemented in a coherent manner, the organization must select a tactical framework that will best facilitate the execution of its corporate defense strategy. In the corporate defense context, the tactical framework in place represents a description of the system of corporate defense practices, which determine how corporate defense activities are performed throughout the organization.

A corporate defense framework is made up of the essential supporting structures that enable the organization's corporate defense activities to operate on an ongoing basis. It represents the underlying configuration of systems in place that facilitates the day-to-day management of the corporate defense program. It represents how the program is organized and engineered, and how this structure will have a significant impact on the effectiveness of the program in executing the corporate defense strategy in the short, medium, and long terms. The corporate defense framework determines how the organization's people, processes, and systems interact in relation to its corporate defense activities.

### 4.4.1 FRAMEWORK DESIGN

The design of the corporate defense framework is extremely important as it determines the logistics of corporate defense activities and lays the foundation for the success of the corporate defense program. This framework includes the infrastructure in place to support corporate defense activities including the processes, systems, and practices in place to achieve this end. It also comprises a technological aspect, including its technological architecture and the various technologies available.

Given that organizations can be complex entities, in many organizations the corporate defense framework has developed organically over the years without any premeditation or the required preplanning associated with the type of framework required by the organization in question. Typically, organic frameworks develop in an ad-hoc fashion and reflect a legacy of how the different critical components developed in the organization over time. In many cases, this development has been sporadic in nature, often the result of a reaction to an immediate incident rather than a phased preplanned approach.

Often a critical component becomes prioritized because it happens to be the *flavor of the month* at a particular point in time, only to later be replaced by another component that has become the focus of attention. This can very often result in operational silos and stovepipe-type structures that operate independently of one another. Silo-type structures can be extremely difficult to manage in an integrated manner as each develops its own people, processes, and systems to suit its own individual requirements in isolation of other organizational activities. Therefore, in many organizations, the framework within which their corporate defense activities operate have developed incrementally over time, rather than by any preplanned holistic development. This can be very challenging in terms of the effectiveness and efficiency of the entire corporate defense program.

A corporate defense program is best placed to succeed when it is managed in an integrated manner, and therefore there is a requirement for the organization to design and implement an integrated framework that will enable the integrated management of the corporate defense program.

#### 4.4.1.1 An Umbrella Framework*

What is required is a coherent framework that enables the smooth integration of corporate defense activities at all levels of the organization. This requires an umbrella-type approach that helps ensure that all relevant corporate defense activities operate under a single umbrella framework, rather than operating independently in isolation of the corporate defense program. An umbrella framework can also facilitate the unification, alignment, and integration of these corporate defense activities. Such an integrated framework can help ensure that all corporate defense activities are unified under the one umbrella so that they share a common purpose, whereby they are all operating in unison toward common strategies, objectives, and goals. The existence of an integrated framework can help to avoid and dramatically reduce any misalignments between any of the critical corporate defense components.

---

* For further information, refer to the corporate defense management (CDM) framework, which is addressed in more detail in Chapter 12.

#### 4.4.1.2 Effective Coordination

An umbrella-type framework also facilitates effective coordination of the corporate defense program at strategic, tactical, and operational levels so that all corporate defense activities both individually and collectively are working toward the common good of the organization as a whole. Effective coordination is required in order to help ensure that there is an appropriate level of communication and information sharing among the corporate defense activities themselves and with the business. Effective coordination helps to enable the required level of co-operation and collaboration among these activities and can help ensure that they are supporting each other and working together. Such an approach is required in order to break down silo-type structures and to integrate corporate defense activities.

### 4.4.2 FRAMEWORK SELECTION

When selecting a suitable corporate defense framework, consideration should be given to how such a framework will facilitate the integration of the critical corporate defense components. A truly comprehensive and integrated framework will facilitate this integration at all levels, top to bottom, side to side, and front to back.

#### 4.4.2.1 Vertical and Horizontal Integration

Vertical integration refers to the framework's capability to help ensure that there is an appropriate integration of activities from the top-down and from the bottom-up. This specifically refers to monitoring and reporting of information so that it flows both downstream all the way from the board, and upstream all the way from the frontlines.

Horizontal integration refers to the framework's capability to help ensure that there is an appropriate cross-functional integration of activities at strategic, tactical, and operational levels. This specifically refers to interdepartmental communication across the business and across the various corporate defense functions.

#### 4.4.2.2 Selection Choice

Each organization must ensure that it selects a framework which it feels is best suited to its organization structure and to address its expectations. The framework selected should be one that provides the organization with the appropriate level of flexibility and agility to suit the organization's individual requirements and circumstances. The focus on selecting a particular framework should be driven by the requirement to execute the corporate defense strategy rather than focusing on the individual frameworks themselves. A particular framework should only be chosen if it is deemed to be a good fit with the execution of the corporate defense strategy and the achievement of corporate defense objectives.

#### 4.4.2.3 Corporate Defense Framework: Stakeholder Questions

The following are examples of basic questions that stakeholders might be expected to ask in relation to the organization's corporate defense framework:

- Does the organization currently have a formal corporate defense framework in place?
- Has this framework developed organically or is it the result of a formal selection process?
- Is this framework currently designed to integrate all corporate defense activities under the one umbrella?

### 4.4.3 CRITICAL COMPONENT FRAMEWORKS

Each of the critical components should also be required to select a subframework that is specifically designed to help manage their area of expertise in an integrated manner. In the majority of these critical components, a number of international best practice frameworks are available that can be incorporated in the overall corporate defense framework (refer to Chapters 9 and 10 for specific details).

## 4.5  CORPORATE DEFENSE PLAN

The corporate defense plan outlines how the organization intends to implement its corporate defense strategy. It is therefore by necessity a function of the organization's corporate defense strategy and its corporate defense framework, as the strategy and framework provide the context from which the plan can be prepared. They serve as drivers for the plan and set the parameters from which the plan can be plotted.

A corporate defense plan is required in order to determine an appropriate plan of action so that the corporate defense strategy can be implemented in practice and in order to help achieve the organization's corporate defense objectives. The plan therefore serves to determine how best the organization's corporate defense resources can be manipulated in order to achieve corporate defense objectives. It lays out a roadmap or game plan of the necessary action steps required to be carried out, and acts as a comprehensive blueprint of the organization's overall corporate defense efforts. At a detailed level, it outlines all of the critical tasks and activities that are required to be performed within specified timescales.

### 4.5.1  CORPORATE DEFENSE PLANNING

Success in business or in corporate defense requires strategy setting, tactical planning, and operational execution. A prerequisite to performing is *planning* (i.e., clearly determining what exactly needs to be performed) and meaningful performing, informing, and holding to account can only be achieved after meaningful planning has first taken place. In the famous words of the former U.S. President Dwight D. Eisenhower "plans are worthless, but planning is everything" (The American Presidency Project 1957). As with all plans, the planning process itself is the critical element, if this is not carried out in a competent manner then the resulting plan will be flawed and unlikely to be successful in achieving the sought after objectives. At a business level, failures in strategy execution are almost always a result of poor planning, and the same challenges apply to the execution of the corporate defense strategy. Corporate defense planning is therefore perhaps one of the most important aspects of the strategy execution.

Each organization may have developed its own preferred planning methodology over time that it feels is the best fit with the organization's culture, structure, and so on. If the organization has a history of successful implementation of plans or projects, it may be advisable to leverage this organizational experience and adopt this preferred methodology in the corporate defense planning process. Alternatively, there are numerous available planning methodologies available in the marketplace that can provide guidance in relation to the planning process.

The corporate defense planning process involves making important decisions on how best to pursue the strategy and acts as step-by-step guide on how to implement the strategy. The planning process must identify the relevant inputs and activities required to produce expected outputs. The corporate defense plan once drafted should make it very clear exactly what work programs and individual tasks or activities are necessary to be performed within a specified time period, and the mix of corporate defense resources required. In the volatile environment of the twenty-first century, the planning process needs to be flexible, adaptable, and subject to continuous improvement. It is no longer advisable to rely on a 5-year, 3-year, or even annual plan; what is required is continuous planning. This means that the planning process needs to be transformed into an ongoing exercise that involves frequent and constant communication among groups of senior leaders in order to take stock of changes in circumstances, and to reprioritize the allocation of resources as required.

An integrated planning process should take a holistic view, and therefore include a dual focus at all times on the achievement of both the corporate defense objectives and the business objectives. It should also be cognizant of the impact and implications that each can have on the other. Integrated planning involves integrating the planning process at strategic, tactical, and operational levels, and wherever possible relevant activities should be performed in a synchronized manner.

#### 4.5.1.1  Situational Analysis: "As Is and to Be"

The corporate defense planning process should begin by taking stock of the current state of affairs within the realm of corporate defense; this is referred to as "As Is." This should involve a review of the current corporate defense environment, including the structure and maturity of the corporate defense initiative and its relationship with the business. It should also involve performing an adequately detailed assessment of the individual critical corporate defense components, their activities, their individual maturity levels, and their ongoing relationships with one another. The purpose of this analysis is to have as clear a picture as possible of the starting point, in order to be able to assess the extent of the journey that needs to be travelled and in order to arrive at the desired destination. This is referred to as "To Be." It becomes very difficult to develop a credible roadmap if you are unsure of your starting point and/or your desired destination. The vision and mission statement therefore provide the necessary guidance on the desired destination.

#### 4.5.1.2  Magnitude and Scope

Once the current state of affairs has been determined, the planning process should perform a gap analysis between the current state and the projected future state as outlined in the corporate defense strategy, and the related corporate defense objectives, in order to ascertain the extent of the work that needs to be performed over the short-, medium-, and long-term time horizons. The plan should reflect the time horizons of the strategy and should be updated regularly with a formal plan prepared at least annually. This will require setting specific short-, medium-, and long-term milestones, in line with corporate defense strategy and objectives.

The associated strategic, tactical, and operational goals that will need to be achieved must then be set in tandem with identifying the precise individual action steps, activities, and tasks that are needed to be performed at strategic, tactical, and operational levels in order to achieve these goals. The process will also involve a prioritization of these actions that is likely to include exercises such as critical path analysis and so on.

It is however important that all aspects of the business will be appropriately safeguarded in order to provide an acceptable level of comfort to stakeholders. It is therefore essential that the scope of the corporate defense plan is comprehensive in nature and it is important that the planning process adopts an enterprise-wide approach. The plan should therefore incorporate all the organization's geographic locations, all business units, and all divisions, departments, and functions. It should also include all branches and subsidiaries. Incomplete coverage can result in inconsistencies, gaps, and vulnerabilities, which can in turn result in unexpected hazard events and potential contagion that could have unknown consequences.

### 4.5.2  Planning Preparation and Groundwork

Preparing the documented roadmap is an important step in the planning process. Outlining the plan on paper can be a technically challenging exercise and can present certain logistical difficulties; however, it is only part of the planning process, and in some instances it may prove to be the easy part. Ensuring that the action plan is realistic and achievable in practice represents a different type of challenge and also requires sufficient preparation and groundwork. Successful implementation requires equally important additional steps that if not dealt with appropriately can lead to implementation problems further down the line, which can ultimately hinder the successful execution of the corporate defense strategy.

#### 4.5.2.1  Delegation of Responsibility

Having identified and prioritized the required actions and tasks, the responsibility for performing these actions and tasks then needs to be allocated to the appropriate individuals and groups throughout the organization. These individuals and groups must determine how the required actions are to be implemented, the approaches to be adopted, the skill-sets required, and tools to be used. Delegation of responsibility typically flows downstream in an organization; however, delegation does not absolve line management from being held accountable. Accountability typically flows upstream, hence the requirement for supervision and oversight. Without clear and appropriate delegation, there may be confusion regarding the responsibility for the performance of required actions, and this can result in ineffective and inefficient implementation and execution.

### 4.5.2.2   Setting Achievable Timescales

The planning process will also involve establishing time frames by which the required actions need to be accomplished and allocating target dates by when they need to be performed. Certain actions may be required to be performed only once with definitive start and end dates, whereas others may be required on a continuous or periodic basis (e.g., daily, weekly, and monthly). Timing is an essential part of any planning process and all required actions should appear as a schedule of planned activities. When scheduling activities, it is important to ensure that there is appropriate alignment and synchronization of interdependent activities and to determine the most appropriate time for each element of the strategy to be implemented, as taking the right action at the right time is critical to the success of the strategy execution.

### 4.5.2.3   Allocation of Resources

The planning process will also involve determining the level of resources that will need to be required and made available in order to execute the required actions. This will involve mobilizing the organization's existing corporate defense resources, and securing approval for the allocation of additional required resources, and any additional investment in order to cover associated additional costs and expenses. Typically, the budget will be finite and therefore certain aspects may need to be prioritized over others. Any such prioritization should take into account the potential impact on achieving the required milestones and the implications of any resulting delays. The planning process must also consider providing appropriate incentives in order to motivate and reward individuals and groups to effectively perform their duties and achieve their targets on schedule.

### 4.5.3   IMPLEMENTATION OF THE CORPORATE DEFENSE PLAN

Once the initial corporate defense plan has been appropriately finalized, it must then be formally approved and ratified at the appropriate level. From a corporate defense perspective, the higher up the organization's hierarchy that formal approval is required, the more seriously the plan will be regarded, and this can send out an important message to the rest of the organization. Each organization needs to determine for itself whether the board needs to approve the precise details of the plan or simply ratify such approval. In terms of the corporate defense program, the more board engagement, the better.

Once this approval has been received, it must then be rolled out and put into practice. The plan, however, is a living entity and may be subject to continuous refinement and amendment depending on the prevailing circumstances. The individuals and groups that have been allocated responsibility for performing the required actions are accountable for achieving their targets. However, changes in the environment can often mean that these targets may not be achieved, and that forecasts and related plans may need to be changed accordingly. Ideally, the plan will have factored in contingencies for unexpected delays and disruptions, but it is nonetheless important that progress is measured on an ongoing basis.

### 4.5.3.1   Measurement of Progress

In order to be able to measure progress, it is important that appropriate targets and goals are set and that their achievement is itself measureable. The targets set should have quantitative and qualitative elements attached to them in addition to pure chronological timescales so that their level of progress can be effectively measured and to help to ensure that all critical milestones are reached and relevant goals achieved. In most instances the quality of the work performed is as important as the quantity of work performed. The status of the implementation of required corporate defense actions, activities, and tasks needs to be closely monitored in order to identify any deviations from the planned outcomes, and to allow adequate time to take any required remedial action to get the plan back on track.

### 4.5.3.2 Managing, Monitoring, and Reporting

The corporate plan should ensure that there is an appropriate system of checks and balances in place to manage and monitor the execution of required action steps and to adequately assess the performance of these tasks. Monitoring can be achieved via ongoing activities or through separate periodic assurance assignments, or through a combination of these two approaches. The existence of ongoing monitoring activities that are embedded into normal day-to-day operations so that monitoring occurs on an ongoing and continuous basis helps to provide real-time or close to real-time supervision. This could include continuous monitoring activities at strategic, tactical, and operational levels in order to oversee, supervise, and verify the appropriateness of the required actions performed, and the extent to which all planned milestones are achieved. The scope and frequency of separate assurance assignments may be subject to the effectiveness of ongoing monitoring activities, the complexity of the activities being undertaken, and the associated risks.

Reporting should flow upstream through the normal reporting channels, and all serious matters noted should be escalated in line with reporting protocols, potentially to the executive management and the board. Effective reporting should include a blending of both qualitative and quantitative metrics in order to help establish the quality and quantity of the work being performed. These can best be measured by identifying a set of key performance indicators (KPIs) in advance and reporting on these KPIs on an ongoing and a periodic basis. Reporting of key risk indicators (KRIs) is also advisable. In such cases, the quality of reporting may be dependent on the quality of the KPIs and KRIs selected by the organization.

### 4.5.3.3 Corporate Defense Plan: Stakeholder Questions

The following are examples of basic questions that stakeholders might be expected to ask in relation to the organization's corporate defense plan:

- Does the organization have a formal corporate defense plan in place?
- Has this plan been formally approved, and at what level has it been approved?
- Is this plan reviewed on a periodic basis and is its implementation status formally reported on a periodic basis? Who receives this report?

### 4.5.4 CRITICAL COMPONENT PLANS

Each of the critical components should also prepare their own individual plans and work programs relevant to their area of expertise. Similar to the overall corporate defense plan, this is necessary so that each discipline or function can identify all required actions, determine how best to execute these actions, identify and receive approval for required resources, allocate appropriate responsibility, and set achievable timescales and targets. They are also required in order to determine how corporate defense activities are to be conducted on a day-to-day basis in the frontline. When setting these plans, it is important that they are in alignment with, and consistent with, the overall corporate defense plan itself. It is also important that the plans of each of the critical components are in alignment and consistent with one another.

# Section II

*A Tactical Perspective*

# 5 Laying the Foundation and Setting the Ground Rules

Shallow men believe in luck. Strong men believe in cause and effect.[*]

**R.W. Emerson**

## 5.1 FUNDAMENTALS OF CORPORATE DEFENSE

How does an organization go about addressing its corporate defense obligations? All organizations are faced with the possibility of potential hazards, and these can arise for numerous reasons. Examples of potential hazards include litigation, fraud, regulatory breaches, crime, espionage, and natural disasters, to name but a few. These hazards represent not only short-term financial risk to the organization, but also a potential knock-on reputational impact, not to mention the human implications and costs. Ultimately, all hazards can have a financial implication, be it in the form of additional costs, reduced profits, or impact on share prices, and so on. These hazards can typically be the result of deficiencies in an organization's corporate defense program, whereby these deficiencies were either intentionally or unintentionally exploited.

### 5.1.1 CORPORATE DEFENSE MEASURES

Every organization is faced with its own unique set of risks, threats, and vulnerabilities, and these will vary depending on the organization's philosophy and culture, the business sector it operates in, its geographic location, and so on. As a result, each organization in turn will need to take its own unique steps to defend against the occurrence of potential hazards in order to help preserve stakeholder value.

---

[*] Per "Worship," *The Conduct of Life*, 1860, Ralph Waldo Emerson.

#### 5.1.1.1   Corporate Defense Disciplines

There are a number of corporate defense components that are generally acknowledged to be required in order to help preserve value and safeguard stakeholder interests (i.e., governance, risk, compliance, intelligence, security, resilience, controls, and assurance). All organizations typically implement a diverse mix of these components to varying degrees in the operation of their business. Each of the critical corporate defense components will have certain specialist disciplines associated with its area of expertise that in themselves require specific technical skills and relevant qualifications. An organization's existing corporate defense measures are a reflection of the extent to which each of these critical components is currently being addressed, and hopefully this mirrors the organization's corporate defense requirements given its own unique circumstances.

#### 5.1.1.2   Current Corporate Defense Efforts

Generally speaking, an organization's corporate defense measures evolve over time as a reaction to its prevailing circumstances. In some organizations, it is acknowledged in advance that certain defense disciplines are necessary and that these require a specific level of experience and expertise. This can result in the setting up of specific departments or functions to act as competence centers for these disciplines (e.g., risk management or compliance functions). In other organizations, their level of experience and expertise in a particular discipline may simply develop organically over time based on the organization's experiences in that particular area. Individual organizations need to be fully cognizant of the extent of its current corporate defense efforts in each of the critical corporate defense components and the level of experience and expertise available within the organization in relation to different corporate defense disciplines.

### 5.1.2   THE CORPORATE DEFENSE RATIONALE

Corporate defense is generally associated with taking appropriate measures to protect the organization and its stakeholders from the occurrence of hazard events. This can include measures to help ensure that its stakeholders are safeguarded from danger, attack, or harm. It can also include taking actions to help shield the organization from experiencing the impact of loss or damage, be it of a financial, physical, or reputational nature. The requirement to defend can be associated with an individual stakeholder, a group of stakeholders, or their associated tangible and intangible assets. Defending against the occurrence of loss or damage is no easy task as it represents an asymmetric challenge in so far as loss or damage can arise as a result of so many different events all of which need to be defended against, and yet only one needs to occur in order to incur a loss or damage. Corporate defense therefore requires constant alertness and continuous vigilance. From a stakeholder perspective, corporate defense represents a fundamental responsibility that is entrusted on their organization and its guardians.

If addressed in an appropriate manner, corporate defense measures can be effective in protecting the organization and its stakeholders from hazard events. These measures can also help support growth, sustainability, and profitability in the long term. If poorly or inadequately addressed however it can result in loss or damage, in poor performance, and lead to ongoing organizational decay in the long term. It can also result in the loss of stakeholder confidence and trust, which in itself can have either an immediate or a long-term catastrophic impact on the organization's achievement of its objectives. The importance of an adequate corporate defense program should therefore never be underestimated.

#### 5.1.2.1   Lessons Learned

Organizations can improve their existing corporate defense efforts by learning lessons from the past. Valuable lessons need to be learned from the organization's own previous hazard experiences, and by ensuring that appropriate remedial action is taken to rectify issues that have been identified as contributing to the occurrence of previous hazard events. Equally valuable and less costly lessons can also be learned by the previous hazard experiences of other organizations. The identified failings of competitors or other similar organizations provide an opportunity to ensure that the organization addresses known vulnerabilities, weaknesses, and deficiencies. In doing so, it can ensure that it is adequately insulated against the occurrence of similar hazard events and help avoid the associated financial, physical, and reputational impact that can result. Learning lessons from past experiences however requires an inquisitive mind-set and a clear appreciation and understanding of the purpose of different corporate defense measures, and the capabilities of their associated specialist corporate defense disciplines.

### 5.1.2.2 Bullet-Proofing and Future-Proofing the Organization

Organizations are faced with a multitude of hazards that can be detrimental to the achievement of its objectives. In such circumstances, the corporate defense program can act as a buffer between the occurrence of hazard events and the potential impact that these events can have on your organization. An effective corporate defense program can in effect help bullet-proof the organization against the occurrence of hazard events so that your organization can not only survive but also thrive during periods of turbulence and chaos when other organizations are struggling or devastated. Bullet-proofing involves providing protection to the organization against the impact of a hazard event, and an effective corporate defense program can in effect act as the organization's bullet-proof vest. The bullet-proof vest provides the organization with an extra level of protection that can actually allow the organization to take risks and reap rewards that other organizations are simply not in a position to do.

An effective corporate defense program can help future-proof the organization to ensure that it has developed measures to anticipate the occurrence of and safeguard against future hazards. Such measures can help minimize the impact of hazards. Future-proofing is concerned with delivering long-term sustainable value and developing the ability to accurately predict and prepare in advance for potential hazard events. It involves building durability, redundancy, flexibility, and adaptability into the organization's structures, so that it is adequately prepared to address the challenges of the future rather than simply addressing the challenges of yesterday and today.

## 5.2 CORPORATE DEFENSE DOMAIN

The corporate defense domain refers to the entire field of expertise that can contribute to an organization's corporate defense program. It relates to the critical corporate defense components and the related specialist disciplines associated with each of these components. It is concerned with the range of corporate defense-related activities, all of which contribute to the defense of the organization and its stakeholder interests. In effect it relates to the extent of the corporate defense jurisdiction and the areas that potentially need to be covered by a corporate defense program. The corporate defense domain can help an organization identify the different aspects of corporate defense that need to be considered when deciding on the corporate defense measures to be put in place.

### 5.2.1 CORPORATE DEFENSE-RELATED ACTIVITIES

Each of the critical corporate defense components has subcategories of defense-related activities that are associated with each component. It must be appreciated that in the modern era each of these components requires specialist skills and expertise that are essential to their effectiveness. Table 5.1 outlines the critical components and provides examples of the associated defense-related activities (Lyons 2009b). As can be seen, the corporate defense domain can encompass a broad range of areas, and as a result the corporate defense program can have a very wide scope. It is unreasonable to expect any one person to be an expert in all of these activities or to possess the deep level of technical knowledge required to be proficient in each of these areas.

**TABLE 5.1**

**Corporate Defense-Related Activities**

**Governance**
- Environment/culture/philosophy
- Organization/design/structure
- Ethics and integrity
- Stakeholder relations
- Strategy and planning
- Frameworks and methodologies
- Policies and procedures
- Processes and practices
- Responsibility and accountability
- Oversight and supervision

**Risk**
- Enterprise risk
- Operational risk
- Credit risk
- Market risk
- Strategic risk
- Reputation risk
- Financial risk
- Project risk
- Environmental risk

**Compliance**
- Regulatory compliance
- Legal compliance
- Workplace compliance
- Industry codes
- Best practice guidelines
- Internal standards

**Intelligence**
- Business intelligence (B.I.)
  - Operational intelligence
  - Market intelligence
  - Competitive intelligence
- Knowledge management
  - Data/content management
  - Record management
  - Document management
  - Filing/storage/archive management
- Communication
  - Monitoring and reporting
  - Telecommunications

**Security**
- Physical security
  - Premises security
  - People security
  - Materials security
  - Facility security
  - Operations security
- Information security
  - Endpoint security
  - Application security
  - Operating system security
  - Database security
  - Network security
  - Gateway security

**Resilience**
- Incident response
- Emergency operations
- Crisis management
- Disaster recovery
- Contingency planning
- Continuity management
- Interruption protection
- Health and safety
- Insurance

**Controls**
- Internal controls
- Monitoring controls
- Operational/processing controls
- Financial/compliance/security controls
- Preventative/detective controls
- Primary/compensating controls

**Assurance**
- Inspection review
- Internal/external audit
- Regulator review
- Rating agency review
- Standards certification
- Self-assessment review
- Due diligence review
- Fraud examination
- Forensic investigation
- Litigation support

Each of these activities represents an important aspect of corporate defense in order to help the organization to address potential risks, threats, and vulnerabilities, which can arise both internally and externally to the organization. In fact, each of these activities should be considered to be an essential *link in the chain*, and effective corporate defense must be all inclusive as *the chain is only as strong as its weakest link*. To be most effective, all corporate defense-related activities need to be functioning in unison.

#### 5.2.1.1 An Inclusive Mind-Set Required

Given the complexity of the corporate defense domain, the organization's corporate defense initiative requires an inclusive mind-set in order to incorporate all these defense activities under one umbrella. An inclusive mind-set can help ensure the effective and efficient coordination of these diverse corporate defense activities in a systematic and coherent manner. Such an approach will help facilitate the convergence and alignment of their multiple perspectives so that they can be managed in a professional and competent manner.

### 5.2.2 CORPORATE DEFENSE AND MARTIAL ARTS

The right to self-defense by an individual and by groups has historically been regarded as a fundamental human right. Since the earliest times human beings, and groups of human beings, have engaged in physical combat when exerting this right to self-defense, whether it be motivated by pride, food, dominance, or mere survival. In the twenty-first century, the organization not only has a right to self-defense, but also an obligation, and perhaps the organization still has a lot to learn from developments in the human art of self-defense.

#### 5.2.2.1 Origins of Hand-to-Hand Combat

Hand-to-hand combat is perhaps the most ancient known form of self-defense. It dates back to primitive times when typically the individual who fared best in hand-to-hand combat became the alpha male and took his place at the top of the food chain. With the stakes so high, it gradually became apparent that self-defense through close quarter combat was not something to be left to chance. As in business the chance of success in hand-to-hand combat can depend on a large number of parameters. On the one hand, it is influenced by the threat poised by the attacker, whereas on the other hand it is also influenced by the mental and physical preparedness of the defender. Over time hand-to-hand combat began to be seen as an art form in itself that involved infinite measures and countermeasures, which could be perfected with diligence and practice. At its highest level, hand-to-hand combat is similar to a game of chess in that for every move there is a corresponding countermove. Like chess, the more knowledgeable and prepared the player, the better the chances of victory. Consequently, almost every culture has developed its own version of self-defense in hand-to-hand combat, and developed its own methods of practicing and training in the intricacies of the skills required in close quarter combat.

#### 5.2.2.2 Art of Self-Defense and Emergence of Martial Arts

The art of self-defense has been practiced for thousands of years using many different styles and techniques; however, it has only been since the twentieth century that western culture has shown a mainstream interest in what is referred to as the *martial arts*. The term *martial arts* has become heavily associated with the fighting arts and with sophisticated combat systems. Generally speaking, the martial arts represent an extensive system of codified practices and traditions of combat, exercised for a variety of reasons, including self-defense, competition, physical health, and fitness, as well as for mental and spiritual development. The mid- to late nineteenth century marks the beginning of the history of the martial arts as a modern sport that developed out of earlier traditional fighting systems.

Unarmed combat as a martial art can be broadly grouped into two distinctly different approaches. The first approach concentrates primarily on what can be referred to as stand-up fighting, whereby different styles of martial arts have developed elaborate offensive and defensive moves based on fighting from a standing position. Offensive moves can include punching with the fists, kicking with the feet, as well as striking with different parts of the body, including the open hands, elbows, and knees. Defensive moves can not only include blocking with the arms and legs but also rely on rapid reactions, movement, and agility in order to evade oncoming attacks. Examples of traditional martial arts classified as stand-up fighting styles can include *Boxing, Muay Thai, Karate, Kung Fu,* and *Taekwondo.* The second approach concentrates primarily on what can be referred to as ground fighting or grappling, whereby different styles of martial arts have developed elaborate offensive and defensive moves based on fighting on the ground. Offensive moves can include striking from the ground and grappling techniques such as throws, choke holds, and locking of joints. Defensive moves can include redirecting the force of the attacker and intricate body movements and shifting of the weight in order to counter the attacker's movement. Examples of traditional martial arts classified as ground fighting styles can include *Wrestling, Aikido, Judo, Jiu-jitsu,* and more recently *Brazilian Jiu-jitsu.*

Under both approaches, each competitor needs to be physically and mentally conditioned in order to be in a position to both inflict and absorb more pain than their opponent in order to prevail. Each of these different self-defense fighting styles has developed over time to help individuals defend themselves under specific sets of prevailing parameters and any one of these styles may prove the most successful depending on the prevailing parameters. To become a master in any one of these disciplines requires instruction, dedication, and self-discipline over a prolonged period of time; however, a basic level of knowledge in each of these can often be of benefit.

Similar to self-defense and the development of the different martial arts, corporate defense has developed its own critical components that have evolved over time to defend against the occurrence of specific issues that could threaten the stability of the organization. Each of the critical corporate defense components is designed to best address a specific set of parameters, and every organization is required to have at least a basic knowledge of all of them and may require a deeper level in certain components depending on its circumstances. The sharing of knowledge across these disciplines and functions is also to the overall benefit of the organization.

### 5.2.3  CORPORATE DEFENSE DYNAMICS

To appreciate the challenge of implementing a successful corporate defense program, it is vital that all concerned have a sound understanding of corporate defense dynamics. An effective corporate defense program is impacted by each of the corporate defense components and is reliant on each of these components to be operating effectively as each is considered an important element of successful corporate defense. In fact, each one of these critical components contributes to and receives from each of the other critical components. Therefore, a weakness or deficiency in one component could have an adverse impact on all of the other components. Alternatively, when each is operating effectively, each of the other components can benefit from this. In this way when the corporate defense program is operating effectively, the whole of the defense program is far greater than the sum of its individual parts.

#### 5.2.3.1  Corporate Defense Ecosystem

A growing number of business commentators (thought leaders, analysts,  industry experts, etc.) already acknowledge the critical interdependences that exist among these critical components. Hence, the corporate defense domain can be said to represent what can be described as a corporate defense ecosystem, as it relates to the symbiotic relationships that exist among these components. The symbiotic relationship refers to the fact that the effectiveness of each one of the components relies on the effectiveness of each of the other components. This relationship again highlights the fact that all defense-related activities are linked, and, as previously stated, each could be said to represent a link in a chain. Like any chain, it is only as strong as its weakest link, and therefore it could be said that this represents something of an asymmetric challenge for an organization, as it is the weakest link that is typically exploited. The corporate defense program therefore needs to ensure that all of these components are operating at a consistent level with similar levels of performance expected. An inconsistent or poor level of performance in any one component is capable of undermining the entire program.

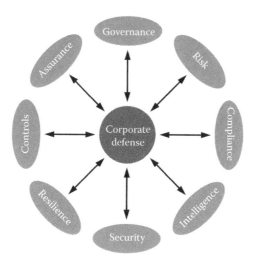

**FIGURE 5.1**   The corporate defense ecosystem.

Figure 5.1 outlines the eight critical components that make up what can be referred to as the corporate defense ecosystem (Lyons 2009c).

The challenge therefore facing the corporate defense program is to somehow unify, align, and integrate the management of all these critical corporate defense components so that they are collectively working together toward a common set of objectives.

### 5.2.3.2   An Interdisciplinary Methodology

The corporate defense program requires the adoption of a proactive approach in coordinating and integrating all of these interrelated disciplines and activities, which taken together can help protect the organization from the occurrence of potential hazards. In light of these complexities, it becomes self-evident that the function of corporate defense is unending, as corporate defense in effect is a constantly evolving multidiscipline or superdiscipline. Coordinating all of these disciplines requires an interdisciplinary methodology in order to ensure that all of these disciplines are fully engaged and contributing to the overall program. What needs to be created is a cybernetic loop whereby communication includes multidimensional feedback, both top-down and bottom-up, as well as operating horizontally across all of the critical components. It requires a strategic outlook and the alignment of all of the critical components, which  need to be coordinated in a strategic manner. This requires tactical organization and planning, which needs to be implemented with military precision and accuracy.

## 5.3   CORPORATE DEFENSE CYCLE

The challenge of defending the organization against the occurrence of hazard events is ongoing and without end. It represents a constantly evolving process that requires ongoing vigilance and an iterative approach in order to ensure constant revision and continuous improvement. The corporate defense cycle addresses the key drivers that should be present in all corporate defense-related activities. For most corporate defense-related activities, their defensive mission is generally to anticipate, prevent, detect, and react to potential risks, threats, and vulnerabilities, which in turn could contribute to the occurrence of a hazard event. The critical issue is to do this in as timely a manner as possible in order to minimize any damage or loss. The corporate defense cycle therefore visually captures how these key drivers interact on a continuous basis within the corporate defense process. For effective corporate defense, these key drivers need to be the driving force behind all corporate defense activities. Perhaps for this reason, it has been said that anticipation,

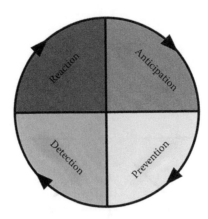

**FIGURE 5.2**   The corporate defense cycle.

prevention, detection, and reaction represent the four cornerstones of a corporate defense program. The corporate defense cycle therefore represents the foundations on which an effective corporate defense program can be built upon. The extent to which each corporate defense activity applies this cycle and the speed at which it is applied can help determine the success of these individual defense activities. Figure 5.2 illustrates the corporate defense cycle (Lyons 2006c).

### 5.3.1   Unifying Corporate Defense Objectives

The corporate defense cycle comprises what have also been described as the unifying defense objectives, as these are objectives common to all corporate defense activities. As previously mentioned, this cycle operates in a continuous loop, and these underlying objectives need to be embedded in the mind-set throughout the organization and need to be continuously present in day-to-day activities. They represent four individual layers to any corporate defense activity. The degree to which these objectives are present in the corporate mind-set could be said to represent the DNA of corporate defense within the organization, which will ultimately determine an organization's robustness. The most robust organizations will have the highest pre-emptive capabilities in place because it is the reaction times to potentially devastating events that will determine the magnitude of the initial impact and the subsequent collateral damage.

#### 5.3.1.1   Anticipation

In the context of the corporate defense cycle, *anticipation* refers to the timely identification and assessment of existing risks, threats, and vulnerabilities, as well as the prediction of future risks, threats, and vulnerabilities. Anticipation is concerned with knowing what needs to go right and anticipating what could possibly go wrong. As the predictive element of the corporate defense cycle, it is concerned with being forward looking and future oriented in nature so that corporate defense-related activities can help successfully future-proof the organization. It can involve continuous education in order to be best able to recognize potential matters of concern and an ability to identify and evaluate matters of particular concern to the organization. In essence, anticipation is about being ahead of the curve and requires an appropriate level of planning and preparation in order to be in possession of the necessary intelligence and to be in the best possible position to be able to foretell likely upcoming matters.

#### 5.3.1.2   Prevention

In the context of the corporate defense cycle, *prevention* refers to taking sufficient measures to shield the organization against anticipated risks, threats, and vulnerabilities. Once there is an anticipation that certain matters are of concern to the organization, appropriate measures need to be put in place to help prevent these matters from having a detrimental impact on the organization. This involves considering viable alternatives that have the capability to prevent the organization being exposed to the matters in question. Preventative measures can include focusing on deterrence measures, protection measures, interception measures, and resilience measures. From a corporate defense perspective, the old maxim that *an ounce of prevention is worth a ton of cure* always applies.

### 5.3.1.3 Detection

In the context of the corporate defense cycle, *detection* refers to the identification of activity types (e.g., exceptions, deviations, and anomalies) that indicate a breach of corporate defense protocol. Detection is concerned with ensuring that the organization is made aware of the occurrence of any matters of concern or red flags as early as possible so that these matters can be appropriately addressed. Detective measures can include focusing on the organization's ability to capture, monitor, investigate, diagnose, and communicate data and information in a speedy manner. Detective measures are required in the event that the preventative measures are either not in place or are not effective, and a degree of detective measures should be present throughout the organization and across all aspects of the business at strategic, tactical, and operational levels.

### 5.3.1.4 Reaction

In the context of the corporate defense cycle, *reaction* refers to the timely response to a particular event or series of events in order to both mitigate the current situation and to take further corrective action in relation to deficiencies identified, and to prevent these events from reoccurring in the future. As soon as matters of concern have been detected, the speed of the reaction can well be the difference between the success or failure of containing the matter at hand. Reaction is primarily concerned with the required action steps and keeping response times to a minimum. Reaction measures can include focusing on the available options, deciding on the best option, and taking precise action as quickly as is deemed possible. It also involves identifying the root cause of the matter of concern so that appropriate remedial action can be taken to prevent a reoccurrence going forward.

## 5.3.2 CORPORATE DEFENSE DNA

As can be seen, the corporate defense cycle is an iterative cycle whereby reaction in turn leads back to anticipation, and so on and so forth. This cycle represents a simple yet effective approach to the challenges facing corporate defense, and for an organization it represents what has been described as the art and practice of learning. There are valuable lessons to be learned from the experiences of failing to anticipate a particular hazard event, of failing to take appropriate measures to prevent an anticipated hazard event, of failing to appropriately detect an unprevented hazard event, and of failing to appropriately react to a detected hazard event. Each of these lessons should help steer efforts to continuously improve the organization's corporate defense measures so that such failures do not occur again in the future. Therefore, applying the corporate defense cycle can help spur constant innovation, reinvention, and improvement.

### 5.3.2.1 A Continuous Improvement Process

There are certain aspects about corporate defense that need to be fully appreciated by all concerned. Corporate defense is not a once-off point in time assignment, but rather it is a constantly evolving exercise without end. The corporate defense program itself requires continuous revision and constant improvement. All those involved in corporate defense-related activities must be cognizant of the key corporate defense drivers and their importance in the corporate defense process. They need to be constantly alert to potential risks, threats, and vulnerabilities, and there needs to be an ongoing level of vigilance present throughout the organization at all levels.

### 5.3.2.2   Corporate Defense Cycle Revisited

The corporate defense cycle contains the four unifying corporate defense objectives that should be present in all corporate defense activities and represent their key drivers. Those involved in any corporate defense activity throughout the organization should take appropriate measures to anticipate what could possibly go wrong, where to take possible appropriate measures to prevent these matters from occurring, or at a minimum take appropriate measures to ensure their early detection, and take appropriate measures to ensure a timely reaction to address the occurrence of these matters. The degree to which these four processes are in operation on a day-to-day basis throughout the organization can be said to represent the organization's corporate defense DNA.

## 5.4   CORPORATE DEFENSE PROGRAM EXPECTATIONS

In order to deliver an effective corporate defense program, it is essential to start by first establishing the extent of the organization's corporate defense ambitions and then setting clear expectations of what can realistically be achieved by the program. This also applies to the individual subprograms of each of the critical corporate defense components.

The corporate defense vision and strategy that was addressed in Chapter 4 should adequately deal with the extent of the program's overall ambitions. Following the setting of strategic corporate defense objectives, it is important to set clear and more detailed corporate defense objectives at a tactical and operational level in order to help further clarify the program's expectations.

### 5.4.1   Lower-Level Corporate Defense Objectives

Lower-level corporate defense objectives need to be determined by the organization well in advance of any rolling-out of the corporate defense program. The setting of these objectives should be guided by the corporate defense vision, strategy, and strategic objectives. These objectives should be determined with the successful implementation of the corporate defense strategy in mind. Specific program roll-out objectives should also be determined in relation to effectively rolling out the program. These objectives may be more logistical in nature and should focus on achieving an effective roll-out and implementation of the program, which in turn should contribute toward the successful execution of the corporate defense strategy.

#### 5.4.1.1   Setting Clear Objectives

Clear and concise corporate defense objectives need to be determined from the off-set. It is important to consider these objectives within the organization's overall corporate defense context and their potential impact on the achievement of the program's strategic objectives. These lower-level objectives also need to add value to the organization by complementing the achievement of the organization's business objectives and assisting in the successful execution of the business strategy. At all levels (whether strategic, tactical, or operational), corporate defense objectives should be as clear as possible and clearly contribute toward the execution of the corporate defense strategy. They should be relevant to the corporate defense vision and mission, measureable in outcome, and realistic in terms of being achievable.

#### 5.4.1.2   Alignment with Business Objectives

In principle, corporate defense objectives should complement and be in alignment with the business objectives at all times as both should be geared toward the long-term sustainable success of the organization. While there may at times be a healthy tension between the objectives of the business and those involved in corporate defense activities, this should not result in fundamental conflicts if the corresponding business and corporate defense strategies are in alignment. In an ideal world, corporate defense should be seen as a business enabler rather than a disabler, and the objectives should help support and enhance business objectives rather than be a hindrance to the achievement of business objectives. In such circumstances where any fundamental conflict exists between the business objectives and corporate defense objectives, this represents a red flag to the organization and needs to be addressed in a timely manner. Such conflicts are likely to represent a misalignment between business objectives and corporate defense objectives, and will need to be considered at the very highest levels within the organization and the necessary modifications made to one or the other or both.

### 5.4.1.3   Aligning Strategic, Tactical, and Operational Objectives

Corporate defense objectives need to be established at strategic, tactical, and operational levels and these also need to be in alignment with, and complement, one another.

> *Strategic objectives*: As noted in Chapter 4, at a strategic level the corporate defense strategy should incorporate setting clear strategic objectives and how it is intended to achieve these objectives. Strategic objectives should be of a high level in nature and focus on the long-term achievement of the corporate defense vision and mission. The strategic objectives should cascade and flow down through the various levels of the organization, thereby enabling the setting of relevant complementary tactical and operational objectives. Such an approach should also help ensure that these tactical and operational objectives are also in alignment with and complement the tactical and operational objectives of the business.

> *Tactical objectives*: Tactical objectives should flow from strategic objectives. Once clear and concise strategic corporate defense objectives have been established, this should make it easier to set the relevant interdependent and interconnected tactical corporate defense objectives. Tactical objectives therefore should be in alignment and complement the achievement of strategic objectives. These objectives should be of a more infrastructural nature and focus on the organization's medium-term corporate defense goals that are required in order to deliver on its strategic objectives. Basic examples of tactical corporate defense objectives include the following:
> - To design and implement a comprehensive corporate defense framework that helps to manage all corporate defense activities under a single umbrella
> - To manage the setting and alignment of individual programs for each of the critical corporate defense components
> - To coordinate and align the setting of objectives for each of the critical corporate defense components

> *Operational objectives*: At an operational level, the corporate defense objectives should flow from the tactical objectives, and reflect efforts to help support the achievement of strategic and tactical corporate defense objectives. Operational objectives should focus more on the day-to-day operations of the critical corporate defense components, and on delivering on the organization's short-term corporate defense goals. In setting operational objectives for the different critical components, it is essential to ensure that all of these components are *on the same page* in order to support and complement one another. Basic examples of operational corporate defense objectives include the following:
> - To set clear operational objectives for each of the critical corporate defense components
> - To effectively execute the required actions to help achieve the operational objectives of the individual, critical corporate defense components
> - To monitor the performance of each of the critical corporate defense components

### 5.4.1.4   Critical Component Objectives

In order to effectively deliver on the corporate defense strategy, it is important that each of the critical components set its own individual objectives at strategic, tactical, and operational levels. For each critical component, these objectives need to be in alignment with one another, in alignment with the objectives of the other critical components, in alignment with the overall corporate defense objectives, and in alignment with the objectives of the business. The setting of clear objectives can help direct the day-to-day activities of each of these critical components. Achieving this required level of alignment involves effective coordination and communication that can only be achieved by adopting an integrated approach.

### 5.4.1.5 Corporate Defense Objectives: Stakeholder Questions

The following are examples of basic questions that stakeholders might be expected to ask in relation to the organization's corporate defense objectives:

- Has the organization set clear corporate defense objectives at strategic, tactical, and operational levels?
- Have clear objectives been set for each of the critical corporate defense components at strategic, tactical, and operational levels?
- Are all of these corporate defense objectives in alignment with one another and with the objectives of the business?

### 5.4.2 CORPORATE DEFENSE POLICY

Similar to business policies, the organization needs to be aware of the requirement to determine clear corporate defense policies at strategic, tactical, and operational levels. Corporate defense policies need to be established in order to provide clear guidance to both the business and corporate defense practitioners in dealing with corporate defense issues.

### 5.4.2.1 Policy Setting

Policies can help drive discussion on delicate topics that have a corporate defense element to them and where there may be conflicting views on how these issues could be dealt with. Policies can help provide parameters within which to operate on a daily basis and clearly outline the boundaries within which the organization is prepared to operate. Where considered appropriate, corporate defense policy setting should follow the same process and format that is followed in the setting of business policy. When setting corporate defense policy, it should be set in the context of business policy and due consideration should be given to the intended and unintended impact these corporate defense policies could have on the achievement of business objectives. Therefore, policy setting can require an element of collaboration between the corporate defense functions and the business.

### 5.4.2.2 Strategic, Tactical, and Operational Policies

The existence of policies can help clarify what the organization deems to be acceptable practices at strategic, tactical, and operational levels. While the authority to set policy at strategic, tactical, and operational levels in the organization may be delegated, these corporate defense policies nonetheless should be in alignment with one another and with the corporate defense objectives. Strategic policies can be broad in nature, and subsequent tactical and operational policies can gradually become more detailed and specific. In the corporate defense context, strategic policy should be set at a strategic level such as the board committee for corporate defense and tactical policy should be set at a tactical level such as the corporate defense function or department, while operational policy should be set at a critical component level such as the risk management function or the compliance function. Operational policies will in turn drive corporate defense practices and procedures in the frontlines.

### 5.4.2.3 Critical Component Policies

Each of the critical components should set its own individual policies at strategic, tactical, and operational levels. For each critical component, these policies need to be fully in alignment with the overall corporate defense policies and business policies.

#### 5.4.2.4 Corporate Defense Policy: Stakeholder Questions

The following are examples of basic questions that stakeholders might be expected to ask in relation to the organization's corporate defense policy:

- Has the organization set clear corporate defense policy at strategic, tactical, and operational levels?
- Have clear policies been set for each of the critical corporate defense components at strategic, tactical, and operational levels?
- Are all of these corporate defense policies in alignment with one another and with the objectives of the business?

### 5.4.3 CORPORATE DEFENSE INTERNAL STANDARDS

In determining how to set and apply corporate defense standards within the organization, it will be necessary to consider how best to balance the use of a principles-based approach and the use of a rules-based approach.

#### 5.4.3.1 Principles-Based Direction

A principles-based approach places greater reliance on principles and less reliance on prescriptive standards and rules (FSA 2007). This involves moving away from the dictatorial approach of detailed prescriptive rules on how the business should operate in practice and toward a high-level outcome-focused approach. The aim is to focus more clearly on the outcomes the organization wishes to achieve, thereby leaving more discretion to the senior management of the business to make individual judgment calls on how to achieve those outcomes.

A principles-based approach to corporate defense involves the setting of overarching requirements for all of the organization's corporate defense activities in order to help steer the expectations of business and the way it deals with corporate defense. Principles focus on what the corporate defense program is trying to achieve, and therefore should be expressed in terms of preferred outcomes and behaviors rather than processes, practices, or procedures. They should clearly express the actions and behaviors expected of the organization as a means of driving the corporate defense agenda.

#### 5.4.3.2 Rules-Based Direction

A rules-based approach places greater reliance on prescriptive standards and rules, and this approach may be best suited under certain circumstances. Although an organization may have a preference for a principles-based approach, it will never get completely away from prescriptive rules, and a rules-based approach can have an important continuing role in certain aspects of the business. While principles can set out the highest level outcomes the organization is seeking to achieve, more detailed rules should however remain a part of the organization's toolkit, whereby principles may still need to be underpinned with further prescriptive rules. There may be a range of scenarios in which prescriptive rules will be the most appropriate way to secure the required outcomes. In certain areas, there may not be any discretion but to apply detailed standards, and therefore prescriptive rules and processes will be required to ensure conformance with mandatory requirements (i.e., legal and regulatory). However, a large volume of detailed, prescriptive, and highly complex rules can overburden business resources and divert attention toward adhering to the letter of the law, rather than the spirit of the law.

#### 5.4.3.3 A Blended Approach

Past experience would suggest that neither approach on its own has resulted in successful outcomes, or has been able to prevent misconduct that has been damaging to organizations. In reality, effective corporate defense will always require a mixture or blending of high-level principles and prescriptive rules. Setting high-level desirable outcomes guided by more detailed processes can help enable constructive engagement with the business; however, a degree of flexibility and adaptability is also required in the pursuit of these outcomes. It is important that the business can respond rapidly to changing events and while in some circumstances adherence to prescriptive rules may facilitate rapid response, under different circumstances innovation may be necessary and overly prescriptive rules may simply result in delays and actually prevent a timely response. This would make it less likely that the organization will achieve its goals. The challenge is getting the balance right between these two approaches and this means the flexibility to exercise a degree of judgment on a case-by-case basis within the overall framework. The business needs to be responsible for deciding on how best to implement corporate defense requirements in order to achieve desirable outcomes while receiving support and advice from corporate defense practitioners, within reason of course.

### 5.4.4  CRITICAL COMPONENT EXPECTATIONS

The individual programs of each of the critical components (e.g., the governance program and the compliance program) should also set its own individual strategies, objectives, policies, and internal standards relevant to its area of expertise. These are necessary in order to determine how best these components can help contribute to the corporate defense program and how they are expected to help achieve corporate defense objectives. They are also required in order to determine how corporate defense activities are to be conducted on a day-to-day basis in the frontline. In setting these objectives, policies, and standards, it is important that they should be in alignment with, and consistent with, corporate defense objectives, policies, and standards. It is also important that the objectives, policies, and standards of each of the critical components are in alignment and consistent with one another. For example, the risk management objectives should complement and be consistent with the compliance objectives and so on. Where there are inconsistencies, these need to be resolved judiciously. By managing all of the critical components in an integrated manner, the easier it is to coordinate them in a coherent fashion. The more integrated the corporate defense program is, the closer it is to adopting an enterprise approach, and the easier it will be to ensure that all defense-related activities are in alignment and operate in unison toward common objectives.

# 6 An Enterprise-Wide Approach to Corporate Defense

By failing to prepare, you are preparing to fail.[*]

**Benjamin Franklin**

## 6.1 TOWARD ENTERPRISE DEFENSE

A comprehensive corporate defense program should help ensure the adoption of an enterprise-wide approach to corporate defense. Enterprise defense includes the methods, systems, and processes used by the organization to help ensure that its corporate defense objectives are achieved. It refers to the complete framework for responsibility and accountability of corporate defense activities throughout the entire organization. Organizations typically address corporate defense activities in a variety of ways across business units, divisions, departments, and functions. Each of these may vary in its corporate defense capability and capacity and in its willingness to collaborate with one another. The challenge of an enterprise-wide approach to corporate defense is to help improve the organization's corporate defense capability and capacity across the organization.

### 6.1.1 A HOLISTIC OUTLOOK

Developing a truly integrated approach to corporate defense requires a holistic perspective, which means considering the organization and its activities as a whole rather than separately focusing on

---

[*] Per *Critical Infrastructure: Homeland Security and Emergency Preparedness*, Third Edition, 2013, R. Radvanovsky & A. McDougall, CRC Press, Boca Raton, FL.

its individual parts. This means understanding corporate defense in terms of the big picture and how corporate defense activities are increasingly interconnected and interdependent both among themselves and with other business activities. Adopting a single unified view of corporate defense is essential in order to produce robust organization-wide policies and standards, which can help address corporate defense challenges across the multiple organization units.

#### 6.1.1.1 From Separation to Integration

A holistic perspective encourages a move toward integrating and coordinating corporate defense activities across the organization as a whole, and in some cases this means moving away from separate specialist structures (i.e., silos) and toward more broadly focused integrated structures in order to achieve a single consistent view of corporate defense across the entire organization. While specialist knowledge and skills are still required, a holistic view encourages an understanding of how these activities may potentially impact on other areas and vice versa, and how other areas may impact on them. Such an understanding facilitates the adoption of a more integrated approach to managing these activities.

#### 6.1.1.2 A Top-Down and Bottom-Up Perspective

A holistic outlook means considering the complete picture, and this requires a top-down strategic focus in order to help ensure that all corporate defense activities are aligned and operating in unison toward the achievement of the strategic objectives of the organization. It also requires a bottom-up focus in order to fully understand the operations and implications of day-to-day corporate defense activities and the possible impact they may have on the achievement of the organization's strategic objectives. In order to help develop as complete an understanding as possible, a top-down and bottom-up focus requires an appropriate structure. This involves a structure that includes top-down oversight, supervision, and monitoring, and also includes bottom-up feedback, reporting, and assurance.

### 6.1.2 CORPORATE DEFENSE AS A TEAM SPORT

The adoption of a holistic perspective means that the organization needs to begin to view corporate defense as a team sport where every player has an important role to play. A holistic perspective means that the corporate defense team is no longer seen as being restricted to corporate defense practitioners or those working directly in corporate defense activities, but is now viewed as an expanded team that incorporates a much wider group of players across the entire organization, including those involved in the business and support services. The expanded team includes both management and staff working across all the organization's divisions, business units, departments, and functions, and includes front, middle, and back office staff. This expanded group must now be treated as a team and is required to work as a team and conform to the expected level of teamwork.

#### 6.1.2.1 Corporate Defense Teamwork

Corporate defense teamwork involves each team member being educated and trained in relation to their corporate defense responsibilities and being held to account for delivering on these responsibilities. Each team member is expected to do his or her part and recognize that he or she is contributing to the achievement of the greater good. Such teamwork includes continuous interaction, cooperation, and collaboration among team members. It also involves ongoing communication, support, and sharing of information among team members. The slicker the interactions among team members, the more effective and efficient the end product, but this requires continuous practice. Teamwork requires all team members to contribute their fair share to the team, and this includes sacrificing personal ambitions from time to time for the greater good.

#### 6.1.2.2 Influence the Organization's Culture

The corporate defense team has a responsibility to help develop, foster, and promote an appropriately positive and proactive corporate defense culture throughout the organization. By helping to embed a strong corporate defense culture, it is also helping to influence a healthy overall organizational culture that appreciates the requirement to balance its offense and defense responsibilities in order to help the organization achieve a long-term sustainable success. The corporate defense team therefore has an important role to play in influencing corporate culture for the better and should take pride in its duties in this regard.

## 6.2  CORPORATE DEFENSE ORGANIZATION AND STRUCTURE

A corporate defense program should not be very different from any other enterprise-wide program in its approach. In order to develop and foster an integrated corporate defense program, an appropriate structure first needs to be put in place in order to facilitate the smooth implementation of the program. An appropriate structure needs to give guidance on how the corporate defense initiative is to be organized across the organization and the infrastructure required to be put in place to support this initiative.

### 6.2.1  THE CORPORATE DEFENSE CHARTER

An appropriate starting point is the preparation of a formal corporate defense charter that should clearly state the terms of reference of the corporate defense program (Lyons 2006c). The charter defines the corporate defense program and provides guidance for managing corporate defense by describing its governance, responsibilities, and operations. It serves to act as a focal point and provides an overview reference document that outlines the reasons for and the purpose of the program, and should clearly state the main corporate defense objectives and goals. The charter should clearly outline the scope of the program and how it is intended to achieve the objectives and goals. From a relationship management perspective, it should outline the main participants and also identify the main stakeholders. The charter should be formally approved by the board of directors.

#### 6.2.1.1  Responsibility and Accountability

The charter should establish the authority of the various corporate defense players and clearly outline their delegated roles and responsibilities at strategic, tactical, and operational levels. This sends out a clear signal to the organization and also provides a basis to hold these individuals to account for their responsibilities. The delegation of responsibility and the maintenance of accountability are important aspects of managing the corporate defense program. The charter should also clearly state the obligation of all corporate defense players to observe both the spirit and letter of all relevant policies, standards, principles, and rules in the performance of their duties.

#### 6.2.1.2  Clarity and Transparency

Two of the essential elements of an effective corporate defense charter are clarity and transparency. Clarity is essential in order to avoid any possible confusion that may arise and to ensure that all the participants are all on the same page and singing from the same hymn sheet. Transparency is essential in order to ensure that there is a clear chain of command and clear reporting lines. This is of particular importance in relation to the delegation of responsibility for decision making and in holding individuals and groups to account for the fulfillment of their duties and responsibilities. A lack of transparency can lead to obfuscation and a lack of accountability, which in turn can seriously hinder the effectiveness of the corporate defense program.

### 6.2.2  THE CORPORATE DEFENSE COMMITTEE

At a strategic level, a supervisory committee should be established with responsibility for supervising the entire corporate defense program. This committee should be responsible for overseeing all of the organization's corporate defense activities and ensuring that these activities are in alignment with the organization's corporate defense strategy. It is often said that at a certain level all strategies and plans are basically similar; however, it is their execution that sets them apart. The corporate defense committee should be fully committed to monitoring the organization's execution of its corporate defense strategy and plan.

### 6.2.2.1   A Committee/Subcommittee of the Board

Ideally, the corporate defense committee should be a board-level committee. It should be an operating committee of the board of directors charged to assist the board to fulfill its corporate defense oversight responsibilities, and should report to the board in relation to the implementation of the organization's corporate defense strategy and issues of strategic importance. Its role should be to provide advice and recommendations to the board within the scope of its terms of reference as outlined in the corporate defense charter. The board's responsibility for overseeing the corporate defense program may be delegated to this committee; however, this does not take away from the board having the ultimate responsibility for corporate defense oversight. As a committee of the board, it has a strategic oversight and monitoring role that is primarily concerned with strategic issues. It will therefore rely on executive management and the corporate defense function to manage the tactical and operational aspects of corporate defense on a day-to-day basis. The committee should be empowered to acquire external expertise where deemed necessary to help in the performance of their duties. Basic examples of the responsibilities of the corporate defense committee include the following:

- The preparation of the corporate defense vision, mission statement, and strategy for board approval
- The approval of the strategic corporate defense objectives, policies, and principles
- The oversight of the ongoing execution of the corporate defense program

### 6.2.2.2   Committee Composition

Members of the committee should be selected from the organization's board with a chairperson selected from among the committee members. For the purposes of independence, this committee should be chaired by a nonexecutive director (NED) of the board. At least one member of the committee should have relevant qualifications in terms of corporate defense knowledge, expertise, and competence, although appropriate education and training should be provided to the committee members as a whole or tailored individually as required. Each organization must decide for itself as to the skills and experience required for its members. As with other board committees, a suitable diversity of members can prove beneficial in terms of avoiding potential blind spots. It is advisable that the organization's chief corporate defense officer is in attendance at the meetings of the committee as well as with other relevant heads of the critical corporate defense components as required. For example, there may be a requirement for the chief risk officer, chief compliance officer, or chief security officer to attend the meetings similar to national defense, whereby the Joint Chiefs of Staff may be required to attend a Department of Defense meeting.

### 6.2.2.3   Assimilation of Critical Component Committees

In some organizations, similar board committees may already be in place to address certain critical corporate defense components, such as a governance committee, a risk committee, a compliance committee, and an audit committee. In such circumstances, there are a number of options available. Ideally, these critical component committees could become assimilated into a new overarching corporate defense committee or round table, whereby these committees may continue to exist but now become subcommittees of the corporate defense committee. Alternatively, the scope of one of these existing committees could be expanded to include all corporate defense-related matters and effectively act as a corporate defense committee. Either way it is preferable to have one board committee responsible for addressing all corporate defense activities and reporting to the board with one unified voice rather than a number of competing voices seeking and clamoring for board attention.

## 6.2.3   THE CORPORATE DEFENSE FUNCTION

At a tactical level, there are examples of corporate defense operating in a number of different ways. First, it can operate in a completely decentralized manner, whereby each business unit is separately responsible for its own corporate defense efforts as the challenges faced by each business unit may be very different. Second, it can operate in a centralized silo-type manner, whereby each individual critical corporate defense component is responsible for managing its specific component area across the entire organization, but each of these components operates independently of the other components. Finally, it can operate in an integrated manner, whereby a centralized corporate defense function is established with responsibility for the tactical management of all critical corporate defense components across the entire organization. An integrated corporate defense function could be likened to the Department of Defense at a national level, whereby it is responsible for overseeing all the defense forces, including the Army, the Navy, and the Air Force.

### 6.2.3.1   An Integrated Function

Ideally, the corporate defense function would be an integrated function with responsibility for the tactical management of all corporate defense-related activities. This function should also be responsible for liaising with the executive management and the business in order to help ensure that corporate defense activities become embedded throughout the whole organization. It should be responsible for ensuring that corporate defense activities follow a logical sequence in order to help ensure that the corporate defense strategy is executed in practice and that the organization's corporate defense objectives are achieved in the short, medium, and long terms. Such an integrated approach would operate in a similar manner to the Joint Forces approach taken by the Department of Defense.

### 6.2.3.2   Integrated Command and Control

The establishment of a centralized corporate defense function facilitates an integrated command and control structure, which is necessary for the implementation of all corporate defense activities at a consistent level throughout the organization. However, the fact that the corporate defense function and the critical corporate defense components operate in a guidance, advisory, and support role with the business, rather than being directly responsible for the performance of corporate defense activities in the frontline, also allows for a necessary degree of flexibility. The fact that the business is ultimately responsible for implementing corporate defense activities in the frontline enables each of the business units to adapt the precise measures implemented to the needs of the business. The corporate defense function and the critical components in their tactical role provide oversight of the corporate defense activities in the frontlines. By establishing a corporate defense committee at a strategic level, a corporate defense function at a tactical level, and an aligned business workforce at an operational level, it becomes possible to manage the corporate defense program in an enterprise-wide manner.

## 6.2.4   CORPORATE DEFENSE STRUCTURE: STAKEHOLDER QUESTIONS

The following are examples of basic questions that stakeholders might be expected to ask in relation to the organization's corporate defense structure:

- Does the organization have a formal corporate defense charter in place?
- Does the organization have a board-level corporate defense committee in place?
- Does the organization have a corporate defense function in place with responsibility for managing, coordinating, and integrating the critical corporate defense components?

## 6.3    DIRECTING THE CORPORATE DEFENSE PROGRAM

In essence, the corporate defense program is the process in place for coordinating and guiding a number of interrelated subprograms or projects in order to help ensure that their overall performance is greater than the sum of its parts. It is also anticipated that such an approach can help maximize their combined added value contribution to the overall business strategy. The corporate defense program must therefore focus on the end game for the organization as a whole, and consider the required aggregate result, based on how each of the subprogram outputs can contribute to the required outcome of the overall program. This can be a complex undertaking and will initially require a sufficient level of direction, leadership, and insight in order to have any realistic expectation that the overall program will deliver on its objectives.

### 6.3.1    STEERING THE PROGRAM

Like any successful initiative, the corporate defense program requires appropriate steering and direction from the top of the organization to help ensure it is in alignment with the business strategy. Appropriate steering is required to ensure that the program itself and all related subprograms or projects are facing in the same direction and ready to collectively move forward together in unison. There are a multitude of corporate defense-related activities operating within an organization and, to operate effectively, these activities will need to be managed within the corporate defense program. Effective steering will require linkages that connect the various corporate defense activities at strategic, tactical, and operational levels so that the organization's strategic decisions effectively steer the subsequent tactical and operational decisions.

#### 6.3.1.1    Program Governance

In order to effectively roll out the corporate defense program on an enterprise-wide basis, it is important that certain crucial governance issues are first addressed. Governance is more than addressing the delegation of authority and the allocation of responsibility. Good governance can help ensure that the program is appropriately directed and controlled at strategic, tactical, and operational levels. It is basically concerned with creating an appropriate environment, designing an appropriate infrastructure, setting appropriate behavior, outlining appropriate practices and procedures, and ensuring appropriate supervision and oversight (the issue of governance is addressed in more detail in Chapter 9).

#### 6.3.1.2    Corporate Defense Champions

Successful corporate defense requires a variety of corporate defense champions throughout the organization across all functional activities at strategic, tactical, and operational levels. A corporate defense champion represents an individual who by virtue of their authority and expertise can act as an advocate for the corporate defense program within their sphere of influence. Such champions should have sufficient status to help drive and support the corporate defense process within their areas and possess the necessary skills, knowledge, and leadership qualities to inspire confidence and trust in their opinions and recommendations. Corporate defense champions should have a genuine interest and at least a basic understanding about the overall corporate defense process and show a passion and commitment to their area of interest.

Corporate defense champions are of particular importance within the business itself as by advocating support for corporate defense activities, they can help communicate the benefits of corporate defense in the language of the business. They can show how corporate defense can help the business meet its own objectives and how corporate defense can better position the organization in the long term. The corporate defense program should be designed to seek out appropriate champions and provide them with sufficient guidance, instruction, and assistance so that they fully understand their important roles and responsibilities.

### 6.3.1.3 Leaders and Leadership

Napoleon Bonaparte is reported to have stated, "If you build an army of 100 lions and their leader is a dog, in any fight, the lions will die like a dog. But if you build an army of 100 dogs and their leader is a lion, all dogs will fight like a lion." Inspirational leaders are required in every walk of life, and the corporate defense program is no different. Leaders are individuals who can help drive the corporate defense initiative especially during times of stress and times of opposition or conflict. In order to help promote an appropriate corporate defense environment and culture, both leaders and leadership are required throughout the organization. This leadership begins at the top, but needs to travel all the way down the chain of command.

*Strategic leaders*: At a strategic level, the board should appoint a corporate defense sponsor to ensure that corporate defense has a seat at the boardroom table. While ultimately the entire board is responsible for the organization's corporate defense program, the sponsor should be delegated with responsibility for overseeing and agreeing the corporate defense activity across the organization. This should specifically include the preparation of the organization's corporate defense vision, mission statement, and strategy to be approved by the board, the receipt of reports on corporate defense activity, and the discussion of relevant corporate defense matters at board level. Where relevant, an appropriate sponsor should be identified and agreed in advance of the roll-out of the corporate defense program. A NED would best serve the role of sponsor from an independent perspective, and where there is a board-level corporate defense committee in place, this sponsor should serve as its chairperson. Such a role is perhaps the equivalent of the role of the Secretary or Minister of Defense in the context of national defense.

*Tactical leaders*: At a tactical level a C-suite position should be created by the appointment of the chief corporate defense officer with responsibility for effective management, monitoring, and reviewing of corporate defense activities both functionally and cross-functionally within the organization. This should specifically include establishing a corporate defense framework, coordinating corporate defense functions (i.e., each of the critical components), and driving corporate defense activity throughout the organization. This role would also involve liaising with the heads of each of the critical corporate defense components (i.e., the chief risk officer, chief compliance officer, and chief security officer). Such a role is perhaps the equivalent of the role of the Head of the Joint Chiefs of Staff in the context of national defense.

*Operational leaders*: At an operational level, each critical corporate defense component may also have its own functional head responsible for managing the operational execution of its respective component and its specific area of expertise. These positions should require individuals with a greater technical understanding of the individual corporate defense disciplines in question (e.g., compliance or security). Each functional head should be responsible for managing, reporting, and providing assurance on the component's own program and for ensuring that the component's vision, mission statement, and strategy are in alignment with the overall corporate defense program. Such a role is perhaps the equivalent of the role of the Chief of Staff of the Army, the Navy, or the Air Force in the context of national defense.

*Business leaders*: At a business level, the chief executive officer (CEO) and the C-suite should help promote an appropriate corporate defense environment and culture. They should assign corporate defense champions for each of the functional areas of the business (e.g., sales, marketing, operations, human resources [HR], information technology [IT], and finance). These champions can be charged with addressing corporate defense matters both in their individual functional areas and as a cross-functional business team collaborating on corporate defense across the entire organization. These champions can provide leadership and guidance, but they need not be experts in corporate defense. They should however be the business' liaison person with the corporate defense functions or competence centers, and be responsible for communicating back to the business on corporate defense matters. Effective corporate defense requires close team work and open communication in order to succeed in getting corporate defense practices engrained into day-to-day business activities.

### 6.3.2 INTERNAL AND EXTERNAL DEFENSE RELATIONSHIPS

The corporate defense program also requires that those who are involved in corporate defense, and in particular, in the corporate defense function and the critical components, develop both positive and proactive relationships internally within the business but also with external corporate defense bodies. This is required in order to facilitate collaboration, cooperation, exchange of ideas, and sharing of information in relation to corporate defense activities. Effective corporate defense requires a strong partnership approach both inside and outside the organization, and effective corporate defense professionals display the ability to communicate well, build alliances, and develop relationships. It is therefore advisable that the organization fosters good relationships with a number of relevant external groups, each of which has a potentially different role to play.

#### 6.3.2.1 Professional Representative Bodies

Close liaison with the professional bodies that publically represent professionals engaged in the different critical corporate defense components is advisable as they can help provide the organization with guidance in relation to best practices and facilitate the exchange of corporate defense experiences from corporate defense professionals from around the globe. In many cases, they provide internationally recognized qualifications and professional training in addition to publishing research and best practice guidance in their specialized areas of expertise. Many of the organizations provide educational programs and continuing professional development in their respective fields in addition to thought leadership forums and discussion groups for like-minded individuals. Certain representative bodies actually go as far as developing, setting, and promoting international professional standards in their chosen field in an effort to help promote excellence in managing their particular discipline.*

#### 6.3.2.2 Industry Bodies and Peer Groups

It is also advisable that those involved in the corporate defense function should actively participate and become members of corporate defense peer groups within the organization's particular industry or business sector. The nature of the corporate defense challenges being faced in different industries and business sectors can vary considerably and therefore more specific guidance and advice can prove to be very helpful. Examples of these groups may include peer groups for risk managers or compliance officers in the banking industry. These peer groups can act as useful forums for corporate defense practitioners to swap experiences, exchange ideas, and share information in relation to the particular corporate defense discipline being addressed within a particular industry. Practitioners can discuss their common challenges with their peers from other organizations in their industry and learn from the experiences of their peers. It is an opportunity to treat these groups as a sounding board and to obtain advice from fellow practitioners in similar circumstances. It also provides the opportunity to gauge the corporate defense activities of their peers and to benchmark their own organization's corporate defense efforts against those of their peers.

## 6.4 THE CORPORATE DEFENSE FORCE

In a narrow sense, the corporate defense force refers to all those specifically involved in corporate defense activities within the organization. It refers to those directly employed in the corporate defense function with responsibility for the day-to-day coordination and implementation of

---

* For more information on these professional representative bodies please refer to Chapters 9 and 10.

the corporate defense program. It also refers to those directly employed in the coordination and implementation of the individual critical corporate defense component programs (i.e., governance program, compliance program, assurance program, etc.) and those with expert knowledge and technical skills in each of these specialist disciplines. Finally, it refers to all staff who are dedicated full-time to corporate defense activities or whose role is solely focused on corporate defense matters.

In a broader sense, the corporate defense force also refers to those who are employed in the business but are engaged in corporate defense activities as part of their day-to-day operations. This includes executive management, middle management, and staff working in the frontlines of the business. An effective corporate defense program requires close interaction between all relevant parties in order to project a unified approach where all corporate defense forces are operating in unison in order to collectively defend the interests of the stakeholders. In military parlance, the corporate defense forces need to be rallied and organized into a cohesive unit in order to operate effectively.

## 6.4.1 Managing Corporate Defense Activities

Throughout the organization, the corporate defense forces are engaged in corporate defense-related activities at strategic, tactical, and operational levels. These activities need to be managed in a coordinated and coherent manner, and this requires appropriate organization, supervision, and administration at all levels.

### 6.4.1.1 The Corporate Defense Hierarchy

At a strategic level, the board is ultimately responsible for overseeing the strategic forces and their strategic corporate defense activities. The board, via the corporate defense committee, is responsible for managing the strategic forces and their strategic corporate defense activities. At a tactical level, the corporate defense function is responsible for managing the tactical forces and their tactical corporate defense activities. This includes overseeing the activities of the critical corporate defense components (i.e., risk management, compliance, security, etc.). At an operational level, the critical corporate defense components are responsible for managing the operational forces and their operational corporate defense activities. This includes overseeing the activities of the business. The business management team is responsible for managing and overseeing the corporate defense activities of line management, who in turn are responsible for managing and overseeing the execution of corporate defense activities in the frontline of the business. Table 6.1 outlines the corporate defense forces hierarchy.

### 6.4.1.2 Operations and Support Functions

A number of business operations and support functions although not directly involved in corporate defense activities are also an important link in the chain. For example, IT support will be relied upon to deliver and support the required corporate defense IT governance infrastructure and technology

## TABLE 6.1
## Corporate Defense Forces

|  | Group Responsibility | Individual Responsibility |
|---|---|---|
| Strategic forces | • Board | • Chairman of the corporate defense committee |
|  | • Corporate defense committee |  |
| Tactical forces | • Corporate defense function | • Chief corporate defense officer |
| Operational forces | • Critical component functions | • Heads of critical components |
|  | • Business management | • Line managers |

architecture. The office supplies function will be relied upon to source and fit the required office equipment, office furniture, and so on. Of particular importance is the HR function, as the HR staff can play an important role in recruitment, and in facilitating the education and training of business staff in relation to their understanding of corporate defense and their corporate defense responsibilities. The corporate defense function and the critical component functions should work closely with the HR function in order to help ensure the smooth coordination of corporate defense recruitment, training, and education.

### 6.4.2   The Key Corporate Defense Players

As previously stated, corporate defense is a team sport, where all those involved in corporate defense activities have an important role to play. Certain key roles however have a more central role to play than others and represent the spine of the corporate defense program. These key roles need to be in place at strategic, tactical, and operational levels to help ensure the effective execution of the corporate defense strategy. Therefore, these roles need to be carefully filled with suitably qualified candidates so that the appropriate individuals are in place to help with the smooth implementation of the corporate defense program on an ongoing basis.

#### 6.4.2.1   Chairman of the Corporate Defense Committee

The appointment of the chairperson of the corporate defense committee should be regarded as a very senior appointment that has a great deal of responsibility attached to the role, somewhat similar to the appointment of the Secretary of Defense in the context of national defense. Ideally, the chairperson should be a member of the board of directors, be regarded as the board-level corporate defense sponsor, and represent the voice of corporate defense at board meetings. From an independence perspective, the appointment of the chair is best suited to a NED who reports directly to the board. As chairperson, this role is responsible for chairing all the meetings of the corporate defense committee and for ensuring that the committee fulfills all its duties and responsibilities in a professional manner.

#### 6.4.2.2   Chief Corporate Defense Officer

The appointment of a chief corporate defense officer should be regarded as a key role in the corporate defense process, somewhat similar to the role of the Head of the Joint Chiefs of Staff in the context of national defense. Ideally, as head of the corporate defense function, this person should be a member of the C-suite, report directly to the corporate defense committee and its chairperson, and liaise with the CEO and executive management on matters relating to corporate defense that could impact on the business. For practical and pragmatic reasons, there may be cause for this role to administratively report to the CEO on a day-to-day basis. This role should manage the corporate defense function and oversee the workings of each of the critical corporate defense components.

#### 6.4.2.3   Heads of the Critical Corporate Defense Components

The appointment of the individual heads of each of the critical corporate defense components should be regarded as critical roles in the corporate defense program, somewhat similar to the Chiefs of Staff in the context of national defense. Ideally, the heads of these functions (i.e., chief risk officer, chief compliance officer, etc.) would report directly to the chief corporate defense officer and act as liaison officers with the corporate defense champions within the business units. These roles should manage their individual functions (i.e., the risk management function and the security function) and oversee the implementation of these activities in the business frontlines. The existence of these roles may vary from organization to organization, as may their precise duties and responsibilities. Table 6.2 lists examples of the key critical component players.

**TABLE 6.2**
**Key Critical Component Players**

| | |
|---|---|
| Chief governance officer | Head of information technology |
| Company secretary | Chief security officer |
| Chief risk officer | Chief information security officer |
| Chief ethics officer | Chief resilience officer |
| Chief compliance officer | Chief business continuity officer |
| Chief legal officer | Chief controls officer |
| General counsel | Chief assurance officer |
| Chief intelligence officer | Chief audit executive |
| Chief information officer | |

The aforementioned key roles and key players are considered very important to the success of the corporate defense program by providing the leadership required to implement an effective program. As previously mentioned, corporate defense is however a team sport and this means that everyone in the organization has a role to play in corporate defense, including those directly employed in the critical corporate defense components as well as those employed in the business that are expected to execute corporate defense practices and procedures in the frontlines on a day-to-day basis.

# 7 Oversight and the Five Lines of Corporate Defense

What Washington needs is adult supervision.*

**Barack Obama**

## 7.1 OVERSIGHT OF THE CORPORATE DEFENSE PROGRAM

Corporate defense oversight involves the review, monitoring, and supervision of the corporate defense program. Although the primary responsibility for corporate defense oversight rests with the board of directors and how the board administers its oversight duty, oversight needs to be performed throughout the organization and this involves oversight at strategic, tactical, and operational levels. Strategic oversight involves monitoring the implementation of its corporate defense vision, mission, and strategy, and it also involves understanding and monitoring the critical corporate defense assumptions, which underlie the corporate defense strategy. Tactical oversight involves monitoring the ongoing workings of the corporate defense framework and adjusting the framework as required. Operational oversight involves monitoring the execution of policies and procedures in practice and ensuring that the practices are in accordance with the corporate defense objectives and goals. Although the term oversight is often an implied responsibility, for best results and for the purposes of clarity and transparency, it is best if this responsibility is clearly outlined in advance.

---

* Per *Barack Obama: In His Own Words*, 2009, Lisa Rogak, PublicAffairs, New York, NY.

### 7.1.1  An Oversight Framework

Even though the ultimate responsibility for overseeing the corporate defense program lies with the board, to operate effectively as a board it cannot and should not be involved in day-to-day corporate defense activity. The corporate defense framework in place should enable the board to satisfy itself that effective corporate defense processes are in place and functioning effectively at strategic, tactical, and operational levels. Adequate oversight of the corporate defense program involves establishing an appropriate oversight framework with appropriate oversight roles and an understanding of the relationship dynamics among the various players. An oversight framework is a means by which the board can determine that the organization has robust corporate defense processes in place and that these processes are operating effectively. The oversight framework forms part of the system of checks and balances that help to ensure the effectiveness and efficiency of the execution of the corporate defense program, and adequate oversight requires a comprehensive framework that stretches all the way from the boardroom to the frontlines.

#### 7.1.1.1  Purpose of Oversight

Board oversight is sometimes referred to as the supervision or monitoring of the management team or management process. Management oversight is different from board oversight, as it is the responsibility of the organization's executive management team. Success in corporate defense requires vigilant oversight in order to help ensure that often complex corporate defense activities are appropriately managed across the entire enterprise. Although the board should not be involved in day-to-day corporate defense, the financial crisis highlighted the need for more proactive and direct engagement over and above the traditional oversight of corporate defense processes. What is now required is a degree of greater oversight accompanied by a level of deeper insight. Such improved oversight and insight should help to better identify and address potential hazards, understand how hazards are interconnected, and recognize the potential compounding of hazards should unfavorable events occur at the same time.

A comprehensive corporate defense oversight model needs to help provide a clear structure of responsibility and accountability for the organization's corporate defense systems and processes. It needs to provide transparency over the organization's corporate defense roles, responsibilities, and accountabilities so that all parties have a clear mandate and share a practical understanding of their corporate defense oversight responsibilities. Relevant stakeholders bear responsibility for satisfying themselves that effective corporate defense processes are in place and are functioning effectively within the scope of their mandate. Going forward, corporate defense oversight needs to be proactive and assertive, including continuously monitoring and reviewing the planning and operational execution of corporate defense processes. Ultimately, a robust corporate defense oversight process should help build a solid foundation from which to manage corporate defense activities on an enterprise-wide basis, thus being capable of helping the organization to enhance performance and improve stakeholder value.

### 7.1.2  Lines of Defense Approach

In order to gain a measure of comfort that critical activities are being appropriately addressed, stakeholders commonly rely on various lines of defense to be in place and to operate as oversight layers within their organizations. These internal lines of defense are responsible for providing stakeholders with a degree of confidence that the organization is operating effectively and in an appropriate manner (Lyons 2011).

#### 7.1.2.1  The Lines of Defense Concept

The lines of defense oversight approach is intended to operate on the principle of providing transparency in the assignment of oversight responsibilities, and in holding individuals (or groups) to account for these responsibilities. The logic of such an approach is that each line of defense has specific oversight responsibilities for monitoring and reporting on the performance of the activities of other lines of defense. Each line of defense therefore has *skin in the game* and has the capability to provide separate and additional levels of comfort, which can be relied upon in the event that a subordinate line of defense fails to operate effectively.

A number of different hierarchical lines of defense therefore exist to help ensure that appropriate corporate oversight is in place at all levels within the organization itself and beyond. Each of these lines of defense has differing oversight roles, duties, and responsibilities, and if operating effectively all are expected to make a valuable contribution to the overall corporate oversight framework. A line of defense approach can facilitate both vertical and horizontal oversights of the organization's activities, thereby helping to provide it with both *defense-in-depth* and *defense-in-breadth* in the process.

### 7.1.2.2 The Traditional Three Lines of Defense Model

The three lines of defense model is a commonly applied concept that has been in operation across different industries and geographic regions for some time. This model represents a common approach to providing oversight. It recognizes operational line management (OLM),[*] tactical oversight functions,[†] and independent internal assurance[‡] as individual lines of defense. "All three lines should exist in some form at every organization, regardless of size or complexity. Risk management normally is strongest when there are three separate and clearly identified lines of defense" (IIA 2013a). The three lines of defense model has historically often been the preferred model of regulators when they review an organization's oversight structures. Figure 7.1 outlines the three lines of defense model.

Unfortunately, although this model recognizes an oversight role for executive management and the board of directors, it does not recognize these specific roles as important additional strategic lines of defense, and this can lead to a degree of confusion as to their precise roles and responsibilities within the three lines of defense model. As far as many stakeholders are concerned, however, these two groups are considered to be the most important lines of defense, particularly from a strategic perspective. The financial crisis has already served to highlight how a lack of adequate strategic oversight can be a cause for concern. "Boards are being asked…could they have done a better job in overseeing the management of their organization's risk exposures, and could improved board oversight have prevented or minimized the impact of the financial crisis on their organization?" (COSO 2009).

## 7.2 THE FIVE LINES OF CORPORATE DEFENSE MODEL

The global financial crisis clearly highlighted the inherent weakness in placing sole reliance on the oversight roles of the first three lines of defense. Given that failures in board and executive management oversight of risk was commonly identified as a contributing factor to the crisis, an increasing number of regulators and other commentators are now focusing specific attention on the specific strategic oversight roles of these two additional lines of defense. "Signals from some regulatory bodies now suggest that there may be new regulatory requirements or new interpretations of existing requirements placed on boards regarding their risk oversight responsibilities" (COSO 2009). In fact, many observers are now beginning to regard these as the most important lines of defense from a strategic perspective. For this reason, it would appear logical and prudent for organizations to focus on implementing the more comprehensive extended five lines of corporate defense model (Lyons 2011) that specifically includes the important strategic oversight roles of the board and executive management. This model addresses the oversight requirement at strategic, tactical, and operational levels. Figure 7.2 outlines the five lines of corporate defense vertical.

Given that every organization faces a unique set of circumstances, there is no *silver bullet* when it comes to assigning and delegating specific corporate defense activities; however, each of these

---

[*] Sometimes referred to as *management* or *the business.*
[†] Sometimes referred to as *business enabling functions, risk functions,* or *control functions.*
[‡] Sometimes referred to as *internal audit.*

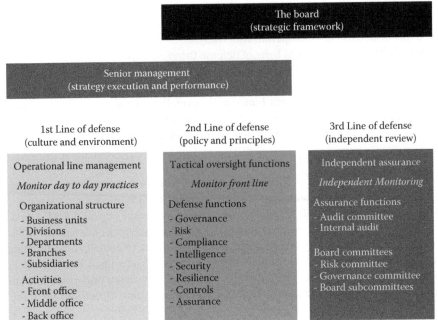

(Lyons 2011)

**FIGURE 7.1** Three lines of defense model. (Adapted by author from various *Three Lines of Defense* frameworks, including material from FERMA & ECIIA, *Guidance on the 8th EU Company Law Directive Article 41*, Federation of European Risk Management Associations and European Confederations of Institutes of Internal Auditing, http://www.eciia.eu/wp-content/uploads/2013/09/Blog-4.4-Avoid-reg-part-1. pdf, September 2010; KPMG, *Enterprise Risk Management: The 3 Lines of Defense*, Audit Committee Forum Volume 1, KPMG, Thailand, http://www.acithailand.org/aci/event/AC_forum/vol01/ACIWebsite-Vol1_20Oct.pdf, October 2009; Booz & Co, *Bringing Back Best Practice in Risk Management: Banks' Three Lines of Defense*, Booz & Co, http://www.strategyand.pwc.com/media/file/Bringing-Back-Best-Practices-in-Risk-Management.pdf, 2008; PWC, *Three Lines of Defence: How to Take the Burden Out of Compliance*, PricewaterhouseCoopers (PWC), Insurance Digest, European Edition, http://www.pwc.com/gx/en/insurance/ pdf/three_lines_of_defence.pdf, April 2008; Burden, P., *Three Lines of Defence Model*, ACCA IA Bulletin, http://newsweaver.co.uk/accaiabulletin/e_article001026154.cfm?x=b11,0,w, February 2008.)

five lines of defense has an important role in providing oversight over assigned corporate defense duties and responsibilities. The existence of each of these lines of defense provides an additional layer of protection to the organization's stakeholders in the event that an earlier line of defense is not operating in an effective manner. Figure 7.3 outlines the five lines of corporate defense horizontal.

### 7.2.1 THE FIRST LINE OF DEFENSE: OLM

OLM has an oversight role in relation to the day-to-day activities of the business. Business and operations teams act as frontlines through the enforcement of clear segregation of duties, and the implementation of procedures that should be designed to ensure that corporate defense activities are embedded into all relevant decisions and operations.

#### 7.2.1.1 The Oversight Role of the First Line of Defense

As the first line of defense, OLM is responsible for overseeing day-to-day business operations, both internally (front, middle, and back office) and in its interaction with the external world (clients, supply chain, etc.). OLM has the responsibility for the oversight of all corporate defense mechanisms

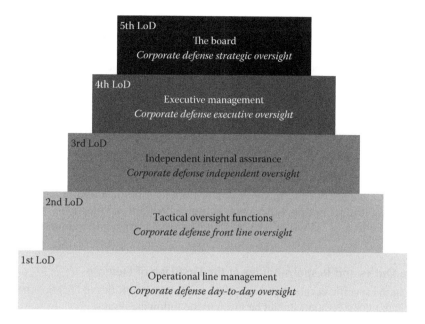

**FIGURE 7.2** The five lines of corporate defense—vertical.

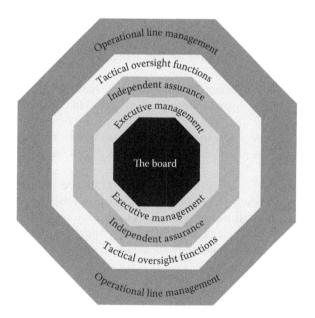

**FIGURE 7.3** The five lines of corporate defense—horizontal.

(i.e., practices, processes, and systems) operated by staff in daily operations. As the frontline of defense, it has the ultimate ownership, responsibility, and accountability for the execution of corporate defense activities on an ongoing basis, within its sphere of influence, in accordance with established corporate defense protocols, and consistent with the corporate defense values of the organization. OLM is responsible for ensuring there is an appropriate operational environment in place and that an appropriate operational culture is prevalent across the entire business. This line of defense is accountable to the other lines of defense for ensuring that its corporate defense practices are in accordance with the organization's overall corporate defense policies.

OLM assigns corporate defense responsibilities at an operational level to individual line managers in specific processes, functions, or departments. Accordingly, these line managers play a more hands-on role in executing particular day-to-day corporate defense practices. For instance, they identify, assess, and determine appropriate corporate defense practices through the development of procedures. OLM is responsible for the delegation, supervision, and routine verification of the execution of corporate defense procedures and should be in a position to provide the other lines of defense with up-to-date information about key indicators (i.e., key performance indicators [KPIs], key risk indicators [KRIs], etc.) associated with its corporate defense activities. OLM's effectiveness is dependent on a number of issues, such as the support received from executive management and the board for its corporate defense objectives. This will generally determine the organization's corporate defense maturity, its allocation of resources, and the extent to which these corporate defense activities are embedded into day-to-day operations. The relationship between OLM and the tactical oversight functions (and the support received from these functions) will also have an impact on the effectiveness, as will be the commitment to education and training in the corporate defense space.

### 7.2.1.2 The Duties and Responsibilities of the First Line of Defense

In determining the specific corporate defense duties and responsibilities of OLM as the first line of defense, particular consideration should be given to the following issues:

*Corporate defense ownership*: The extent of its duty to ensure the acknowledgment by the business itself that it has the ultimate ownership of corporate defense in the day-to-day activities of the business operations.

*Corporate defense execution*: The extent of its duty to appreciate that the business itself is responsible for the ongoing execution of corporate defense practices, which form part of the day-to-day business.

*Corporate defense people*: The extent of its duty to ensure the clear and transparent allocation of corporate defense roles, responsibilities, and accountabilities to staff in the performance of their business duties.

*Corporate defense processes*: The extent of its duty to ensure that appropriate corporate defense processes are in place and are in accordance with the organization's corporate defense policies.

*Corporate defense practices*: The extent of its duty to ensure that appropriate corporate defense practices (including procedures) are in place in order to adequately safeguard against the potential hazards that the business is exposed to on a daily basis.

*Corporate defense systems*: The extent of its duty to ensure that the organization's corporate defense systems are designed, implemented, and operated in accordance with their intended use.

As can be seen, OLM operating in the frontline has a very important corporate defense oversight role in relation to the ongoing effectiveness and efficiency of a corporate defense program on a day-to-day basis.

### 7.2.2 The Second Line of Defense: Tactical Oversight Functions

Tactical oversight functions represent centralized functions (or competence centers), which have been put in place to provide subject matter guidance and expertise on the critical corporate defense components, and to provide oversight and tactical support for the first line of defense in this regard. The operational culture, which is set out by the first line of defense, is supported and enabled by the second line of defense through the clear allocation of roles, delegation of responsibilities, and the establishment and implementation of appropriate organizational infrastructure and technological architecture. Examples of tactical oversight functions include the risk management function, compliance function, and security function.

In an ideal world, one corporate defense function would act as the central tactical oversight function and as the second line of defense. This centralized function would be responsible for coordinating and integrating all of the individual tactical oversight functions (i.e., risk management function, compliance function, and security function, etc.). Where no centralized corporate defense function exists, the individual tactical oversight functions operate as the immediate second line of defense working in conjunction with one another.

### 7.2.2.1 The Oversight Role of the Second Line of Defense

Tactical oversight functions are established to provide oversight over the execution of frontline critical component activities. These functions are expected to monitor, facilitate, and coordinate the consistent, competent, adequate, and effective operation of critical component activities established by OLM. This oversight role does not in any way diminish the duties and responsibilities of OLM for managing these critical component activities in the frontline. Tactical oversight functions help to design the various critical component systems that address essential requirements deemed necessary to safeguard the organization. In addition, they have a responsibility for providing the corporate defense committee, executive management, and the board with supplementary support and corporate defense assurance. Tactical oversight functions have the responsibility for developing a consistent enterprise-wide approach to critical components activities and therefore require specialist skills and knowledge in their own areas of expertise. They have the responsibility for overseeing the day-to-day activities of OLM in relation to the critical components. These functions have the responsibility for setting critical policy and outlining principles in relation to critical component activities, which in turn need to be executed in practice by the first line of defense on a daily basis, in order to become embedded in the business. Such tactical supervision should help set implementation of goals, as well as provide (and review) the critical component frameworks for implementation, in addition to monitoring, advising, and providing guidance to OLM. Tactical oversight functions have therefore been described as a combination of both watchdog and trusted advisor.

The effectiveness of each tactical oversight function as the second line of defense will very much depend on the level of its collaboration with other tactical oversight functions. This involves cooperating with and leveraging from the other defense-related functions within the organization. Success will also depend on the functional and cross-functional capability and maturity that exists within the organization. The more mature the organization, the easier it will be for the various tactical oversight functions to work hand in hand and to implement an integrated holistic approach to ensure alignment of the objectives.

Depending on the organization's governance structures, these tactical oversight functions may be accountable directly to the corporate defense function, to executive management, to the board committees (e.g., risk committee and compliance committee), or to the board of directors itself. From a corporate defense oversight perspective, the extent of their level of independence from executive management will increase their authority and status within the organization.

### 7.2.2.2 The Duties and Responsibilities of the Second Line of Defense

In determining the specific corporate defense duties and responsibilities of these tactical oversight functions as the second line of defense, particular consideration should be given to the following issues:

*Critical component framework*: The extent of its duty to ensure that the organization selects appropriate critical component frameworks that are suitable for their organization's needs.
*Critical component classifications*: The extent of its duty to ensure that there is an appropriate system in place to ensure consistent classification of all critical component matters.

*Critical component obligations*: The extent of its duty to ensure that there is an appropriate system in place to address all critical component obligations.

*Critical component appraisal*: The extent of its duty to ensure that there is an appropriate system in place to appraise and evaluate all critical component matters.

As can be seen, the tactical oversight functions have a very important corporate defense oversight role in relation to the design, implementation, and monitoring of the critical component programs. Where a central corporate defense function is in place the aforementioned duties and responsibilities apply at an integrated corporate defense level rather than at a critical component level. For example, the corporate defense function needs to consider the extent of its duty to ensure the organization selects and adopts an appropriate corporate defense framework, corporate defense taxonomy, corporate defense classification, and so on.

### 7.2.3   THE THIRD LINE OF DEFENSE: INDEPENDENT INTERNAL ASSURANCE

Independent internal assurance as the third line of defense provides the board (and to a lesser extent executive management) with a level of independent assurance in relation to the effectiveness of the activities of OLM, tactical oversight functions, and to varying degrees the activities of the executive management. This line of defense typically includes the board committees and subcommittees such as the audit committee (and the internal audit function). In terms of the corporate defense program, the board corporate defense committee ideally operates as the third line of defense and advises the board on corporate defense strategy, policy, and exposure. In the absence of a corporate defense committee, other critical component board committees such as the risk committee, compliance committee, and audit committee can provide the board with this service; however, they will need to be coordinated by the board itself.

#### 7.2.3.1   Oversight Role of the Third Line of Defense

The corporate defense oversight responsibilities of this line of defense include overseeing both the corporate defense activities of OLM, the tactical oversight functions, and certain corporate defense activities of the executive management function. This line of defense can help provide an independent perspective on the overall corporate defense program through the provision of independent challenge and assurance. Independent internal assurance provides the board with independent assurance in relation to the effectiveness of the organization's corporate defense systems so that it can be satisfied that these systems are fit for purpose and are robust and defensible. This involves the reviewing of the adequacy of the organization's corporate defense systems, and among other things, monitoring the effectiveness of these systems. The tactical oversight functions can play an important role in assisting the third line of defense in the performance of its duties, and therefore they may sometimes have a reporting line to the third line of defense. The extent of this reporting line may however impact the independence of the assurance provided by the third line of defense. The independence of the corporate defense committee ideally requires a committee of nonexecutive directors (NEDs) chaired by a senior independent director.

The audit committee (and internal audit) can also play an important role as the third line of defense as the functioning of the organization's corporate defense systems (including the corporate defense committee) should be the subject of internal audit review. The internal audit function reports to the audit committee and is required to provide objective and impartial assurance to the audit committee, board, and executive management on the effectiveness of the organization's corporate defense activities. Internal audit has a responsibility to undertake a series of independent tests and regular reviews of the adequacy of the overall corporate defense program (and related critical component programs), which should cover all aspects of the first and second lines of defense (including the manner in which the corporate defense function operates itself). Generally, there is at least a reasonable expectation that internal audit will identify weaknesses in the first and second lines of defense and recommend the appropriate remedial action. Internal audit can take some degree of assurance from the work undertaken by the second line functions and reduce or tailor its checking of the first line activity accordingly. The degree of assurance taken will depend on its view of the quality of the second line, and to avoid the duplication of effort, internal audit will need to coordinate its work with the second line functions. As well as assessing their work, internal audit can also add value by serving as an in-house consultant, suggesting improvements in the structure and operation of the organization's corporate defense program.

The effectiveness of the third line of defense will be determined by a number of factors, including the existence and structure of corporate defense committee, the competence of the individual committee members, their terms of reference, and the quality of corporate defense information received. Ultimately, the third line of defense must have the appropriate status and authority to empower it to enforce its recommendations. Where no corporate defense committee exists, the board will need to rely on the advice and support of the audit committee and other critical component committees (i.e., risk committee, compliance committee, etc.).

### 7.2.3.2 Duties and Responsibilities of the Third Line of Defense

In determining the specific corporate defense duties and responsibilities of independent internal assurance as the third line of defense, particular consideration should be given to the following issues:

*Corporate defense program*: The extent of its duty to ensure that it has the capability to provide independent assurance in relation to the effectiveness and efficiency of the overall corporate defense program.

*Strategic assurance*: The extent of its duty to ensure that it has the capability to provide independent assurance in relation to how corporate defense activities are being addressed at a strategic level.

*Tactical assurance*: The extent of its duty to ensure that it has the capability to provide independent assurance in relation to how corporate defense activities are being addressed at a tactical level.

*Operational assurance*: The extent of its duty to ensure it has the capability to provide independent assurance in relation to how corporate defense activities are being addressed at an operational level.

Examples of specific corporate defense-related questions, which independent internal assurance may also need to consider, include the following. Is there an appropriate mechanism in place to ensure that the

- Corporate defense strategy is being implemented in practice?
- Corporate defense framework is fit for purpose?
- Required corporate defense infrastructure is in place?
- Design of corporate defense architecture is capable of delivering on the organization's corporate defense requirements?
- Execution of corporate defense operations (e.g., assessment, monitoring, and reporting) is functioning effectively?

As can be seen, independent internal assurance has a very important corporate defense oversight role in relation to the provision of independent assurance over the corporate defense program.

### 7.2.4 FOURTH LINE OF DEFENSE: EXECUTIVE MANAGEMENT

The fourth line of defense involves the executive team appointed by the board of directors to run the business, and to provide assurance to the board that the objectives of the organization are being achieved. Executive management provides leadership to line management and staff in relation to the corporate defense program, and provides assurance to the board that the objectives of the corporate defense program are being achieved.

### 7.2.4.1   The Oversight Role of the Fourth Line of Defense

As the fourth line of defense, executive management contributes to the corporate defense program by helping to set the corporate defense *tone at the top* (along with the board) and by providing adequate corporate defense oversight of those they manage. Executive management is responsible for ensuring that the organization's activities are consistent with the organization's corporate defense strategy and policies approved by the board. Executive management is accountable to the board and has a responsibility for discussing, debating, and agreeing upon corporate defense strategy and policies for approval by the board.

The chief executive officer (CEO) has a personal responsibility for helping to set the *tone at the top* within the organization and assumes the ultimate executive ownership for corporate defense. The CEO has the responsibility for overseeing the corporate defense activities of the executive management team while at the same time supporting this team in its responsibilities. Central to executive management's role is to provide leadership and direction on corporate defense to both OLM and the corporate defense function, while also prioritizing the limited corporate defense resources of the organization. Executive management also has the responsibility for aligning an organization's corporate defense strategy with its broader business strategy, and for converting this strategy into operational objectives. Members of executive management have the responsibility for managing corporate defense activities within their fields of responsibility and for monitoring any misalignment with the corporate defense strategy. Typically, executive management has the responsibility for overseeing both the activities of OLM and the corporate defense function.

The effectiveness of this fourth line of defense will be dependent on attracting the right caliber of people to the executive management team and on the delegation, accountability, and transparency of their individual roles and responsibilities in relation to corporate defense. This includes the caliber of the CEO and the individual members of the C-suite in terms of their corporate defense acumen and skills.

### 7.2.4.2   The Duties and Responsibilities of the Fourth Line of Defense

In determining the specific corporate defense duties and responsibilities of executive management as the fourth line of defense, particular consideration should be given to the following issues:

> *Corporate defense program*: The extent of its duty to ensure that the design of the corporate defense program is appropriate in helping to deliver the organization's business strategy and for monitoring and reporting on its performance to the board of directors.
>
> *Corporate defense environment*: The extent of its duty to ensure that there is an appropriate corporate defense environment in place throughout the organization.
>
> *Corporate defense awareness*: The extent of its duty to ensure that there is an appropriate amount of education and training provided to help ensure a suitable level of corporate defense awareness throughout the organization.
>
> *Corporate defense profile*: The extent of its duty to ensure that the organization's corporate defense profile is acceptable, and that it is in accordance with its corporate defense strategy.
>
> *Corporate defense coverage*: The extent of its duty to ensure that corporate defense coverage is extended to all areas of business and operations.
>
> *Strategic corporate defense*: The extent of its duty to ensure that all significant strategic corporate defense matters are being appropriately managed.

Examples of specific corporate defense-related questions, which executive management may also need to consider, include the following.

Is there an appropriate mechanism in place to ensure that

- Executive management has a robust framework and comprehensive process in place to manage the corporate defense issues facing the organization?
- Executive management has a clear understanding of all hazard types and sources of hazards facing the organization?
- Executive management has a firm appreciation of the interconnectivity of hazard events and the associated speed and velocity of this interconnectivity?
- Executive management has a clear understanding of its role in determining and setting the *tone at the top* for corporate defense within the organization?
- Executive management has a clear understanding of the financial and nonfinancial implications of the potential hazard events facing the organization?

As can be seen, executive management has a very important corporate defense oversight role in relation to the strategic oversight of the corporate defense program.

### 7.2.5 THE FIFTH LINE OF DEFENSE: BOARD OF DIRECTORS

The board of directors as the fifth and last line of defense involves the elected board members with the responsibility for jointly overseeing the activities of the organization, and are accountable to the shareholders for the organization's strategy and performance. The board exercises a supervisory role as responsibility for actually managing the organization is delegated to the executive management team. The board has the overall responsibility for corporate defense oversight; however, the delegation of responsibility for corporate defense oversight is an important tool in strengthening the board's corporate defense oversight capacity.

#### 7.2.5.1 The Oversight Role of the Fifth Line of Defense

The corporate defense oversight responsibility of the board includes periodically reviewing the adequacy and effectiveness of the corporate defense program, and overseeing the activities of its corporate defense committee (and subcommittees thereof), its audit committee, and of its executive management. The board has the ultimate responsibility for ensuring that executive management is fulfilling its corporate defense obligations and responding appropriately to ongoing issues. Other duties include helping executive management to formulate a corporate strategy. It also has the responsibility for ensuring the availability of adequate financial resources for corporate defense, and for approving corporate defense appointments, policies, and budgets.

The chairperson as the highest office in the organization is elected to lead the board of directors and has the corporate defense oversight responsibility for presiding over the meetings of the board and for ensuring that the board's corporate defense business is conducted in an orderly fashion. Individual board members can be either nonexecutive or executive. Independent NEDs do not form part of the executive management team and are therefore in a position to provide independent corporate defense oversight of executive management. As the last custodians of the corporate defense oversight process, board members should constructively challenge executive management and provide independent views and contributions in relation to all board corporate defense matters. Executive directors being board representatives from the executive management team are not independent of executive management and therefore do not add an additional level of corporate defense oversight at board level.

From a corporate defense perspective, the board has the responsibility for providing direction, strategic oversight, and support in relation to the organization's corporate defense activities and the corporate defense oversight framework in place to address these obligations. The board should ultimately remain accountable to the stakeholders for the quality of the organization's corporate defense structure and capabilities. The board also has the responsibility for reviewing and approving the corporate defense program on an ongoing basis, taking into consideration the organization's changing circumstances and the constantly mutating challenges it is faced with. Ultimately, the primary responsibility for effective corporate defense oversight within the organization rests with the full board.

The effectiveness of this fifth line of defense in its corporate defense oversight role will be dependent on the board's composition, independence, and qualification. It will be dependent on the board having the appropriate balance of corporate defense skills, experience, and knowledge. The NEDs contribution will be dependent on their dedicated support and overall time commitment to their role, in addition to their corporate defense knowledge and understanding. From a stakeholder perspective, the separation of the roles of the chairman and CEO can provide additional corporate defense oversight independence and reduces many of the risks associated with the concentration of power lying with the CEO.

### 7.2.5.2   Duties and Responsibilities of the Fifth Line of Defense

In determining the specific corporate defense duties and responsibilities of the board of directors as the fifth line of defense, particular consideration should be given to the following issues:

*Corporate defense culture*: The extent of its duty to ensure that it sets the appropriate *tone at the top* to help foster an appropriate corporate defense culture within the organization.

*Corporate defense agenda*: The extent of its duty to ensure that the corporate defense agenda is appropriately prioritized within the organization, particularly at a strategic level.

*Corporate defense program*: The extent of its duty to ensure that an appropriate corporate defense program is put in place to reflect the organization's business strategy and business model.

*Strategic Corporate Defense*: The extent of its duty to ensure that all strategic corporate defense matters are identified, understood, and being appropriately managed and monitored within the organization. Of particular interest is the organization's reputation.

Examples of specific corporate defense-related questions, which the board of directors may also need to consider, include the following:
Is there an appropriate mechanism in place to ensure that

- The board possesses the appropriate corporate defense knowledge, experience, and expertise required to address the corporate defense matters facing the organization?[*]
- The board has an enterprise-wide view and clear understanding of the organization's corporate defense measures and all the significant hazards the organization is exposed to?
- The board clearly articulates and approves the organization's corporate defense program and strategy?
- The board sets clear delegations of authority and has sufficient communications with delegated corporate defense oversight parties?
- The board has access to all requested information, and receives all relevant corporate defense information from executive management and the corporate defense committee(s)?

As can be seen, the board of directors as the last line of defense has the ultimate responsibility for the governance and oversight of the corporate defense program.

---

[*] Are there any professional biases or blind spots that particularly need to be addressed?

## 7.2.6 FIVE LINES OF DEFENSE IN PRACTICE

In order for the corporate defense oversight model to operate effectively in practice, each line of defense must play its part both individually and collectively as *the chain is only as strong as the weakest link*. Such an integrated approach means that each line of defense must fulfill its corporate defense oversight duties within a holistic framework. Accordingly, each line of defense must acknowledge and accept its own individual requirement to both collaborate with and challenge the other lines of defense as part of their own enlightened self-interest. Enhanced cooperation and communication between these lines of defense is required and can be facilitated by better interaction between stakeholders through regular dialogue that is based on mutual understandings of the organization's objectives. This, however, must be achieved without allowing respective responsibilities and accountabilities to become blurred in the process.

### 7.2.6.1 Oversight at Strategic, Tactical, and Operational Levels

It is essential that each line of defense recognizes that it has specific oversight responsibilities in relation to the functioning of an effective corporate defense program at strategic, tactical, and operational levels. This requires clarity of responsibilities and accountabilities at every line of defense. These oversight responsibilities are end, to end and begin at the boardroom, but run right through the organization all the way to the frontline. Within the model itself, each line of defense must independently review the adequacy and effectiveness of the assurance it is capable of providing to the other lines of defense. Above all, effective corporate defense oversight requires an appropriate level of due diligence, vigilance, and escalation at every oversight layer.

### 7.2.6.2 Telescope and Microscope

Fundamentally, what an effective corporate defense oversight framework seeks to achieve is an appropriate balance between trust and supervision. Appreciating the boundary between providing oversight and actually interfering with the delegated management can be a challenge. As a rule, the maxim *noses in, fingers out* should be applied. Corporate defense oversight requires macromanagement rather than micromanagement; however, recent experience has highlighted the genuine requirement for greater oversight (telescope) and better insight (microscope). The implementation of the extended five lines of defense model represents an opportunity to address this challenge and in the process creates a more robust oversight in order to help better safeguard stakeholder interests going forward. This means that there needs to be a healthy tension in place between the different lines of defense while still working together in harmony. Corporate defense oversight relies on a system of *checks and balances* that both support and challenge the status quo, thereby enabling the organization to achieve its business objectives in the short, medium, and long terms. In truth, corporate defense oversight is a relentless challenge that requires ongoing scrutiny, constant learning, and continuous improvement. Like so many challenges in life, the focus therefore needs to be both on the ongoing journey and final destination.

### 7.2.6.3 Lines of Defense Weaknesses

It is common for postmortem investigations into the causes of large-scale corporate failures or scandals to typically identify the lines of defense weaknesses in the organization(s) concerned as being a significant contributing factor. The occurrence of weaknesses in a number of lines of defense indicates an ineffective lines of defense framework and a lack of a clear defense focus. Such weaknesses can lead to unnecessary large-scale losses, significant reputation damage, and negatively impact on stakeholder interests. The following example may help to illustrate this point.

## JPMORGAN CHASE—LONDON WHALE

In 2012, JPMorgan Chase incurred large trading losses in its chief investment office (CIO) based on transactions booked through its London branch, the so-called London Whale case. The case related to its London branch trading losses in excess of $6.2 billion was associated with a hedging strategy involving a synthetic credit portfolio. In two released internal reports from JPMorgan, the bank itself highlighted weaknesses at a number of its lines of defense.[*]

*First LoD*: It was noted that CIO London office traders (including Bruno Iksil "The Whale") lacked an understanding of their complex trades, that they did not monitor these complex trades, and did not listen to questions from the risk function. It was also noted that they did not communicate the full extent of trading losses. It was reported that the CIO headquarters failed to review or monitor the trading strategy and that it failed to ensure that the risk and finance functions were providing appropriate oversight and control of the portfolio.

*Second LoD*: The risk and finance functions were criticized for inadequacies inside the CIO. It was noted that the risk function failed to provide appropriate oversight and control of the portfolio in question and also failed to spot the trouble. It was noted that the risk function did not always ask questions, share information, and have granular limits in place on the risks undertaken.

*Third LoD*: There were no specific comments raised in relation to the audit committee and the internal audit function. The risk policy committee was exonerated as risks were not elevated in a timely manner; therefore, it was not provided with the opportunity to directly address the risks. Based on the information provided, it was noted that it discharged its duties with respect to the oversight of the firm and the CIO. There were however a number of recommendations focusing on how it could better function going forward (perhaps by implication suggesting there were deficiencies in previous practices).

*Fourth LoD*: The executive management, and in particular the CEO Jamie Dimon, was criticized for failure to understand warning signs in a unit reporting directly to him. It also noted that he should have scrutinized the CIO more, and challenged the CIO strategy more robustly.

*Fifth LoD*: The board was exonerated as the information received did not suggest significant problems. The debacle did however raise issues in relation to board oversight of both corporate governance and risk management. The fact that Jamie Dimon held the dual role of the CEO and chairman of the board raised concerns in some circles in relation to the board's oversight of the executive management.

In September 2013, JPMorgan Chase agreed to pay $920 million in fine to the U.S. and the U.K. regulators to settle charges related to unsafe and unsound practices concerning the "London Whale" trading debacle. In September 2015, JPMorgan Chase & Co. shareholders won court permission to pursue their securities fraud lawsuit against the bank's oversight of the "London Whale" scandal as a class action. This case serves as a good example of the importance of adequate oversight at each line of defense and how stakeholders may rely on effective oversight to identify issues before they escalate out of control.

---

[*] 1. Report of the Review Committee of the Board of Directors of JPMorgan Chase & Co., Relating to the Board's Oversight Function with Respect to Risk Management, January 15, 2013.

2. Report of JPMorgan Chase & Co. Management Taskforce, Regarding 2012 CIO Losses, January 16, 2013.

## 7.3 EXTERNAL GATEKEEPERS AND WATCHDOGS

Parties external to the organization also perform certain oversight functions and often provide information useful for carrying out the duties of the organization. Although stakeholders may place a certain degree of reliance on these parties as additional lines of defense, they are not traditionally considered to be a part of the organization's own defense program. However, the oversight responsibility and accountability associated with these external parties do not necessarily follow the same linear pattern as outlined in the internal lines of defense.

### 7.3.1 EXTERNAL AUDITORS

External audit professionals who are independent of the organization can provide a degree of oversight through their unbiased and independent evaluation of the financial statements of that organization. The primary role of the external auditors is to express an opinion on whether an organization's financial statements are free of material misstatements. The auditor can therefore provide the organization's stakeholders (including shareholders, the board, and senior management) with a true and fair view of the organization's preparation of accounts.

#### 7.3.1.1 Controls over Financial Reporting

During the audit process, an external auditor may review the organization's internal control procedures when assessing and evaluating the organization's overall internal controls. However, given the specific scope and objectives of its mission, the information gathered by external auditors is limited to financial reporting only. This process generally does not include assurance on the way the board or executive leaders are managing corporate defense activities, the second and third lines of defense separately provide certain assurance for these. Assessments and evaluations by the second and third lines of defense can provide significant information for the external auditors' assessment of risks and controls affecting the financial statements.

#### 7.3.1.2 External Auditor Assurance

The effectiveness of stakeholder assurance received from external auditors depends on the relationship between the external auditors and the organization that appoints them and pays them for their services. It will also be dependent on the agreement of the scope of work to be undertaken, the methodology adopted, and the audit coverage. The external audit team's experience, expertise, and knowledge of the organization are also factors.

### 7.3.2 SHAREHOLDERS

Shareholders, when they participate to guard their investments in the organization as legal owners, can provide a degree of oversight. Although the shareholders cannot control the board directly by acting together in the organization's general meetings (i.e., annual general meeting [AGM], extraordinary general meeting [EGM], etc.), they can exert a level of control indirectly by appropriately exercising their rights. Through the constructive use of the AGM, they are in a position to raise issues about the organization's strategy, the direction of the organization, and the performance of the board. The general meeting can only interfere with the board's exercise of power by altering the articles of association by special resolution. The right to vote on the appointment or removal of directors nominated by the board, the right to propose directors themselves, the right to propose shareholder resolutions, and to vote on proposals—are all fundamental to the shareholders' role in corporate oversight.

#### 7.3.2.1 Shareholder Activism

Any oversight depends on the active participation of the shareholders. Although not a primary oversight role, shareholder activism represents an opportunity for public scrutiny of the board.

In recent times, shareholder activists have made significant progress in gaining more information and in shifting power away from the corporate boards and management toward shareholders (particularly institutional investors) so that they can wield greater influence. By participating actively, shareholders can exert pressure on the board to be more transparent, thereby encouraging openness, integrity, and above all the accountability of the board and, in doing so, further enhance effective oversight.

### 7.3.3 RATING AGENCIES

Independent professional agencies and research analysts, who specialize in analyzing, benchmarking, and rating organizations with their expertise in credit, corporate governance, risk management, and so on, represent another level of oversight. Although these agencies are hired by the organization, the question of whether their accountability should be to market forces or to more stringent regulation has been the subject of much debate.

#### 7.3.3.1 Rating Agency Reputation

In essence, the rating agency's role is to formulate and publish its neutral opinion through ratings, which serve as a yardstick to stakeholders. Ratings can reduce the level of work required by stakeholders (particularly investors) in evaluating an organization themselves. In such cases, the reputation and trustworthiness of the rating agency matter. To be rated by one of the more reputable rating agencies sends a signal that the organization takes the issue of its rating seriously. An organization can therefore expect to acquire a more favorable reputation among its stakeholders if it is willing to operate under a rating agency's ongoing scrutiny. Employing and collaborating with a highly regarded rating agency is one way to distinguish the organization from its competitors.

Similar to external auditors, the effectiveness of rating agencies will in turn depend on whether the agency is "free from material conflicts of interest that might compromise the integrity of their analysis or advice" (OECD 2009). It will also depend on both the quality of the review process itself and on the stakeholders' perception of the reputation of the rating agency. The rating agency's reputation is determined by its history and on the level of endorsements and certifications it publicly receives. Although these ratings do provide a degree of assurance, stakeholders must also be aware of that to a certain extent, the rating agency acts as an information intermediary between the organization and its stakeholders, and therefore it very much relies on the information provided by the organization in question.

There is now some anecdotal evidence that credit rating agencies (e.g., S&P) are placing more emphasis on corporate defense initiatives (e.g., enterprise risk management [ERM] programs) than was previously the case. This implies that the rating agency's overall assessment may be affected by the quality of the organization's defense initiatives. Consequently, such ratings should increase the level of transparency surrounding the quality of corporate defense.

### 7.3.4 REGULATORS

Typically regulators are responsible for codifying and enforcing rules and regulations, and for imposing supervision or oversight of a particular industry or service for the benefit of the public at large, and in this capacity they also provide protection for stakeholders. The government generally determines the level of regulation or deregulation deemed appropriate in a particular market, industry, sector, or profession, and is accountable to its electorate.

#### 7.3.4.1 State Regulation and Self-Regulation

Where a market or profession is self-regulated, a nongovernment agency is typically established by representatives within that industry or profession that is accountable only to market forces. Government regulators oversee whether organizations comply with administrative law or other rules that outline specific requirements, restrictions, or guidelines, applicable within the mandated territory. The regulator's role might also involve licensing, supervision of entrants, enforcement of requirements, and discipline for misconduct. In certain cases, regulators will perform specific investigations and ongoing reviews. The sanctions available to regulators can vary considerably and include the authorization to revoke a business license, the imposition of fines, or even the initiation of criminal proceedings against organizations and their officers. This level of oversight is effective when the regulator is perceived to be competent, and has good standing within its industry or with the general public.

### 7.3.5 OTHER EXTERNAL STAKEHOLDERS

A complete circle of accountability is essential to ensure that the oversight system works as a whole. In this regard, such a complete circle of accountability should also include other external stakeholders such as the government, the electorate, and the society.

#### 7.3.5.1 The Government

In democratic countries, the government tends to reflect the appetite among the electorate for regulation and the level of regulation demanded by the electorate. Politicians are the elected representatives of the people and therefore they have certain oversight duties and responsibilities to fulfill on behalf of the people they represent. Generally speaking, the government of the day is expected to provide a degree of oversight over the workings of the government regulators and is expected to hold these regulators to account for the quality of their performance. The political opposition parties in turn provide a level of scrutiny of the government in their performance of these responsibilities.

#### 7.3.5.2 The Electorate

The electorate represents the registered adults who are eligible to vote in a democracy. The electorate must therefore shoulder responsibility for electing politicians who they feel most closely represent their viewpoints and aspirations. Therefore, the electorate's passive or aggressive stance toward regulation will likely be reflected by those who chose to exercise their franchise in the ballot box. The extent to which the electorate can hold the politicians accountable for their level of oversight will certainly contribute to the level of oversight provided by the government on their behalf.

#### 7.3.5.3 Society

Society refers to the people, not only the citizens, who live in a country, regardless of their age, sex, religion, or occupation, and so on. It includes both adults and children, and tax payers and nontax payers. Although not every member of society may have a right to vote in political elections, society has other means available to it in order to make an impression on the electorate and impact on the politicians. Typically, society can avail of the right of assembly, the right to march, the right to protest, the right to boycott, and so on, in order to bring attention to issues of concern. The attitude of society to regulation and oversight generally reflects the culture of the country, and this culture is likely to be prevalent throughout the entire oversight system. Society relies on a number of additional players such as the market and the media (including social media) to also contribute to corporate oversight and in helping to ensure that stakeholder interests are being adequately defended. Market analysts and media commentators are increasingly providing stakeholders with additional information channels.

# 8 Managing the Critical Corporate Defense Components

To succeed as a team is to hold all members accountable for their expertise.[*]

**Mitchell Caplan**

## 8.1 ALIGNING THE CRITICAL COMPONENTS

Successful corporate defense requires a number of related activities to be operating in an effective and efficient manner. Where any one of these activities is not operating to the required standard, it can undermine all of the other efforts and result in unnecessary loss or damage. A number of corporate defense-related activities have been identified as constituting the critical components of an organization's corporate defense program. Each of these components is inherently interconnected and interdependent, and therefore its effectiveness is contingent on one another, as each contributes to and receives from each of the other components in the course of its duties. Effective corporate defense requires the alignment, integration, and coordination of all of these specialist components.

---

[*] Per *The Executive Calling: Corporate Success Without Selling Your Soul*, 2008, Roger D. Andersen, Creation House, Lake Mary, FL.

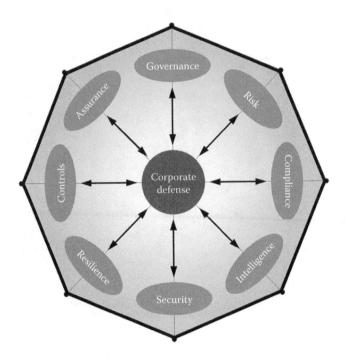

**FIGURE 8.1**   The corporate defense umbrella.

### 8.1.1   THE CORPORATE DEFENSE UMBRELLA

A comprehensive and coherent corporate defense program involves managing and coordinating each of the critical corporate defense components under one umbrella. These critical components address corporate defense from different perspectives and form part of the necessary system of checks and balances required to help ensure that the organization has taken appropriate measures to help preserve stakeholder value and safeguard stakeholder interests. Figure 8.1 illustrates the corporate defense umbrella.

## 8.2   CORPORATE DEFENSE AS AN INTEGRATED DISCIPLINE

Overall corporate defense needs to be regarded as an integrated multidiscipline whereby all of the critical corporate defense components are managed in a truly integrated manner. Prudence and common sense would suggest that this requires an integrated corporate defense program. A corporate defense program therefore involves the individual and collective management of all these components in order to help maximize their potential added value. Their integrated management is required as recent developments in each of these disciplines have meant that the boundaries between these activities have become somewhat blurred, and therefore it is now increasingly difficult to determine where one component ends and another begins, as each includes and contains elements of the others.

### 8.2.1   ASSESSING COMPONENT MATURITY AND COMPETENCE

Every organization addresses each of the critical corporate defense components to some extent, whether consciously or not, or whether formally or not. Certain organizations may address individual components in an ad-hoc manner as specific circumstances arise, some may address them via individual formal structured programs, while others may address them collectively via an integrated corporate defense program.

#### 8.2.1.1 Level of Maturity[*]

Depending on the approach taken to address corporate defense, the maturity of each individual component may vary from one component to the next, and may vary considerably from one organization to another. The required maturity levels in each of the critical components may well be dependent on the maturity of the organization itself and where it fits into a classical organizational lifecycle. For example, new or start-up entities are much less likely to have the same level of structure and formality present in these critical components as would be expected of multinational global conglomerates. Each organization however should be keenly aware of the level of maturity present in each of its critical components, and any variances should be fully understood and appreciated. Organizations should also evaluate if the current levels of maturity are considered to be adequate going forward into the future, particularly if the organization is planning to expand, or if the business environment is perceived to have become more dynamic.

#### 8.2.1.2 Level of Competence

An organization's level of competence in each of the critical components may also vary considerably from one component to another and from one organization to another. Typically, this will be a reflection of the industry the organization is operating in, the type of business it is involved in, and its geographic location. Different organizations will have different requirements in terms of the level of qualifications, skills, and expertise needed in each of the critical components. Each organization should however assess its existing levels of competence in each of these critical corporate defense components and evaluate the extent to which it currently possesses the desired level of competence, or whether remedial action is required in order to reach the required levels.

### 8.2.2 INDIVIDUAL SPECIALIST DISCIPLINES

Each of these critical components represents a specialist corporate defense discipline in its own right, with each involving specific training, education, and expertise. It is unreasonable to expect everyone in the organization to be fully proficient in any one, much less all of these disciplines. It is however considered prudent that the organization has individuals or groups in its employment with a sufficient grasp of these disciplines and has external access to more specialized knowledge if and when required. Each organization should therefore consider how it intends to address each of these specialist disciplines within its business, and the precise level of specialist skills required. In order to ensure that due consideration is given to each of these disciplines, the organization should review the extent of its program, formal or otherwise, for each of these components.

#### 8.2.2.1 Expert Competence Centers

Depending on the organization's circumstances, and given that it is considered unreasonable to expect any one individual to have a deep technical knowledge in each of these critical components, it may be advisable to develop centralized competence centers in particular disciplines as required. Such centers can help proactively develop individuals and groups with the required qualifications and experience so that the competence center can provide direction, advice, and support in their specialized field to the other areas of the business. These in-house centers may become a center of excellence in their particular areas of expertise or they may also rely on the support of external specialists as required.

## 8.3 INDIVIDUAL CRITICAL COMPONENT PROGRAMS

Each of the critical components needs to be systematically and consistently managed in its own right. In order to do them justice each requires its own individual program, and the level of structure and degree of formality present in such programs can help provide a good indication of the

---

[*] The matter of maturity levels is specifically addressed in more detail in Chapter 11.

organization's attitude to each component as well as the level of maturity present. It is important to be aware that each of these components may be addressed differently in different organizations, and that they all do not necessarily need to be operating at the same level in every organization. It is however important to know what these differences are, where they occur, and why they occur.

### 8.3.1   THE KEY TO READING CHAPTERS 9 AND 10

Chapters 9 and 10 help provide the reader with a high-level appreciation of the individual program requirements for each of the critical components.* The following headers in this section therefore represent the *key* to understanding and appreciating the next two chapters. To emphasize its individual contribution, each critical component is addressed in a systematic fashion, and for reasons of consistency and comparability, each one is treated equally and addressed in a similar manner. Owing to the generic nature of this approach, there are certain sections where similar wordings have been used in each component section. This is considered essential in order to emphasize the importance of each of these sections and the impact they will have on the management of that individual component. It is believed that such an approach will help each organization identify inconsistencies in its approaches to various components, and help recognize the extent to which each component has been consciously prioritized by the organization. The following sections and headings have been used in all cases.

### 8.3.2   THE CRITICAL COMPONENT (DESCRIPTION)

A brief description of each critical component is provided at the beginning of each section in order to quickly introduce the concept of each of the individual critical components.

### 8.3.3   THE CRITICAL COMPONENT AS A DISCIPLINE

Organizations need to learn to appreciate each individual critical component as a specialist discipline. They need to fully understand the individual purpose of each critical component, and how each critical component can help add value to the organization. It is of utmost importance that organizations fully appreciate the corporate defense role each critical component has to play and how each component can help the organization in the achievement of its objectives.

#### 8.3.3.1   Role of the Critical Component in Corporate Defense

Each of the critical components has an important and specific role to play in helping to safeguard the organization's assets and in helping to achieve the organization's objectives. For a critical component to be in a position to optimize its contribution to an organization, there should be an appropriate recognition and understanding of its purpose as a corporate defense discipline. This is a prerequisite to appreciating the potential for each to add value to the organization. For example, certain critical components are perhaps more focused on helping the organization to anticipate certain events in advance, others may be more focused on helping the organization to prevent the occurrence of negative events, some others may be more focused on helping the organization to detect when events have occurred, while still others may be more focused on helping the organization to react to the occurrence of events. Each can add value in its own unique ways. Again the level of focus on each of these defense objectives may vary from one organization to another, and may also vary considerably by each component, depending on how the organization chooses to manage the component.

---

* Chapters 9 and 10 provide a basic introduction to these disciplines. For those wishing to develop a deeper technical understanding of these disciplines, further reading of the materials in the frameworks and guidance sections is recommended.

### 8.3.3.2 Management of the Critical Component

Effective management of the component means addressing the component matters throughout the organization. Management includes developing an in-depth profile of each component, including its objectives and required capabilities. It involves setting a clear agenda for an individual component program and ensuring that this agenda is endorsed at the highest levels in the organization in order to set the appropriate *tone at the top*. It involves not only setting an appropriate critical component tone and developing an acceptable critical component culture, but it also involves adequately addressing specific component issues that the organization may face from time to time or on an ongoing basis. Each component requires appropriate oversight at strategic, tactical, and operational levels (i.e., *governance oversight, risk oversight, compliance oversight, intelligence oversight, security oversight, resilience oversight, controls oversight*, and *assurance oversight*). Generally speaking, the more formal the critical component program is, the more structured the management of the critical component will tend to be.

### 8.3.3.3 Key Component Program Players

In each case, an effective critical component program requires that all members of the organization fulfill their various component duties and responsibilities at strategic, tactical, and operational levels. There are however a number of key groups and individuals who specifically occupy important strategic roles in relation to each one of the critical corporate defense components. These include the following:

*Board members*: The board of directors and all of its members individually have important oversight roles and responsibilities for the existence and performance of each of the organization's individual critical corporate defense component programs.
*Chairman of the board*: The chairman of the board has a specifically important role in setting the appropriate tone at the top of the organization for each of the individual critical corporate defense component programs.
*Executive management*: The senior management team, and all of its members individually, have oversight roles and responsibilities for the effective enterprise-wide implementation of each of the critical corporate defense component programs.
*Chief executive officer (CEO)*: The CEO has a specifically important role in fostering the appropriate critical component culture throughout the organization and in overseeing the execution of the individual component activities across the entire organization on an ongoing basis.

While the ultimate responsibility rests with the aforementioned individuals as the leaders within the organization, the responsibility for managing the organization's individual critical component activities and practices will normally rest with groups and individuals with specific roles and responsibilities within the critical component programs.* It is therefore essential that there is a clear and transparent understanding of the issue of ownership of the individual critical component obligations, and this ownership issue needs to be addressed at strategic, tactical, and operational levels. In instances where no specific roles relating to a critical component are present within the organization, this potentially represents a red flag or warning, and is a strong indication that the component is not considered a priority by the organization.

### 8.3.3.4 Component Deliverables

Organizations need to understand and appreciate the potential for each critical component to deliver on their objectives. This involves assessing each critical component's capability and capacity to deliver on these objectives. In setting these deliverables, due consideration needs to be

---

* These specific roles and responsibilities will be addressed further in Chapters 9 and 10.

given to not only how they will positively impact on the achievement of the organization's objectives, but also on how realistic these expectations are given the prevailing capability and capacity.

### 8.3.4  CRITICAL COMPONENT MATTERS

To operate effectively, each component needs to be operating in an appropriate working environment that facilitates the execution of the individual component programs and the subsequent delivery of component objectives. In every organization, the working environment is impacted by the organization's culture. As part of the overall organizational culture, an appropriate component culture needs to be fostered and nurtured for each of the critical components.

#### 8.3.4.1  Component Philosophy and Culture

How the organization manages each individual component will generally be influenced by the organization's component philosophy and ethos. The component philosophy helps to set expectations, which in turn will dictate the approach to the component program. The organization's component philosophy refers to how the organization, in particular the board and senior management, appreciates, understands, and regards the importance of the role of the component in their organization. This component philosophy will set the tone for the organization's component culture, which in turn will influence the overall organizational culture. The component culture will have a big influence on the organization's approach to the component activities, which in turn will have a strong impact on the day-to-day working environment in which the organization's staff are expected to perform their component duties on a daily basis. In this way, the component philosophy and ethos become pervasive throughout the organization and can become embedded into the organization's culture.

#### 8.3.4.2  Component Issues for Consideration

For each corporate defense component, there are certain matters of concern that an organization must give due consideration to before deciding on its requirements and its approach to that specific component. Many of these matters should not be considered in isolation as they may impact on or be impacted by matters of concern in other critical components.

### 8.3.5  THE CRITICAL COMPONENT PROGRAM

Ideally, there should be a formal program put in place for each of the individual components (i.e., a *governance program*, a *risk program*, a *compliance program*, an *intelligence program*, a *security program*, a *resilience program*, a *controls program*, and an *assurance program*). Such programs can obviously vary by individual component and by organization; however, the existence of a formal program for each individual component demonstrates that the organization has at least given due consideration to the individual component and the organization's precise requirements in relation to the component concerned. A transparent process should be in place to help ensure that each individual component program covers all aspects and areas within the business for that component.

#### 8.3.5.1  Component Program Particulars

A formal program needs to begin with a formal structure that addresses its approach to issues at strategic, tactical, and operational levels. As such the program itself requires good governance from the outset and needs to follow the sound governance practices that should be applied to all component programs. A comprehensive component program therefore should be structured, so that at a minimum it addresses certain matters at strategic, tactical, and operational levels. Table 8.1 outlines these matters.

#### 8.3.5.2  Component Program Standing

A component program must have appropriate standing within the organization in order to help ensure it operates effectively. Invariably, its standing can be defined by its positioning within the

**TABLE 8.1**

**Component Program Particulars**

| | Program Particulars |
|---|---|
| Strategic level | • Program vision |
| | • Program mission statement (including program charter) |
| | • Program strategy (including program objectives) |
| Tactical level | • Program plan |
| | • Program framework |
| | • Program policies |
| Operational level | • Program systems |
| | • Program processes |
| | • Program procedures |

organization and the perceived level of its station vis-à-vis other similar programs. The program's standing and station may well be ascertained by the structure of the program and the composition of those engaged in the program. It may also be ascertained by its chain of command and direct reporting lines. The program's standing may also be reflected by the level of funding that the program has available to it and the level of resources at its disposal.

Adequate measures need to be taken in order to help ensure that there is appropriate awareness of the requirement for each of the individual critical component programs at strategic, tactical, and operational levels within the organization. At the end of the day, it may be the perceived status, authority, and influence of those engaged in the component program that will determine the extent to which the component program is prioritized within and throughout the organization.

### 8.3.6 CRITICAL COMPONENT PROGRAM FRAMEWORKS AND GUIDANCE

An appropriate operating framework needs to be selected for each of the individual critical component programs in order to help provide guidance on suitable infrastructure, architecture, and processes. There needs to be an appropriate infrastructure (e.g., people, processes, and systems) put in place to help ensure the effective operational execution of each of the individual component programs.

#### 8.3.6.1 National and International Guidance

Fortunately, when it comes to each of these components, there is no shortage of codes of practice and frameworks available from many national and international bodies. In most cases, there is an abundance of frameworks from which to choose from, many of which provide structure and guidance for somewhat different purposes. These range from frameworks that provide generic broad-based guidance that can be applied by practically all organizations regardless of industry or sector, to others with a more technical narrow focus that are designed for specific industries or sectors. Given that the level of detail required may vary from one organization to another, organizations can selectively utilize what is most applicable to their individual circumstances. Each organization needs to determine for itself which specific component framework, combination of frameworks, or unique bespoke framework to adopt based on its own unique requirements. Whatever framework is selected, it is advisable that the framework be flexible enough to address varying levels of complexity and adaptable enough to address the continuously evolving environment.

Most of the critical components are relatively new as distinct disciplines, and these disciplines are continuously evolving and developing. Both as theoretical academic topics and as practical subject matters, they have increasingly become the focus of technical attention. Given the nature of this publication, it is only possible to provide a high-level account of these components (see Chapters 9 and 10) and due to pragmatic restrictions it is not possible to explore their precise technical aspects in greater detail. There is however an abundance of literature (e.g., guidelines, best practices, standards, and principles) available addressing different aspects of these components for those who wish to further explore these topics.

### 8.3.7   INDIVIDUAL CRITICAL COMPONENT ORGANIZATIONS

In recent years, a number of organizations have developed internationally, regionally, and nationally that are specifically devoted to developing and promoting these critical components as specialist disciplines. These organizations provide a wide variety of services and resources to their members in their respective regions. It is therefore advisable that those involved in the planning and execution of individual critical components avail of the knowledge, resources, and support on offer by these organizations in order to benefit from their prior experience, lessons learned from past incidents, and the array of technical skills available (for further details, refer to Chapters 9 and 10).

## 8.4   REVIEW AND ASSESSMENT OF CRITICAL COMPONENT PROGRAMS

The level of preparation, formality, and structure devoted to a critical component program may differ by individual component and from one organization to another. In some organizations, no such programs may be in operation for any of the critical components, but rather each business unit is responsible for addressing corporate defense activities within the business unit itself. In other organizations, there may be some form of these programs in operation, but these programs may be not be formal or structured and may have evolved organically over the years in reaction to particular incidents and events. In certain organizations, there may be some formal, structured programs in place for certain critical components but not for all. Finally in some very mature and progressive organizations, as part of a proactive initiative, there may in fact be formal structured programs in place for all of the critical components. In many organizations, it is likely that there will be a mixture of varying levels of these scenarios.

### 8.4.1   ASSESSMENT OF CRITICAL COMPONENT PROGRAM STATUS

In any event, each organization needs to reflect on its current situation as it stands and evaluate the adequacy of its current efforts for each of the critical components. Such assessment should occur on an ongoing basis and should address its critical component efforts at strategic, tactical, and operational levels. On such reflection, it must consider if its current approach is considered appropriate going forward or if changes to the approach are required.

#### 8.4.1.1   Current Status and Future Requirement

Where there is no program in place for a particular critical component, the organization needs to review the circumstances that led to this situation, assess the implications, and determine if the organization is content to continue without some form of plan going forward. The lack of a formal program in any one of the critical components suggests that the organization does not consider the critical component in question to be of critical importance to the achievement of its objectives.

Where an informal or unstructured program is in operation for a particular critical component, the organization needs to reassess the logic of adopting such an approach and reconsider the requirement to add formality and structure to such a program. Informal unstructured programs can in some cases achieve the required objectives; however, prudence and common sense would suggest that a formal structured program will be more effective and efficient than an informal unstructured program.

Where formal structured programs are in place for all of the critical components, the organization should compare these programs in order to help ensure that a consistent approach is being adopted in each case, and where inconsistencies are noted, the organization must satisfy itself that there are valid reasons for such inconsistencies, or alternatively take appropriate remedial action to address these inconsistencies.

## 8.4.2 INTERDISCIPLINARY SCRUTINY

Like all aspects of business, it is important to have appropriate *checks and balances* in place at all levels of the organization. In order to determine the robustness of each individual program, it can be useful to apply an interdisciplinary approach to scrutinize these programs. This involves continuously cross-referencing these critical components. For example, each individual critical component should be assessed to ensure that it has adequately addressed the governance, risk, compliance, intelligence, security, resilience, controls, and assurance issues relating to its program. (For more details, refer to Figure 14.1 in Chapter 14)

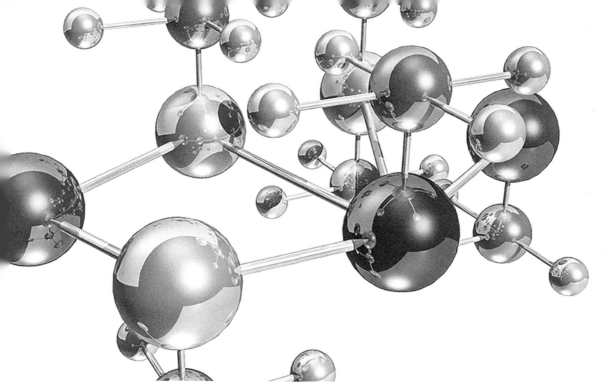

# 9 Critical Corporate Defense Components (Part I)*

The greatest enemy of knowledge is not ignorance, it is the illusion of knowledge.†

**Stephen Hawking**

## 9.1 GOVERNANCE

Governance, and the management of the governance process, is considered to be one of the critical components of an organization's corporate defense program. In simple terms, this refers to how the organization is directed, controlled, and held to account all the way from the boardroom to the frontlines. The Organization for Economic Co-operation and Development (OECD) in a paper titled "OECD Principles of Corporate Governance" defines corporate governance as "the system by which business corporations are directed and controlled. The governance structure specifies the distribution of rights and responsibilities among different participants in the corporation, such as the board, managers, shareholders and other stakeholders, and spells out the rules and procedures for making decisions on corporate affairs. By doing [so], it also provides the structure through which the company objectives are set, and the means of attaining those objectives and monitoring performance" (OECD 2004).

---

* Please refer to Chapter 8, Section 8.3.1 "The Key to Reading Chapters 9 and 10".
† Per *Uncertainty Modelling and Analysis in Engineering and the Sciences*, 2006, B.M. Ayyub and G.J. Klir, Chapman & Hall/CRC, Boca Raton, FL.

### 9.1.1  Governance as a Discipline

Governance is considered by some to be a somewhat abstract term. In its broadest sense it could be said to represent how an organization is directed and managed. It therefore involves multidimensional layers, both vertical and horizontal, which reflect the measures, processes, and mechanisms in place throughout the organization in order to achieve this objective. In order to effectively contribute to the overall corporate defense program, this component needs to be managed in a structured and systematic manner. When considering governance as a specialist discipline, it can be considered from two differing perspectives. First, governance with an uppercase "G" focuses on corporate governance from a strategic perspective, whereby the board is considered to be the focal point of governance activities, and the custodian of corporate governance within the organization. This includes the board structure, its responsibilities, and relationship dynamics. Second, governance with a lowercase "g" focuses on governance from a management perspective and the measures taken by management to direct and control business activities in order to achieve the objectives of the organization. This includes the management structures and processes in place, and the governance issues addressed by management on the course of its duties.

#### 9.1.1.1  Role of Governance in Corporate Defense

In a conversation in 2014 entitled "Ira Millstein: Why governance is our best defence,"[*] corporate governance legend Ira Millstein states: "Governance is a necessary defence against entrenched interests, greed, corruption, incompetence and indifference." In an interview in 2008,[†] governance expert Richard Steinberg (former head of the corporate governance advisory practice at PricewaterhouseCoopers), when asked for his views on where the role of governance currently fits into the broader concept of an organization's program for self-defense, stated: "Effective governance at the board level, and what's done throughout the management structure, is critical to defend against a broad range of challenges and threats. Processes and related activities at all levels must be established and executed effectively to avoid harm. But just as important is ensuring the organization is well positioned to react positively to potential events with upside impact, in order to take advantage to changes in the environment and marketplace. It's not a case of 'either-or', but rather both. That's how successful companies avoid the downside and achieve their goals to grow the business and add share value" (Lyons 2009c).

#### 9.1.1.2  Management of the Governance Component

Management of the governance component is required in order to help ensure that there is a system in place to address how the organization is directed and controlled, all the way from the boardroom to the frontlines. It involves specifying the distribution of rights and responsibilities among different stakeholders and spelling out the rules and procedures for decision making. It therefore involves multidimensional layers, both vertical and horizontal, which reflect the measures and mechanisms in place throughout the organization for setting and achieving organization's objectives and the means for monitoring performance at strategic, tactical, and operational levels. The governance component is both impacted by and impacts on the management of all of the other critical components. Each component should address the governance issue within its individual program (e.g., *risk governance, compliance governance, intelligence governance, security governance, resilience governance, controls governance,* and *assurance governance*).

---

[*] This was in an interview with David W. Anderson, which was published by *Listed Magazine* on October 30, 2014 (www.listedmag.com).

[†] In 2008, the author conducted a series of Q&A interviews with expert commentators on the critical components that constitute an organization's program for self-defense. This series was titled "Corporate Defense Insights: Dispatches from the Front Line" and was originally published during 2008 by the RiskCenter, a New York financial risk management media company then based on Wall Street (www.riskcenter.com).

### 9.1.1.3   Key Governance Players

An effective governance program requires all members of the organization to fulfill its governance duties. Although the ultimate responsibility for governance rests with the board and executive management, the responsibility for managing the organization's governance practices can typically rest with a number of key individuals who specifically occupy important governance positions.

*Chairman of the governance committee*: The chairman of the governance committee (should one exist) has an important intermediary role between the board and management. The chairman has the responsibility for the effective operation of the governance committee and its oversight of the implementation of the governance program.

*Company secretary*: The company secretary can play an important role in board governance by providing vital support to the board in the fulfillment of its governance duties and responsibilities.

*Chief governance officer*: The chief governance officer (should one exist) has an important role in overseeing the work of the governance function (should one exist) and in monitoring and advising on the ongoing governance activities of the organization.

### 9.1.1.4   Governance Deliverables

The purpose of addressing the governance component is to help deliver certain governance attributes that contribute to the organization's achievement of its business objectives. The following are some examples of what effective governance can hope to deliver:

*Leadership and direction*: Governance includes providing effective leadership at all levels within the organization. Leadership involves providing management and staff with appropriate direction, guidance, and stewardship. It involves taking the necessary steps to ensure that the organization is setting the right *tone at the top* through not only words but also in actions that permeate the culture of the organization.

*Integrity and ethics*: Governance includes instilling a sense of ethical purpose throughout the organization in order to help foster a culture of integrity. It involves the development of ethics policies and codes of conduct that espouse the organization's values and in communicating and reinforcing these values in order to encourage acceptable behavior throughout the organization in a manner consistent with appropriate ethical standards.

*Roles and responsibilities*: Governance includes the establishment of appropriate roles throughout the organization and the assignment of specific and general responsibilities to these roles via job descriptions, and so on. Clear delegation of authority and assignment of responsibility is essential in order to help ensure all required duties are performed by the appropriate individuals and groups and to avoid any possible confusion that might otherwise arise.

*Accountability*: Governance includes not only setting and enforcing clear lines of responsibility but also holding individuals and groups accountable for the performance of their duties throughout the organization. The formalization of roles and responsibilities provides a structure by which individuals can be held to account for the performance of their duties. Accountability requires appropriate oversight, supervision, and monitoring, and it requires appraisal via formal performance evaluations, and so on.

*Transparency*: Governance includes creating an environment that is transparent so that key information can be readily reported to relevant stakeholders. It involves identifying and divulging potential conflicts of interest and removing any impediments to transparency, so that there is transparent disclosure of both financial and nonfinancial information.

*Clarity*: Governance includes helping to provide clarity over the organization's vision and mission so that the key activities of the organizations are performed in a manner that helps the organization achieve its strategic objectives. It involves the creation of a predetermined strategy accompanied by comprehensive supporting plans, policies, methodologies, and procedures for all processes, so that the organization does the right things in the right way.

*Capability*: Governance includes providing an appropriate infrastructure so that the organization is capable of achieving its objectives. It involves designing the physical and technological architecture required and providing appropriate funding and resources to ensure that the required people, processes, and systems are made available to the organization as required.

### 9.1.2 Governance Matters

Sound corporate governance has an extremely important role to play in positively influencing an organization's culture. It is considered one of the primary mechanisms available to an organization in helping to ensure that it is managed and operating in an appropriate manner and is considered one of the essential ingredients required to deliver an appropriate working environment.

#### 9.1.2.1 Governance Philosophy and Culture

In a broader sense, the governance philosophy will influence the nature of the organization's relationships with its shareholders and with its other key stakeholders. From a structural perspective, it will influence how the organization itself is organized in terms of how it is designed and the nature of its infrastructure. The governance philosophy will influence how the organization goes about formulating strategy and the setting of its plans. Importantly, it will also influence how the organization goes about determining its corporate responsibilities, allocating these responsibilities, delegating authority, and holding individuals and/or groups to account for meeting their responsibilities. It will determine the extent to which formal frameworks and methodologies are required to be in place and the required formality and consistency of the organization's policies, practices, and procedures.

#### 9.1.2.2 Governance Issues for Consideration

Organizational governance covers a very broad spectrum and needs to address the multilevel requirements (and perhaps the often conflicting interests) of the various stakeholders of the organization (i.e., shareholders, clients, business partners, management, staff, etc.). The following are some examples of selected governance issues that organizations are required to consider:

*The board*: Organizations need to consider the structure, composition, and duties of its board. This involves determining the structure of the board in terms of its numbers and the process for nomination, appointment, and reelection of board members. It involves clearly determining the board objectives and understanding the board dynamics that come into play so that appropriate protocols exist to ensure a properly organized and functioning board. Organizations need to consider the composition of the board in terms of issues such as experience, independence, and diversity. This involves making sure that board members possess suitable qualifications and knowledge so that they have a clear understanding of their governance role and their required time commitment. Organizations need to consider the assignment of responsibility and accountability at board level and the mechanisms to be used to assess and evaluate board performance and competence. This involves ensuring that board members receive sufficient information, education, and training in order to develop a sound knowledge of the affairs and operations of the organization, and enable them to competently direct, monitor, evaluate, and take appropriate actions where necessary.

*Board committees and subcommittees*: Organizations need to consider how the board can best perform their governance duties and provide an adequate level of oversight where required. This involves an appreciation that although overall responsibility rests with the full board, many responsibilities can be best dealt with at a board committee level or a subcommittee level. Typically, boards may establish a number of board committees such as a nomination committee and a compensation committee. Specifically relating to corporate defense, boards may decide to establish a corporate defense committee or specialized

committees to oversee vital corporate defense activities and functions such as a governance committee, an audit committee, a risk committee, a compliance committee, and so
on. Ultimately, however, the board is responsible for adequately overseeing the operations
of these individual committees.

*Remuneration*: Organizations need to consider not only their personnel recruitment
policies and talent development processes but also be mindful of how individuals are
rewarded for their contributions to the organization. This involves ensuring that compensation policies and practices especially in relation to the board and senior management are transparent and in alignment with the organization's strategy, objectives, and
ethical values. It involves making sure not only that compensation metrics are performance based but also that performance measures are in alignment with the achievement of long-term strategy rather than short-term rewards. An organization's approach
to remuneration should not only motivate the management and staff through appropriate compensation but should also encourage appropriate behavior in the fulfillment of
their duties.

*Stakeholder relations*: Organizations need to consider how it can best communicate and
develop trusted relationships with its external stakeholders. This specifically involves how
it communicates with its shareholders (private and institutional investors), including transparency in reporting financial and nonfinancial information. It includes developing and
maintaining open channels of communication with all major stakeholders and managing
these stakeholder relationships by paying appropriate attention to stakeholder issues. In the
broader sense, it involves how the organization promotes itself as a good corporate citizen
and undertakes its corporate social responsibilities.

### 9.1.3   THE GOVERNANCE PROGRAM

The governance program in place must therefore be seen as a critical component of successful value
preservation, and it must operate in association with the other critical defense components that are
inherently interconnected and interdependent. A comprehensive governance program should also
incorporate these defense components into the program itself, and therefore should address issues
such as *governance risk*, *governance compliance*, *governance intelligence*, *governance security*,
*governance resilience*, *governance controls*, and *governance assurance*.

The objective of the governance program is to help direct and control the activities of the organization at strategic, tactical, and operational levels. Therefore, the governance program is concerned
with ensuring that the performance of each activity, regardless of what level within the organization,
is guided and directed by a *vision* and a *mission statement*, a *strategy* and a *plan*, a *framework* and a
*methodology*, and a *policy* and a *procedure*. This also applies to the governance program itself and
to the other critical component programs.

#### 9.1.3.1   Governance Program Particulars

Stakeholders of an organization can ascertain the extent to which the organization has adopted a
formal structured approach to its governance program by receiving coherent answers to their questions. The following are examples of basic questions that stakeholders might be expected to ask in
relation to the organization's governance program:

- Does your organization have a formal board-approved governance program in place?
- Does your organization have a formally approved governance vision in place?
- Does your organization have a formally approved governance mission statement in place?
- Does your organization have a formally approved governance strategy in place?
- Does your organization have a formally approved governance plan in place?

#### 9.1.3.2   Governance Program Standing

Stakeholders of an organization can ascertain the standing of the organization's governance program by receiving coherent answers to their questions. The following are examples of basic questions that stakeholders might be expected to ask in relation to the standing of the organization's governance program:

- Is there a board governance committee (or subcommittee) in place?
- Is there a specialist governance function (or competence center) in place?
- Has a chief governance officer been appointed?
- Where or to whom does the chief governance officer directly report?
- What is the governance program's budget as a percentage of the organization's overall budget?

### 9.1.4   GOVERNANCE FRAMEWORKS AND GUIDANCE

There are numerous versions of governance frameworks and guidance available to organizations. The following are examples of selected governance frameworks, codes, and other guidance:

**SELECTED GOVERNANCE FRAMEWORKS AND GUIDANCE**

- G20/OECD Principles of Corporate Governance: OECD Report to G20 Finance Ministers and Central Bank Governors (OECD 2015)
- UK Corporate Governance Code (FRC 2014)
- ICGN Global Corporate Governance Principles: Revised 2009 (ICGN 2014)
- NYSE: Corporate Governance Guide (NYSE 2014)
- Principles of Corporate Governance (Business Roundtable 2012)
- Basel Committee on Banking Supervision: Principles for Enhancing Corporate Governance (BCBS 2010)
- King Code of Governance for South Africa 2009 (IOD SA 2009)

### 9.1.5   INTERNATIONAL GOVERNANCE ORGANIZATIONS

There are numerous international organizations that are specifically devoted to developing and promoting governance as a discipline. Table 9.1 outlines notable international organizations that specifically focus on governance as a subject matter.

**TABLE 9.1**
**Selected Governance Organizations**

| Organization | Website |
| --- | --- |
| International Corporate Governance Network (ICGN) | www.icgn.org |
| European Corporate Governance Institute (ECGI) | www.ecgi.org |
| Hawkamah, Institute for Corporate Governance | www.hawkamah.org |
| International Corporate Governance Society (ICGS) | www.icgssociety.org |
| National Association of Corporate Directors (NACD) | www.nacdonline.org |
| Institute of Directors (IOD) | www.iod.com |
| Australian Institute of Company Directors | www.companydirectors.com.au |
| Society of Corporate Secretaries and Governance Professionals | www.governanceprofessionals.org |
| Institute of Chartered Secretaries and Administrators (ICSA) | www.icsa.org.uk |

## 9.2 RISK

Risk, and the management of risk, represents a necessary component of an organization's program for self-defense. In simple terms, this refers to how the organization identifies, measures, and manages the risks it is exposed to. There are a number of somewhat varying definitions of risk in circulation; however, in its simplest form, risk can be defined as "the chance of something happening that will have an impact on objectives" (AS/NZS 2004). A joint group of the U.K. Risk Management bodies describes risk management as follows: "Risk Management is a central part of any organisation's strategic management. It is the process whereby organisations methodically address the risks attaching to their activities with the goal of achieving sustained benefits within each activity and across the portfolio of all activities" (AIRMIC et al. 2002).

### 9.2.1 RISK AS A DISCIPLINE

The management of risk is concerned with addressing the relationship between potential risks and their related potential rewards. It is therefore effectively about how an organization manages its risk, so that it delivers a balance between maximizing the potential gains from realized opportunities while minimizing the potential losses incurred from risk exposures. Traditionally, the discipline of risk management tended to be restricted to *credit risk management*, *market risk management*, and *operational risk management*; however, in recent years, organizations are now also seeing the use of such terms as *corporate risk management*, *strategic risk management*, *enterprise risk management (ERM)*, and *integrated risk management*.

When considering the management of risk as a specialist discipline, one must first have a clear appreciation that risk taking is a prerequisite of doing business (i.e., *no risk, no reward*) and each organization will need to make its own informed decisions in relation to the risks that it is willing to take. This requires a sound understanding and cognition of risk as a concept, and more specifically an awareness of the nature of the trade-off between individual risks and the associated rewards. This may require tailored education and training at different levels throughout the organization, so that the fundamentals and principles of risk management are clearly understood and appreciated.

First, it is important that the organization clearly understands and differentiates between those risks that may be within the organization's own sphere of influence (i.e., *controllable risks*), and those risks that may be outside of the organization's control (i.e., *uncontrollable risks*). Controllable risks tend to be risks that are internal to the organization itself, or risks over which the organization has a choice to accept or avoid. Organizations need to be aware of their precise level of control when considering such risks. Uncontrollable risks on the other hand tend to be risks that are external to the organization itself or risks over which the organization has no choice. Having a risk strategy in place can help control against negative outcomes; however, in certain cases, the organization may have to accept uncontrollable risks for which there are very little associated rewards but rather the cost of doing business. Second, the organization must be conscious of the difference between the risks it intends to take in the course of its business (i.e., *intended risks*), which may result in expected losses, and the risks that it does not intend to take (i.e., *unintended risks*), which may result in unexpected losses. Each organization therefore needs to be clear as to the risks that it considers to be desirable in achieving its objectives and those that are considered to be undesirable and likely to hinder the achievement of these objectives. Third, the organization must clearly understand the distinction between engaging in risks that may be regarded as acceptable by its stakeholders (i.e., *acceptable risks*) and engaging in risks that may not be regarded as acceptable (i.e., *unacceptable risks*). It also needs to be recognized that not all stakeholders may be in agreement on what is regarded as acceptable. Fourth, the organization must clearly understand that although risk relates to uncertainty, the manifestation of some risks is predictable to a certain degree (i.e., *conventional risks*) and other risks are far more unpredictable in nature (i.e., *unconventional risks*). The fixed and variable nature of risk is therefore a constant challenge when prioritizing the management of risk.

Finally, the organization must clearly understand its own capacity to be able to absorb risks and be cognizant that although different risks may be appealing, the organization may only have the capacity to absorb certain risks and others may not be within its risk capacity. A clear understanding and appreciation of the nature of risk is a prerequisite to addressing individual risks.

### 9.2.1.1  Role of Risk in Corporate Defense

McKinsey and Co. in a paper titled "Enterprise Risk Management: What's different in the corporate world and why" states the following: "A common framework for risk management, especially in the financial sector, is that of 'three lines of defense,'...This framework is typically brought to emphasize that the risk-management function does not operate in isolation, and that robust risk management requires all three defensive lines to be in place" (McKinsey and Co. 2012). In an interview in 2008, risk management expert, Dr. David M. Rowe, director of the Professional Risk Managers' International Association (PRMIA), when asked for his opinion on where the role of risk management currently fits into the broader concept of an organization's corporate defense program and how he sees its role developing going forward, stated: "In my view risk management is effectively synonymous with the corporate defense function leavened with the recognition that some risks are necessary for a business to survive and prosper. It is the breadth of the potential dangers that makes the emerging role of the CRO [chief risk officer] especially challenging. As in politics so it is in risk management, there are no final victories. One requirement for long-term corporate success is constant vigilance and the will to act when threats emerge" (Lyons 2009c). Philip H. Martin, chairman of the Institute of Operational Risk (IOR), when asked in 2008 for his view on where operational risk management (ORM) currently fits into the broader concept of an organizations program of self-defense and how do you see it developing going forward, stated: "Operational Risk Management ought to be front and centre in a company's program of self-defense. If you go back to the empty-space definition of 'if it's not market or credit risk, it must be operational risk', then this would suggest that ORM must take the lead. I would like to think that the discipline of Operational Risk Management will continue to grow in importance, but this will depend on the skills of the ORM professionals" (Lyons 2009c).

### 9.2.1.2  Management of the Risk Component

Managing the risk component is required in order to systemically address how the organization identifies, measures, and manages the risks it is exposed to, whereby risk is generally understood to be the uncertainty or possibility that an event will occur that can have an adverse or undesired impact on the achievement of the organization's objectives (ISO 2009). The idea of managing risk on an enterprise-wide basis while in existence for some time began to evolve as a formal concept in the 1990s with the development of a heightened concern and focus on risk management, and as it became increasingly clear that a need existed for a robust framework to effectively identify, assess, and manage risk. ERM as a discipline began to gain considerable traction when the Committee of Sponsoring Organizations of the Treadway Commission (COSO) finally launched its *Enterprise Risk Management—Integrated Framework* in 2004 and it became the benchmark for ERM frameworks.* "Enterprise risk management is a process, effected by an entity's board of directors, management and other personnel, applied in strategy setting and across the enterprise, designed to identify potential events that may affect the entity, and manage risk to be within its risk appetite, to provide reasonable assurance regarding the achievement of entity objectives" (COSO 2004).

The risk component is both impacted by and impacts on the management of all of the other critical components. Each component should address the risk issue within its individual programs (e.g., *governance risk, compliance risk, intelligence risk, security risk, resilience risk, controls risk,* and *assurance risk*).

---

* On October 21, 2014 COSO announced a project to update the 2004 Enterprise Risk Management—Integrated Framework.

### 9.2.1.3 Key Risk Players

An effective risk program requires all members of the organization to fulfill their risk duties. Although ultimate responsibility for risk rests with the board and executive management, the responsibility for managing the organization's risk practices can typically rest with a number of key individuals who specifically occupy important risk positions.

*Chairman of the risk committee*: The chairman of the risk committee (should one exist) has an important intermediary role between the board and management. The chairman has responsibility for the effective operation of the risk committee and its oversight of the implementation of the risk program.

*Chief risk officer*: The chief risk officer (should one exist) has an important role in overseeing the work of the risk function (should one exist) and in monitoring and advising on the ongoing risk activities of the organization.

*Chairman of the audit committee*: The chairman of the audit committee can have an important intermediary role between the board and the oversight of the organization's management of its risk program, particularly in the absence of a risk committee.

*Heads of credit risk, market risk, and operational risk*: Where these risks are considered specialist risks, separate individuals may have important roles in the monitoring of, and advising on, the management of these unique risks.

### 9.2.1.4 Risk Deliverables

Organizations naturally face a variety of different risks in the course of their business, and therefore they need to have an adequate system in place to manage risk at strategic, tactical, and operational levels. It is generally accepted that an effective risk management system should ensure that the following processes are in operation[*]:

*Risk environment*: There should be an appropriate process in place to consider the environment in which the organization operates in order to establish the context in which risk needs to be addressed. The risk environment can be influenced by factors both internal and external to the organization. This includes internal issues such as the organization's risk culture, risk philosophy, and risk governance, all of which set the tone for how risk is viewed and addressed. It also includes external issues such as its market and the legal, social, and political environment in which it operates. Risk should be considered in the context of the achievement of the organization's business objectives and in the context of its stakeholders' expectations and interests.

*Risk identification*: There should be an appropriate process in place to establish the organization's risk profile and clearly identify the risks the organization is exposed to, which may affect the achievement of its business objectives. This should include identifying, documenting, and describing the types and sources of risk the organization is exposed to, be they financial and/or nonfinancial risks. The risk identification process requires an intimate knowledge of the organization's environment and a sound understanding of its strategic, tactical, and operational objectives. It requires an understanding of risk drivers and causes, types of risk, distinct risk events, and an appreciation of current and future risks. A risk register is often used to help the organization to capture all relevant risks.

*Risk assessment*: There should be an appropriate process in place to effectively analyze and evaluate the identified risks to which the organization is exposed. This should involve analyzing these risks and developing an understanding of each risk in order to consider the range of potential consequences and how these occur. It should involve evaluating and

---

[*] All of these risk processes are addressed in the major international risk management frameworks and standards, including COSO 2004, AIRMIC et al. 2002, and AS/NZS 2004. See "Risk Frameworks and Guidance" section.

ranking the organization's risk exposure in quantitative and qualitative terms, and comparing the estimated risk exposures against the organization's established risk criteria in order to determine how this risk should be managed. It should involve initially assessing the organization's level of inherent risk present, evaluating the mitigating influence of existing controls, and estimating the residual level of risk remaining.

*Risk response*: There should be an appropriate process in place to help ensure that the organization's response to the level of residual risk is in alignment with preestablished risk criteria (e.g., risk appetite and risk tolerances). This involves choosing from a selection of response options. These typically include decisions on whether to (1) tolerate the risk by simply accepting the residual risk, (2) treat the risk in order to reduce the residual risk to an acceptable level, (3) transfer the risk by sharing the residual risk with another party, or (4) terminate the risk by removing the source of the risk. Risk treatment may involve reducing the probability or the impact of the risk by improving existing controls or developing new controls. Policies and procedures are required to help ensure risk responses are effectively implemented.

*Risk communication*: There should be an appropriate process in place to help ensure that relevant risk intelligence is communicated to internal and external stakeholders. Different stakeholders require different information in different forms and time frames to enable them to perform their responsibilities. Relevant information, reporting formats, and time frames, should be determined through regular consultation with stakeholders. Risk reporting and consultation should occur as appropriate in relation to the risk management process as a whole and at each individual phase of the process. Risk intelligence should be communicated vertically (i.e., top-down and bottom-up) and horizontally (i.e., cross-functionally and across) throughout the organization.

*Risk monitoring*: There should be an appropriate process in place to help ensure that the entire risk management system is continuously monitored and regularly reviewed. The system should be continuously monitored to take account for changes in existing circumstances and the emergence of a new set of circumstances that may result in an altering of priorities or objectives. All phases of the risk management process need to be reviewed to measure progress and determine risk response implementation status and the quality of execution. The efficiency and effectiveness of performance need to be evaluated in order to help ensure continuous improvement. Where considered appropriate, modifications to the system or enhancements to individual phases in the process should be made as deemed necessary.

In theory, if these risk processes are applied in practice at strategic, tactical, and operational levels within the organization, it should result in an effective risk management system, and thereby help the organization to better identify, measure, and manage its risk.

## 9.2.2 Risk Matters

Every organization is exposed to a multitude of different risks; however, it is the organization's approach to identifying, measuring, and managing these risks that defines its risk culture and the risk environment in which risk activities are performed and executed on a day-to-day basis.

### 9.2.2.1 Risk Philosophy and Culture

In a broader sense, the risk philosophy will influence the nature of the organization's attitude to taking risk, which is expressed in its risk appetite statement. It will influence whether the organization views risk as the potential for downside only or as the potential for downside and upside. It will influence whether the organization views risk as simply a compliance exercise or as an important element in helping the organization to take advantage of opportunities, optimize performance, and realize its objectives. It will influence whether risk is addressed as an afterthought, or whether it is integrated into business decision making at all levels of the organization, be it strategic, tactical, or operational. It will influence whether the ownership of risk is considered to be the responsibility of the risk management function or whether everyone in the organization is considered to be a risk manager with the responsibility for managing the risk in its sphere of influence. Finally, it will influence human behavior throughout the organization and whether its conduct is risk averse or risk taking in the course of its ongoing duties.

### 9.2.2.2   Risk Issues for Consideration

Risk management involves ensuring that all risk issues that may impact on the organization's achievement of its objectives are appropriately considered and dealt with in an adequate manner. The following are some examples of selected risk issues that organizations are required to carefully consider:

*Risk profile*: Organizations need to consider what constitutes its desired risk profile and continuously compare this to its current risk profile in order to identify the extent of the gap and specific deviations or anomalies so that the appropriate corrective action can be taken. A clear insight into an organization's risk profile, being the sources of risks (i.e., economic risk, industry risk, product risk, environmental risk, etc.) that an organization is exposed to, is essential in order to be in a position to actively address these risks in a manner that also creates appropriate opportunities.

*Risk criteria*: Organizations need to carefully consider the terms of reference by which risks will be measured and assessed. This should include establishing precise criteria against which inherent risk and residual risk will be evaluated. Such risk criteria may typically include analyzing the probability or likelihood of the occurrence of a risk event, and the maximum impact or consequence should such an event occur, in addition to the speed at which the impact will be felt. It may also include considering multiple possible outcomes or a range of outcomes, and the potential interconnectivity of related risks and the risk-speed or the velocity of the risk contagion and the potential acceleration of the cascade of consequences once a risk event has occurred.

*Risk appetite*: Organizations need to consider and document the extent of their risk appetite, and whether it considers itself to be conservative (risk averse) or liberal (risk taker) in its engagement with risk. Its risk appetite should in reality be a reflection of the organization's capacity to absorb risk. An organization's risk appetite statement should clearly address the amount of risk that it considers desirable to take in the course of its ongoing activities. Such a statement can help act as a necessary link between the organization's strategy and its day-to-day operations. The risk appetite framework can help ensure that the risks being taken on an ongoing basis are in alignment with the business strategy set by the board and senior management. In this regard, it can empower staff in decision making by providing guidance and direction, as well as giving them the confidence to make the appropriate trade-offs between being overly cautious and being reckless in the performance of their duties.

*Risk tolerances*: An organization needs to consider how it determines the quantifiable metrics associated with the level of risk that it is willing to tolerate for the different types of risks the organization is exposed to. It needs to consider the level of risk that is considered acceptable in its different business activities throughout the organization. It needs to consider the maximum level of its aggregated risk exposure, the levels of risk concentration in any particular business sector, its market risk positions, and its risk boundaries, limits, or other parameters down to a granular level. Risk tolerances form an important part of the risk appetite framework.

*Risk categorization*: Organizations need to consider how they intend to classify the risk categories to be used at strategic, tactical, and operational levels in order to establish a clear risk profile and facilitate risk aggregation reporting. Risks may be categorized in many different forms, including market, credit, and operational risk, or more specifically as commercial risk, legal risk, financial risk, technology risk, behavior risk, and so on. Risks may also need to be categorized at strategic, tactical, and operational levels. Each organization needs to decide on risk categories that best suit its circumstances.

*Risk measurement*: An organizations needs to consider how it intends to measure the risks it is exposed to, in terms of both quantitative and qualitative metrics. There should be a clear understanding of the organization's risk quantification and aggregation methodologies so that risk strategy and risk tolerances are aligned to capital allocation and capital structure. The use of risk models and risk scoring techniques need to be professionally validated and approved and their underpinning assumptions clearly understood by all relevant parties. The interpretation of the results produced, their potential limitations, and the level of confidence associated with the results should also be clearly understood by those who may rely on these results to make critical decisions on behalf of the organization.

### 9.2.3  THE RISK PROGRAM

A risk management program addresses how an organization deals with uncertainty and the nature of the organization's approach to the risk and reward dynamic. In the business world, there is always an element or a degree of uncertainty associated with taking a particular course of action, and as a result of this uncertainty doing business involves risk taking. Successful business requires due consideration of the possible positive and negative outcomes, and choosing a course of action that is based on a trade-off between these possible outcomes. Positive outcomes are associated with the upside and the possibility of opportunities and rewards resulting from a particular course of action. Negative outcomes are associated with the downside and the possibility of threats and risks resulting from a particular course of action.

Traditionally, risk management as a discipline has focused on the mitigation or control of the possible downside. In recent times however there has been a trend to move the definition of risk away from the *chance or probability of loss* and toward the *effect of uncertainty on objectives* (ISO 2009) leading some practitioners to refer to the concepts of both *upside risk* and *downside risk*. Although traditionalists continue to argue that risk is only attached to the downside and the risk associated with an undesired outcome (there is no risk associated with a desired outcome), most practitioners would however agree that risk management needs to be aligned to business strategy and therefore needs to be mindful of the business drivers. COSO states: "Events can have negative impact, positive impact, or both. Events with a negative impact represent risks, which can prevent value creation or erode existing value. Events with positive impact may offset negative impacts or represent opportunities. Opportunities are the possibility that an event will occur and positively affect the achievement of objectives, supporting value creation or preservation. Management channels opportunities back to its strategy or objective-setting processes, formulating plans to seize the opportunities" (COSO 2004). Managing risk across the organization requires a holistic approach to help ensure that risks are appropriately managed at strategic, tactical, and operational levels. A comprehensive risk program should also incorporate the other defense components into the program itself, and therefore should address issues such as *risk governance, risk compliance, risk intelligence, risk security, risk resilience, risk controls,* and *risk assurance.*

#### 9.2.3.1  Risk Program Particulars

Stakeholders of an organization can ascertain the extent to which the organization has adopted a formal structured approach to its risk program by receiving coherent answers to their questions. The following are examples of basic questions that stakeholders might be expected to ask in relation to the organization's risk program:

- Does your organization have a formal board-approved risk program in place?
- Does your organization have a formally approved risk vision in place?
- Does your organization have a formally approved risk mission statement in place?

- Does your organization have a formally approved risk strategy in place?
- Does your organization have a formally approved risk plan in place?

### 9.2.3.2  Risk Program Standing

Stakeholders of an organization can ascertain the standing of the organization's risk program by receiving coherent answers to their questions. The following are examples of basic questions that stakeholders might be expected to ask in relation to the standing of organization's risk program:

- Is there a board risk committee (or subcommittee) in place?
- Is there a specialist risk function (or competence center) in place?
- Has a chief risk officer been appointed?
- Where or to whom does the chief risk officer directly report?
- What is the risk program's budget as a percentage of the organization's overall budget?

### 9.2.4  Risk Frameworks and Guidance

There are numerous versions of risk frameworks and guidance available to organizations. The following are examples of selected risk frameworks, codes, and other guidance:

### SELECTED RISK FRAMEWORKS AND GUIDANCE

- Professional Risk Managers' Handbook—2015 Edition: A Comprehensive Guide to Current Theory and Best Practices (PRMIA 2015)
- Principles for the Sound Management of Operational Risk (BCBS 2011)
- ISO 31000:2009: Risk Management—Principles and Guidelines (ISO 2009)
- Enterprise Risk Management: Frameworks, Elements, and Integration (IMA 2006)
- Enterprise Risk Management—Integrated Framework (COSO 2004)
- Risk Management AS/NZS 4360:2004 (AS/NZS 2004)
- A Risk Management Standard (AIRMIC et al. 2002)

### 9.2.5  International Risk Organizations

There are numerous international organizations that are specifically devoted to developing and promoting risk as a discipline. Table 9.2 outlines notable international organizations that specifically focus on risk management as a subject matter:

**TABLE 9.2**
**Selected Risk Organizations**

| Organization | Website |
| --- | --- |
| Federation of European Risk Management Associations (FERMA) | www.ferma.eu |
| Institute of Risk Management (IRM) | www.theirm.org |
| Professional Risk Managers' International Association (PRMIA) | www.prmia.org |
| Global Association of Risk Professionals (GARP) | www.garp.org |
| Risk and Insurance Management Society (RIMS) | www.rims.org |
| Risk Management Association (RMA) | www.rmahq.org |
| International Risk Management Institute (IRMI) | www.irmi.com |
| Association of Insurance and Risk Managers (AIRMIC) | www.airmic.com |
| Institute of Operational Risk (IOR) | www.ior-institute.org |

## 9.3　COMPLIANCE

Compliance, and the management of compliance, is considered one of the critical components of an organization's corporate defense program. In simple terms, this refers to how the organization ensures that its activities are in conformance with all relevant mandatory and voluntary requirements. The Open Compliance and Ethics Group (OCEG) describes compliance as follows: "Compliance is the act of adhering to, and the ability to demonstrate adherence to, mandated requirements defined by laws and regulations, as well as voluntary requirements resulting from contractual obligations and internal policies" (OCEG 2009).

### 9.3.1　COMPLIANCE AS A DISCIPLINE

Management of the compliance component is required in order to help ensure that the organization's activities are in compliance with accepted protocols. It involves clearly defining applicable laws and regulations, and being able to demonstrate how the organization manages to ensure that it is in strict adherence with all relevant requirements. In its broadest sense, compliance encompasses not only compliance with legal, regulatory, and contractual requirements but also includes compliance with market conventions, industry codes, and best practices, as well as internal standards, policies, protocols, and procedures. There are various sources of laws, regulations, and standards; therefore, the frameworks and/or sound principles and/or precise rules may vary significantly across different jurisdictions and geographical regions. Each organization must therefore ensure that appropriate compliance measures are in place in all of its business activities, particularly if these interests are geographically dispersed.

Ongoing efforts by lawmakers and regulators globally to further enhance sound corporate practices mean that the compliance imperative in many organizations is motivated by the threat of sanctions against the institution and the threat of prosecution against individuals. The sanctions available to regulators can vary considerably and include the authorization to revoke a business license, the imposition of fines, or even the initiation of criminal proceedings against organizations and their officers. Given the increasing volume of laws and regulations that an organization is already required to comply with, and the number of new laws and regulations continuously in the pipeline, in many organizations, compliance represents a reactionary function that is constantly struggling just to keep pace with the organization's current compliance requirements. Certain more progressive organizations however believe that a proactive approach to compliance can also help add value, in addition to simply avoiding possible sanctions. From a corporate defense perspective, a proactive compliance culture can have a considerable positive impact.

#### 9.3.1.1　Role of Compliance in Corporate Defense

The U.S. Securities and Exchange Commission (SEC) certainly considers compliance to have an important role to play in corporate defense. In 2012 Carlo V. di Florio, Director, Office of Compliance Inspections and Examinations (OCIE) at the SEC stated: "Key support functions, such as compliance and ethics or risk management, are the second line of defense. They need to have adequate resources, independence, standing and authority to implement effective programs and objectively monitor and escalate risk issues."[*] Such views were further reinforced by SEC Chair Mary Jo White in 2013, when in a section of her speech to compliance professionals titled "A Strong Line of Defense against Non-Compliance," she stated: "So at the SEC, we see you as a critical line of defense against violations of the securities laws and regulations, inadequate policies, procedures

---

[*] Remarks made on January 31, 2012 at the Compliance Outreach Program, SEC Headquarters, Washington, D.C. www.sec.gov/News/Speech/Detail/Speech/1365171489759.

and systems, and inadvertent errors—all of which may harm investors or your firms. But you are not and should not be the only line of defense."[*]

In an interview in 2008, compliance expert Roy Snell, chief executive office of the Society of Corporate Compliance and Ethics (SCCE), when asked for his views on where compliance currently fits into the broader concept of an organization's program of self-defense, and how he sees it developing going forward, stated: "If you want to eliminate the need to defend yourself, don't do anything that would require you to defend yourself. Implement a compliance program, avoid all of the distractions, find and fix problems, and you will reduce the need to defend yourself. Compliance (finding and fixing problems) is the single most effective use of your time and money" (Lyons 2009c).

### 9.3.1.2 Management of the Compliance Component

Management of the compliance component is required in order to help ensure there is a system in place to address how the organization ensures it is adhering to required protocols. This involves establishing an enterprise-wide system to identify all relevant mandatory and voluntary compliance boundaries, to analyze the organization's specific compliance requirements, to outline general policies and specific procedural requirements, and to monitor the implementation of these policies and procedures. Compliance requirements can have an impact on the organization's activities at strategic, tactical, and operational levels, including the composition of the board of directors at the very top of the organization. The compliance program is a reflection of the measures taken by the organization to address its compliance obligations at strategic, tactical, and operational levels. The compliance component is both impacted by and impacts on the management of all of the other critical components. Each component should address the compliance issue within its individual programs (e.g., *governance compliance, risk compliance, intelligence compliance, security compliance, resilience compliance, controls compliance,* and *assurance compliance*).

### 9.3.1.3 Key Compliance Players

An effective compliance program requires all members of the organization to fulfill their compliance duties. Although the ultimate responsibility for compliance rests with the board and executive management, the responsibility for managing the organization's compliance practices can typically rest with a number of key individuals who specifically occupy important compliance positions.

> *Chairman of the compliance committee*: The chairman of the compliance committee (should one exist) has an important intermediary role between the board and management. The chairman has responsibility for the effective operation of the compliance committee and its oversight of the implementation of the compliance program.
> *Chief compliance officer*: The chief compliance officer (should one exist) has an important role in overseeing the work of the compliance function (should one exist) and in monitoring and advising on the ongoing compliance activities of the organization.
> *Company secretary and general counsel*: Both these positions can have important roles to play in the monitoring of, and advising on, the specific compliance matters that fall within their area of expertise.

### 9.3.1.4 Compliance Deliverables

The purpose of addressing the compliance component is to help deliver on its duties (fiduciary and moral) and certain specific compliance requirements in order to facilitate the organization in the achievement of its objectives. As part of this process the organization must clearly identify its mandatory and voluntary compliance requirements and establish its compliance expectations

---

[*] Remarks made on October 22, 2013 at National Society of Compliance Professionals, National Membership Meeting, Washington D.C. www.sec.gov/News/Speech/Detail/Speech/1370539960588.

accordingly. The following are some examples of what effective compliance management can hope to deliver:

*Legal compliance*: Compliance with the requirements of all applicable laws and legislation across all relevant jurisdictions. Legal compliance is generally considered to be a mandatory compliance commitment and examples include compliance with relevant international law, criminal law, contract law, employment law, privacy law, and so on.

*Regulatory compliance*: Compliance with the requirements of all applicable principles and rules as outlined by relevant regulatory bodies. Regulatory compliance is generally considered to be a mandatory compliance commitment and examples include compliance with relevant environmental regulation, financial regulation, health and safety regulation, and so on.

*Industry compliance*: Compliance with the requirements of all applicable industry codes of practice and industry best practices as outlined by relevant industry associations and/ or government agencies. Industry compliance is generally considered to be a voluntary compliance commitment unless also addressed by law or regulation (including industry self-regulation). Examples include compliance with the relevant codes of practice, best practices, and professional standards specific to the organization's industry sector.

*Internal compliance*: Compliance with the requirements of all applicable internal protocols as approved by relevant internal parties. Internal compliance is generally considered to be a voluntary compliance commitment (unless also addressed by law or regulation) and examples include compliance with the relevant codes, policies, protocols, practices, and procedures specific to the organization in question.

*Ethical compliance*: Compliance with the requirements of all generally accepted principles of honesty, integrity, and morality as expected by the stakeholders of the organization. Ethical compliance is generally considered to be a voluntary compliance commitment (unless also addressed by law or regulation) and examples include compliance with the expected conduct, morals, and ethical values of the society in which the organization operates its business.

### 9.3.2  Compliance Matters

Effective compliance means addressing compliance requirements at all levels of the organization and across all relevant jurisdictions and geographic regions. This involves not only setting an appropriate compliance tone and fostering an acceptable compliance culture but also ensuring that there is a documented system in place to facilitate the organization in demonstrating that it is doing the right things, that it is doing them in the right way, and that such standards are maintained so that it occurs in a repeatable fashion.

#### 9.3.2.1  Compliance Philosophy and Culture

The compliance philosophy will determine the organization's appetite for compliance and ultimately the compliance culture and its level of commitment to compliance. This commitment will reflect the standards that the organization sets for itself during the course of its business activities. It will reflect the extent to which the organization is concerned with making minimum efforts to merely comply to the *letter of the law,* or the degree to which it strives to make every effort to observe the *spirit of the law,* particularly when faced with difficult ethical challenges. The compliance ethos will determine whether the organization's commitment to compliance is seen in terms of a straightforward financial calculation or in terms of a moral obligation or an ethical decision. A financial trade-off may involve carefully considering the benefits of compliance with its associated costs, and the final decision on the level of the compliance commitment may be determined purely by the extent of the possible sanction for a specific violation, rather than any moral or ethical decision. Failure however to consider the possible negative stakeholder impact may result in significant reputational damage, even if no law has been broken, and this may well have unforeseen long-term financial consequences. The organization's compliance ethos will therefore determine whether or not the organization wishes to go beyond what is considered to be legally binding and emphasize higher standards of honesty, integrity, and ethical conduct.

The compliance philosophy starts at the top of the organization, with the board and senior management leading by example and setting the tone for the organization's compliance culture. The compliance ethos should be part of the culture of the organization, and compliance should be viewed as an integral part of the organization's corporate defense and business activities. The approach to the compliance program should concern every member of the organization and should not be viewed solely as the responsibility of the compliance function or specialist compliance staff.

#### 9.3.2.2 Compliance Issues for Consideration

When prioritizing compliance activities, each organization should begin by carefully considering the risks associated with its identified compliance obligations. *Compliance risk* can be interpreted as the potential impact of the failure to comply with its compliance obligations and specified requirements resulting in legal or regulatory sanctions, negative financial consequences, or damage to the organization's reputation, which could negatively impact on the achievement of its objectives. Compliance risk should be managed along with other risks as part of the organization's risk program.

Compliance covers an extremely broad spectrum and each organization will face its own unique compliance challenges and requirements, and these may vary depending on factors such as the company's size, the nature and complexity of its structure, its geographic locations, and the business sector it operates in. The following are some examples of selected generic compliance issues that organizations are required to consider:

| | | |
|---|---|---|
| • Fraud prevention | • Conflicts of interest | • Health and safety |
| • Bribery and corruption | • Insider dealing | • Privacy legislation |
| • Anti-money laundering | • Price manipulation | • Corporate taxation |

Ultimately, the extent of an organization's compliance obligations will be very much influenced by the maturity and complexity of the legal and regulatory frameworks within which it operates its business activities. Each organization must therefore assess its own compliance universe in order to identify the jurisdictions of relevant legal and regulatory bodies in order to determine all applicable laws and regulations. The related principles and rules must then be carefully interpreted to establish the effect on the organization and its precise requirements, before sound compliance advice and guidelines can be developed.

### 9.3.3 THE COMPLIANCE PROGRAM

Compliance as a specialist discipline is required to be managed on an enterprise-wide basis and ideally requires a structured program of its own that operates at strategic, tactical, and operational levels. A comprehensive compliance program should incorporate the other defense components into the program itself, and therefore should address issues such as *compliance governance, compliance risk, compliance intelligence, compliance security, compliance resilience, compliance controls,* and *compliance assurance.*

There is no perfect way to deliver a compliance program, and organizations need to be free to choose what works best for them in accordance with their own unique circumstances and the potential for compliance to add value to their business. A formal compliance program should however address certain generally agreed elements. Essential elements of a compliance program should include the following:

*Oversight*: Establish sufficient oversight over the management of the compliance program. This should involve the creation of a compliance committee and the designation of a compliance officer. There should be an appropriate reporting mechanism to ensure that the management of the compliance program reports to the board of directors who are ultimately responsible for compliance oversight.

*Protocols*: Establish appropriate policies and procedures to help ensure that the organization is able to fulfill its compliance obligations and to help prevent and detect compliance violations. These should clearly outline the standards of expected behavior and highlight unacceptable behavior. It should include matters such as an integrity statement, an ethics policy, a code of conduct, and industry best practices. It should provide staff with clear compliance guidelines by incorporating required compliance behavior into day-to-day business procedures.

*Due diligence*: Exercise appropriate due diligence when appointing individuals to leadership positions to help ensure that authority is not delegated to unethical individuals. It is essential that those with a leadership role in your compliance program have been appropriately vetted in order to establish that they are of sound character and to minimize the potential for unethical behavior. Ethical leadership is the foundation that the organization needs to be built upon in order to stand the test of time.

*Education*: Establish an education program to educate staff on the organization's compliance obligations in order to raise staff awareness and help foster a culture of compliance within the organization. The organization should ensure that all staff members receive appropriate compliance training regarding their individual obligations, and that there is continuous communication with staff to advise them on compliance issues in order to ensure that they are kept abreast of new compliance requirements and other relevant changes as they occur.

*Monitoring*: The effectiveness of the organization's compliance efforts needs to be regularly and continuously monitored and evaluated. All levels of the compliance program should be audited and reviewed in order to assess the effectiveness of compliance education and to test that adherence to compliance protocols is implemented in practice. Monitoring systems should be in place to monitor changes to the compliance environment both internal and external to the organization.

*Enforcement*: The compliance program should be continuously and consistently enforced through a range of appropriate incentives and disciplinary measures. Confidential lines of communication should be established to facilitate inquiries and anonymous reporting of potential compliance breaches. All suspected compliance violations or allegations of misconduct should be recorded and appropriately followed up via a system developed to help ensure that they are appropriately examined and investigated.

*Response*: An appropriate system needs to be established to help ensure a prompt response to identified incidents of criminal offense and other compliance violations. Detected incidents of misconduct should be appropriately reported to the board and the relevant authorities. Corrective measures should be put in place to help ensure that weaknesses are identified as a result of compliance failures, and that appropriate improvements are made to prevent further similar incidents occurring in the future.

### 9.3.3.1  Compliance Program Particulars

Stakeholders of an organization can ascertain the extent to which the organization has adopted a formal structured approach to its compliance program by receiving coherent answers to their questions. The following are examples of basic questions that stakeholders might be expected to ask in relation to the organization's compliance program:

- Does your organization have a formal board approved compliance program in place?
- Does your organization have a formally approved compliance vision in place?
- Does your organization have a formally approved compliance mission statement in place?

- Does your organization have a formally approved compliance strategy in place?
- Does your organization have a formally approved compliance plan in place?

#### 9.3.3.2 Compliance Program Standing

Stakeholders of an organization can ascertain the standing of the organization's compliance program by receiving coherent answers to their questions. The following are examples of basic questions that stakeholders might be expected to ask in relation to the standing of organization's compliance program:

- Is there a board compliance committee (or subcommittee) in place?
- Is there a specialist compliance function (or competence center) in place?
- Has a chief compliance officer been appointed?
- Where or to whom does the chief compliance officer directly report?
- What is the compliance program's budget as a percentage of the organization's overall budget?

### 9.3.4 Compliance Frameworks and Guidance

There are numerous versions of compliance frameworks and guidance available to organizations. The following outlines examples of selected compliance frameworks, codes, and other guidance:

#### SELECTED COMPLIANCE FRAMEWORKS AND GUIDANCE

- The Complete Compliance and Ethics Manual (SCCE 2015)
- A Compliance and Ethics Program on a Dollar a Day: How Small Companies Can Have Effective Programs (SCCE 2010)
- Red Book: Foundation Guidelines (OCEG 2006)
- Compliance and the Compliance Function in Banks (BCBS 2005)
- United States Sentencing Commission Guidelines Manual (USSC 1991)

### 9.3.5 International Compliance Organizations

There are numerous international organizations that are specifically devoted to developing and promoting compliance as a discipline. Table 9.3 outlines notable international organizations that specifically focus on compliance as a subject matter.

**TABLE 9.3**

**Selected Compliance Organizations**

| Organization | Website |
| --- | --- |
| Society of Corporate Compliance and Ethics (SCCE) | www.corporatecompliance.org |
| Open Compliance and Ethics Group (OCEG) | www.oceg.org |
| Regulatory Compliance Association (RCA) | www.rcaonline.org |
| International Federation of Compliance Associations (IFCA) | www.ifca.co |
| Australasian Compliance Institute (ACI) | www.acigrc.com |
| Compliance Institute of South Africa | www.compliancesa.com |
| Ethics and Compliance Officer Association (ECOA) | www.theecoa.org |
| National Society of Compliance Professionals (NSCP) | www.nscp.org |

## 9.4  INTELLIGENCE

Intelligence, and the management of intelligence, is considered to be one of the critical components of an organization's corporate defense program. In simple terms this refers to how the organization ensures that it gets the right information, for the right purpose, in the right format, to the right person, in the right place, and at the right time. Professor William E. Halal, professor of management at George Washington University, described an organization's intelligence component as follows: "Organizational Intelligence (OI) is the capacity of an organization to create knowledge and use it to strategically adapt to its environment or marketplace. It is similar to I.Q. [Intelligence Quotient] but framed at an organizational level. While organizations in the past have been viewed as compilations of tasks, products, employees, profit centers and processes, today they are increasingly seen as intelligent systems designed to manage knowledge. Scholars have shown that organizations engage in learning processes using tacit forms of intuitive knowledge, hard data stored in computer networks and information gleaned from the environment, all of which are used to make sensible decisions. Because this complex process involves large numbers of people interacting with diverse information systems, OI is more than the aggregate intelligence of organizational members; it is the intelligence of the organization itself as a larger system" (Halal 1997).

### 9.4.1  Intelligence as a Discipline

Business is complex and the degree of an organization's intelligence generally determines its long-term success or failure. Some organizations display acute intelligence, the ability to learn quickly, and to successfully adapt to their ever-changing business environment, whereas others appear to display lower levels of intelligence, are much slower to learn, fail to detect signals of change, and hence fail to respond accordingly. Intelligent organizations recognize that intelligence helps an organization to understand complexities and informs decision making. When considering intelligence as a discipline within the corporate context, it is therefore important to appreciate that the scope of the intelligence component is much more than traditional information management. It also encompasses such aspects as integrated thinking and communications, business intelligence (BI) and analytics, market and competitive intelligence, and knowledge management and organizational learning.

#### 9.4.1.1  Role of Intelligence in Corporate Defense

In the context of national defense, the concept of intelligence has long been regarded as a critical element. In December 2008, the Center for Strategic & International Studies (CSIS) stated: "One of the central responsibilities of the Secretary of Defense is to maintain a coherent and adequately resourced defense intelligence program. Diverse defense intelligence functions and activities are housed in a number of different organizations and are designed to support both the warfighter and national defense and intelligence requirements" (CSIS 2008). A similar sentiment is emphasized on the Central Intelligence Agency (CIA)'s twitter account @CIA where it clearly states "We are the Nation's first Line of defense."* Clearly, intelligence is considered to have an important role to play in national defense.

The corporate world appears to be somewhat reticent to embrace the important role that intelligence systems have to play in corporate defense efforts; however, there are indications that this is changing. In an interview in 2008, intelligence specialist Stephen Walker, a technology markets analyst at the Aberdeen Group, when asked for his views on where intelligence currently fits into the broader concept of an organization's program of self-defense and how he sees the role

---

* As per September 2015 twitter account @CIA states "We are the Nation's first line of defense. We accomplish what others cannot accomplish and go where others cannot go."

of intelligence developing going forward, stated that "Currently, the maturity level of intelligence initiatives is rather low and still primarily approached from an ad-hoc or siloed basis, rather than an enterprise-wide perspective. Going forward, intelligence needs to be integrated into every aspect of a company's broader self-defense program. A prerequisite for the success of these overall programs is ensuring and maintaining the breadth, depth, and comprehensiveness of intelligence-enabling capabilities at all levels of the organizational structure" (Lyons 2009c).

### 9.4.1.2   Management of the Intelligence Component

Management of the intelligence component is required in order to help ensure that the organization makes the best decisions based on the best available intelligence. It relates to mechanisms, processes, and systems in operation as an organization identifies, obtains, interprets, and communicates the data, information, and knowledge available within (and outside) the organization in order to be in the best position to make the timely and informed decisions that are necessary for the achievement of its objectives. It refers to both the larger organization's capacity to create and use intelligence and the aggregate intelligence capacity of its stakeholders. The intelligence component is therefore a critical element in the decision-making process.

The intelligence component involves addressing intelligence at different levels within the organization and therefore includes strategic intelligence, tactical intelligence, and operational intelligence. For example, intelligence at a strategic level involves the communication of required intelligence insight that is needed in order to enable strategic decisions that can help ensure the achievement of the organization's strategic objectives. It also incorporates strategic reporting and disclosure requirements. Intelligence at a tactical level as well as being concerned with the communication of required tactical intelligence insights also involves the organization's intelligence architecture and infrastructure. Intelligence at an operational level as well as being concerned with the communication of required operational intelligence insights also involves scanning the horizon in order to identify, source, gather, and collate relevant data and information. In essence the management of an organization's intelligence involves its ability to think and act at different levels within the organization in order to achieve objectives, guide behavior, and aide in decision making.

The intelligence component is both impacted by and impacts on the management of all of the other critical components. Each component should address the intelligence issue within its individual programs (e.g., *governance intelligence, risk intelligence, compliance intelligence, security intelligence, resilience intelligence, controls intelligence,* and *assurance intelligence*).

### 9.4.1.3   Key Intelligence Players

An effective intelligence program requires all members of the organization to fulfill their intelligence duties. Although ultimate responsibility for intelligence rests with the board and executive management, the responsibility for managing the organization's intelligence practices can typically rest with a number of key individuals who specifically occupy important intelligence positions.

> *Chairman of the intelligence committee*: The chairman of the intelligence committee (should one exist) has an important intermediary role between the board and management. The chairman has responsibility for the effective operation of the intelligence committee and its oversight of the implementation of the intelligence program.
> *Chief intelligence officer:* The chief intelligence officer (should one exist) has an important role in overseeing the work of the intelligence function (should one exist) and in monitoring and advising on the ongoing intelligence activities of the organization.
> *Chief financial officer and head of information technology (IT)*: Both these positions can have important roles to play in the monitoring of, and advising on, the specific intelligence matters that fall within their area of expertise.

#### 9.4.1.4   Intelligence Deliverables

In some respects intelligence can be seen as representing the oxygen or lifeblood of an organization as it is linked to decision making at every aspect of the business, and it is not very difficult to appreciate that the quality of the intelligence flow will have a direct impact on the organization's decision making and resulting performance. As such the importance of the effective management of the intelligence component cannot be overstated. The following are some examples of what an effective intelligence system is expected to deliver:

*Accurate intelligence*: Intelligence should be as accurate as possible in order for decision makers to make informed decisions. It should be free from processing errors; in particular, it should be free from errors relating to data conversion, transcription, translation, or other errors of data transformation. Accurate information is a critical aspect of any decision-making process and it is essential that decisions are not arrived at based on faulty or inaccurate information.

*Reliable intelligence*: Intelligence should be reliable so that the decision makers can put their faith in the source of the information and can trust that the information is of a high quality. Decision makers need to be confident that the information provided represents the single version of the facts. This means that information should be appropriately validated to ensure that it is free from any unintended interference or manipulation.

*Relevant intelligence*: Intelligence should be relevant to the decision-making process and help provide a relevant insight that will facilitate good decisions. Decision makers must be of the view that the information received is usable in the context of their decision-making process and useful in the context of helping to achieve objectives.

*Up-to-date intelligence*: Intelligence should be current and reflect the most recent set of circumstances. In a corporate world facing an accelerating rate of change, it is essential that decision-making information is up-to-date at all times and as close to real time as is possible. The time lapse between the information provided within the organization and events in real time can be the difference between success and failure.

*Objective intelligence*: Intelligence should be objective and free from possible subjective bias wherever possible. Information should be presented in a factual manner and where information is of a subjective nature, this should be clearly referenced as such so that decision makers can factor this into their own decision making. It should however be noted that any decision-making process by its very nature involves an element of subjectivity on behalf of the decision maker(s).

*Accessible intelligence*: Intelligence should be readily available and accessible when required, meeting both static and variable stakeholder requirements. Intelligence is a service that needs to be promptly provided, either through regular periodic reporting, through event-driven reports, or through on-demand self-service mechanisms. The speed at which an organization can provide its information can be the source of significant competitive advantage.

#### 9.4.2   INTELLIGENCE MATTERS

Decision making lies at the heart of success in business and because corporate intelligence has such a logical link to an organization's decision-making processes, its importance should never be underestimated. The nature of intelligence requirements can vary by industry, business type, and geographic region; therefore, each organization needs to establish its own precise intelligence requirements at strategic, tactical, and operational levels.

### 9.4.2.1 Intelligence Philosophy and Culture

Peter Drucker, widely regarded as the founder of modern management, once stated that "Knowledge has become the key economic resource and the dominant, if not the only, source of competitive advantage" (Drucker 1993). An organization's prioritization of the intelligence component is generally influenced by the extent to which knowledge is regarded as power, and intelligence is recognized to represent the lifeblood of the organization. The organization's intelligence philosophy, culture, and ethos will generally reflect the extent to which the organization buys into these notions. Its philosophy can influence whether the organization strives to become an intelligence leader or is content to remain a laggard in this particular field. Its culture can influence whether the organization chooses integrated thinking or segregated thinking, integrated intelligence or segregated intelligence, and integrated technology or segregated technology. Its ethos can influence whether an organization chooses a centralized viewpoint or a decentralized viewpoint, a formal approach or an informal approach, and a structured program or an unstructured program. Its attitude can influence whether an organization chooses a consistent methodology or an inconsistent methodology, streamlined information or congested information, and consolidated reporting or unconsolidated reporting. Its approach to technology can influence whether the organization chooses compatible solutions or incompatible solutions, standardized tools or nonstandardized tools, and scalable options or nonscalable options.

Typically, the intelligent organization of the twenty-first century considers organizational intelligence to be an intellectual property or an intellectual capital that is regarded as a valued intangible asset. Intelligence is therefore seen as a business driver, a business enabler, and a source of competitive advantage to be harnessed. Such organizations tend to adopt an integrated enterprise-wide philosophy and embrace technology as a means to facilitate and support the workings of its intelligence component. This involves ensuring that it has a mature technological infrastructure and architecture in place in order to empower its workforce. The existence of integrated thought processes and compatible systems helps to avoid information overload and helps to deliver a *single version of the truth*.

### 9.4.2.2 Intelligence Issues for Consideration

The intelligence component is about people, processes, and systems (increasingly technological), it therefore involves incorporating and combining aspects of business performance management, business process management, and the latest advances in technology. The following are some examples of selected intelligence issues that organizations are required to carefully consider:

*Business intelligence*: Consideration of the organization's approach to addressing its BI requirements. This includes how it intends to address issues such as its market intelligence, competitive intelligence, and operational intelligence requirements on an ongoing basis. It involves its use of people and processes in satisfying these requirements and the use of BI technology (e.g., BI tools, BI analytics, and BI models).

*Knowledge management*: Consideration of how the organization intends to manage the knowledge accumulated within the organization. This includes its approach to issues such as data management, content management, document management, and record management. It needs to consider its approach to filing, storing, retaining, and archiving information and knowledge over the short, medium, and long terms.

*Communication*: Consideration of how the organization intends to communicate intelligence to its various stakeholders. This includes whether to use verbal or written communication, and for written communication whether there is a requirement for a physical hard copy or an electronic copy, and so on. Consideration is required in relation to reporting, such as whether to use dashboard reporting, balanced scorecards, or more detailed reports. This includes choosing an appropriate user interface and the location of these reports.

*Education and training*: Consideration of the requirement to educate, develop, and train the workforce at all levels of the organization. This involves determining the specific intelligence requirements for each level and deciding on how best to address these requirements. Examples include whether to use in-house training or more formal academic-based education. In relation to training, whether it is more appropriate to use open access computer-based training, group-based training, personalized one-on-one training, and so on.

### 9.4.3 THE INTELLIGENCE PROGRAM

The intelligence program should include the development of an appropriate intelligence culture in order to help align intelligence practices throughout the organization. This will require appropriate training and education so that intelligence practices becomes integrated into all parts of the business process and become embedded into day-to-day operations on an enterprise-wide basis. A comprehensive intelligence program should also incorporate the other defense components into the program itself, and therefore should address issues such as *intelligence governance, intelligence risk, intelligence compliance, intelligence security, intelligence resilience, intelligence controls,* and *intelligence assurance*. Examples of essential elements of an intelligence program include the following:

*Business requirements*: Appropriate mechanisms need to be in place to identify business and stakeholder requirements. The identification of intelligence requirements should be closely linked to the requirements of the business and the organization's stakeholders. It needs to be determined in advance how the intelligence program can best help the organization in the achievement of its objectives. The business and stakeholder requirements should drive the needs of the intelligence program and internal and external intelligence needs.

*Data*: Appropriate mechanisms need to be in place to address data issues within the organization. This includes measures for sourcing, gathering, collecting, compiling, and organizing data throughout the organization. It includes the use of tools for extracting, loading, converting, and modeling data. It includes the use of databases, data warehouses, data marts, and data mining.

*Information*: Appropriate mechanisms need to be in place to analyze and make sense of available data and transform it into usable information. Measures need to be in place to address both quantitative and qualitative information, and to ensure that appropriate metrics and formats are selected. Information needs to be analyzed, evaluated, synthesized, and streamlined to help ensure it is relevant, reliable, complete, timely, and contextual.

*Insight*: Appropriate mechanisms need to be in place to help ensure that available information can be meaningfully interpreted and converted into the necessary insight required for sound decision making. Measures need to be in place to ensure that information can be accessed, disseminated, and communicated to the decision makers and relevant parties in order to help provide not only hindsight but also predictive foresight.

*Action*: Appropriate mechanisms need to be in place to help ensure that the necessary insight provided leads to sound decision making at all levels of the organization. Measures need to be in place to ensure that all decisions are promptly acted upon and that these actions are appropriately monitored and their performance appropriately reviewed and outcomes reported so that the findings form part of a continuous feedback process.

*Knowledge*: Appropriate mechanisms need to be in place to ensure that the knowledge gleaned from the past experience is retained in the organization's memory bank. Measures need to be in place to ensure that a knowledge repository and interface are developed and continuously updated so that the organization retains such knowledge and experience for future reference, and to create a breadth and depth of knowledge that can be tapped into going forward.

*Organizational learning*: Appropriate mechanisms need to be in place to ensure that the organization is continuously learning and developing from its experiences, both good and bad. Measures need to be in place to ensure that access to knowledge and experience results in the organization continuously innovating, improving, and adapting. By developing a continuous communication loop, the organization can learn to share and exchange knowledge and information in a cooperative and collaborative manner. Learning from both success and failure can contribute to an evolving process that can help foster creativity and innovation, in addition to helping to assist with ongoing education and training.

### 9.4.3.1 Intelligence Program Particulars

Stakeholders of an organization can ascertain the extent to which the organization has adopted a formal structured approach to its intelligence program by receiving coherent answers to their questions. The following are examples of basic questions that stakeholders might be expected to ask in relation to the organization's intelligence program:

- Does your organization have a formal board approved intelligence program in place?
- Does your organization have a formally approved intelligence vision in place?
- Does your organization have a formally approved intelligence mission statement in place?
- Does your organization have a formally approved intelligence strategy in place?
- Does your organization have a formally approved intelligence plan in place?

### 9.4.3.2 Intelligence Program Standing

Stakeholders of an organization can ascertain the standing of the organization's intelligence program by receiving coherent answers to their questions. The following are examples of basic questions that stakeholders might be expected to ask in relation to the standing of organization's intelligence program:

- Is there a board intelligence committee (or subcommittee) in place?
- Is there a specialist intelligence function (or competence center) in place?
- Has a chief intelligence officer been appointed?
- Where or to whom does the chief intelligence officer directly report?
- What is the intelligence program's budget as a percentage of the organization's overall budget?

### 9.4.4 Intelligence Frameworks and Guidance

There are numerous versions of intelligence frameworks and guidance available to organizations. The following are examples of selected intelligence frameworks, codes, and other guidance:

## SELECTED INTELLIGENCE FRAMEWORKS AND GUIDANCE

- International Integrated Reporting <IR> Framework (IIRC 2013b)
- ITIL Lifecycle Publication (ITIL 2011)
- AS 5037–2005 Knowledge Management Guide (Standards Australia 2005)
- European Guide to Good Practice in Knowledge Management (Parts 1–5) (CEN 2004)
- PAS 2001 Knowledge Management: a guide to good practice (BSI 2001)

#### 9.4.5 International Intelligence Organizations

There are numerous international organizations that are specifically devoted to developing and promoting intelligence as a discipline. Table 9.4 outlines notable international organizations that specifically focus on intelligence as a subject matter.

**TABLE 9.4**
**Selected Intelligence Organizations**

| Organization | Website |
| --- | --- |
| European CIO Association | www.eurocio.org |
| U.S. Chief Information Officer and Federal CIO Council | www.cio.gov |
| Strategic and Competitive Intelligence Professionals (SCIP) | www.scip.org |
| International Integrated Reporting Council (IIRC) | www.integratedreporting.org |
| Global Reporting Initiative (GRI) | www.globalreporting.org |
| The Data Warehouse Institute (TDWI) | www.tdwi.org |
| Organizational Intelligence Institute (OII) | www.oi-institute.com |
| Knowledge Management Association (KMA) | www.kmassociation.org |

# 10 Critical Corporate Defense Components (Part II)[*]

The time to repair the roof is when the sun is shining.[†]

**John F. Kennedy**

## 10.1 SECURITY

Security, and the management of security, is considered to be one of the critical components of an organization's corporate defense program. In simple terms, this refers to how the organization ensures that it protects its critical assets from threats and danger, its people, information, technology, and facilities. In their book entitled *The Manager's Handbook for Corporate Security*, G.L. Kovacich and E.P. Halibozek state the following: "No business is without security problems and assets protection risks. These risks and problems take many forms. Effectively mitigating them is not a happenstance occurrence. Problem elimination and risk mitigation require planning and an understanding of security needs, conditions, threats and vulnerabilities. Assessing security conditions and planning for appropriate levels of asset protection should begin with the basics: risk management" (Kovacich and Halibozek 2003).

---

[*] Please refer to Chapter 8, Section 8.3.1 "The Key to Reading Chapters 9 and 10"
[†] Per *Public Papers of the Presidents of the United States: John F. Kennedy, 1962*, U.S. Government Printing Office 1963, Washington D.C.

### 10.1.1 SECURITY AS A DISCIPLINE

In a world of global economies and ever-increasing e-business, there is an increasing realization in the corporate boardroom of the increased need to adequately secure and protect their corporate assets. Whether it is the prevention of internal security threats, such as the theft of office equipment or malicious external attacks, such as hackers and industrial saboteurs, top management is entrusted to anticipate security vulnerabilities, to protect its organization, and to provide a safe environment for employees and their belongings. Although in the past it was common for security systems to be deployed as a reaction to an event, this approach is no longer sustainable in a more dynamic market environment where infrastructures, business transactions, and technologies have become more complex.

Corporate security generally falls into two categories: physical security and information security. Historically, most organizations have addressed security concerns through a number of different functions within the organization, typically operating in a nonintegrated fashion. As new technologies emerge, the need to unify security functions throughout the entire enterprise is now being recognized. This involves the integration of physical and information security systems and related technologies.

#### 10.1.1.1 Role of Security in Corporate Defense

The National Institute of Standards and Technology (NIST) in a paper entitled "Managing Information Security Risk: Organization, Mission, and Information System View" describes the following security defense capabilities: "Defense-in-Depth: Information security strategy integrating people, technology, and operations capabilities to establish variable barriers across multiple layers and missions of the organization. Defense-in-Breadth: A planned, systematic set of multidisciplinary activities that seek to identify, manage, and reduce risk of exploitable vulnerabilities at every stage of the system, network, or subcomponent life cycle (system, network, or product design and development; manufacturing; packaging; assembly; system integration; distribution; operations; maintenance; and retirement)" (NIST 2011).

In an interview in 2008, security expert Professor Stephen Northcutt, president of the SANS Technology Institute, when asked for his views on where the role of security management currently fits into the broader concept of corporate defense and how do you see its role developing going forward, stated: "It all comes back to risk. The first question an organization needs to ask is how much of their total value is comprised of information assets. If you are a software company or an intellectual property holding company, it is probably 99%. If the majority of employees in an organization use computers daily to do their work, it is probably 80% or higher. Next, we need to understand that the focus of both nation state attackers and identity theft motivated attackers is to locate and steal your information. If they can steal 99% of the value of your organization, what is your organization worth? In terms of the role of security management, the greater the percent of value our information assets are, the closer to the top the information security leadership needs to be. It seems like the value of information in an organization is not decreasing, so this may be even more true in five years" (Lyons 2009c).

#### 10.1.1.2 Management of the Security Component

Management of the security component is required in order to help ensure that the organization has the ability to protect its assets (i.e., people, information, technology, and facilities) from threats or danger. This involves the ongoing management of both physical and information security issues in order to secure the assets of the organization. It requires the deterrence, prevention, or preemption of threats facing the organization and mitigating these threats or minimizing any possible vulnerability that might exist. Assessing security requirements and planning for appropriate levels of asset protection involves consideration of each of the other critical components. The security component is both impacted by and impacts on the management of all of the other critical components. Each component should address the security issue within its individual programs (e.g., *governance security, risk security, compliance security, intelligence security, resilience security, controls security,* and *assurance security*).

### 10.1.1.3  Key Security Players

An effective security program requires all members of the organization to fulfill their security duties. Although the ultimate responsibility for security rests with the board and executive management, the responsibility for managing the organization's security practices can typically rest with a number of key individuals who specifically occupy important security positions.

*Chairman of the security committee*: The chairman of the security committee (should one exist) has an important intermediary role between the board and management. The chairman has the responsibility for the effective operation of the security committee and its oversight of the implementation of the security program.

*Chief security officer*: The chief security officer (should one exist) has an important role in overseeing the work of the security function (should one exist) and in monitoring and advising on the ongoing security activities of the organization.

*Heads of information security and physical security*: Both these positions can have important roles to play in the monitoring of, and advising on, the specific security matters that fall within their area of expertise.

### 10.1.1.4  Security Deliverables

The purpose of addressing the security component is to help deliver a safe and secure environment in order to facilitate the organization in the achievement of its objectives. As part of this process, the organization must clearly identify its assets (both tangible and intangible) and establish its security requirements and expectations accordingly. The following are some examples of what effective security management can hope to deliver:

*Safety*: Adequate measures need to be in place to help ensure that the organization's assets (people, information, technology, facilities, etc.) are being protected from threats of a physical and/or logical nature. The creation and maintenance of a safe environment can help to ensure that the assets of the organization are protected from undergoing or causing any danger, damage, hurt, harm, injury, or loss.

*Privacy*: Adequate measures need to be in place to help ensure that the privacy of data submitted to the organization is appropriately safeguarded. Stakeholders' right to privacy needs to be fully respected, and stakeholders need to be assured that access to their data is adequately protected and that such data will only be used in accordance with the organization's privacy statement.

*Confidentiality*: Adequate measures need to be in place to help ensure that appropriate rules are in place to limit access to information. Restrictions need to be in place to ensure that only authorized individuals have access to sensitive information and to ensure that only the right people view the information in question. Appropriate information classification is required in order to help ensure that information of a confidential nature is adequately secured and does not get into the wrong hands.

*Integrity*: Adequate measures need to be in place to help ensure that there is an acceptable level of security over the integrity of the organization's information. Information needs to be adequately secured to help ensure that the organization's information is trustworthy at all times. This means that there need to be controls in place to prevent unauthorized access and tampering with information, which could affect the validity, accuracy, or completeness of the organization's information.

*Availability*: Adequate measures need to be in place to help ensure that there is reliable access to the organization's information for authorized individuals. Appropriate security steps should be taken to provide and maintain uninterrupted access to required information. This includes appropriate measures to guard against downtime and prevent malicious actions that could potentially result in a lack of access to required information.

## 10.1.2  Security Matters

Corporate security has an important role to play in positively influencing stakeholder confidence in the organization. Alternatively, corporate scandals relating to security incidents can seriously undermine stakeholder confidence and cause damage to the organization's reputation. In addition, sound corporate security is considered as one of the essential ingredients required to deliver an appropriate working environment.

### 10.1.2.1  Security Philosophy and Culture

The organization's security philosophy will dictate the organization's approach to security. It will determine the extent to which the organization considers security to be a high, medium, or low priority for the organization, and the security protection level required by the organization. The security ethos will determine the extent to which the organization strives toward delivering security best practices, good practices, or simply minimum practices. Its security culture will determine the extent to which the organization adopts a proactive or reactive approach to its security component. It will determine the extent to which the organization adopts an integrated *strategy-centric* approach to security or merely *a nice to have* a *security-centric* approach, which can be somewhat divorced from the organization's objectives.

### 10.1.2.2  Security Issues for Consideration

Historically, security has always been associated with corporate defense and the requirement to safeguard and protect the assets of the organization. This requirement is now increasingly being applied to both tangible and intangible assets of the organization. The following are some examples of selected security issues that organizations are required to carefully consider:

*Asset inventory*: Consideration of the assets of the organization across all businesses and geographic regions, and the identification of those assets that are considered to be critical to the achievement of the organization's objectives. This should involve an inventory of all assets that are classified in terms of their critical nature. Critical assets can include people, property, premises, processes, equipment, materials, technology, data, and intellectual property (IP).

*Security domains*: Consideration of the different domains in which the critical assets of the organization reside and which require specific security attention. This includes both the physical security domain, which focuses on the protection of physical assets, and the IT or information security domain, which focuses on the protection of information and the intellectual property (IP) of the organization.

*Threat analysis*: Consideration of potential threats that could negatively impact on the critical assets of the organization. Analysis should include the existence, characteristics, history, intentions, and capability of any potential threats and the likely targets, being the assets of the organization. The impact of potential threats to the organization's critical assets needs to be assessed and security requirements considered in light of the potential impact and likelihood of these potential threats. A variety of threat scenarios should be evaluated and assessed.

*Types of threats*: Consideration of the identification of the types of security threats to critical assets, both tangible and intangible assets. Examples of typical threats include such matters as sabotage resulting in the destruction or damage to critical assets, fraud resulting from the interference or tampering with a critical asset, or espionage resulting from the unauthorized access to or theft of a critical asset. Awareness of different threat types should be promoted and individual threat types fully understood.

*Sources of threats*: Consideration of the sources of potential threats and whether these are internal or external to the organization itself. Sources of threats can arise from many vectors, and these range from internal sources, such as incompetent, unethical, or disgruntled employees, to external sources, such as competitors, hackers, organized crime, thieves or vandals, terrorists groups, or political protesters. The source of potential threats should be considered in the light of most likely targets.

*Vulnerability*: Consideration of where the organization may be vulnerable to the potential threats it faces. An organization may be vulnerable where it has not taken the necessary measures to safeguard against a specific threat. Possible vulnerabilities can be identified by assessing historical events, industry or police warnings, system redundancies, operational requirements, and so on. The extent of the vulnerability should be considered in the light of the potential consequence, be it monetary, performance, legal, or reputational in nature.

*Security measures*: Consideration of the security measures required to protect the organization's critical assets from identified threats. Security measures can range from anticipative measures such as penetration testing to deterrence measures such as warnings, to preventative measures such as access controls, to detective measures such as surveillance, to responsive measures such as interception and containment, and so on. The decision on which measures best suit the organization in different individual circumstances needs to be carefully evaluated and assessed.

*Security level*: Consideration of the level of security protection required both throughout the organization itself and in specific areas, based on anticipated threat levels and perceived vulnerabilities. The required level of security vigilance may vary depending on point in time occurrences such as security warnings or alerts, or where different perceived threat levels exist in different parts of the organization. This should also be considered in relation to how business requirements may be impacted by security measures.

### 10.1.3   THE SECURITY PROGRAM

The security program in place should be seen as a critical component of successful value preservation, and it should operate in association with the other critical defense components that are inherently interconnected and interdependent. A comprehensive security program should also incorporate the other defense components into the program itself, and therefore should address issues such as *security governance, security risk, security compliance, security intelligence, security resilience, security controls*, and *security assurance*.

Security management involves utilizing a broad array of security capabilities in order to help ensure *defense-in-depth. Defense-in-depth* denotes the practice of having multiple and independent layers of safeguard systems. It involves deploying successive overlapping layers of security that employ a diverse set of tactics, techniques, and technologies to protect against threats, thereby helping to mitigate the risk of a single security measure being compromised or circumvented. The deployment of complementary layers helps to fortify each other, creating a solution that is stronger than the sum of its parts. Therefore, the organization never relies on one single security measure alone. A well-planned *defense-in-depth* strategy will deploy forces in mutually supportive positions, in appropriate roles, and will include a combination of techniques, each of which will attempt to deter, prevent, detect, or respond to security threats (Lyons 2010).

In particular, physical and information security requirements should be considered at all of the organization's entry and exit points, as well as security requirements for the storage of assets and while in transit. Table 10.1 outlines examples of layers of security that include the following.

#### 10.1.3.1   Security Program Particulars

Stakeholders of an organization can ascertain the extent to which the organization has adopted a formal structured approach to its security program by receiving coherent answers to their questions. The following are examples of basic questions that stakeholders might be expected to ask in relation to the organization's security program:

- Does your organization have a formal board-approved security program in place?
- Does your organization have a formally approved security vision in place?

**TABLE 10.1**
**Security Layers**

| Physical Security | Information Security |
|---|---|
| Site security | Perimeter security |
| Building security | Network security |
| People security | Endpoint security |
| Operations security | Operating system security |
| Facilities security | Application security |
| Materials security | Database security |

- Does your organization have a formally approved security mission statement in place?
- Does your organization have a formally approved security strategy in place?
- Does your organization have a formally approved security plan in place?

### 10.1.3.2 Security Program Standing

Stakeholders of an organization can ascertain the standing of the organization's security program by receiving coherent answers to their questions. The following are examples of basic questions that stakeholders might be expected to ask in relation to the standing of organization's security program:

- Is there a board security committee (or subcommittee) in place?
- Is there a specialist security function (or competence center) in place?
- Has a chief security officer been appointed?
- Where or to whom does the chief security officer directly report?
- What is the security program's budget as a percentage of the organization's overall budget?

### 10.1.4 SECURITY FRAMEWORKS AND GUIDANCE

There are numerous versions of security frameworks and guidance available to organizations. The following are examples of selected security frameworks, codes, and other guidance.

> ## SELECTED SECURITY FRAMEWORKS AND GUIDANCE
>
> - The Standard of Good Practice for Information Security (ISF 2014)
> - National Cybersecurity Workforce Framework 2.0 (NICE 2014)
> - Framework for Improving Critical Infrastructure Cybersecurity (NIST 2014)
> - ISO/IEC 27001:2013 Information Security Management (ISO 2013)
> - An Introduction to the Business Model for Information Security (ISACA 2009)
> - Facilities Physical Security Measures Guideline (ASIS 2009a)
> - Governing for Enterprise Security (Allen 2005)
> - Readings in Security Management: Principles and Practices (McCrie 2002)

### 10.1.5 INTERNATIONAL SECURITY ORGANIZATIONS

There are numerous international organizations that are specifically devoted to developing and promoting security as a discipline. Table 10.2 outlines notable international organizations that specifically focus on the security as a subject matter.

**TABLE 10.2**

**Selected Security Organizations**

| Organization | Website |
| --- | --- |
| Information Systems Security Association (ISSA) | www.issa.org |
| American Society for Industrial Security (ASIS) International | www.asisonline.org |
| International Information Systems Security Certification Consortium, Inc (ISC)[2] | www.isc2.org |
| Information Security Forum (ISF) | www.securityforum.org |
| European Network and Information Security Agency (ENISA) | www.enisa.europa.eu |
| Security Executive Council (SEC) | www.securityexecutivecouncil.com |
| The SANS Institute | www.sans.org |

## 10.2 RESILIENCE

Resilience, and the management of resilience, is considered to be one of the critical components of an organization's corporate defense program. In simple terms, this refers to how the organization ensures that it has the capacity to withstand, rebound, or recover from the direct and indirect consequences of a shock, disturbance, or disruption. The World Economic Forum (WEF) in its Global Risks Report 2011 stated: "We define 'resilience' as the ability of a system to reorganize under change and deliver its core function continually, despite the impact of external or internally generated risk" (WEF 2011). The computer emergency response team (CERT) at Carnegie Mellon University in a podcast entitled "Adapting to Changing Risk Environments: Operational Resilience" stated the following: "Operational resilience is the ability of an organization to adapt to changing risk environments, and to manage the hazard risk that is inherent in day-to-day operations. In business terms, operational resilience represents the organization's ability to protect its critical assets and keep its critical business processes and services up and running, even in the face of a disruption or security event…Resiliency engineering is the process by which an organization designs, develops, implements, and manages the protection and sustainability of business-critical services, related processes, and associated assets such as people, information, technology, and facilities."[*] (CERT 2007).

### 10.2.1 RESILIENCE AS A DISCIPLINE

From a business perspective, resilience refers to an organization's ability to sustain the impact of an emergency or business interruption, and its capacity to recover from a disaster scenario, in order to resume its operations and continue to provide services. This requirement includes ensuring that adequate measures have been taken in order to sufficiently and proactively protect the continuity of the business and the individual staff members. Adequate continuity and recovery measures need to prepare the organization to address a variety of contingency scenarios. Sufficient planning and testing give an organization the capacity to endure planned and unplanned events with confidence, so that its critical services can be supported by resilient operations in order to ensure the availability, reliability, and recoverability of key processes and systems.

Organizational resilience typically involves an integrative approach to the implementation and management of resilience processes across the entire organization, including the creation of appropriate integrated strategies, plans, and mechanisms to help address resilience challenges. Effective resilience requires a proactive approach that needs to be embedded at strategic, tactical, and operational levels in order to help the organization predict, avoid, withstand, and

---

[*] CERT Podcast: Adapting to Changing Risk Environments: Operational Resilience, featuring Richard A. Caralli and Stephanie Losi. Posted on May 1, 2007. Podcast Categories: Risk Management and Resilience, available at www.cert.org/podcasts/.

quickly recover from disruptive events. A resilience strategy involves integrating and aligning several disparate strategies to ensure continuity against the threat of emergency, disruption, or disaster scenario.

### 10.2.1.1 Role of Resilience in Corporate Defense

Booz & Co. in a paper entitled "The Root Causes of Value Destruction: How Strategic Resiliency Can Help" stated the following: "Adopt strategic resiliency thinking: Managers need to consider how strategic decisions can affect resiliency, incorporate resiliency into all decision making, and always be on the look out for more strategically resilient alternatives in order to build greater corporate agility" (Booz & Co. 2012). IBM in a paper entitled "Business resilience: The best defense is a good offense" stated the following: "True business resilience starts with understanding exactly what your business needs in order to survive unexpected events and plan ahead for challenges that could come at any time. Whether an event is IT related, business related, or a natural disaster, there will always be challenges to overcome. Think of business resilience as your ticket to continued business service and operational continuity-proper planning, readiness, and the ability to respond quickly to any threat or opportunity" (IBM 2009).

In an interview in 2008, resilience expert Kathleen Lucey, president of the Business Continuity Institute (BCI) US Chapter, when asked for her views on where does resilience currently fit into the broader concept of an organization's program of self-defense and how do you see it developing going forward, stated: "All control disciplines should be integrated: Information Security (computer security, data security), Records Management, Emergency Management, Crisis Management, Business Continuity Management (disaster recovery, contingency planning, resilience). All of the control disciplines work to minimize the probability and severity of incidents and all are concerned with controls to reduce incident-related effects: injuries and/or damages" (Lyons 2009c).

### 10.2.1.2 Management of the Resilience Component

Management of the resilience component is required in order to help ensure that the organization has the capacity to adequately absorb or adapt so that it remains stable under conditions of stress. A resilient organization has the capability to fulfill its obligations and continue to achieve its objectives under challenging circumstances. Resilience is concerned with focusing on the organization's ability to sustain the impact of an emergency or interruption, and its capacity to recover from a disaster scenario, in order to resume its operations and continue to provide services with a minimum impact on performance and productivity. Organizational resilience relates to survivability and sustainability, and involves adapting to the constantly changing business environment. It represents an organization's ability to keep its business critical processes, services, and assets up and running in the face of adversity.

The resilience component is both impacted by and impacts on the management of all of the other critical components. Each component should address the resilience issue within its individual programs (e.g., *governance resilience*, *risk resilience*, *compliance resilience*, *intelligence resilience*, *security resilience*, *controls resilience*, and *assurance resilience*).

### 10.2.1.3 Key Resilience Players

An effective resilience program requires all members of the organization to fulfill their resilience duties. Although the ultimate responsibility for resilience rests with the board and executive management, the responsibility for managing the organization's resilience practices can typically rest with a number of key individuals who specifically occupy important resilience positions.

*Chairman of the resilience committee*: The chairman of the resilience committee (should one exist) has an important intermediary role between the board and management. The chairman has the responsibility for the effective operation of the resilience committee and its oversight of the implementation of the resilience program.

*Chief resilience officer*: The chief resilience officer (should one exist) has an important role in overseeing the work of the resilience function (should one exist) and in monitoring and advising on the ongoing resilience activities of the organization.

*Chairman of the audit committee*: The chairman of the audit committee may have an important intermediary role between the board and the oversight of the organization's management of resilience, particularly in the absence of a resilience committee.

*Heads of IT and operations*: Both these positions can have important roles to play in the monitoring of, and advising on, the specific resilience matters that fall within their area of expertise.

### 10.2.1.4   Resilience Deliverables

The purpose of addressing the resilience component is to help develop a robust, agile, and antifragile organization that is capable of delivering on the long-term objectives of its stakeholders. The resilience process involves developing the capability to anticipate, avoid, absorb, adapt, recover, and rebound from minor hazard events to major disaster events. It involves recognizing an early warning signal, assessing the risk involved, determining the appropriate response, managing the response, resolving the situation, recovering from the event, learning from the event, and improving as a result of the event. This involves anticipating the potential impact of hazard events, engineering the organization so that it is agile and adaptable enough to minimize the initial impact, developing the organization's capacity to absorb or endure this impact, and being responsive enough to adapt in order to minimize any subsequent collateral damage. The following are some examples of what effective resilience can hope to deliver:

*Preparedness*: The organization is well prepared in advance to deal with the occurrence of hazardous situations with a minimum disruption to its operations. Preparedness is a result of a proactive approach to preparing for the impact of potential hazard events by considering various scenarios, by planning and developing appropriate responses, and by rehearsing and testing these responses in order to help ensure they are smoothly executed in practice.

*Agility*: The organization is sufficiently agile to avoid the impact of flagged hazardous events. Agility is a result of anticipating the impact of likely hazardous events in advance and taking appropriate action to avoid or at least minimize the potential impact should such events occur. The organization is flexible enough to change its behaviors as required with minimum difficulty in order to minimize possible disruption or damage.

*Robustness*: The organization is robust enough to withstand the impact of hazardous events should they occur with a minimum disruption to its operations. Robustness is achieved as a result of a hardening of critical areas so that they can withstand the stress of hazardous events without suffering excessive damage or loss that could fatally disrupt the organization's critical operations. Stress testing can help measure the organization's level of robustness.

*Redundancy*: The organization has sufficient redundancy in place to ensure that an adequate buffer exists that can be relied upon to absorb the potential impact of hazardous events. Adequate redundancy can be achieved by determining the additional level of capacity required to meet functional requirements under stressful conditions, and by putting structures in place to be able to achieve these levels if required. Redundancy can apply to many areas of the business, including human resources, financial capital, and information technology (IT) systems capacity.

*Ingenuity*: The organization has developed sufficient innovative capabilities to be able to successfully manage disruption during the occurrence of hazardous events. Ingenuity involves being resourceful and creative in times of chaos, and possessing the ability to identify problems, establish priorities, and manage available resources in order to avoid or cope with the impact of hazardous events. It represents the ability to make the most out of available resources in order to continue to deliver on objectives despite the challenging environment.

*Speediness*: The organization has developed sufficient capability to be able to respond to hazard incidents or events in a speedy manner, in order to help prevent a minor incident from escalating into a crisis situation or a full-blown disaster scenario. Speediness involves an accelerated reaction or a rapid response to circumstances during stressful situations and the ability to deliver on priorities and achieve goals in a timely manner.

*Adaptive learning*: The organization has developed the adaptive capacity to continuously learn from its stressful experiences in order to not only restore operations to normal levels but also to actually improve the organization based on lessons learned from these experiences. Adaptive learning involves evolving as an organization and continuously considering new ideas for the future. It involves developing new capabilities (e.g., technologies and processes) in order to better withstand, rebound, and recover from adverse situations, and adapting to changing, new, or unexpected circumstances.

### 10.2.2 RESILIENCE MATTERS

A reactive approach of simply waiting for disruptive events to occur is no longer acceptable if organizations want to protect their people, operations, and shareholder value. The high-risk fire fighting or crisis management mind-set of the past is now being replaced by the requirement for an enterprise philosophy of anticipation and prevention.

#### 10.2.2.1 Resilience Philosophy and Culture

The business world accepts that shocks will occur from time to time, which can negatively impact on the organization's achievement of its objectives. The resilience philosophy of the organization will determine the extent to which the organization aspires to be prepared to deal with such eventualities. Its resilience ethos will therefore determine the extent to which the organization proactively addresses its resilience capabilities or the extent to which it adopts a more reactive approach. A proactive approach is reflected in prioritizing resilience at strategic, tactical, and operational levels within the organization. It involves moving beyond simply focusing on *what could go wrong* (a *risk-centric* focus) to focusing on *what needs to go right* (a *resilience-centric* focus). A *resilience-centric* focus is therefore easily aligned to the achievement of the organization's objectives and encourages a holistic view of the organization. A reactive approach, on the other hand, is reflected in a lower level of attention afforded to proactive resilience activities and a higher degree of reliance on day-to-day fire-fighting, case-by-case trouble-shooting, and a greater reliance on insurance as a method of dealing with the occurrence of hazardous events.

An organization that fosters a truly resilient culture is recognizable by the fact that the concept of resilience is contemplated at all levels within the organization (e.g., strategic, tactical, and operational) and across all time frames (e.g., short, medium, and long terms). Examples of this would include contemplating resilience requirements in relation to matters such as portfolio resilience (i.e., market exposure, business sector concentration, and product or service diversification), financial resilience (i.e., capital adequacy, solvency, liquidity, etc.), human resource resilience (i.e., succession planning, cross-training, outsourcing, etc.), supply chain resilience (internal—performance and productivity, external—suppliers and customers, etc.), and so on.

#### 10.2.2.2 Resilience Issues for Consideration

Impact analysis and assessment is at the center of resilience management. At its best, this requires a high level of critical thought and the adoption of a systems thinking approach that understands the complexities of existing relationships and can help map the potential levels of interdependence and interconnectivity. A systems approach can help identify potential points of failure or weakness and can help predict how a disruptive incident or event might occur and subsequently escalate throughout the organization. The following are some examples of selected resilience issues that organizations are required to carefully consider:

*Hazard analysis*: Due consideration should be given to the source, cause, and nature of hazard events and the resulting impact on the organization. The source of hazard events can emerge from both inside and outside the organization itself and generally can be the result of unintentional acts (accidents, errors, incompetence, etc.), intentional acts (e.g., fraud, cybercrime, and vandalism), or natural causes (e.g., hurricane, earthquake, and tsunami). Hazard events can vary and range from expected incidents that should be specifically prepared for, to unexpected incidents that are known and therefore can be specifically prepared for, to unforeseen incidents that by their nature are very difficult to specifically prepare for.

*Asset impact analysis*: Due consideration should be given to the potential impact of a hazard event on the assets and resources that form the critical infrastructure of the organization. For example, the extent to which a hazard event may impact on the health and safety of the organization's people (e.g., fire, pandemic, and terrorism), on the availability of the organization's premises (e.g., picketing, flooding, and ice and snow, etc.), on the organization's power supply (e.g., power surge, interruption, and outage), on the organization's systems performance (e.g., processing speed, capacity, and downtime), and on the availability of the organization's critical data (e.g., live, back-up, and storage).

*Objective impact analysis*: Due consideration should be given to the potential impact of hazard events on the achievement of the objectives of the organization. For example, the extent to which a hazard event may impact on the organization's performance (quality) and productivity (quantity), on the organization's legal position (e.g., fines, criminal charges, and civil litigation), on the organization's reputation (e.g., media coverage, shareholder activists, and stakeholder trust), and ultimately on the organization's financial circumstances (e.g., sales, profit, and share price).

### 10.2.3 THE RESILIENCE PROGRAM

The resilience management program in place must be seen as a critical component of successful value preservation, and it must operate in association with the other critical defense components that are inherently interconnected and interdependent. A comprehensive resilience management program should also incorporate the other defense components into the program itself, and therefore should address issues such as *resilience governance, resilience risk, resilience compliance, resilience intelligence, resilience security, resilience controls*, and *resilience assurance*.

Resilience management is concerned with an organization's aptitude to deal with a turbulent environment. It is about being best prepared to cope with a variety of stressful situations that can range from minor incidents to emergency situations, to complex crises, to extreme abnormal events, and to full-blown disaster scenarios. It requires critical thinking so that sufficient thought has been given to how challenging events might transpire in practice. It is about enhancing the organization's ability to respond quickly to events as they emerge and evolve, as the implications have been reasoned out in advance and the required actions have been fully thought through. This should enable the organization to respond in a logical and rational manner rather than in a frantic haphazard manner, which might otherwise be the case. A resilience program therefore involves developing a strategy to address this requirement. It involves maintaining and upgrading relevant plans to address these wide-ranging scenarios. It involves regularly testing the execution of these plans and their related processes and procedures through an assortment of simulation exercises and periodic full-blown rehearsals. Essential elements of a resilience program should include the following:

*Resiliency engineering*: A prepared approach to building resilience into the organization's infrastructure, thereby helping to ensure that there is minimum disruption or inconvenience to the operation of its activities. Resiliency engineering involves identifying and eliminating potential faults or weaknesses in the organization's processes and systems that could result in a point of failure under stressful conditions. It involves developing end-to-end resilience by ensuring that an appropriate level of resilience is built into all the components of its infrastructure (e.g., human resources, architecture, technology, practices, and supply chain) by developing redundancy and sufficient capacity to best resist stress without changing the primary functions of the components.

*Incident response*: A prepared approach to dealing with individual incidents as they occur in a timely and competent manner. The everyday occurrence of seemingly minor incidents may have the potential to escalate into more serious issues. The occurrence of one minor incident, or the simultaneous occurrence of a number of minor incidents, if not dealt with in a timely manner may have the potential to create a major incident. A swift response can help resolve and contain the matter as close to source as possible, thereby avoiding any possible contagion.

*Emergency operations*: A prepared approach to dealing with major incidents in an urgent manner. Emergency situations typically reflect the sudden occurrence of an unexpected event that requires immediate attention or action. Emergency operations require the rapid response to evolving circumstances that present an immediate threat of loss (i.e., human, physical, financial, or nonfinancial) to the organization and may have the potential to develop into a crisis situation.

*Crisis management*: A prepared approach to effectively managing a crisis situation, which if not adequately contained, has the potential to develop into a disaster scenario that could destabilize the organization. A crisis situation represents an unstable condition requiring urgent attention in order to help protect life, assets, or the environment. Crisis management requires a holistic approach to managing multiple responses to a crisis situation in an appropriate and a consistent manner than helps to safeguard the organization's operations, brand, and reputation from damage. Clear lines of communication (both internal and external) are essential for effective crisis management.

*Continuity management*: A prepared approach to help ensure the continuity of the business under stressful conditions. This involves developing adequate capabilities at strategic, tactical, and operational levels to respond to situations and events as they arise in order to continue to perform critical activities at acceptable predefined levels. The focus is on the successful continuity of the business and being as prepared as possible for all eventualities, regardless of the extent of any possible disruption.

*Contingency planning*: A prepared approach to determining contingency options in advance of minor or major disruptions to the critical operations of the organization. Contingency planning involves identifying suitable alternatives and solutions, which can be invoked in order to avoid or minimize possible disruptions to the business. It requires a clear command and decision-making structure, and clearly documented roles, responsibilities, and required actions. Examples of contingency scenarios can range from restoring data from back-up operations, to the in-house relocation of staff, or to the access to external premises (hot-site) and systems.

*Disaster recovery*: A prepared approach to addressing disaster scenarios that could disrupt the critical business processes and that could cause significant damage to the organization or result in the collapse of the organization. Disaster recovery planning involves prioritizing the organization's people, processes, systems, data, facilities, and premises, bearing in mind the potential loss that may incur as a result of any unavailability of the organization's critical activities. It involves taking the necessary actions to speedily restore these critical activities and help the organization rebound as quickly as possible once adverse circumstances have passed.

### 10.2.3.1 Resilience Program Particulars

Stakeholders of an organization can ascertain the extent to which the organization has adopted a formal structured approach to its resilience program by receiving coherent answers to their questions. The following are examples of basic questions that stakeholders might be expected to ask in relation to the organization's resilience program:

- Does your organization have a formal board-approved resilience program in place?
- Does your organization have a formally approved resilience vision in place?
- Does your organization have a formally approved resilience mission statement in place?
- Does your organization have a formally approved resilience strategy in place?
- Does your organization have a formally approved resilience plan in place?

### 10.2.3.2 Resilience Program Standing

Stakeholders of an organization can ascertain the standing of the organization's resilience program by receiving coherent answers to their questions. The following are examples of basic questions that stakeholders might be expected to ask in relation to the standing of the organization's resilience program:

- Is there a board resilience committee (or subcommittee) in place?
- Is there a specialist resilience function (or competence center) in place?
- Has a chief resilience officer been appointed?
- Where or to whom does the chief resilience officer directly report?
- What is the resilience program's budget as a percentage of the organization's overall budget?

### 10.2.4 RESILIENCE FRAMEWORKS AND GUIDANCE

There are numerous versions of resilience frameworks and guidance available to organizations. The following are examples of selected resilience frameworks, codes, and other guidance:

---

#### SELECTED RESILIENCE FRAMEWORKS AND GUIDANCE

- BS 65000:2014 Guidance on Organizational Resilience (BSI 2014)
- ISO 22301:2012 Societal security—Business continuity management systems—Requirements (ISO 2012)
- Enabling and Managing End to End Resilience (ENISA 2011)
- CERT Resilience Management Model: A Maturity Model for Managing Operational Resilience (CERT 2010)
- AS/NZS 5050:2010 Business continuity—Managing disruption-related risk (AS/NZS 2010)
- Resiliency Framework (ICOR 2010)
- ASIS SPC.1-2009 Organizational Resilience Standard (ASIS 2009b)

---

### 10.2.5 INTERNATIONAL RESILIENCE ORGANIZATIONS

There are numerous international organizations that are specifically devoted to developing and promoting resilience as a discipline. Table 10.3 outlines notable international organizations that specifically focus on resilience as a subject matter:

**TABLE 10.3**
**Selected Resilience Organizations**

| Organization | Website |
|---|---|
| Computer Emergency Response Team (CERT) Division, Software Engineering Institute, Carnegie Mellon University (CMU) | www.cert.org |
| Business Continuity Institute (BCI) | www.thebci.org |
| Business Continuity Management Institute (BCMI) | www.bcm-institute.org |
| Disaster Recovery Institute International (DRII) | www.drii.org |
| International Consortium for Organizational Resilience (ICOR) | www.theicor.org |
| Business Resilience Certification Consortium International (BRCCI) | www.brcci.org |

## 10.3   CONTROLS

Controls, and the management of the controls process, are considered to be one of the critical components of an organization's corporate defense program. In simple terms, this refers to how the organization ensures that it has taken appropriate actions in order to address risk and to help ensure that the organization's objectives will be achieved. The Committee of Sponsoring Organizations of the Treadway Commission (COSO) in their publication entitled "Internal Control—Integrated Framework" stated the following: "Internal control is broadly defined as a process, effected by an entity's board of directors, management and other personnel, designed to provide reasonable assurance regarding the achievement of objectives in the following categories: • Effectiveness and efficiency of operations, • Reliability of financial reporting, • Compliance with applicable laws and regulations" (COSO 1992). Furthermore, the Basel Committee on Banking Supervision in a paper entitled "Framework for the Evaluation of Internal Control Systems" described internal control as follows: "Internal Control is a process effected by the board of directors, senior management and all levels of personnel. It is not solely a procedure or policy that is performed at a certain point in time, but rather it is continually operating at all levels within the bank. The board of directors is responsible for establishing the appropriate culture to facilitate an effective internal control process and for monitoring its effectiveness on an ongoing basis; however, each individual within the organisation must participate in the process" (BCBS 1998).

### 10.3.1   CONTROLS AS A DISCIPLINE

The system of internal controls represents how an organization ensures that it has taken the necessary actions to manage risk in order to ensure that the organization's objectives and goals will be achieved. These actions include the methods, measures, and procedures employed by the organization in order to provide the board with at least reasonable comfort that the organization's objectives will be achieved in an effective, efficient, and economical manner. Organizations are required to identify, design, implement, monitor, and test internal controls, in order to adequately safeguard their business resources, assets, and processes. Therefore, a system of effective internal controls is considered fundamental to the operation of safe and sound business practices, and is considered a critical component in an organization's corporate defense infrastructure. This includes an effective internal control reporting system that enables the timely communication of intelligence. Appropriate internal controls are required to help ensure that the organization is in compliance with both internal and external standards and protocols. In fact, a properly designed and consistently enforced system of internal controls, both operational and financial, can help mitigate risks and adequately prepare for contingency scenarios. It can assist in the prevention of the occurrence of undesirable events, and help in the timely detection and remediation of these events should they occur.

The generally acknowledged criterion for an effective internal control structure is the installation of an integrated framework of internal controls. The implementation of such an integrated framework enables line management to assess, evaluate, and report to the board on the quality, integrity, and adequacy of the organization's internal control system. The COSO integrated internal control framework (COSO 1992) identifies five critical elements to an effective internal control system.[*] The first is the control environment in which controls operate on a day-to-day basis (i.e., governance component). The second is the process in place by which the organization assesses its risks (i.e., risk component). The third is actual control activities themselves that are put in place to mitigate the organization's risks (i.e., controls component). The fourth is the system in place to share information and communicate among stakeholders (i.e., intelligence component). The fifth and final element is the process in place for monitoring activities on an ongoing basis (i.e., assurance component).

Historically, internal control was very much regarded as a domain reserved for auditors, accountants, and financial controllers. Today however with the advancements in technology and corporate governance requirements, internal control means far more than simply financial control, and this change of attitude needs to be reflected in the overall control environment. The control environment reflects the tone set by top management and the overall attitude, awareness, and actions of the board of directors, management, and others, concerning the importance of internal controls and the emphasis placed on controls in the company's policies, procedures, methods, and organizational structure. The control environment is the foundation for all other elements of the internal control framework, providing both discipline and structure to the internal control system.

### 10.3.1.1 Role of Controls in Corporate Defense

The US General Accounting Office (GAO) stated the following: "Internal control comprises the plans, methods, policies, and procedures used to fulfill the mission, strategic plan, goals, and objectives of the entity. Internal control serves as the first line of defense in safeguarding assets. In short, internal control helps managers achieve desired results through effective stewardship of public resources" (GAO 2014).

In an interview in 2008, internal controls expert Jim Kaplan, founder and chief executive officer (CEO) of AuditNet, when asked for his views on where do internal controls currently fit into the broader concept of corporate defense and how do you see its impact developing going forward, stated: "Internal controls are an important component of the corporate defense scheme and will continue as long as a business exists. Organizations must also implement other initiatives such as employee fraud awareness programs to highlight that fraud and internal controls are the responsibility of each and every employee within an organization" (Lyons 2009c).

### 10.3.1.2 Management of the Controls Component

Management of the controls component is required in order to help ensure that the organization is effectively balancing risks and controls so that the level of risk exposure is decreased to a level which is considered acceptable to the organization. It is also important to appreciate that although internal controls can help an organization achieve success, they cannot guarantee success. It is also important to appreciate that the existence of a sound system of internal controls can provide reasonable but not absolute assurance that the objectives of the organization will be achieved. The reasons why it cannot provide absolute assurance include the fact that many hazard events are outside of the organization's control, in addition to the cost-effective business restrictions that apply. The concept of reasonable assurance therefore acknowledges that an internal controls system should be developed and implemented, which, while not completely eliminating risk, helps provide an appropriate level of control to ensure that business objectives are achieved. In this way internal controls help to keep an organization on course to achieve its objectives while at the same time helping to minimize unwelcome surprises.

The controls component is both impacted by and impacts on the management of all of the other critical components. Each component should address the controls issue within its individual

---

[*] The updated COSO Integrated Internal Control Framework 2013 has continued to retain these five elements.

programs (e.g., *governance controls*, *risk controls*, *compliance controls*, *intelligence controls*, *security controls*, *resilience controls*, and *assurance controls*).

### 10.3.1.3 Key Controls Players

An effective controls program requires all members of the organization to fulfill their controls duties. Although the ultimate responsibility for controls rests with the board and executive management, the responsibility for managing the organization's controls practices can typically rest with a number of key individuals who specifically occupy important controls positions.

> *Chairman of the controls committee*: The chairman of the controls committee (should one exist) has an important intermediary role between the board and management. The chairman has the responsibility for the effective operation of the controls committee and its oversight of the implementation of the controls program.
>
> *Chief controls officer*: The chief controls officer (should one exist) has an important role in overseeing the work of the controls function (should one exist) and in monitoring and advising on the ongoing controls activities of the organization.
>
> *Internal auditor and financial controller*: Both these positions can have important roles to play in the monitoring of, and advising on, the specific controls matters, which fall within their area of expertise.

### 10.3.1.4 Controls Deliverables

Internal controls need to be built into the management decision process, and when operating effectively can help an organization mitigate risk and achieve its business objectives. Internal controls can reduce the risk of financial and asset loss, promote the effectiveness and efficiency of business operations, and help ensure compliance with laws and regulations. The following are some examples of what effective controls can hope to deliver:

> *Financial reporting objectives*: Financial controls are required to help achieve financial reporting objectives. Financial controls help ensure the integrity of the information (i.e., intelligence controls) contained in the published financial statements and the reliability of the preparation of the organization's financial reports. The integrity of information systems requires appropriate controls to help ensure the validity, accuracy, and completeness of all transactions involving the organization. Effective financial controls should help ensure that all transactions are correctly calculated, appropriately summarized, and accurately recorded in the organization's books and records.
>
> *Operations objectives*: Operational controls are required to help achieve operations objectives, which contribute to the achievement of strategic and tactical objectives. Operational controls address the effectiveness and efficiency of operations and help ensure that the organization's assets and resources are appropriately safeguarded (i.e., security controls and resilience controls), and help enhance the performance and productivity of business operations (i.e., governance controls and assurance controls). Operational controls can vary considerably by business sector; however, they should always be focused on enhancing profitability and protecting against loss.
>
> *Compliance objectives*: Compliance controls are required to help achieve compliance objectives. Compliance controls primarily help ensure that the organization is complying with all relevant mandatory external laws and regulations to which the organization is subject to. They can also help ensure that the organization's activities are being conducted in accordance with the organization's own voluntary internal standards. Compliance controls need to address external expectations and are therefore subject to modification to address changing external requirements. These external requirements may also differ by industry, geographic region, and so on.

## 10.3.2　Controls Matters

Every organization must consider the multitude of risks to which it is exposed. Before considering how controls can help mitigate these risks, there must be a clear distinction between which of these risks are considered to be controllable risks and which are considered to be uncontrollable risks. Uncontrollable risks represent risks that are outside of the control of the organization and therefore are difficult if not impossible to mitigate, while controllable risks represent risks that are within the control of the organization and are therefore easier to mitigate.

### 10.3.2.1　Controls Philosophy and Culture

The controls philosophy will be shaped by the organization's business objectives and its attitude to risk taking, which is reflected in its risk appetite. In simple terms the greater the organization's risk appetite, the less emphasis may be placed on the importance of controls and vice versa. An organization that simply views controls as an external requirement (Sarbanes Oxley Act 2002, etc.) imposed on the business may ultimately regard controls as an unnecessary expense. Due to their time-consuming nature and financial cost, it may be unlikely to prioritize controls or to foster a positive and proactive attitude to controls. In contrast, an organization that recognizes that effective internal controls can create competitive advantage and can actually result in the creation and preservation of value, is more likely to prioritize controls and foster a positive and proactive attitude to controls. In the latter case, the organization recognizes that the right kind of controls can enable the organization to capitalize on opportunities while actually saving time and money in the process. It also recognizes that effective controls not only offset risks but can also allow the organization to actually take on additional risk.

The controls culture will also be heavily influenced by the extent to which the organization is predisposed to a control and command approach to managing its operations, or is prepared to delegate authority and trust throughout its operations. The level of autonomy delegated to business units, branches, subsidiaries, and so on will impact the organization's overall control culture. An organization with a heavily centralized operating structure will therefore differ considerably with an organization that operates in a mainly decentralized manner.

### 10.3.2.2　Controls Issues for Consideration

In order to achieve an appropriate balance, it is important that internal controls not only address risk exposure but are also cost-effective. This means that the cost of a control should not exceed the benefit derived from the existence of that control. The following are some examples of selected controls issues that organizations are required to carefully consider:

*Control objectives*: Consideration needs to be given to the purpose of a required control and the control objective that is hoped to be achieved. Precise control objectives can vary depending on the individual circumstances and different controls may be required to help achieve different control objectives. Examples of control objectives can include providing a level of comfort in relation to issues such as the validity, accuracy, completeness, timeliness, and confidentiality of transactions. Not all controls will be capable of providing comfort in all of these areas and therefore specific controls may be required in order to achieve specific control objectives.

*Level of risk*: Consideration needs to be given to the level of risk associated with a particular area, event, process, and so on. Inherent risk represents the anticipated level of risk present before the organization takes any risk-mitigation measures (including internal controls), while residual risk represents the risk that remains after the organization has taken measures to mitigate the level of inherent risk. The required controls will be influenced by the level of residual risk, which the organization deems to be at an acceptable level.

*Levels of comfort*: Consideration needs to be given to the level of comfort required by a control in order to satisfy a control objective. In general, an effective system of internal control is said to provide an overall reasonable level of comfort; however, different levels of comfort may be required in each unique situation, depending on the risk levels involved. Examples of levels of comfort can vary from no comfort, to limited comfort, to reasonable comfort, to dependable comfort, to complete comfort, and so on. These can also be measured in terms of percentages or degrees of confidence. Different controls are capable of providing different levels of comfort, however, a complete level of comfort may not be realistically attainable and it may not be cost-effective in the long run.

*Control types*: Consideration needs to be given to the range and types of controls required to provide the required level of comfort in order to achieve the control objective. A selection of control types are available ranging from preventative controls to detective controls, from manual (physical) controls to automated (IT) controls, or from primary controls to secondary compensating controls. The individual control or range of controls selected should depend on the risks that need to be addressed. For example, high-risk processes may require preventative controls while detective controls may be considered acceptable for low-risk processes, where corrective action may be more easily taken on the detection of an anomaly.

*Control locations*: Consideration needs to be given to the actual location of controls during the course of the business. Each organization must determine for itself the appropriate location of different controls. For example, controls over-strategic risk may need to be located at the board level, while controls over operational risk may be best located in the front office, the middle office, or the back office depending on the business processes and the type of business involved. Oversight controls may also be spread over the different lines of defense as deemed appropriate based on defined roles and responsibilities.

### 10.3.3   The Controls Program

An effective internal controls program is achieved when all the control program elements operate successfully together across the entire organization. Control elements are closely connected and involve people, processes, and systems, which need to be operating in unison in order to be effective. Establishing an effective controls program is not a once-off exercise, it requires continuous monitoring and continuous improvement in order to take account of newly emerging risks, control failures, and changes to the organization's circumstances and expectations. A comprehensive controls program should also incorporate the other defense components into the program itself, and therefore should address issues such as *controls governance*, *controls risk*, *controls compliance*, *controls intelligence*, *controls security*, *controls resilience*, and *controls assurance*. Any controls program should however address the following:

*Controls program execution*: The formality and structure of a controls program can vary depending on the organization's size, the complexity of operations, and its risk profile. Each organization needs to carefully design, implement, monitor, test, and report on the controls program that can achieve its business control objectives. Regardless of the level of formality or structure, it is important that the organization is aware of the importance of each of these stages and their contribution to the overall effectiveness of the controls program.

*Control assessment*: The assessment of the internal control system and the identification of possible weaknesses or deficiencies that need to be considered is an ongoing challenge for any organization. Where weaknesses or deficiencies are identified, an organization must choose from a range of available options. It may decide to improve existing controls, increase existing controls, introduce new controls, or accept the risk associated with the identified control weaknesses. At the end of the day, the final decision on the required level of control may be a matter of sound business judgment after weighing up the associated costs and benefits.

*Control activities*: A controls system does involve the establishment of policies and procedures in addition to addressing issues such as the prevention of fraud, conflict of interests, and the implementation of appropriate segregation of duties; however, it is also much more than that. It involves a blending of different control activities in order to deliver the appropriate checks and balances required to deliver an effective integrated internal controls system. For example, supervisory or management controls involve a level of monitoring or review in order to provide appropriate oversight of activities under direct supervision at strategic, tactical and operational levels. Business process controls involve controls that are in-built into the business process and are in operation on a day-to-day basis. Financial controls involve controls over the integrity of financial information, and nonfinancial controls such as operational controls, compliance controls, physical controls, and IT controls are all critical in supporting decision-making and helping the business to achieve its intended results. Individual control activities can include approvals, authorizations, verifications, reconciliations, and reviews of performance. Although effective controls can reduce the risk of erroneous and inappropriate actions, the precise mix of the required control activities needs to be determined by each organization individually.

### 10.3.3.1 Controls Program Particulars

Stakeholders of an organization can ascertain the extent to which the organization has adopted a formal structured approach to its controls program by receiving coherent answers to their questions. The following are examples of basic questions that stakeholders might be expected to ask in relation to the organization's controls program:

- Does your organization have a formal board-approved controls program in place?
- Does your organization have a formally approved controls vision in place?
- Does your organization have a formally approved controls mission statement in place?
- Does your organization have a formally approved controls strategy in place?
- Does your organization have a formally approved controls plan in place?

### 10.3.3.2 Controls Program Standing

Stakeholders of an organization can ascertain the standing of the organization's controls program by receiving coherent answers to their questions. The following are examples of basic questions that stakeholders might be expected to ask in relation to the standing of organization's controls program:

- Is there a board controls committee (or subcommittee) in place?
- Is there a specialist controls function (or competence center) in place?
- Has a chief controls officer been appointed?
- Where or to whom does the chief controls officer directly report?
- What is the controls program's budget as a percentage of the organization's overall budget?

### 10.3.4 CONTROLS FRAMEWORKS AND GUIDANCE

There are numerous versions of controls frameworks and guidance available to organizations. The following are examples of selected controls frameworks, codes, and other guidance:

#### SELECTED CONTROLS FRAMEWORKS AND GUIDANCE

- Standards for Internal Control in the Federal Government (GAO 2014)
- Integrated Internal Controls Framework (COSO 2013)
- Evaluating and Improving Internal Control in Organizations (IFAC 2012)
- Internal Control: Revised Guidance for Directors on the Combined Code (FRC 2005)
- Framework for Internal Control Systems in Banking Organizations (BCBS 1998)
- The Criteria of Control (CoCo) Framework (CICA 1995)

### 10.3.5    INTERNATIONAL CONTROLS ORGANIZATIONS

There are numerous international organizations that are specifically devoted to developing and promoting controls as a discipline. Table 10.4 outlines notable international organizations that specifically focus on controls as a subject matter.

---

**TABLE 10.4**
**Selected Controls Organizations**

| Organization | Website |
| --- | --- |
| Committee of Sponsoring Organizations of the Treadway Commission (COSO) | www.coso.org |
| Chartered Professional Accountants of Canada (CPA Canada) | www.cpacanada.ca |
| International Federation of Accountants (IFAC) | www.ifac.org |
| The Institute for Internal Controls | www.theiic.org |
| International Control Institute (ICI) | www.internalcontrolinstitute.org |

---

## 10.4    ASSURANCE

Assurance, and the management of assurance, is considered to be one of the critical components of an organization's corporate defense program. In simple terms this refers to the system in place to provide a degree of confidence to stakeholders that everything is operating in a satisfactory manner. The International Auditing and Assurance Standards Board (IAASB) in a paper entitled "International Framework for Assurance Engagements" has described an assurance engagement as follows: "Assurance engagement means an engagement in which a practitioner expressed a conclusion designed to enhance the degree of confidence of the intended users other than the responsible party, about the outcome of the evaluation or measurement of a subject matter against criteria. The outcome of the valuation or measurement of a subject matter is the information that results from applying the criteria to the subject matter" (IAASB 2005).

### 10.4.1    ASSURANCE AS A DISCIPLINE

Obtaining assurance involves the expression of a conclusion designed to provide a degree of confidence to those concerned about the evaluation of a subject matter against specific predefined criteria. This requires the performance of an objective examination of evidence, in order to provide an impartial assessment on a particular subject matter. If boards and stakeholders are to obtain their required degree of confidence, it is imperative that an appropriate assurance framework is in place. This framework should incorporate a combination of assurance options, and should be tailored to reflect the structure, which best fits the organization, in order to obtain a balanced view. For example, an effective audit committee should primarily be responsible for ensuring that the financial position of the company is accurately reflected in its reports, and for overseeing the necessary internal controls to achieve this result. In order to achieve this objective, an audit committee should make full use of line management assurance, its internal audit function, and seek independent assurance from its external auditors, and indeed from other third-party professionals where required.

With the ever increasing speed, complexity, and uncertainty of business today, obtaining high-quality assurance regarding the effectiveness of key business processes, risks, and controls has never been more vital to the organization. Adequate and comprehensive assurance across the entire enterprise is needed to meet the assurance needs of forward-looking boards of directors. By utilizing the appropriate combination of the assorted assurance services available, a board can gain increased confidence that due diligence is being exercised throughout the organization, and that an appropriate corporate defense framework is in place and operating effectively.

### 10.4.1.1 Role of Assurance in Corporate Defense

The U.K.'s HM Treasury in a paper entitled "Assurance Frameworks" states the following: "Assurance can come from many sources within an organization. A concept for helping to identify and understand the different contributions the various sources can provide is the Three Lines of Defense model. By defining the sources of assurance in three broad categories, it helps to understand how each contributes to the overall level of assurance provided and how best they can be integrated and mutually supportive. For example, management assurances could be harnessed to provide coverage of routine operations, with internal audit activity targeted at riskier or more complex areas" (HM Treasury 2012). Booz & Co. in a paper entitled "First and Last Line of Defense: How Business Assurance Makes Organizations Resilient to Risk" state the following: "The challenge in creating a business assurance program resides in striking the right balance between facilitating integration and building capabilities. For instance, developing an integrated assurance organization without paying enough attention to building the right assurance capabilities will yield an organization that is incapable of effectively responding to specific types of risks. Similarly, an organization that develops the functional capabilities but does not effectively address the management of these capabilities risks developing functional 'stovepipes', along with weak coordination and no clear accountability" (Booz & Co. 2009).

In an interview in 2008, assurance expert Michael Parkinson, a director of the Institute of Internal Audit (IIA), when asked for his views on where does assurance currently fit into the broader concept of an organization's program of self-defense and how do you see it developing going forward, stated: "The assurance processes are like an instrument panel. They are not the controls, but they tell the organization's board and top management how the organization is performing and whether the controls are operating correctly. While more effective ways of reporting may be developed, the basic controls and the knowledge that they are working will always be required" (Lyons 2009c).

### 10.4.1.2 Management of the Assurance Component

Management of the assurance component is required in order to help provide a degree of confidence to the stakeholders of the organization. A comprehensive assurance framework focuses on assurance from a holistic perspective and addresses assurance requirements, both internal and external to the organization. Internal assurance can therefore be provided on strategic, tactical, and operational activities. Stakeholders may also require assurance in relation to the organization's supply chain and external business partners. In such cases a certain degree of confidence may be drawn in a variety of sources, including warranties and guarantees, the brand and reputation of the external party, their process maturity and professional competence, and any assurance certifications received. Where additional assurance is required, the case for the external party's product or service may require material evidence as proof to support or substantiate any claims made by the party concerned. Any assurance engagement, be it internal or external, needs to establish that the appropriate mechanisms are in place, that they are all operating as intended, and that they deliver a high- quality end product. The ultimate test of assurance is the extent to which assurance is demonstrable, repeatable, and defensible.

The assurance component is both impacted by and impacts on the management of all of the other critical components. Each component should address the assurance issue within its individual programs (e.g., *governance assurance, risk assurance, compliance assurance, intelligence assurance, security assurance, resilience assurance,* and *controls assurance*).

### 10.4.1.3 Key Assurance Players

An effective assurance program requires all members of the organization to fulfill their assurance duties. Although ultimate responsibility for assurance rests with the board and executive management, the responsibility for managing the organization's assurance practices can typically rest with a number of key individuals who specifically occupy important assurance positions.

*Chairman of the assurance committee*: The chairman of the assurance committee (should one exist) has an important intermediary role between the board and management. The chairman has the responsibility for the effective operation of the assurance committee and its oversight of the implementation of the assurance program.*

*Chief assurance officer*: The chief assurance officer (should one exist) has an important role in overseeing the work of the assurance function (should one exist) and in monitoring, and advising on, the ongoing assurance activities of the organization.

*Chairman of the audit committee*: The chairman of the audit committee has an important intermediary role between the board and management. The chairman has responsibility for the effective operation of the audit committee and its oversight of the implementation of the audit program.

*Chief audit executive*: The chief audit executive has an important role in overseeing the work of the internal audit function and in monitoring, and advising on, the ongoing internal audit activities of the business.

### 10.4.1.4 Assurance Deliverables

The purpose of addressing the assurance component is to help ensure that the assurance requirements of the stakeholders of the organization are met in a satisfactory manner. The precise stakeholder assurance requirements may vary from one organization to another; however, certain general assurance requirements are to be expected in all cases. The following are some examples of what effective assurance can hope to deliver:

*General assurance*: The provision of adequate assurance that in general the organization is being managed in an appropriate manner and is likely to achieve its stated objectives. Based on the assurance provided stakeholders are satisfied with the overall operation of the organization and have developed sufficient confidence and trust in the organization to believe that the required objectives will be achieved within the stated time frames. Such assurance may be the result of a combination of assurance providers.

*Financial assurance*: The provision of adequate assurance that the organization's financial statements and financial reporting satisfies financial reporting standards. Based on the assurance provided stakeholders are satisfied that the organization's financial controls are operating appropriately, and that the organization's financial reporting is accurate, reliable, and free from any material misstatements. Stakeholders generally rely on financial assurance to be provided by the organization's external auditors.

*Nonfinancial assurance*: The provision of adequate assurance that the organization's nonfinancial activities are operating in a satisfactory manner. Based on the assurance provided stakeholders are satisfied that the organization's operational and other nonfinancial practices are appropriately controlled and operating in accordance with expected standards of effectiveness, efficiency, reliability, and quality management. This type of assurance is typically provided by the internal audit function.

*Ongoing assurance*: The provision of adequate assurance that on an ongoing basis the organization's controls are operating effectively, its risks are being managed at an acceptable level, and that its objectives are being successfully achieved. Stakeholders receive ongoing assurance in relation to the organization's activities. This includes a blending of assurance via real-time or continuous monitoring, periodic audits or inspection reviews, and specific point-in-time assurance engagements on hot topics. Any such blending will

---

* An Assurance Committee should be assigned responsibility for the oversight of the assurance component program. In many organizations the Audit Committee is regarded as the primary assurance committee; however, its remit is often more narrow in scope. Where its remit is extended to include the oversight of the assurance component program, this may also be regarded as diluting or compromising its independence.

ultimately be dependent on the stakeholder expectations and requirements. Ongoing assurance can be provided by a variety of assurance providers over the course of the year and over a number of years.

*Engagement assurance*: The provision of adequate assurance that specific issues are being addressed in a satisfactory manner. Stakeholders receive specific assurance that an individual issue is being appropriately addressed. Individual assurance engagements are required where matters of specific concern arise, which are deemed to require review or investigation. Such issues may be the result of red flags raised via whistleblower or a hotline and can include matters such as allegations of corruption or suspected fraud and so on. Such a matter may require fraud examination or forensic investigation and can potentially shake stakeholder confidence or negatively impact on the organization's reputation. Specialist external firms are often employed to provide this type of assurance.

## 10.4.2 ASSURANCE MATTERS

Every organization needs to establish its own precise assurance requirements at strategic, tactical, and operational levels. Assurance requirements can vary considerably from informal verbal assurance received over the telephone to formal written assurance received in a structured report format. Organizations can typically use a variety of different assurance sources and different types of assurance techniques in order to fulfill their assurance requirements, depending on their precise assurance needs. Each organization will invariably be influenced by time and cost restrictions when deciding on the exact trade-off considered to be acceptable to its stakeholders at any given point in time.

### 10.4.2.1 Assurance Philosophy and Culture

The assurance philosophy will be influenced by the organization's management focus. An organization with a *strategy-centric* focus may expect assurance on the execution of the strategy, one with an *objective-centric* focus may expect assurance on the achievement of objectives, one with a *risk-centric* focus may expect assurance on the management of risk, while one with a *control-centric* focus may expect assurance on the effectiveness of controls. The assurance ethos will to some extent be influenced by the manner in which management delegates authority within the organization. The delegation of authority requires supervision and monitoring of activities by those to whom authority has been delegated, and these individuals are in turn expected to provide assurance on the performance of activities based on their supervision. Typically, in an organizational context, responsibility and monitoring flow downward, while accountability and assurance flow upward. An organization's attitude to assurance is in part a reflection of the level of trust or faith that an organization is prepared to put in individuals and groups within the organization itself. The precise level and type of assurance required of its assurance providers is a good indication of the organization's assurance philosophy and of the assurance culture being fostered in the organization.

Typically, a traditional command and control-type organization may require a systematic disciplined approach to the provision of assurance throughout the organization, while a more organic organization with a flatter control structure may prefer to operate a less rigid approach to the provision of assurance. Likewise, the assurance culture of an organization that operates on a *trust but verify* basis may differ significantly from one that operates on an *ethics and trust* basis. It should be remembered however that these differences may prove to have either positive or negative consequences for the organization, depending on other organizational cultural factors that can come into play. For example, an organization that fosters a culture of *ethics and trust* may benefit by the fact that each staff member in turn feels more trustworthy and a *trust but verify* approach may actually undermine the level of existing trust. Nevertheless, there are certain assurance aspects, which will require compliance with mandatory external standards (i.e., financial reporting, etc.).

### 10.4.2.2 Assurance Issues for Consideration

Assurance requirements both individually and collectively need to address the purpose of the assurance, the subject matter requiring assurance, the criteria for providing the assurance, the individual or group responsible for the provision of the required assurance, and the method of providing assurance. The following are some examples of selected assurance issues that organizations are required to carefully consider:

*Assurance purpose*: Organizations need to consider the purpose of fulfilling their assurance requirements in terms of what it is that they are hoping to achieve. What are their assurance objectives in the short, medium, and long term and how do these objectives contribute to the achievement of the organization's business objectives? The purpose of assurance should determine the level of due diligence required whether it relates to internal (e.g., internal controls) or external (e.g., merger and acquisition) activities. The assurance purpose should be carefully considered at each stage whether it relates to an individual assurance engagement or the entire assurance program.

*Assurance subject matter*: Organizations need to consider the subject matter over which it requires assurance and the precise scope of the assurance undertaking. The assurance subject matter may vary considerably in complexity ranging from a specific issue such as a fraud examination to a range of practices performed by a specific function or business unit, to the business processes relating to a product or service, to activities of a particular subsidiary or in a particular geographic region, or finally to the entire assurance universe of the organization. Clarity over the strategic, tactical or operational nature and scope of the assurance subject matter is an essential element of the assurance process.

*Assurance provider*: Organizations need to carefully consider the assurance provider being entrusted to provide assurance on a particular subject matter. The organization needs to consider important issues such as the integrity (e.g., honesty, diligence, and responsibility) of the assurance provider and the level of independence, objectivity, and impartiality that can realistically be provided. It needs to consider matters such as the required level of professional competence and confidentiality from the selected assurance provider, and the sufficiency of resources available to them to ensure that the engagement will be conducted with proficiency and due professional care. It needs to consider the authority and the formality of the mandate of the assurance provider, and any restrictions to the access granted to them in conducting its assurance undertakings.

*Assurance criteria*: Organizations need to carefully consider the assurance criteria to be applied to the subject matter in order to provide a frame of reference. The organization needs to consider the requirement and relevance of both quantitative and qualitative assurance. It needs to consider the level of due diligence expected of the assurance provider in a specific engagement, including the nature and level of work required, and the resulting evidence (i.e., quantity and quality) required to substantiate any assurance provided. It needs to consider the type of evidence required and whether it relates to the environment, people, processes, or systems. It needs to consider the requirement to benchmark with industry best practices or any required conformance with internationally accepted codes or professional standards. It needs to consider the time frame within which the assurance undertaking is required and the timescales over which the assurance is expected to cover.

*Assurance delivery*: Organizations need to consider the most suitable communication mechanism for delivering the required assurance. The organization needs to consider the materiality of the assurance required and how it should best be communicated to the relevant stakeholders. It should consider whether verbal or written representation is expected and provide due consideration to the type of language to be used for specific intended users. It needs to consider the precise format in which the required assurance should be provided particularly if written assurance is required. It needs to consider the delivery expectations of its audience and any particular stakeholder requirements.

### 10.4.3 THE ASSURANCE PROGRAM

A comprehensive assurance program involves the management of the organization's sources of assurance and all assurance resources in order to optimize the quality of assurance provided to its stakeholders. An assurance program therefore should incorporate the management and coordination of the various assurance providers available to the organization so as to improve the quality and coverage of available assurance and to eliminate any unnecessary duplication of assurance activities. It should incorporate the management of the different assurance techniques in order to provide assurance under different circumstances and over different time frames. Assurance is required to be managed on an enterprise-wide basis and the best results can be achieved when all the assurance elements form part of a structured assurance program. A comprehensive governance program should also incorporate the other defense components into the program itself, and therefore should address issues such as *assurance governance, assurance risk, assurance compliance, assurance intelligence, assurance security, assurance resilience*, and *assurance controls*.

A structured assurance program should incorporate the potential assurance that can be provided from all of the organization's internal lines of defense. In order to optimize the organization's potential level of assurance, clear roles, expectations, and required standards need to be established in advance for each line of defense as follows:

*Business line management*: Operational line management can provide fundamental operational assurance based on its supervisory and monitoring efforts in the frontline of the organization's activities, its ongoing quality-assurance mechanisms, and the completion of self-assessments. Line management is required to regularly verify, assess, and report on the integrity of the organization's internal controls. In order to fulfill this responsibility from both a prudence and regulatory perspective, line management is expected to undertake an enterprise-wide comprehensive approach, in order to provide dependable reports on internal controls.

*Specialist support functions*: Various corporate defense functions can provide a degree of assurance in relation to their particular areas of expertise (i.e., governance, risk, compliance, intelligence, security, resilience, and controls) based on the fulfillment of their oversight roles. In addition other specialist oversight functions such as the human resources function, the finance function, and the IT function can provide useful complimentary assurance based on their specialist knowledge, the performance of their oversight responsibilities and performing periodic audits.

*Internal audit*: Internal Audit as the primary provider on independent internal assurance can provide the essential objective and impartial assurance on all aspects of the organization's activities based on the findings of detailed inspection reviews, ongoing internal audits, and high-level assessments of the organization's circumstances. The use of the internal audit function should also provide the audit committee and management with an objective and impartial assessment of internal controls, by performing assurance services in a systematic and disciplined manner. Increasingly what is being required from the internal audit function is to be strategic in outlook, and yet also provide a continuous auditing process.

*Senior management*: Executive management can provide a useful holistic assurance based on its oversight of business-line management and of specialist support functions. The quality of assurance provided by senior management will invariably determine the success or failure of the organization given their unique position, their responsibility for managing the organization on behalf of the board, and their strategic, tactical, and operational knowledge and understanding of the organization's activities.

*Board of directors*: The board of directors as the guardians of the organization can provide important strategic assurance based on their oversight of executive management and the various subcommittees of the board such as the nomination committee, remuneration committee, and so on (in addition to the various corporate defense committees). The use of board committees (audit committee, risk committee, compliance committee, and so on) to assist the board in fulfilling its oversight responsibilities should include the provision of assurance that risks are managed to an acceptable level, and that controls are adequate and effective.

*External third parties*: External assurance can be provided by firms who conduct independent specialist reviews of the organization's activities. Examples include the organization's external auditors who can provide useful assurance in relation to the organization's financial reporting, and various other specialist firms can also provide valuable assurance on matters requiring external specialist support such as external law firms, providers of standards certifications, other specialist consultancy firms, and so on. The independent attestation provided by external audit firms, or the use of other external consultants, can provide organizations with independent assurance over their systems, processes, and calculations so that stakeholders can have confidence in the information produced. This can include benchmarking to best practices, or certifications against recognized international standards. In extreme cases, corporate lawyers are now recommending organizations employ independent third-party specialists for special engagements concerning such areas as fraud examination or forensic investigations.

### 10.4.3.1 Assurance Program Particulars

Stakeholders of an organization can ascertain the extent to which the organization has adopted a formal structured approach to its assurance program by receiving coherent answers to their questions. The following are examples of basic questions that stakeholders might be expected to ask in relation to the organization's assurance program:

- Does your organization have a formal board-approved assurance program in place?
- Does your organization have a formally approved assurance vision in place?
- Does your organization have a formally approved assurance mission statement in place?
- Does your organization have a formally approved assurance strategy in place?
- Does your organization have a formally approved assurance plan in place?

### 10.4.3.2 Assurance Program Standing

Stakeholders of an organization can ascertain the standing of the organization's assurance program by receiving coherent answers to their questions. The following are examples of basic questions that stakeholders might be expected to ask in relation to the standing of organization's assurance program:

- Is there a board assurance committee (or subcommittee) in place?
- Is there a specialist assurance function (or competence center) in place?
- Has a chief assurance officer been appointed?
- Where or to whom does the chief assurance officer directly report?
- What is the assurance program's budget as a percentage of the organization's overall budget?

### 10.4.4 Assurance Frameworks and Guidance

There are numerous versions of assurance frameworks and guidance available to organizations. The following are examples of selected assurance frameworks, codes, and other guidance:

## SELECTED ASSURANCE FRAMEWORKS AND GUIDANCE

- Framework for Assurance Engagements (AASB 2014)
- International Standards for Assurance Engagements (IAASB 2013)
- Standards and Guidance—International Professional Practices Framework (IPPF) (IIA 2013b)
- ITAF™—Professional Practices Framework for IS Audit/Assurance, 3rd Edition (ISACA 2013)
- Assurance Frameworks (HM Treasury 2012)
- Internal Audit Guide: Assessing Governance, Risk, Compliance and Ethics Capabilities (OCEG 2007)
- Internal Audit in Banks and the Supervisor's Relationship with Auditors (BCBS 2001)

### 10.4.5 International Assurance Organizations

There are numerous international organizations that are specifically devoted to developing and promoting assurance as a discipline. Table 10.5 outlines notable international organizations that specifically focus on assurance as a subject matter.

**TABLE 10.5**
**Selected Assurance Organizations**

| Organization | Website |
| --- | --- |
| International Auditing and Assurance Standards Board (IAASB) | www.iaasb.org |
| Institute of Internal Audit (IIA) | www.theiia.org |
| Information Systems Audit and Controls Association (ISACA) | www.isaca.org |
| American Institute of Certified Public Accountants (AICPA) | www.aicpa.org |
| Association of Chartered Certified Accountants (ACCA) | www.accaglobal.com |
| The Associations of Accountants and Financial Professionals in Business (IMA) | www.imanet.org |
| Chartered Institute of Management Accountants (CIMA) | www.cimaglobal.com |
| Financial Executives International (FEI) | www.financialexecutives.org |

# 11 Developments in Approaches to Corporate Defense

We shall not cease from exploration, and the end of all our exploring will be to arrive where we started and know the place for the first time.*

**T.S. Eliot**

## 11.1 A CHANGING MIND-SET EMERGING

Since the turn of the twenty-first century, the corporate world has seen something of a change in mind-set in relation to how organizations are approaching corporate defense and in relation to how corporate defense components themselves are changing. It must be said that much of this has been the result of enforced change as a result of regulator reactions to incidents; however, there are also promising signs that at least some firms are adopting a more proactive approach to developing their corporate defense capability.

### 11.1.1 PROGRESS TO DATE

It would certainly be unfair to suggest that organizations have historically ignored addressing risks, threats, and vulnerabilities; however, the manner in which these challenges are now being addressed is changing quite dramatically. Over time many top organizations, in their attempts to safeguard their stakeholder value, have introduced specialist functions with more and more sophisticated

---

* Per *Little Gidding*, Poem, 1942, T.S. Eliot.

techniques and services. This progress however has been slower than required and has been somewhat reactive rather than proactive.

#### 11.1.1.1 Part of Normal Business

In the past, the various critical components were often considered just part of doing business as normal, where issues were addressed on a case-by-case basis as circumstances arose. Many organizations adopted a best efforts approach to value preservation mainly relying on instinct or intuition. There was a very basic level of understanding of the potential complexity of issues facing the organization or the requirement for specialist knowledge in the various corporate defense areas. In fact, many of the critical components themselves were still very much in their infancy and were still evolving as disciplines in their own right.

#### 11.1.1.2 Corporate Defense as an Additional Add-On Task

Over time, there was an increasing degree of appreciation that certain corporate defense aspects needed to be addressed from time to time. In many cases, the responsibility for addressing these aspects was delegated as additional add-on tasks to individuals who already had primary responsibilities in other areas of the business, and were therefore treated as secondary to their business responsibilities. Invariably these individuals often only possessed general business skills and therefore often only possessed a low level of knowledge in the corporate defense realm.

#### 11.1.1.3 The Need for Specialist Skills

Gradually many organizations began to identify the need to take their corporate defense components to the next level and began to acknowledge a requirement for certain individuals with a specialist focus in a particular area of corporate defense. This required individuals with a deeper level of understanding and technical knowledge in a particular area. Generally these individuals were still employed within the business functions and may also have had additional business duties and responsibilities. There was however a recognition of the need for higher levels of corporate governance, risk management, and compliance and so on.

### 11.1.2 TOWARD A SILO ENVIRONMENT

Once this requirement for a specialist focus was recognized, it was not long before many firms decided to take the next step and to move toward the development of specialist critical component functions within their organization. The setting up of critical component functions involved the training or recruitment of individuals with specific skills in certain required components, which by now were being regarded as required specialist disciplines within the organization. The critical components identified as being required however were still very much in reaction to a crisis within the industry or the organization itself.

#### 11.1.2.1 A Recognition of Required Specialist Functions

As organizations began to increasingly recognize the value of these critical components, groups of individuals were now required in order to staff specialist functions that were now being setup to address the particular critical component, which was deemed important to the organization's operations. This meant that these individuals were required to possess specialist know-how, including relevant knowledge, qualifications, skills, experience, and expertise in particular areas of corporate defense.

#### 11.1.2.2 Development of Specialist Disciplines

Members of these critical component functions now required relevant education and training, which included attending specialist seminars, conferences, and other courses tailored for these individual corporate defense disciplines. In some instances, education providers began offering academic and professional qualifications to meet this growing demand. This demand also saw the development of professional representative bodies in each of the different critical component fields, with a view to developing these particular disciplines. This in turn facilitated the coming together of like-minded individuals with similar backgrounds and interests in order to further cultivate their specialist niche.

### 11.1.2.3  Functional Silos

In many instances however these corporate defense functions were set up as stand-alone functions somewhat removed from the everyday business. The creation of these silo-type structures in isolation of the business in turn resulted in the creation of silo environments, and this led to silo-type thinking within these functions where they understandably developed a narrow discipline-focused (i.e., *risk-centric*, *compliance-centric*, and *control-centric* and so on) approach, rather than a more holistic and aligned *business strategy-centric* focus. In many instances, this had the result of creating tension and conflict with business units and such an approach did not lend itself to the fostering of positive relationships between these corporate defense activities and the business itself.

## 11.2  FUNCTIONAL MATURITY MODEL

Developments in each of the corporate defense components have however been continuous at a functional level, so much so that it has been referred to as an evolutionary process, which is commonly described in terms of a maturity model. This evolution seems to be occurring in practically all of the critical components, although some are generally at a more advanced phase of maturity than others. The maturity models applied, of which there are many variations, are generally based on an adaptation of the capability maturity model (CMM), which was developed for defense software purposes by the Software Engineering Institute (SEI) at the Carnegie Mellon University in the mid 1980s (Humphrey 1989). Derivatives or variations of this maturity model can be found in practically all corporate defense-related activities. Figure 11.1 outlines the functional maturity model.

### 11.2.1  Phases of Maturity

The functional maturity model outlines how each corporate defense component typically progresses through a number of different phases of maturity. At each of these phases of maturity, the corporate

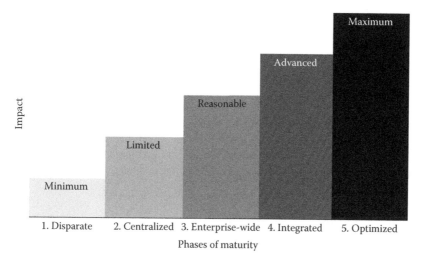

**FIGURE 11.1**  The functional maturity. (Data from Lyons S. October 16, 2006b. Corporate Defence Management: A Strategic Imperative. The Bank Director [www.bankdirector.com]. http://papers.ssrn.com/sol3/papers.cfm?abstract_id=1032576.)

defense component is in a position to be able to offer a different level of positive contribution to business impact. The earlier the phase of maturity of a particular corporate defense component, the less it will be in a position to positively contribute to the organization.

### 11.2.1.1　The Disparate Phase

Initially, the individual business units within the organization tend to be left to their own devices in developing their approach or methods in relation to the management of any one of these components, representing something of a disparate or fragmented type approach. This often results in these approaches being developed on an inconsistent basis and consequently the management of a given component across the business units is generally unsystematic and unstructured (e.g., ad-hoc risk management). The business impact associated with this phase of development is considered minimum as the activity tends to be performed in an ad-hoc manner and often operates in a crisis mode whereby the business unit is continuously fire fighting on a day-to-day basis.

### 11.2.1.2　The Centralized Phase

In order to help develop a more consistent approach, organizations next attempt to consolidate a particular component by introducing a centralized function. These centralized functions have the responsibility of managing the component from a centralized source requiring specialist skills and expertise (e.g., risk management and compliance functions). This phase could be described as first-generation convergence, pulling related issues together under one umbrella, using a centralized-type approach. The business impact associated with this phase of development is improving but is still considered to be limited. The activity is now seen as a specialist area and is considered a defined professional discipline within the organization.

### 11.2.1.3　The Enterprise-Wide Phase

The next phase of maturity is designed to involve a push to embed agreed specialist principles and processes associated with the component throughout the entire organization or on an enterprise-wide basis. This promotion of an enterprise approach is an attempt to help ensure that all areas within the organization are adopting common practices so that all areas are addressing the relevant component in a systematic and structured manner (e.g., enterprise risk management [ERM] program). The business impact associated with this phase of development is now considered to be increasing to reasonable as the organization now agrees on its enterprise objectives and to a defined set of methodologies that are required to be the standard or benchmark for a particular component's activity.

### 11.2.1.4　The Integrated Phase

The next phase of maturity involves an organization's attempt to integrate the component's activities by taking advantage of advances in technology. Such an integrated approach is the natural progression beyond the enterprise-wide phase to where a component's activities are now integrated enabling the organization to effectively manage the component by migrating from a manual to an automated environment (e.g., integrated risk solution). By using available technological solutions, it is now becoming possible for organizations to move toward an end-to-end vertical and horizontal integration of the component's activities. The business impact associated with this phase of development is now considered advanced as it becomes possible to report essential measurement metrics relating to performance and productivity.

### 11.2.1.5　The Optimized Phase

The final maturity phase involves the organization focusing on deliberate process improvement and optimizing the use of the organization's resources. This is possible because the organization now has its people, processes, and systems fully integrated, and its workforce has now become empowered. The business impact associated with this phase of development represents the organization's opportunity to deliver maximum impact. By constant efforts at continuous improvement and by adopting accelerated learning techniques, the organization helps ensure that processes are continually enhanced and that performance becomes more innovative. This phase involves continually improving process performance through both established and pioneering improvements. Quantitative and qualitative improvement objectives are determined, continually revised to reflect changing business objectives, and used as benchmark criteria in managing improvement. Both the defined goals and the organization's set of benchmarks are targets for constant evaluation and assessment (e.g., optimized risk management).

## 11.3   CONTEMPORARY CORPORATE DEFENSE EVOLUTION

As developments in each of the critical components continue to evolve and mature at a functional level, there appears to be a move away from silo-type thinking toward a more open minded and impartial perspective. Given that these developments are occurring across all of the critical corporate defense components at a functional level, this can provide an opportunity for a common interdisciplinary corporate defense focus; however, if not adequately addressed, it can also result in certain cross-functional tensions and operational inefficiencies. Such issues therefore need to be addressed and resolved at a cross-functional level.

### 11.3.1   TOWARD CROSS-FUNCTIONAL CONVERGENCE

In an attempt to address some of the cross-functional issues that arise, similar developments are now also occurring at a cross-functional level. What is now emerging is an evolution in cross-functional convergence, in what could be referred to as the second-generation convergence in this space. These cross-functional developments represent a reaction to the functional silo-type environments that have developed over time within organizations, and represent an attempt to reduce the resulting operational inefficiencies (e.g., overlaps, duplications, and redundancies).

#### 11.3.1.1   Interdisciplinary Progression

Perhaps more important than deconstructing functional silos is that a common interdisciplinary focus is resulting in an opportunity for different corporate defense components to collaborate and work together in order to help achieve common objectives. This sharing and exchange of ideas and practices has resulted in organizations now choosing to apply a blending of what it considers to be the best practices present within different critical components. Such an interdisciplinary approach has also facilitated a progression away from a singular functional perspective (e.g., *control-centric*) and toward a multidisciplinary cross-functional perspective (e.g., *strategy-centric*) aimed at best helping the organization to achieve its objectives.

### 11.3.2   FIRST-ORDER CONVERGENCE

The interdisciplinary progression referred to above begins at a functional level, whereby individual functions, which have consolidated their position, have reached a level of maturity that enables them to operate their component on an enterprise-wide basis. Such consolidation and maturity levels can help encourage functions to stretch outside of their own comfort zones so that they can recognize elements within the practices of other components that are complimentary to their own practices, and could help improve their own contribution to the organization.

#### 11.3.2.1   Unilateral Consolidation

An enterprise-wide management approach is now a common approach to each of the critical corporate defense components. The following are a number of examples of where individual corporate defense components have consolidated their approach at a functional level:

*Risk*: In many organizations, there has been a progression from addressing market risk management, credit risk management, and operational risk management as individual risk management silos toward a more uniform approach to the management of all risks.

The adoption of a consolidated approach to risk management enables an organization to incorporate the management of market risk, credit risk, and operational risk under the one risk management umbrella. This can help ensure that all risks are addressed in a consistent, disciplined, and systematic manner and that appropriate risk principles and procedures are embedded throughout the organization regardless of the type of risks being managed.

*Security*: As new technologies emerge, the need to unify security functions throughout the entire enterprise is now being recognized. In many organizations, there has been a progression from managing physical security and information security separately, toward a convergence of the management of both. A unified approach to security management has now been made possible by advances in technology and it involves the integration of information technology (IT) and physical security systems and related technologies. An effective converged security approach should ideally reach across people, processes, and technology, and enable organizations to prevent, detect, and respond to any type of security-related incident.

*Compliance*: Since the introduction of the Sarbanes–Oxley Act 2002, there has been a heightened focus on the importance of the compliance component in many organizations. In many cases, this has resulted in the management of compliance being extended beyond traditional regulatory compliance to also address legal compliance (e.g., commercial and non-commercial law) and compliance with internal standards. Although an enterprise-wide approach to all types of compliance would appear to be a prudent approach, certain tensions regarding reporting lines between regulatory teams and legal teams have proven to be a difficult obstacle for certain organizations.

*Intelligence*: Efforts by some organizations to introduce the concept of organizational intelligence (OI) is an attempt to manage various streams of the intelligence component under the one umbrella. OI management seeks to collectively manage streams such as business intelligence (BI), knowledge management (KM), and management reporting in a consistent manner across the organization. This represents an effort to standardize strategies, techniques, and tools in order to help educate organizations on how to design, build, and maintain both information systems and KM practices. While there have been some advances made in the consolidation of management of the intelligence component, it is still at a lower level of maturity relative to most of the other corporate defense components.

## 11.3.3 SECOND-ORDER CONVERGENCE

Following on from the consolidation developments occurring among critical components at a functional level, there has also been a raft of interdisciplinary collaboration at a cross-functional level involving two corporate defense perspectives.

### 11.3.3.1 Bilateral Integration

Bilateral integration involves a blending of ideas, knowledge, and practices between two corporate defense disciplines resulting in a bilateral approach to a given challenge. The following are common examples of bilateral developments:

*Governance and risk*: The acknowledgment that poor governance in an organization actually represents a risk has led to a focus on managing *governance risk*, while the acknowledgment that risk management requires good governance has led to the development of *risk governance*. Risk governance refers to the integration of sound governance and risk practices, and also recognizes the importance of their complimentary roles (Scandizzo 2013). Effective risk management requires sound governance practices surrounding how an organization undertakes its risk management. It refers to the governance structures and practices put in place to address the management of risk in an organization. The National Association of Corporate Directors (NACD) describes risk governance as how directors "might improve their processes for overseeing the company's risk management activities" (NACD 2009). Risk governance therefore begins with the board and includes how the organization addresses the responsibility and accountability for the management of risk throughout the organization, and in turn provides guidance for informed decision-making and effective allocation of resources. It has become increasingly recognized as an essential element of both sound corporate governance and sound risk management.

*Risk and intelligence*: The acknowledgment that poor intelligence in an organization actually represents a risk has led to a focus on managing *intelligence risk*, although the alignment and integration of the risk and intelligence components have resulted in the development of the concept of *risk intelligence*. The risk intelligence objective is to help ensure that an organization can make faster, better, more informed business decisions in terms of dealing with the risks it is faced with. It is concerned with making better use of the information an organization already possesses. How organizations cope with risk and how they develop their risk intelligence determines their competitive advantage in terms of their competition. It has been described as an organization's ability, compared to its competitors, to assess a risk, and it depends on an organization's informational advantages and how these advantages are applied (Apgar 2006). Its premise is that organizations with low risk intelligence tend to be continually in a reactive mode and will tend to face far more unwelcome surprises going forward; therefore, organizations should strive to create a risk intelligent enterprise (Funston and Wagner 2010).

*Risk and security*: The acknowledgment that poor security in an organization actually represents a risk has led to a focus on managing *security risk*. The alignment and integration of the risk and security components have resulted in the development of the concept of *security risk management*. It refers to the requirement to acknowledge the importance of security risk and the application of risk management steps in the security management process in order to help ensure that all security risks are identified, measured, and managed in an appropriate manner. *Enterprise security risk management* is a term that is currently being used by many professionals involved in security roles (AESRM 2007).

### 11.3.3.2 Other Bilateral Developments

The above are specific examples of bilateral integration; however, there is a growing list of other bilateral developments that involve the alignment and integration of different critical components. This can best be seen by the services now on offer from the various consultancy firms operating in the corporate defense space. Table 11.1 highlights examples of some of these services on offer.

**TABLE 11.1**

**Bilateral Corporate Defense Services**

| Governance assurance | Compliance controls | Security assurance |
|---|---|---|
| Risk and compliance | Compliance assurance | Resilience risk |
| Risk resilience | Security governance | Resilience assurance |
| Risk controls | Security intelligence | Controls governance |
| Risk assurance | Security resilience | Controls assurance |

### 11.3.4    THIRD-ORDER CONVERGENCE

There are also signs of interdisciplinary collaboration occurring that involves three of the critical corporate defense components. These developments involve the convergence of three corporate defense disciplines and the alignment of three different perspectives on how to address corporate defense issues.

#### 11.3.4.1    Trilateral Integration

Trilateral integration involves a fusion of ideas, knowledge, and practices between three corporate defense disciplines, resulting in a trilateral approach to a given challenge. The following are common examples of trilateral developments:

*Governance, risk, and compliance (GRC)*: The alignment and integration of the governance, the risk, and the compliance components have resulted in the vendor-driven concept of GRC. It has been described by some as compliance management plus the integration of governance and risk management, and by others as the integration of these three areas (OCEG 2009). It represents the recognition that these activities share a number of common objectives and can result in the occurrence of a considerable degree of intersections, overlaps, and duplications throughout the organization. By adopting technology platforms that help to unify the functionality of these components, organizations can hope to overcome the problems caused by business fragmentation and disjointed approaches in these three areas.

*Governance, risk, and control (GRC)*: The alignment and integration of the governance, risk, and controls components have resulted in the internal audit-driven concept of GRC (not to be confused with above). Under this approach an internal auditor's remit is seen to include bringing a systematic and disciplined approach to evaluating and improving the effectiveness of an organization's governance, risk, and control processes. Such an approach helps to ensure that these three areas are in alignment in relation to contributing to the achievement of the organization's objectives. By specifically focusing on these three components, internal auditors gain an understanding of how these components fit together in a cohesive manner. The use of the same acronym as is used in the previous example above has however led to an element of confusion when organizations begin to discuss the topic of GRC.

#### 11.3.4.2    Other Trilateral Developments

A number of other trilateral developments have also been occurring, which involve the alignment and integration of different corporate defense components. Although not yet as prevalent or mature as either type of GRC, these developments are reflected in the services being offered in the corporate defense space. Table 11.2 highlights examples of some of these services on offer.

---

**TABLE 11.2**
**Trilateral Corporate Defense Services**

| | |
|---|---|
| Governance risk and assurance | Compliance controls assurance |
| Governance controls assurance | Intelligence security and resilience |
| Risk security and resilience | Security risk intelligence |
| Risk controls assurance | Security controls assurance |

---

### 11.3.5  Fourth-Order Convergence

Convergence developments at this level are somewhat less complete and less mature in their development. A number of interdisciplinary concepts are now emerging however that involve learning from, and borrowing certain aspects of, four different corporate defense components. Although these concepts do not necessarily represent component convergence in its purest sense, this does involve the alignment of these disciplines as part of a broader objective that indicates continued interdisciplinary progression involving corporate defense practitioners.

#### 11.3.5.1  Quadrilateral Integration

The level of integration here may not be as comprehensive or clear-cut as the earlier orders of convergence referred to above; however, concepts at this level highlight the continued fusion of ideas, knowledge, and practices between corporate defense disciplines, this time involving four different components. The following are examples of quadrilateral developments:

*Integrated assurance framework*: This is a recent concept that has emerged out of the assurance component and an increasing number of assurance seminars and conferences are now setting time aside in both sessions and workshops to address this topic. An integrated assurance framework is fundamentally concerned with the practicalities of harnessing the additional assurance that can be gleaned by assurance providers from the governance, risk, and controls components. Such an approach is also commonly referred to as *collective assurance* and *combined assurance*. This framework represents an attempt to reengineer the assurance operating model so that values and synergies can be unlocked. By linking these areas, it is hoped that organizations can create a more dynamic and sustainable assurance model. South Africa's King III describes it as follows: "Combined Assurance: Integrating and aligning assurance processes in a company to maximize risk and governance oversight and control efficiencies, and optimise overall assurance to the audit and risk committee, considering the company's risk appetite" (IOD SA 2009).

*Integrated reporting framework*: This concept has emerged out of the reporting element of the intelligence component and appears to be gaining increasing international recognition. The integrated reporting international framework (IIRC 2013b) represents a broader initiative to expand the remit for corporate reporting beyond financial and sustainability reporting. The framework itself does however incorporate aspects of the intelligence component through its recognition of intellectual capital as one of an organization's primary forms of capital and of course its guiding principles focus on addressing reporting issues. The framework specifically addresses governance and risk components in its content elements and a separate initiative has separately been undertaken to address the assurance requirements of integrated reporting (IIRC 2015).

### 11.3.6  Fifth-Order Convergence

Convergence developments at this level are somewhat limited or restricted in the scope of their convergence; however, certain long-established and emerging interdisciplinary concepts do include elements of five different corporate defense components.

#### 11.3.6.1  Pentalateral Integration

The following concepts involve a certain degree of interdisciplinary integration involving five critical components. The level of integration of each component is not necessarily equal; however, they serve to highlight an acceptance that certain aspects of each of these components are required to be in alignment in order to help achieve common objectives. The following are examples of pentalateral developments:

*Internal control—integrated framework*: This long established COSO internal control framework (COSO 1992)* was designed to provide a reasonable level of assurance regarding the achievement of the entity's objectives (i.e., operations, financial reporting, and compliance). The framework views internal control as consisting of five interrelated components that imprecisely correspond to critical corporate defense disciplines. First, the *control environment* whose associated principles relate to the governance discipline. Second, *risk assessment* whose associated principles relate to the risk discipline. Third, *control activities* whose associated principles relate to the controls discipline. Fourth, *information and communication* whose associated principles relate to the intelligence discipline. Finally, *monitoring activities* whose associated principles relate to the assurance discipline. While one of its stated objectives relates to compliance, it does not assign a specific component for compliance.

*ERM integrated framework*: This well-established COSO ERM framework (COSO 2004) was geared toward achieving the entity's objectives (i.e., strategic, operations, reporting, and compliance). It is expected to provide reasonable assurance of achieving those objectives. The framework views ERM as consisting of eight interrelated components that imprecisely correspond to critical corporate defense disciplines. They are the *control environment* and *objective setting* components whose associated principles relate to the governance discipline; the *event identification*, *risk assessment* and *risk response* components whose associated principles relate to the risk discipline; the *control activities* component whose associated principles relate to the controls discipline; the *information and communication* component whose associated principles relate to the intelligence discipline; and, finally, the *monitoring activities* whose associated principles relate to the assurance discipline. Although one of its stated objectives relates to compliance, it does not assign a specific component for compliance.

*Business resilience model*: The concept of business resilience has emerged from the IT sector whereby resilience is now viewed not only as a business continuity and disaster recovery issue but increasingly in terms of a number of other imperatives, which also encompass compliance and risk management as well as security and intelligence perspectives (IBM 2004). Business resilience is concerned with aligning these imperatives in order to deliver a resilient IT strategy. Significant attention is also now being focused on resilience outside of the IT sector and its important role in delivering long-term sustainability. This has seen the development of concepts such as enterprise resilience (BAH 2004), resiliency engineering (SEI 2007), and resilient dynamism (WEF 2013), all of which to varying degrees promote a more collaborative approach to resiliency.

### 11.3.6.2 Going Forward

Obviously supporters of individual disciplines or components may quite naturally have a preference for one particular approach over another, depending on their own skill set. In some cases, a number of these approaches may be separately developing within an organization with different critical components as the drivers. As contemporary corporate defense continues to develop and evolve, the cross-functional convergence and interdisciplinary integration of the corporate defense components have a significant part to play in this ongoing evolutionary process.

---

* The COSO Internal Control—Integrated Framework has since been updated in 2013.

## 11.4   A CROSS-FUNCTIONAL CORPORATE DEFENSE ROADMAP

Corporate defense developments at a cross-functional level are ongoing; however, without a clear vision such developments are likely to be sporadic, erratic, and inconsistent. Logically such development is best served by a deliberate roadmap that clearly outlines the journey ahead and the critical destination points along the way.

### 11.4.1   MOVING TOWARD CROSS-FUNCTIONAL MATURITY

The cross-functional developments previously described only serve to highlight the fact that there is an acknowledgment of the requirement to break new ground if organizations are to continue to improve on the effectiveness and efficiency of their corporate defense efforts. It also serves to highlight a willingness to explore different new approaches in the search for this improvement. Unfortunately, the advances made appear to have occurred in a somewhat random order as the integration of different corporate defense components appears to be occurring in a somewhat haphazard manner. It would also appear that these advances are being organically driven from the bottom-up, rather than being strategically driven from the top-down. To some extent this is reflected in the indiscriminate nature of these developments. It has also resulted in a disorganized approach whereby instead of complementing and supporting ongoing progression, many of these developments are often competing with each other and are therefore a drag on the limited resources available.

#### 11.4.1.1   Strategic Corporate Defense Direction

In order to accelerate this development process and arrive at a common objective in an organized and systematic manner, what is now required is a level of clear strategic direction that focuses on the eventual long-term strategic objective rather than ad-hoc short-term goals. In this particular scenario, the end game represents a fully developed and mature corporate defense framework that involves the multilateral collaboration, the interdisciplinary integration, and the cross-functional convergence of all of the critical corporate defense components.

### 11.4.2   THE CROSS-FUNCTIONAL MATURITY MODEL: A FIVE-STEP ROADMAP

The concept of introducing a corporate defense program that integrates all of these critical components has a definite commonsense appeal. Many commentators have however expressed reservations as to the complexity of implementing such a program. The solution to this perceived dilemma is perhaps more simple than many realize. Rather than introducing yet another new framework, organizations need to carefully reorganize their existing activities into a more efficient structure and actually leverage from the work already being done. Simply by taking a more strategic cross-functional view, organizations can quite easily apply the functional maturity model referred to above, only this time apply it in a cross-functional context. The resulting five-step roadmap helps to clearly envision this cross-functional journey, while also acknowledging that certain more progressive organizations may already have progressed some way down the road on this journey whether by accident or by design.

#### 11.4.2.1   Step 1: The Disparate Phase

Step 1 is to recognize that the organization is currently operating in the disparate phase. At a cross-functional level, this phase represents an organization with a traditional view of corporate defense as its corporate defense components tend to operate in silo-type structures. This means that they are not in alignment with one another, but rather they operate in isolation as there tends to be little or no interaction, sharing of information, or indeed collaboration. Frequently, there is also very little cross-functional support among these activities as each activity is operating toward its own narrow view and objective, and as a result they can very often be the subject of internal power struggles. Very often the overall responsibility and accountability for corporate defense is dispersed or fragmented, diluted or ambiguous. In certain scenarios, it can sometimes even be non-existent.

The cross-functional organizational value associated with this phase of development is considered minimum. In fact as a consequence of this type of traditional mind-set, an organization can be subject to typically negative impacts. Confusion relating to overall responsibility and accountability can result in omissions or gaps, and these in turn can create vulnerabilities that can later be exploited, rendering many other related best efforts ineffective in the process. Silo-type structures typically result in multiple intersections, duplications, and overlaps of activities that can result in considerable inefficiencies and unnecessary redundancies from an operational perspective. In worst-case scenarios, the power struggles that can occur from silo-type environments can actually develop into full-scale turf wars, and this can be extremely detrimental to its corporate health and leads to the creation of a dysfunctional organization.

### 11.4.2.2   Step 2: The Centralized Phase

Step 2 is to move toward consolidating all of these critical components under one umbrella and introduce a centralized corporate defense unit or function. At a cross-functional level, this phase represents an organization that is developing a strategic view of corporate defense and a more comprehensive understanding of the complexities of the task of managing the critical components collectively. There is now recognition of both the links and interconnections that exist between the organization's defense-related activities and the symbiotic nature of their interdependence. There is also a clearer appreciation of the correlations that exist between these activities and the possible cascade of consequences that can result, not only direct first-order consequences but indirect second- and third-order consequences that can occur further down the road.

The cross-functional organizational value associated with this stage of development is improving but is still considered to be limited. By converging all of these components under a unified management approach, the organization can help to eliminate any confusion that may exist in relation to responsibility and accountability, which in turn diminishes the potential negative issues that can result from any lack of clarity. Corporate defense is now recognized as a holistic discipline requiring a strategic focus and begins to acquire appropriate status and authority within the organization. There is also the opportunity to introduce an improved stakeholder focus in terms of strategically safeguarding the varying interests of its multiple stakeholders.

### 11.4.2.3   Step 3: The Enterprise-Wide Phase

Step 3 is to take the organization to the next level by focusing on ensuring that the organization's corporate defense philosophy and standards are tactically embedded into the culture of the enterprise. From a cross-functional perspective, this phase represents a move toward a more sustainable approach to defending the organization as it now knows exactly where it needs to go, knows how to get there, and recognizes the need to build the required components into their tactical processes. Agreed standards form the basis for the consistent application of corporate defense throughout the organization. The resulting tactical planning will help align defense policies and best practices and will also help in the education of the organization.

The cross-functional organizational value associated with this stage of development is now considered to be increasing to reasonable as enterprise standards are now in place enabling the adoption of a coherent approach to corporate defense throughout the organization. As consistent policies are applied, there are now similar expectations in all areas as the organization is now able to manage its corporate defense in a systematic manner, which means that where intersections do occur they can now be engineered in a structured manner. The result is cost savings associated with the identification and elimination of duplications, and reductions in overlaps and redundancies, which were inherited from the silo-type environment.

### 11.4.2.4   Step 4: The Integrated Phase

Step 4 represents a move toward a seamless real-time integration of its corporate defense compo-nents. From a cross-functional perspective, this phase represents both the vertical and horizontal integration of its people, processes, and systems via a cybernetic loop that enables the real-time communication of intelligence, which is vital in order to make accurate and timely decisions. This level of integration facilitates the achievement of both top-down and bottom-up buy-in among management and staff, which is necessary to encourage increased operational collaboration and knowledge sharing across all of the components. It also helps to foster cross-functional support, which is required to ensure that corporate defense becomes part of the organization's DNA at a pro-cedural level. Responding to the business needs of more progressive organizations, many leading vendors in this space are now developing and providing end-to-end technology solutions that are enabling this level of integration to become possible.

At this phase of development, an organization now begins to see superior value being added in this space. The organization now has fully integrated reporting in place for its corporate defense activities and has now determined its essential measurement metrics. This means that goals now become quantifiable and therefore performance becomes more predictable. Using these measurement metrics, management can now begin to anticipate and evaluate its corporate defense performance in totality. Management can now determine methods to modify and amend its corporate defense procedures to suit particular circumstances without significant reductions in quality or divergence from its defined benchmarks. Its defense activities are now operating in unison toward common objectives resulting in increased transparency and accountability. There is now improved process alignment resulting in further reductions in associated costs, thus lead-ing to superior efficiency and effectiveness while at the same time also resulting in enhanced stakeholder support.

### 11.4.2.5   Step 5: The Optimized Phase

Step 5 represents arriving at the phase whereby the organization is now optimizing the use of its corporate defense resources. By further education and partnership, the organization begins to empower its workforce, thus enabling it to unlock its latent potential. Through this part-nership, the organization now has the opportunity to further synchronize and synthesize its cross-functional activities creating an optimization of its capabilities. This involves leveraging operational processes and maximizing the possible synergies that exist. Optimized processes are flexible, adaptable, and innovative, dependent on the participation of an empowered workforce, and the alignment with business values and the objectives of the organization. By focusing on the pursuit of excellence, practices begin to evolve in a flexible and adaptable way. Through constant vigilance, the organization is now able to accelerate its reaction times in terms of anticipating, preventing, detecting, and reacting to potential vulnerabilities thereby improving its preemp-tive capabilities and reducing potential liability. By collectively defending the organization the robustness of its defense program is hardened, resulting in both increased resilience and ulti-mately increased stakeholder comfort.

At this phase of development an organization now begins to realize optimal value from its defen-sive investments. Constant revision results in process streamlining, leading to optimal efficiency and effectiveness and resulting in sustainable value creation. The effects of the organization's efforts to improve activities are now assessed and evaluated against the quantitative and qualitative improvement benchmarks. The organization's ability to rapidly react to changes and identify oppor-tunities is enhanced by finding ways to accelerate learning and share knowledge. At this phase, business processes are concerned with addressing root causes of process exceptions, variations, and anomalies, and continuously adapting its processes in order to constantly improve business perfor-mance and productivity. This means diminishing overheads, improved performance, and increased productivity resulting in a competitive advantage for the organization.

## 11.5  TOWARD A HOLISTIC VISION

Evolutionary developments, both functional and cross-functional, should not necessarily be viewed in a traditional linear context as in some organizations many of these developments may be occurring concurrently, at both a functional and a cross-functional level. This can result in a variety of different maturity levels developing across the different corporate defense components at a functional level, while the organization is concurrently attempting to improve its maturity level at a cross-functional level. Progress is not necessarily dependent on all the "*T*"s being crossed and "*i*" 's being dotted; however, it is important to be aware of where inconsistent maturity levels do exist among the different corporate defense components. Regardless of the individual developments, there is no denying that the overall motivation for this seemingly endless exploration is the ongoing quest for a more holistic solution in this space.

### 11.5.1  COLLECTIVE REQUIREMENTS

The developments described above represent varying levels of progression in the area of corporate defense at tactical and operational levels. If one takes a more strategic view however it becomes possible to see that these cross-functional developments have in fact identified a number of collective requirements. Organizations need to recognize that these collective requirements will form the basis for future progress in this area. Table 11.3 highlights examples of these common requirements.

### 11.5.2  THE NEXT EVOLUTIONARY STEP

From an overall perspective, it would appear that there is still quite some distance to be traveled before the corporate defense stage of this evolutionary journey is near completion. The final destination, if there is such a thing, must surely involve a more comprehensive and holistic view of corporate defense and a multilateral integration of different skills and expertise from all of the critical corporate defense components. In this way, the important challenges facing the organization can be simultaneously viewed from different perspectives, thereby incorporating much needed *checks and balances* and reducing the risk of blind spots due to any personal or professional bias.

**TABLE 11.3**
**Common Requirements**

| | |
|---|---|
| A strategic focus | The convergence of complimentary disciplines |
| An enterprise-wide vision | A continuous improvement process |
| A comprehensive strategy | An adaptable approach |
| A strategic plan | The integration of systems and processes |
| The alignment of objectives | The implementation of flexible solutions |
| A unified management structure | |

# 12  The Corporate Defense Management Framework

You cannot conceive the many without the one.[*]

**Plato**

## 12.1  THE REQUIREMENT FOR A HOLISTIC APPROACH

Everyday in the media we hear and read about corporate scandals or corporate failures where organizations have found themselves in difficulties all of their own making. These are often as a result of an event and/or a series of events, which in retrospect the organization could have and should have better anticipated, prevented, detected, or reacted to. In-depth analysis of almost any recent corporate scandal or corporate failure will inevitably expose common corporate defense frailty and fragility and result in the identification of both deficiencies in a number of critical corporate defense components and oversight weaknesses at each line of corporate defense. Such frailty and fragility have led to unnecessary large-scale losses and significant reputation damage, and negatively impacted on stakeholder interests (Lyons 2013).

Prior to the global financial crisis, risk management (enterprise risk management [ERM] in particular) was being touted as the best approach to successful value preservation. Ironically, financial institutions had been among the earliest adopters of the ERM framework and up until then had been well publicized as having the most mature and sophisticated ERM programs in place. Unfortunately, in the aftermath of the global financial crisis, numerous reviews identified that the crisis was a result

---

[*] Per *Parmenides*, 2015, Plato, Aeterna Press, London, UK.

of weaknesses and failures in how risks were identified, assessed, and managed. The financial system in particular was accused of ignoring warnings and failing to question, understand, and manage evolving risks (Lyons 2015). One of the key messages outlined by the United Nations Conference on Trade and Development (UNCTAD) in their report entitled "Corporate Governance in the Wake of the Financial Crisis" stated the following: "In particular, reform efforts should focus on: a) strengthening board oversight of management; b) positioning risk management as a key board responsibility, and; c) encouraging remuneration practices that balance risk and long-term performance criteria" (UNCTAD 2010).

The global financial crisis served to highlight that a singular focus on any one discipline, no matter how advanced it is perceived to be, can ultimately result in a false sense of confidence. Focusing on any one corporate defense discipline in isolation of the other critical disciplines can result in blind spots that, if they remain undetected, can be potentially devastating to the organization. Blind spots can be the result of a myopic view, or in an overreliance on any one particular perspective; therefore, effective corporate defense requires a holistic perspective.

### 12.1.1 A Holistic Vision of Corporate Defense

A holistic corporate defense program should be designed to help ensure that the organization's defense-related activities are in alignment with and actually reinforce corporate strategy to maximize their added value. In the process, it should provide an appropriate system of checks and balances to help ensure that an organization's defense-related activities are strategically aligned, tactically integrated, and operating in unison toward common objectives. The introduction of such a formal systematic defense program can help an organization to arrive at balanced, informed decisions, and help support the achievement of business objectives while also providing both *defense-in-depth* and *defense-in-breadth* (Lyons 2012b).

#### 12.1.1.1 Defense-in-Breadth: A Multilateral View

*Defense-in-breadth* in the corporate defense context can be achieved by first acknowledging the essential contributions that need to be made by all of the critical corporate defense components. It involves appreciating their essential individual contributions to the formation of the required robust system of checks and balances. It involves adopting a multilateral view, whereby individual situations are viewed from the perspectives of each of the critical components (e.g., *governance-centric*, *risk-centric*, *compliance-centric*, *intelligence-centric*, *security-centric*, *resilience-centric*, *controls-centric*, and *assurance-centric*). This includes ensuring that the perspectives of all of the critical components are considered at strategic, tactical, and operational levels throughout the organization. *Defense-in-breadth* involves adopting an interdisciplinary and cross-functional perspective in order to help ensure that the essential individual and collective contributions of each of these critical components is harnessed and optimized. A holistic vision of corporate defense means acknowledging that the whole is greater than the sum of its individual parts.

#### 12.1.1.2 Defense-in-Depth: A Multilayered Structure

*Defense-in-depth* in the corporate defense context can be achieved by acknowledging the essential roles that need be played by each of the five lines of corporate defense. It involves appreciating their essential individual roles in the formation of the required robust system of checks and balances. It involves adopting a multilayered structure, whereby each individual line of defense needs to be effectively performing its corporate defense duties and be providing effective oversight of those other lines of defense to which it has been delegated such responsibility. This includes their oversight responsibility for each of the critical corporate defense components. *Defense-in-depth* involves effectively structuring the five lines of corporate defense in order to help ensure that there is effective supervision and oversight in place at all times. A holistic vision of corporate defense means understanding that the chain is only as strong as its weakest link.

## 12.1.2    Toward a New Corporate Defense Paradigm

A holistic vision of corporate defense therefore represents a change in paradigm and a new way of viewing the challenge posed by the value preservation imperative. The traditional narrow silo-type view of individual corporate defense components needs to be replaced with a broader inclusive view that embraces all of the critical corporate defense components. It requires a deeper understanding of the complexities of managing the organization's corporate defense activities from top to bottom. The traditional three lines of defense model needs to be replaced with an extended five lines of corporate defense framework that includes executive management and the board as critical strategic lines of defense.

### 12.1.2.1    An Enterprise-Wide Outlook

Corporate defense needs to be viewed as a wide-ranging requirement that is addressed in a truly enterprise-wide manner. This means that the corporate defense program needs to be complete in its scope in order to ensure that it covers all of the organization's sections, functions, departments, divisions, branches, subsidiaries, and so on. It needs to be comprehensive in its approach in order to ensure that it addresses all of the organizations activities including its front, middle, and back office activities. It needs to be thorough in application in order to ensure it addresses all of the organization's people, processes, and systems. It needs to be all embracing in order to ensure it addresses all of the organization's products and services, and their related supply chains, both upstream and downstream. By viewing corporate defense in an enterprise-wide manner, it becomes possible to introduce a systematic approach to all of the corporate defense activities throughout the organization. This helps to ensure that there is a consistent level of corporate defense in operation in all areas regardless of location and at all times regardless of time zone. An appreciation that *the chain is only as strong as its weakest link* means that all facets of the organization need to be addressed.

### 12.1.2.2    A Multidimensional Approach

Corporate defense needs to acknowledge that the organization represents a complex system, and in order to understand its complexity, an appropriate level of critical thinking is required. A multidimensional approach involves not only adopting a 360 degree view, but also a three-dimensional view, top to bottom, side to side, and front to back. This includes considering the nature and level of the interactions, interconnections, and interdependences that may exist throughout the organization. It includes considering the strategic, tactical, and operational relationships that exist and their potential influence and consequence, be it a financial or nonfinancial impact. It includes considering the potential knock-on ramifications that any one part of the organization may have on other parts, either directly or indirectly, intended or unintended, or expected or unexpected.

A multidimensional approach can help enable an organization to finally see *the forest from the trees* and focus on the bigger picture. The bigger picture is required in order to effectively unify the defense objectives of the critical defense components and to facilitate a robust collective approach to anticipating, preventing, detecting, and reacting to hazard events as they materialize. Furthermore, a multidimensional approach helps to ensure that all of the critical corporate defense components are operating together in unison and in harmony, similar to musical instruments in a symphony orchestra where everyone is reading from the same music sheet.

### 12.1.2.3    Corporate Defense Management and Mixed Martial Arts

In Chapter 5, developments in corporate defense were compared to developments in self-defense, and in particular to the martial arts. Across different continents, various types of traditional martial arts have been developed over the centuries to become disciplined forms of self-defense. In more recent times, many of these forms of unarmed combat have developed into international combat sports. The early hybrid martial art of *kickboxing* has recently been somewhat overtaken by the phenomenon of mixed martial arts (MMA) as a mainstream combat sport. MMA is the story of the evolution of an elite form of self-defense, which has integrated different aspects of traditional martial arts to become a more comprehensive martial art in its own right. Practitioners of MMA have learned that in order to compete at the very highest level, it is necessary to be well versed in both striking and grappling techniques and have therefore been trained in a number of the traditional martial arts in order to acquire the necessary skills. Top MMA fighters are expected to be well versed in stand-up styles such as *Boxing, Muay Thai, Taekwondo*, and *Karate* while also being proficient in on the ground styles by being well versed in styles such as *Wrestling, Judo, Aikido*, and *Brazilian ju-jitsu*. Although training in many of these martial arts styles was traditionally only thought on an individual basis, the challenge for the early exponents of MMA was to figure out how to integrate these very different skills into a coherent fighting style. These early MMA pioneers later set up specialist gyms dedicated to MMA training as a unique martial art where all of these diverse skills can be learned under one roof. The modern MMA fighter is now considered by many to be a much more well-rounded fighter, with a more holistic understanding of the fighting arts than the exponents of the more traditional martial arts. Martial arts legend Bruce Lee, considered by many to be the father of modern MMA, is reported to have stated: "The best fighter is not a Boxer, Karate, or Judo man. The best fighter is someone who can adapt on any style. He kicks too good for a Boxer, throws too good for a Karate man, and punches too good for a Judo man" (Martin 2008).

It is certainly possible to draw similarities between the evolution of MMA as an elite form of self-defense and the ongoing evolution of corporate defense disciplines discussed in the previous chapter. By combining elements of multiple corporate defense disciplines, organizations can learn to adapt to different sets of circumstances, and to be prepared for a multitude of different hazard situations. In this regard, the emerging concept of corporate defense management (CDM) could therefore be considered to be the corporate equivalent of MMA.

## 12.2    THE CORPORATE DEFENSE MANAGEMENT APPROACH

The concept of CDM was conceived in an effort to help organizations come to develop a holistic vision of corporate defense, which is in alignment with its business objectives. The CDM approach is intended to help provide the organization with an enterprise-wide outlook and to help it to adopt a multidimensional approach. The CDM methodology is designed to help an organization get to grips with its corporate defense responsibilities and to help the organization deliver both *defense-in-breadth* and *defense-in-depth* in the process.

### 12.2.1  CORPORATE DEFENSE MANAGEMENT

The concept of CDM could be described as an emerging discipline that has itself been evolving within its own individual maturity cycle. The intention is to help to deliver a more mature perspective on the management of corporate defense activities, and in the process help the organization to deliver on its value preservation imperative. Perhaps similar to MMA, it represents something of a hybrid discipline that recognizes the important roles of the more traditional corporate defense disciplines and appreciates the different skill sets required in order to be proficient in each of these disciplines. While building on the solid foundations laid by these more traditional corporate defense disciplines, CDM leverages from their complementary strengths in order to help mold them into a more coherent and integrated system.

#### 12.2.1.1  The Genesis of CDM

The concept of CDM was initially developed by the author to help address a common weakness in many organizations, which was the lack of alignment and integration of corporate defense activities at a tactical level. This lack of integration was typically a result of silo-type structures, whereby rather than operating together in unison, many corporate defense activities were not only operating in isolation from one another but were often regarded as rivals in direct competition with one another for scarce resources. In many cases, this led to conflict situations resulting in a certain degree of tension among these activities and often developing into friction and indeed open hostility. Such circumstances were considered very damaging for the overall corporate defense cause and presented a serious challenge to be addressed. CDM therefore represented an attempt to provide a practical solution to this dilemma by focusing on the common high-level objective that brings each of these corporate defense activities together, rather than allowing them to continue to focus on their own narrow objectives. The intention of CDM is to provide a blueprint on how these activities can collectively contribute to the achievement of their common high-level objective while in the process also helping to achieve their component-level objectives.

### 12.2.1.2 CDM Explained

Back in 2006, *corporate defense* was a term frequently in use and was perhaps intuitively understood. It was however noted that there was a distinct lack of detail as to its precise meaning that perhaps resulted in the fact that the role and purpose of corporate defense appeared not to be fully understood or indeed its worth fully appreciated. In an effort to explain the concept of the umbrella term *corporate defense* and its inherent objective, an early definition included the following: "Corporate Defence can be defined as an alchemy of both science and art, aimed at defending an organisation from a multitude of possible threats and vulnerabilities" (Lyons 2006a). Similarly in an effort to explain the CDM discipline as a holistic solution to the challenges facing corporate defense, an early definition was as follows: "... the discipline of managing corporate defence in order to adequately defend the interests of the stakeholders. It requires a proactive approach to co-ordinating and integrating a range of interrelated disciplines, which taken together can help to anticipate, prevent, detect and react to potential threats and vulnerabilities, thereby protecting the organisation from potential hazards" (Lyons 2006b).

### 12.2.2 CDM as a Corporate Defense Discipline

CDM as a distinct corporate defense discipline represents both a science and an art in its own right. The CDM approach refers to a specific attitude and mind-set, while also incorporating a system and methodology to help implement such an approach. Although it provides a blueprint on how organizations can integrate and manage their corporate defense activities at strategic, tactical, and operational levels, unfortunately there is no *silver bullet* or *one size fits all* that can be heuristically applied in every organization. Each organization is still required to tailor the CDM approach to best suit its own individual needs and circumstances. Unfortunately, for some organizations this challenge can prove to be an extremely daunting task and one that requires essential direction and support from the very top of the organization in order to have any realistic chance of succeeding.

### 12.2.2.1 First and Foremost a Management Discipline

First and foremost, CDM is a management discipline as it is concerned with the integrated management of the different corporate defense activities. In this regard, it has a number of different facets. At a strategic level, CDM is concerned with aligning corporate defense activities with the organization's business objectives in order to help ensure that corporate defense strategy reinforces and supports business strategy. In this way, corporate defense can ensure that it occupies a more prominent role in overall corporate strategy. At a tactical level, CDM is concerned with aligning individual corporate defense activities with the corporate defense strategy and in steering these activities toward a common purpose. It is concerned with the coordination and integration of these activities into a coherent unit. At an operational level, CDM is concerned with ensuring that operational practices are appropriately contributing toward the achievement of objectives and that reliance can be placed on the technical knowledge and expertise of the critical components to execute required operational practices on a day-to-day basis.

#### 12.2.2.2  Core Principles of CDM

Regardless of how corporate defense is organized within a given organization, certain high-level generic principles should be applied, which should underpin the organization's corporate defense efforts. The following generic issues need to be carefully considered and addressed:

*Board responsibilities*: The responsibilities of the board of directors in relation to corporate defense need to be clearly established and agreed upon in advance.

*Executive management responsibilities*: The responsibilities of executive management in relation to corporate defense need to be clearly established and agreed upon in advance.

*Corporate defense program*: The precise structure, scope, and resourcing of the corporate defense program and the individual corporate defense roles and responsibilities need to be clearly established and agreed upon in advance.

*Relationship guidance*: The nature of the relationship between the business and corporate defense activities needs to be clearly established and agreed upon in advance. In addition, the nature of the relationships among individual corporate defense components needs to be clearly established and agreed upon in advance.

### 12.3  INTRODUCING THE CDM FRAMEWORK

In order to help conceptualize the holistic nature of the corporate defense challenge, the CDM framework was conceived. The framework was envisaged as a practical mechanism to help organizations understand and appreciate the full extent of their corporate defense obligations in the fulfillment of their value preservation imperative. It was developed to help provide a logical structure to dealing with the challenge organizations face when addressing their corporate defense responsibilities and was designed to provide guidance in addressing each of the above principles (Lyons 2012b).

#### 12.3.1  Eight Critical Corporate Defense Components

The CDM framework incorporates each one of the critical corporate defense components within the framework and openly acknowledges the important role each one of these critical components has to play within the organization's corporate defense program.

##### 12.3.1.1  A Horizontal Perspective

Each of the critical corporate defense components can provide an organization with a slightly different perspective on any given subject matter. Although they may often share certain common views, it is fair to say that fundamentally each component's viewpoint will be influenced by its own unique discipline-centric perspective (e.g., *risk-centric, resilience-centric, control-centric*, etc.). By focusing on each of these critical components, both individually and collectively, it is possible to provide a broader overall perspective of how various issues or events could potentially impact on the organization. Although different organizations may place a greater or lesser level of expectation on individual components, each of these components is still required to be operating across the organization at strategic, tactical, and operational levels. It is therefore important that the different levels of the organization consider issues from each of these different perspectives before finalizing decisions. Very often these different perspectives can act as countermeasures and taken together can help provide a more balanced perspective.

##### 12.3.1.2  The CDM Octagon

In recognition that CDM can be seen to represent the corporate equivalent of MMA, the CDM octagon (Figure 12.1) can help organizations to visualize the fact that each of these components is considered specialist disciplines in their own right and help them understand the intricate

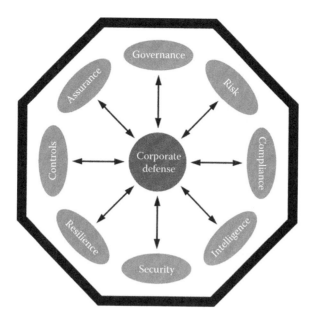

**FIGURE 12.1** The corporate defense management (CDM) octagon.

relationships and interactions that exist between all of these components. It serves to illustrate how each of these components is continuously interlinked, interconnected, and interdependent within a much broader corporate defense ecosystem. It helps to envisage how each of these components contributes to and receives from each of the other components, and therefore how each impacts on and is impacted by each of the other components. It also helps depict how developments in each of these components now mean that each component contains elements of the other components, and it is therefore increasingly difficult to determine where one component ends and another begins.

## 12.3.2 THE FIVE LINES OF CORPORATE DEFENSE

The CDM framework also incorporates the extended five lines of defense model within the framework and acknowledges the important oversight roles that each of these essential lines of defense has to play within the organization. This includes the critical strategic roles of executive management and the board of directors as essential strategic lines of defense. A comprehensive oversight structure is essential in order to transparently address the important issues of responsibility and accountability within the corporate defense program.

### 12.3.2.1 A Vertical Perspective

Each of these essential lines of defense can also provide a somewhat different perspective on any given subject matter at a point in time. Each is positioned at a different level within the organization and as such it provides a unique perspective based on this positioning, particularly in terms of its individual focus on different time horizons. For example, certain lines of defense can provide the organization with a strategic perspective that is more likely to be based on a longer time horizon than lines of defense providing a tactical or operational perspective. Certain lines of defense may in fact be expected to provide more than one perspective from time to time depending on specific circumstances. By relying on the perspectives of each of these essential lines of defense both individually and collectively, it is possible to provide a deeper overall perspective of how various issues or events could potentially impact on the organization over different time horizons.

### 12.3.2.2 From the Boardroom to the Frontlines

The five lines of corporate defense can help provide a comprehensive corporate defense model that operates all the way from the boardroom to the frontlines. Figure 12.2 outlines the five lines of corporate defense model from both vertical and horizontal perspectives.

In order to help ensure that each of the five lines of defense is operating effectively, each line has the dual (top-down and bottom-up) role of overseeing the lines of defense beneath them while also providing assurance to the lines of defense above them. Top-down monitoring and supervision begin at the boardroom and end on the frontlines of the business, thereby helping to provide necessary oversight at strategic, tactical, and operational levels. Bottom-up feedback and reporting begin on the frontlines of business and end at the boardroom, thereby helping to provide necessary assurance at operational, tactical, and strategic levels. Independent internal assurance may however be expected to provide assurance to executive management in relation to the activities of the first and second lines of defense via the use of the internal audit function, and also to the board in relation to not only the activities of the first and second lines of defense, but also in some cases the activities of executive management via the use of subcommittees of the board.

### 12.3.3 A MULTIDIMENSIONAL FRAMEWORK

A truly holistic perspective of corporate defense requires a conceptual integration of the critical corporate defense components with the essential five lines of corporate defense. The multidimensional CDM framework (Figure 12.3) helps to provide this holistic visualization (Lyons 2012c).

The CDM framework incorporates the required management of all of the critical corporate defense components at each of the different lines of defense. As such, the octagon pyramid helps to visualize and conceptualize the integration of the corporate defense components at each line of defense recognizing their continuous interactions, interconnections, and interdependences. The framework addresses the various responsibilities associated with each individual line of defense in relation to each of the critical components.

### 12.3.3.1 A Multidimensional Perspective

The CDM framework helps an organization to address its corporate defense responsibilities and accountabilities in an integrated manner from multiple perspectives. For example, at the board level, the board must be aware of its responsibilities and accountabilities in relation to each of the critical corporate defense components (i.e., *board governance, board risk, board compliance, board intelligence, board security, board resilience, board controls*, and *board assurance*). Similar issues must also be addressed in a systematic manner at each of the other lines of defense. For example, at the frontlines, operational line management (OLM) must also be aware of its responsibilities and accountabilities in relation to each of the critical corporate defense components (i.e., *OLM governance, OLM risk, OLM compliance, OLM intelligence, OLM security, OLM resilience, OLM controls*, and *OLM assurance*).

Each critical component vertical must also be addressed. For example, the governance vertical must address *board governance, executive management governance, independent assurance governance, tactical oversight governance*, and *OLM governance*. A similar process must also be addressed for each of the other critical component verticals (i.e., *board intelligence, executive management intelligence, independent assurance intelligence, tactical oversight intelligence*, and *OLM intelligence*). Such an approach can help an organization to ensure that its corporate defense components are strategically aligned, tactically integrated, and operating in unison toward common objectives. From a strategic perspective, the CDM framework focuses on both the vertical and the horizontal interconnectivities, thereby helping to create a cybernetic loop that enables the organization to continuously learn, improve, adapt, and evolve.

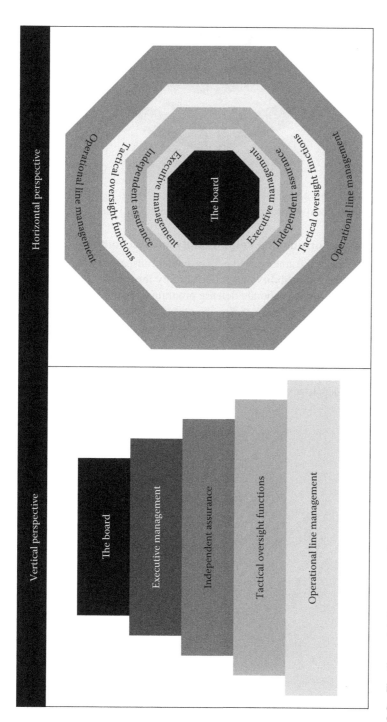

**FIGURE 12.2**  Five lines of defense perspectives.

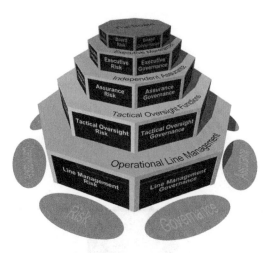

**FIGURE 12.3**   Multidimensional corporate defense management (CDM) framework.

### 12.3.3.2  Transparency Surrounding Responsibility and Accountability

The CDM approach provides a framework to help promote transparency in relation to the management of corporate defense responsibility and accountability throughout the organization. Through the integrated management of the corporate defense program, all parties are aware of not only their own corporate defense responsibilities, but also the corporate defense responsibilities of the other corporate defense parties. Figures 12.4 and 12.5 illustrate how the CDM framework helps promote a more transparent approach to corporate defense.[*]

By addressing corporate defense responsibility and accountability in a disciplined and systematic manner, the CDM framework therefore helps to provide an organization with a logical structure by which it can clearly delegate responsibility and at the same time provide a mechanism for holding

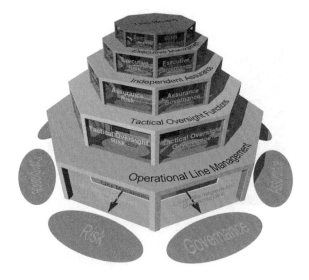

**FIGURE 12.4**   Five lines of defense transparency.

---

[*] In order to further visualize the inner workings of this framework, view a short video entitled "Corporate Defense Management (CDM): A Multi-Dimensional Framework," which is available online on YouTube at http://www.youtube.com/watch?v=vLoA8U0GZHI.

**FIGURE 12.5** Complete transparency.

individuals and groups to account for their responsibilities in an open and transparent manner. The framework helps provide an enhanced level of governance and control by creating a comprehensive system of *checks and balances* over the entire workings of the organization's corporate defense program.

In summary, this CDM multidimensional framework provides an organization with a systematic methodology that enables both the vertical and horizontal management of the organization's defense activities, and provides the organization (and its stakeholders) with both *defense-in-depth* and *defense-in-breadth* in the process. Functioning properly, it can help to ensure that the organization is fulfilling its fiduciary duties, legal obligations, and moral responsibilities, while at the same time helping to create durable value and sustainable economic performance. Such an approach helps the organization to practically demonstrate to its stakeholders that the institution is taking all reasonable steps to ensure that there is an appropriate program in place to help successfully defend its stakeholder interests, thereby providing its stakeholders with an enhanced level of comfort and an additional degree of confidence in this regard.

# Section III

*An Operational Perspective*

# 13 Inside the CDM Framework

Have patience. All things are difficult before they become easy.[*]

**Saadi**

## 13.1 A HOLISTIC VIEW OF CORPORATE DEFENSE

The adoption of a holistic view of the corporate defense challenge involves an appreciation that the purpose of corporate defense is to help the organization to implement its strategy and to achieve its objectives. Within this context, there is also an appreciation that the purpose of individual corporate defense activities is to help the organization to implement its corporate defense strategy and achieve the corporate defense objectives. A holistic view acknowledges that individual corporate defense activities are intimately interconnected and interdependent within a broader corporate defense framework. It also acknowledges that the responsibility for addressing corporate defense extends to all parts of the organization and across all levels. The corporate defense management (CDM) framework enables an organization to develop a holistic view of the corporate defense challenge and provides an organization with a methodology to deliver *defense-in-breadth* and *defense-in-depth*.

### 13.1.1 THE CDM MATRIX

The CDM framework by incorporating the critical corporate defense components and the essential lines of defense into a single framework provides a comprehensive matrix of the required corporate

---

[*] Per *The 15 Invaluable Laws of Growth: Live Them and Reach Your Potential*, 2012, John C. Maxwell, Center Street, New York, NY.

|  | Governance | Risk | Compliance | Intelligence | Security | Resilience | Controls | Assurance |
|---|---|---|---|---|---|---|---|---|
| **Board of directors** | Board governance | Board risk | Board compliance | Board intelligence | Board security | Board resilience | Board controls | Board assurance |
| **Executive management** | Executive governance | Executive risk | Executive compliance | Executive intelligence | Executive security | Executive resilience | Executive controls | Executive assurance |
| **Independent internal assurance** | Independent governance assurance | Independent risk assurance | Independent compliance assurance | Independent intelligence assurance | Independent security assurance | Independent resilience assurance | Independent controls assurance | Independent assurance assurance |
| **Tactical oversight functions** | Tactical governance oversight | Tactical risk oversight | Tactical compliance oversight | Tactical intelligence oversight | Tactical security oversight | Tactical resilience oversight | Tactical controls oversight | Tactical assurance oversight |
| **Operational line management** | Operational governance | Operational risk | Operational compliance | Operational intelligence | Operational security | Operational resilience | Operational controls | Operational assurance |

**FIGURE 13.1**   The CDM matrix.

defense activities at different levels within the organization. In essence, there is an obligation on every organization to engage in each of the critical components to differing degrees throughout the entire organization. The level of engagement may also differ over time depending on the organization's unique circumstances at any given point in time. Each of the fives lines of corporate defense has certain oversight responsibilities in relation to these critical components, in addition to specific direct responsibilities of their own related to these critical components. The CDM framework helps provide a blueprint for the organization on the different corporate defense requirements and responsibilities that exist at each level within the organization both vertically and horizontally. The CDM matrix provides the organization with a holistic snapshot of these multidimensional requirements and could also be incorporated into a high-level corporate defense dashboard if required. Figure 13.1 represents a practical illustration of the CDM matrix.

### 13.1.1.1   A High-Level Overview
Each organization must determine for itself the extent of its corporate defense activities. This includes the precise structure and formality of its corporate defense program. The CDM matrix provides a high-level overview of the corporate defense activities required to be included in a comprehensive corporate defense program. This integrated approach serves to highlight the organization's need to address each of the individual critical corporate defense components at each of the individual lines of defense. The CDM matrix therefore provides a consistent and systematic approach and a much needed structure to help an organization determine the extent of its requirements. The nature of

how each of these components is to be addressed requires due consideration and may vary from one organization to another.

## 13.1.2 Corporate Defense Due Diligence

The CDM matrix provides a clear basis for the organization to perform a corporate defense due diligence exercise in order to help establish its current corporate defense maturity, capability, and capacity. It is becoming increasingly likely that such a due diligence exercise will also become a future requirement of multiple stakeholder groups, including institutional investors, M&A suitors, rating agencies, regulators, and insurance companies.

### 13.1.2.1 Corporate Defense Gap Analysis

The adoption of a holistic view enables an organization to perform a gap analysis and to fully review its current corporate defense efforts, determine its future requirements, and establish what needs to be done in order to deliver on these future requirements. Such rigorous analysis involves examining, assessing, and evaluating its efforts in relation to each of the critical components programs in terms of its strategic, tactical, and operational aspects. It also involves a similar analysis of how these critical components are addressed at each of the essential lines of defense and the degree of clarity present surrounding corporate defense responsibilities and accountabilities at each line of defense.

## 13.2 CDM DEFENSE-IN-BREADTH

The critical corporate defense components help provide *defense-in-breadth* by providing the organization with a broad range of corporate defense perspectives. The CDM framework helps outline how an organization can hope to deliver *defense-in-breadth* by ensuring that each of the critical component initiatives is included in the broader corporate defense program. By incorporating the important aspects of each of the critical components into all aspects of the organization activities, a more concentrated and robust level of *defense-in-breadth* can be achieved.

### 13.2.1 Critical Components—A Vertical Viewpoint

Organizations are expected to undertake at least reasonable steps in each of their critical component initiatives. These initiatives, whether they are formal or informal, or, structured or unstructured, should at a minimum address the core elements of each of these critical components. This involves ensuring that the organization's required efforts in each of these components have been fully considered in relation to the specific component requirements at each of the individual lines of defense. The extent of an organization's individual initiative in each of the critical corporate defense components may vary from organization to organization depending on its type of business and its specific circumstances. Each organization should however be able to demonstrate that it has given due consideration and taken a reasonable approach in each of its critical component initiatives.

### 13.2.1.1 The Governance Initiative

Table 13.1 outlines some basic examples of governance-related matters that require due consideration at each line of defense.

**TABLE 13.1**
**The Governance Initiative**

|  | Governance—Particulars | Governance—Specific Issues |
|---|---|---|
| The board | Board governance oversight | Board composition and duties |
|  | Governance agenda | Board and executive remuneration |
|  | Governance culture | Accountability and audit |
|  | Governance program | Shareholder and stakeholder relations |
|  | Board level governance issues | Governance committee |
| Executive management | Governance environment | Strategy and planning |
|  | Governance awareness | Organizational design and structure |
|  | Governance profile | Delegation of authority |
|  | Governance coverage | Assignment of roles and responsibilities |
|  | Executive governance matters | Stakeholder management |
| Independent internal assurance | Governance program assurance | Risk governance assurance |
|  | Strategic governance assurance | Compliance governance assurance |
|  | Tactical governance assurance | Intelligence governance assurance |
|  | Operational governance assurance | Security governance assurance |
|  |  | Resilience governance assurance |
|  |  | Controls governance assurance |
|  |  | Assurance governance assurance |
| Tactical oversight functions | Governance framework | Charters |
|  | Governance classifications | Tactical plans and objectives |
|  | Governance obligations | Standards and guidance |
|  | Governance appraisal | Policies, principles, and methodology |
| Operational line management | Governance ownership | Operational plans |
|  | Governance execution | Operational objectives |
|  | Governance people | Business process objectives |
|  | Governance practices | Workflow programs and flowcharts |
|  | Governance processes and systems | Procedure manuals |

### 13.2.1.2 The Risk Initiative

Table 13.2 outlines some basic examples of risk-related matters that require due consideration at each line of defense.

**TABLE 13.2**
**The Risk Initiative**

| | Risk—Particulars | Risk—Specific Issues |
|---|---|---|
| The board | Board risk oversight | Enterprise-wide view of risk |
| | Risk agenda | Risk understanding and cognition |
| | Risk culture | Risk appetite |
| | Risk program | Reputation risk |
| | Board level risk issues | Risk committee |
| Executive management | Risk environment | Risk types and sources |
| | Risk awareness | Risk interconnectivity and velocity |
| | Risk profile | Risk tolerances and limits |
| | Risk coverage | Risk quantification and aggregation |
| | Executive risk matters | Risk adjusted capital allocation |
| Independent internal assurance | Risk program assurance | Governance risk assurance |
| | Strategic risk assurance | Compliance risk assurance |
| | Tactical risk assurance | Intelligence risk assurance |
| | Operational risk assurance | Security risk assurance |
| | | Resilience risk assurance |
| | | Controls risk assurance |
| | | Assurance risk assurance |
| Tactical oversight functions | Risk framework | Risk identification |
| | Risk classifications | Risk assessment |
| | Risk obligations | Risk response |
| | Risk appraisal | Risk models and monitoring |
| Operational line management | Risk ownership | Risk register |
| | Risk execution | Risk events |
| | Risk people | Risk probability and impact |
| | Risk practices | Inherent and residual risk |
| | Risk processes and systems | Risk treatment |

### 13.2.1.3   The Compliance Initiative

Table 13.3 outlines some basic examples of compliance-related matters that require due consideration at each line of defense.

**TABLE 13.3**
**The Compliance Initiative**

|  | Compliance—Particulars | Compliance—Specific Issues |
| --- | --- | --- |
| The board | Board compliance oversight | Integrity |
|  | Compliance agenda | Ethics and values |
|  | Compliance culture | Disclosure and transparency |
|  | Compliance program | Code of conduct |
|  | Board level compliance issues | Compliance committee |
| Executive management | Compliance environment | Integrity statement |
|  | Compliance awareness | Ethics program |
|  | Compliance profile | Fiduciary duties |
|  | Compliance coverage | Legal and regulatory |
|  | Executive compliance matters | Compliance attestation |
| Independent internal assurance | Compliance program assurance | Governance compliance assurance |
|  | Strategic compliance assurance | Risk compliance assurance |
|  | Tactical compliance assurance | Intelligence compliance assurance |
|  | Operational compliance assurance | Security compliance assurance |
|  |  | Resilience compliance assurance |
|  |  | Controls compliance assurance |
|  |  | Assurance compliance assurance |
| Tactical oversight functions | Compliance framework | Compliance interpretation and affect |
|  | Compliance classifications | Compliance education and training |
|  | Compliance obligations | Compliance advise |
|  | Compliance appraisal | Compliance testing and review |
| Operational line management | Compliance ownership | Operational compliance |
|  | Compliance execution | Contract compliance |
|  | Compliance people | Policy compliance |
|  | Compliance practices | Procedure compliance |
|  | Compliance processes and systems | Compliance controls |

#### 13.2.1.4 The Intelligence Initiative

Table 13.4 outlines some basic examples of intelligence-related matters that require due consideration at each line of defense.

**TABLE 13.4**
**The Intelligence Initiative**

| | Intelligence—Particulars | Intelligence—Specific Issues |
|---|---|---|
| The board | Board intelligence oversight | Board competency needs |
| | Intelligence agenda | Board education and training |
| | Intelligence culture | Board communications |
| | Intelligence program | Board reporting and access to information |
| | Board level intelligence issues | Intelligence committee |
| Executive management | Intelligence environment | Decision-making protocols |
| | Intelligence awareness | Communications infrastructure |
| | Intelligence profile | Information and knowledge management |
| | Intelligence coverage | Executive reporting |
| | Executive intelligence matters | Dashboards and balanced scorecards |
| Independent internal assurance | Intelligence program assurance | Governance intelligence assurance |
| | Strategic intelligence assurance | Risk intelligence assurance |
| | Tactical intelligence assurance | Compliance intelligence assurance |
| | Operational intelligence assurance | Security intelligence assurance |
| | | Resilience intelligence assurance |
| | | Controls intelligence assurance |
| | | Assurance intelligence assurance |
| Tactical oversight functions | Intelligence framework | Information and intelligence conversion |
| | Intelligence classifications | Knowledge sharing and learning |
| | Intelligence obligations | IT architecture and engineering |
| | Intelligence appraisal | Language and taxonomy |
| Operational line management | Intelligence ownership | Data management |
| | Intelligence execution | Intelligence applications |
| | Intelligence people | Change management |
| | Intelligence practices | Performance metrics |
| | Intelligence processes and systems | Internal and external reporting |

### 13.2.1.5　The Security Initiative

Table 13.5 outlines some basic examples of security-related matters that require due consideration at each line of defense.

**TABLE 13.5**
**The Security Initiative**

|  | Security—Particulars | Security—Specific Issues |
|---|---|---|
| The board | Board security oversight | Board security and protection |
|  | Security agenda | Strategic asset security |
|  | Security culture | Intellectual property (IP) security |
|  | Security program | Data privacy and cyber security |
|  | Board level security issues | Security committee |
| Executive management | Security environment | Executive protection and security |
|  | Security awareness | People protection and security |
|  | Security profile | Tangible and intangible asset security |
|  | Security coverage | Critical infrastructure security |
|  | Executive security matters | Supply chain security |
| Independent internal assurance | Security program assurance | Governance security assurance |
|  | Strategic security assurance | Risk security assurance |
|  | Tactical security assurance | Compliance security assurance |
|  | Operational security assurance | Intelligence security assurance |
|  |  | Resilience security assurance |
|  |  | Controls security assurance |
|  |  | Assurance security assurance |
| Tactical oversight functions | Security framework | Security domains |
|  | Security classifications | Security layers |
|  | Security obligations | Security architecture and engineering |
|  | Security appraisal | Security measures |
| Operational line management | Security ownership | Site and building security |
|  | Security execution | People and equipment security |
|  | Security people | Operations and facility security |
|  | Security practices | Network security |
|  | Security processes and systems | Information and data security |

### 13.2.1.6 The Resilience Initiative

Table 13.6 outlines some basic examples of resilience-related matters that require due consideration at each line of defense.

**TABLE 13.6**
**The Resilience Initiative**

| | Resilience—Particulars | Resilience—Specific Issues |
| --- | --- | --- |
| The board | Board resilience oversight | Board back-up and succession planning |
| | Resilience agenda | Leadership development |
| | Resilience culture | Crisis management |
| | Resilience program | Director and officer liability insurance |
| | Board level resilience issues | Resilience committee |
| Executive management | Resilience environment | Capital adequacy and allocation |
| | Resilience awareness | Emergency operations |
| | Resilience profile | Health and safety |
| | Resilience coverage | Talent management |
| | Executive resilience matters | Supply chain resilience |
| Independent internal assurance | Resilience program assurance | Governance resilience assurance |
| | Strategic resilience assurance | Risk resilience assurance |
| | Tactical resilience assurance | Compliance resilience assurance |
| | Operational resilience assurance | Intelligence resilience assurance |
| | | Security resilience assurance |
| | | Controls resilience assurance |
| | | Assurance resilience assurance |
| Tactical oversight functions | Resilience framework | Incident and emergency response |
| | Resilience classifications | Business continuity management |
| | Resilience obligations | Disaster recovery planning |
| | Resilience appraisal | Insurance |
| Operational line management | Resilience ownership | Back-up systems |
| | Resilience execution | Scenario planning and simulations |
| | Resilience people | Resiliency testing |
| | Resilience practices | Business impact analysis |
| | Resilience processes and systems | Root cause analysis |

### 13.2.1.7 The Controls Initiative

Table 13.7 outlines some basic examples of controls-related matters that require due consideration at each line of defense.

**TABLE 13.7**
**The Controls Initiative**

| | Controls—Particulars | Controls—Specific Issues |
|---|---|---|
| The board | Board controls oversight | Degree of trust and empowerment |
| | Controls agenda | Level of monitoring and supervision |
| | Controls culture | Level of control |
| | Controls program | Centralized v. decentralized approach |
| | Board level controls issues | Controls committee |
| Executive management | Controls environment | Balance autonomy and control |
| | Controls awareness | Segregation of duties |
| | Controls profile | Conflicts of interest |
| | Controls coverage | Whistle-blowing program |
| | Executive controls matters | Cost benefit trade-off |
| Independent internal assurance | Controls program assurance | Governance controls assurance |
| | Strategic controls assurance | Risk controls assurance |
| | Tactical controls assurance | Compliance controls assurance |
| | Operational controls assurance | Intelligence controls assurance |
| | | Security controls assurance |
| | | Resilience controls assurance |
| | | Assurance controls assurance |
| Tactical oversight functions | Controls framework | Preventative and detective controls |
| | Controls classifications | Manual and automated controls |
| | Controls obligations | Primary and secondary controls |
| | Controls appraisal | Controls testing and review |
| Operational line management | Controls ownership | Financial reporting controls |
| | Controls execution | Business control objectives |
| | Controls people | Business process controls |
| | Controls practices | Quality assurance controls |
| | Controls processes and systems | Front, middle, and back-office controls |

### 13.2.1.8 The Assurance Initiative

Table 13.8 outlines some basic examples of assurance-related matters that require due consideration at each line of defense.

**TABLE 13.8**
**The Assurance Initiative**

| | Assurance—Particulars | Assurance—Specific Issues |
|---|---|---|
| The board | Board assurance oversight | Board performance and evaluation |
| | Assurance agenda | Internal audit function |
| | Assurance culture | Executive management |
| | Assurance program | External auditors |
| | Board level assurance issues | Assurance/audit committee |
| Executive management | Assurance environment | Executive oversight |
| | Assurance awareness | Assurance types |
| | Assurance profile | System of checks and balances |
| | Assurance coverage | Sources of assurance |
| | Executive assurance matters | Due diligence |
| Independent internal assurance | Program assurance | Governance assurance |
| | Strategic assurance | Risk assurance |
| | Tactical assurance | Compliance assurance |
| | Operational assurance | Intelligence assurance |
| | | Security assurance |
| | | Resilience assurance |
| | | Controls assurance |
| Tactical oversight functions | Assurance framework | Audit and inspection review |
| | Assurance classifications | Due diligence and benchmarking review |
| | Assurance obligations | Fraud examination |
| | Assurance appraisal | Forensic investigation |
| Operational line management | Assurance ownership | Line management supervision |
| | Assurance execution | Management reviews |
| | Assurance people | Quality assurance |
| | Assurance practices | Continuous monitoring |
| | Assurance processes and systems | Self-assessments |

### 13.2.2  DEFENSE-IN-BREADTH ASSESSMENT

Each organization needs to be aware of the extent to which it provides sound *defense-in-breadth* to its stakeholders. In order to establish the robustness of its *defense-in-breadth,* each organization should review and assess each of the above critical component initiatives and consider the extent to which it is currently addressing its corporate defense requirements for each one of these initiatives at each line of defense.

#### 13.2.2.1  Initiative—Particulars

Due consideration should be given to the *particulars* section in each of the above examples as this can help an organization to assess if it is adopting a consistent approach to each one of the critical component initiatives. It can also help an organization to establish if each initiative is implementing a systematic approach at each individual line of defense.

#### 13.2.2.2  Initiative—Specific Issues

Due consideration should be given to the *specific issues* section in each of the above examples as this can help an organization assess the extent to which it is currently addressing the most important aspects of each critical component initiative. It can also help an organization to establish at which line of defense these important matters are being addressed within the organization.

## 13.3  CDM DEFENSE-IN-DEPTH

The five lines of corporate defense can help provide *defense-in-depth* by providing the organization with an in-depth insight into its corporate defense workings at strategic, tactical, and operational levels. The CDM framework helps outline how an organization can hope to deliver *defense-in-depth* by ensuring that each of the critical lines of defense is included in the broader corporate defense program. By incorporating the important responsibilities of each of the critical lines of defense into the organization's oversight framework, a more concentrated and robust level of *defense-in-depth* can be achieved.

### 13.3.1  LINES OF DEFENSE—A HORIZONTAL VIEW

Organizations are expected to reasonably assign corporate defense responsibilities at each of the lines of corporate defense. A lines of defense agenda, whether it is formal or informal, or, structured or unstructured, should include their responsibilities in relation to each of the critical components. This involves ensuring that the responsibilities associated with each critical component have been fully considered. The extent of an organization's individual line of defense agendas may vary from organization to organization depending on its organizational structure and type of business. Each organization should however be able to demonstrate that it has given due consideration and taken a reasonable approach to assigning corporate defense responsibilities as part of its lines of defense agendas.

### 13.3.1.1  The Board Agenda

Table 13.9 outlines some basic examples of board-related matters that require due consideration for each critical corporate defense component.

**TABLE 13.9**
**The Board Agenda**

|  | Board—Particulars | Board—Specific Issues |
| --- | --- | --- |
| Governance | Board governance oversight | Board composition and duties |
|  | Governance agenda | Board and executive remuneration |
|  | Governance culture | Accountability and audit |
|  | Governance program | Shareholder and stakeholder relations |
|  | Board level governance issues | Governance committee |
| Risk | Board risk oversight | Enterprise-wide view of risk |
|  | Risk agenda | Risk understanding and cognition |
|  | Risk culture | Risk appetite |
|  | Risk program | Reputation risk |
|  | Board level risk issues | Risk committee |
| Compliance | Board compliance oversight | Integrity |
|  | Compliance agenda | Ethics and values |
|  | Compliance culture | Disclosure and transparency |
|  | Compliance program | Code of conduct |
|  | Board level compliance issues | Compliance committee |
| Intelligence | Board intelligence oversight | Board competency needs |
|  | Intelligence agenda | Board education and training |
|  | Intelligence culture | Board communications |
|  | Intelligence program | Board reporting and access to information |
|  | Board level intelligence issues | Intelligence committee |
| Security | Board security oversight | Board security and protection |
|  | Security agenda | Strategic asset security |
|  | Security culture | IP security |
|  | Security program | Data privacy and cyber security |
|  | Board level security issues | Security committee |
| Resilience | Board resilience oversight | Board back-up and succession planning |
|  | Resilience agenda | Leadership development |
|  | Resilience culture | Crisis management |
|  | Resilience program | Director and officer liability insurance |
|  | Board level resilience issues | Resilience committee |
| Controls | Board controls oversight | Degree of trust and empowerment |
|  | Controls agenda | Level of monitoring and supervision |
|  | Controls culture | Level of control |
|  | Controls program | Centralized v. decentralized approach |
|  | Board level controls issues | Controls committee |
| Assurance | Board assurance oversight | Board performance and evaluation |
|  | Assurance agenda | Internal audit function |
|  | Assurance culture | Executive management |
|  | Assurance program | External auditors |
|  | Board level assurance issues | Assurance/audit committee |

### 13.3.1.2 The Executive Management Agenda

Table 13.10 outlines some basic examples of executive management-related matters that require due consideration for each critical corporate defense component.

**TABLE 13.10**

**The Executive Management Agenda**

| | Executive—Particulars | Executive—Specific Issues |
|---|---|---|
| Governance | Governance environment | Strategy and planning |
| | Governance awareness | Organizational design and structure |
| | Governance profile | Delegation of authority |
| | Governance coverage | Assignment of roles and responsibilities |
| | Executive governance matters | Stakeholder management |
| Risk | Risk environment | Risk types and sources |
| | Risk awareness | Risk interconnectivity and velocity |
| | Risk profile | Risk tolerances and limits |
| | Risk coverage | Risk quantification and aggregation |
| | Executive risk matters | Risk adjusted capital allocation |
| Compliance | Compliance environment | Integrity statement |
| | Compliance awareness | Ethics program |
| | Compliance profile | Fiduciary duties |
| | Compliance coverage | Legal and regulatory |
| | Executive compliance matters | Compliance attestation |
| Intelligence | Intelligence environment | Decision-making |
| | Intelligence awareness | Communications infrastructure |
| | Intelligence profile | Information and knowledge management |
| | Intelligence coverage | Executive reporting |
| | Executive intelligence matters | Dashboards and scorecards |
| Security | Security environment | Executive protection and security |
| | Security awareness | People protection and security |
| | Security profile | Tangible and intangible asset security |
| | Security coverage | Critical infrastructure security |
| | Security matters | Supply chain security |
| Resilience | Resilience environment | Capital adequacy and allocation |
| | Resilience awareness | Emergency operations |
| | Resilience profile | Health and safety |
| | Resilience coverage | Talent management |
| | Executive resilience matters | Supply chain resilience |
| Controls | Controls environment | Balance autonomy v control |
| | Controls awareness | Segregation of duties |
| | Controls profile | Conflicts of interest |
| | Controls coverage | Whistle-blowing program |
| | Executive controls matters | Cost benefit trade-off |
| Assurance | Assurance environment | Executive oversight |
| | Assurance awareness | Assurance types |
| | Assurance profile | System of checks and balances |
| | Assurance coverage | Sources of assurance |
| | Executive assurance matters | Due diligence |

### 13.3.1.3 The Independent Internal Assurance (IIA) Agenda

Table 13.11 outlines some basic examples of IIA-related matters that require due consideration for each critical corporate defense component.

**TABLE 13.11**
**The IIA Agenda**

|  | IIA—Particulars | IIA—Specific Issues[a] |
|---|---|---|
| Governance | Governance program assurance<br>Strategic governance assurance<br>Tactical governance assurance<br>Operational governance assurance | Risk governance assurance<br>Compliance governance assurance<br>Intelligence governance assurance<br>Security governance assurance<br>Resilience governance assurance<br>Controls governance assurance<br>Assurance governance assurance |
| Risk | Risk program assurance<br>Strategic risk assurance<br>Tactical risk assurance<br>Operational risk assurance | Governance risk assurance<br>Compliance risk assurance<br>Intelligence risk assurance<br>Security risk assurance<br>Resilience risk assurance<br>Controls risk assurance<br>Assurance risk assurance |
| Compliance | Compliance program assurance<br>Strategic compliance assurance<br>Tactical compliance assurance<br>Operational compliance assurance | Governance compliance assurance<br>Risk compliance assurance<br>Intelligence compliance assurance<br>Security compliance assurance<br>Resilience compliance assurance<br>Controls compliance assurance<br>Assurance compliance assurance |
| Intelligence | Intelligence program assurance<br>Strategic intelligence assurance<br>Tactical intelligence assurance<br>Operational intelligence assurance | Governance intelligence assurance<br>Risk intelligence assurance<br>Compliance intelligence assurance<br>Security intelligence assurance<br>Resilience intelligence assurance<br>Controls intelligence assurance<br>Assurance intelligence assurance |
| Security | Security program assurance<br>Strategic security assurance<br>Tactical security assurance<br>Operational security assurance | Governance security assurance<br>Risk security assurance<br>Compliance security assurance<br>Intelligence security assurance<br>Resilience security assurance<br>Controls security assurance<br>Assurance security assurance |
| Resilience | Resilience program assurance<br>Strategic resilience assurance<br>Tactical resilience assurance<br>Operational resilience assurance | Governance resilience assurance<br>Risk resilience assurance<br>Compliance resilience assurance<br>Intelligence resilience assurance<br>Security resilience assurance<br>Controls resilience assurance<br>Assurance resilience assurance |

*(Continued)*

**TABLE 13.11 (*Continued*)**
**The IIA Agenda**

|  | IIA—Particulars | IIA—Specific Issues[a] |
|---|---|---|
| Controls | Controls program assurance | Governance controls assurance |
|  | Strategic controls assurance | Risk controls assurance |
|  | Tactical controls assurance | Compliance controls assurance |
|  | Operational controls assurance | Intelligence controls assurance |
|  |  | Security controls assurance |
|  |  | Resilience controls assurance |
|  |  | Assurance controls assurance |
| Assurance[b] | Program assurance | Governance assurance |
|  | Strategic assurance | Risk assurance |
|  | Tactical assurance | Compliance assurance |
|  | Operational assurance | Intelligence assurance |
|  |  | Security assurance |
|  |  | Resilience assurance |
|  |  | Controls assurance |

[a] The provision of independent internal assurance on the activities of the organization, including these specific corporate defense issues.

[b] The extent to which the IIA is the primary provider of assurance will determine whether or not it is appropriate for the IIA to provide assurance on the assurance program itself and other assurance that is already being provided by the other lines of defense. There are circumstances where it may be more appropriate to employ an external third party to provide this independent assurance.

### 13.3.1.4  The Tactical Oversight Functions (TOF) Agenda

Table 13.12 outlines some basic examples of TOF-related matters that require due consideration for each critical corporate defense component.

**TABLE 13.12**
**The TOF Agenda**

| | TOF—Particulars | TOF—Specific Issues |
|---|---|---|
| Governance | Governance framework | Charters |
| | Governance classifications | Tactical plans and objectives |
| | Governance obligations | Standards and guidance |
| | Governance appraisal | Policies, principles, and methodology |
| Risk | Risk framework | Risk identification |
| | Risk classifications | Risk assessment |
| | Risk obligations | Risk response |
| | Risk appraisal | Risk models and monitoring |
| Compliance | Compliance framework | Compliance interpretation and affect |
| | Compliance classifications | Compliance education and training |
| | Compliance obligations | Compliance advise |
| | Compliance appraisal | Compliance testing and review |
| Intelligence | Intelligence framework | Information and intelligence conversion |
| | Intelligence classifications | Knowledge sharing and learning |
| | Intelligence obligations | IT architecture and engineering |
| | Intelligence appraisal | Language and taxonomy |
| Security | Security framework | Security domains |
| | Security classifications | Security layers |
| | Security obligations | Security architecture and engineering |
| | Security appraisal | Security measures |
| Resilience | Resilience framework | Incident and emergency response |
| | Resilience classifications | Business continuity management |
| | Resilience obligations | Disaster recovery planning |
| | Resilience appraisal | Insurance |
| Controls | Controls framework | Preventative and detective controls |
| | Controls classifications | Manual and automated controls |
| | Controls obligations | Primary and secondary controls |
| | Controls appraisal | Controls testing and review |
| Assurance | Assurance framework | Audit and inspection review |
| | Assurance classifications | Due diligence and benchmarking review |
| | Assurance obligations | Fraud examination |
| | Assurance appraisal | Forensic investigation |

### 13.3.1.5  The Operational Line Management (OLM) Agenda

Table 13.13 outlines some basic examples of OLM-related matters that require due consideration for each critical corporate defense component.

**TABLE 13.13**
**The OLM Agenda**

|  | OLM—Particulars | OLM—Specific Issues |
|---|---|---|
| Governance | Governance ownership | Operational plans |
|  | Governance execution | Operational objectives |
|  | Governance people | Business process objectives |
|  | Governance practices | Workflow programs and flowcharts |
|  | Governance processes and systems | Procedure manuals |
| Risk | Risk ownership | Risk register |
|  | Risk execution | Risk events |
|  | Risk people | Risk probability and impact |
|  | Risk practices | Inherent and residual risk |
|  | Risk processes and systems | Risk treatment |
| Compliance | Compliance ownership | Operational compliance |
|  | Compliance execution | Contract compliance |
|  | Compliance people | Policy compliance |
|  | Compliance practices | Procedure compliance |
|  | Compliance processes and systems | Compliance controls |
| Intelligence | Intelligence ownership | Data management |
|  | Intelligence execution | Intelligence applications |
|  | Intelligence people | Change management |
|  | Intelligence practices | Performance metrics |
|  | Intelligence processes and systems | Internal and external reporting |
| Security | Security ownership | Site and building security |
|  | Security execution | People and equipment security |
|  | Security people | Operations and facility security |
|  | Security practices | Network security |
|  | Security processes and systems | Information and data security |
| Resilience | Resilience ownership | Back-up systems |
|  | Resilience execution | Scenario planning and simulations |
|  | Resilience people | Resiliency testing |
|  | Resilience practices | Business impact analysis |
|  | Resilience processes and systems | Root cause analysis |
| Controls | Controls ownership | Financial reporting controls |
|  | Controls execution | Business control objectives |
|  | Controls people | Business process controls |
|  | Controls practices | Quality assurance controls |
|  | Controls processes and systems | Front, middle, and back-office controls |
| Assurance | Assurance ownership | Line management supervision |
|  | Assurance execution | Management reviews |
|  | Assurance people | Quality assurance |
|  | Assurance practices | Continuous monitoring |
|  | Assurance processes and systems | Self-assessments |

### 13.3.2 DEFENSE-IN-DEPTH ASSESSMENT

Each organization needs to be aware of the extent to which it provides sound *defense-in-depth* to its stakeholders. In order to establish the robustness of its *defense-in-depth,* each organization should review and assess each of the above critical lines of defense agendas and consider the extent to which it is currently addressing its critical component requirements within each one of these agendas.

#### 13.3.2.1 Agenda—Particulars

Due consideration should be given to the *particulars* section in each of the above examples as this can help an organization to assess if it is adopting a consistent approach at each line of defense. It can also help an organization to establish if each agenda is implementing a systematic approach to each of the critical components.

#### 13.3.2.2 Agenda—Specific Issues

Due consideration should be given to the *specific issues* section in each of the above examples as this can help an organization assess the extent to which each line of defense is currently addressing the more important aspects of each critical component. It can also help an organization establish the extent to which each line of defense is addressing these components in isolation or the extent to which it is adopting a more integrated approach.

## 13.4 A CORPORATE DEFENSE HEALTH CHECK

It is recommended that an initial high-level corporate defense health check be performed at the initial preparation stage of a corporate defense program. This should enable the early identification of existing vulnerabilities and allow for appropriate corrective action to be taken in order to address these vulnerabilities. This exercise will also assist in the prioritization of work to be performed as part of the corporate defense planning process.

### 13.4.1 THE CDM DIAGNOSTIC

The CDM framework provides a blueprint for ensuring that corporate defense activities are addressed across the organization; however, it also provides a basis for performing an initial diagnostic of the health of the organization's current corporate defense activities. The CDM diagnostic involves performing a review of the organization's current efforts in both *defense-in-breadth* and *defense-in-depth.* This CDM diagnostic represents a high-level corporate defense health check that facilitates the early identification of weaknesses, deficiencies, and vulnerabilities in the current corporate defense initiative. By reviewing the organizations corporate defense efforts from the perspective of both *defense-in-breadth* and *defense-in-depth,* it is possible to identify various oversights, inconsistencies, and anomalies that could potentially expose the organization to unnecessary hazards further down the line.

#### 13.4.1.1 Critical Component Diagnosis

Using the CDM framework to review the organization's current critical corporate defense component initiatives will enable the organization to form a clear picture of the extent of its efforts and the level of maturity of these initiatives. It can help determine the extent to which the organization is consciously addressing its *governance, risk, compliance, intelligence, security, resilience, controls,* and *assurance* responsibilities throughout the organization. The following are examples of basic questions that stakeholders might be expected to ask in relation to the organization's critical component initiatives:

- Is each of the critical corporate defense components being clearly addressed at each and every line of defense?
- Has the organization identified any inconsistencies (i.e., oversights, omissions, or anomalies) in how it is addressing each of the critical corporate defense components at each line of defense?
- Where inconsistencies have been identified, have these inconsistencies been given due consideration and has a decision on any required remedial action been determined?

### 13.4.1.2  Lines of Defense Diagnosis

Using the CDM framework to review the organization's current critical lines of defense agendas will enable the organization to form a clear picture of the extent of its efforts and the level of maturity of these agendas. It can help determine the extent to which the organization is consciously operating a comprehensive lines of defense oversight framework in relation to its corporate defense responsibilities. The following are examples of basic questions that stakeholders might be expected to ask in relation to the organization's lines of defense agendas:

- Is each line of defense clearly aware of their corporate defense responsibilities in relation to each of the critical corporate defense components?
- Has the organization identified any inconsistencies (i.e., oversights, omissions, or anomalies) in relation to how individual lines of defense are addressing their critical corporate defense component responsibilities?
- Where inconsistencies have been identified, have these inconsistencies been given due consideration and has a decision on any required remedial action been determined?

# 14 Application of the CDM Philosophy in Practice

Everything is simpler than you think and at the same time more complex than you can imagine.*

**Johann Wolfgang von Goethe**

## 14.1 APPLYING THE CDM PHILOSOPHY

The concept of corporate defense management (CDM) is perhaps every bit as much a philosophy as it is a methodology. Although the CDM framework provides a methodology by which organizations can hope to tackle the many different forms of corporate defense challenges, CDM as a concept is about how an organization thinks about addressing these challenges. It is about how the organization incorporates its value preservation imperative into its thinking and decision making. CDM is a method or technique that should be employed by an organization when considering each challenge it is faced with. Ultimately, CDM represents a mind-set that can be applied across the entire organization at strategic, tactical, and operational levels.

### 14.1.1 Creating a Pervasive Mind-Set

The CDM mind-set needs to become pervasive throughout the organization in order to truly address the value preservation imperative. The CDM mind-set represents an important opportunity to help ensure that the value preservation imperative becomes embedded into the organization's psyche so that it forms part of its culture and becomes part of its DNA. A CDM mind-set should

---

* Per *Knowledge Management, Organizational Intelligence And Learning. And Complexity*, 2009, L. Douglas Kiel, Eolss Publishers Co. Ltd., Oxford, UK.

**TABLE 14.1**
**Multilevel Application**

| | |
|---|---|
| Organization level | Strategic, tactical, and operational etc. |
| Legal entities | Parent company and subsidiaries etc. |
| Business structures | Head office and branches etc. |
| Geographic regions | National and international etc. |
| Business divisions | Wholesale and retail etc. |
| Business units | Lending and treasury etc. |
| Business lines | Products and services etc. |
| Business activities | Front, middle, and back-office etc. |
| Business departments | Sales, underwriting, and completions etc. |
| Business functions | Interdepartmental functions (operations and finance etc.) |

be omnipresent so that it is consistently applied in all decision-making processes, whether they be in the boardroom or on the front lines. It is a mind-set that should be applied not only to specific corporate defense-related decisions but to all business matters in order to help ensure that a truly informed and well-balanced decision is arrived at.

#### 14.1.1.1 Multilevel Application

The CDM mind-set is a technique that can be applied to all aspects of the organization's activities and at all levels. It is a flexible and agile methodology that can equally be applied to strategic, tactical, and operational matters alike. Its multilevel application is sufficiently adaptable to be employed at all different levels within the organization. Table 14.1 outlines some examples of these different levels.

### 14.1.2 THE CDM MIND-SET IN ACTION

By applying the CDM mind-set in practice, an organization can quickly identify matters of importance and ensure that it has adopted a comprehensive approach to its decision making. The best way to gain a clearer understanding of how the CDM mind-set might be applied in practice is to look at how it might be applied in different situations and under different circumstances. To illustrate this effectively, a number of examples have been selected whereby the CDM mind-set can be applied. These examples have been selected to help provide examples of a wide diversity of circumstances in which the CDM approach can be applied. For the purposes of consistency and comparability, each of the examples selected has been approached in a similar manner and addressed in a systematic fashion. Owing to the generic nature of the approach, there are certain sections where similar wordings have been used in the examples chosen. This is considered necessary in order to ensure that each example can be considered in isolation of the other examples and to emphasize the importance of the systematic approach regardless of the circumstances in question. It is believed that such an approach will help the reader to become familiar with the routine application of a systematic CDM process and also help to appreciate the generic aspect of such an approach. Let us now look at examples of how the CDM approach can be applied to some of the above situations.

### 14.2 ORGANIZATION-LEVEL APPLICATION

The CDM mind-set needs to be applied at an organization level in order to help ensure the adequacy and consistency of corporate defense efforts throughout the entire organization. At this level, the organization needs to consider how it is currently addressing the principles of each of the critical components at strategic, tactical, and operational levels. The organization may also need to consider the extent to which it needs to make changes in order to adequately address these components going forward.

### 14.2.1 ORGANIZATION-LEVEL PRECONDITIONS

In order to apply the CDM mind-set at an organization level, it is important to set certain corporate defense preconditions to help facilitate this process. A primary precondition is the expectation that the organization has a responsibility to address each of the critical components at strategic, tactical, and operational levels.

#### 14.2.1.1 Organization-Level Matrix

The CDM matrix can be applied to the organization level and can be a useful tool or checklist for an organization when considering how it is addressing each of the critical components at a strategic, tactical, and operational level. Table 14.2 outlines the organization-level CDM matrix.

### 14.2.2 ORGANIZATION-LEVEL CDM MIND-SET

In order to apply the CDM mind-set at this level, the organization must give due thought and consideration to how it is addressing each critical component at each organization level. The organization-level CDM matrix can help an organization adopt a systematic and comprehensive approach when undertaking this exercise and help to quickly identify any anomalies that require specific attention. It can also help establish which corporate defense initiatives can be classified as the leaders and laggards within the organization and help determine where additional efforts are required.

#### 14.2.2.1 Example: Organization Level—Governance

Due consideration should be given to how the governance initiative (see Chapters 9 and 13 for more detail) is addressed through the different levels of the organization. The following include examples of issues that require due consideration:

*Strategic governance*: Consideration of the organization's strategic governance efforts should include the extent to which the organization has a clear corporate vision and mission statement to help steer it in the long term. It should consider the extent to which there is a formal

---

**TABLE 14.2**
**Organization-Level CDM Matrix**

|  | Strategic | Tactical | Operational |
|---|---|---|---|
| Governance | Strategic governance | Tactical governance | Operational governance |
| Risk | Strategic risk | Tactical risk | Operational risk |
| Compliance | Strategic compliance | Tactical compliance | Operational compliance |
| Intelligence | Strategic intelligence | Tactical intelligence | Operational intelligence |
| Security | Strategic security | Tactical security | Operational security |
| Resilience | Strategic resilience | Tactical resilience | Operational resilience |
| Controls | Strategic controls | Tactical controls | Operational controls |
| Assurance | Strategic assurance | Tactical assurance | Operational assurance |

corporate strategy in place, which outlines how the vision and mission will be achieved, and it should consider the extent to which clear strategic objectives have been established.

*Tactical governance*: Consideration of the organization's tactical governance efforts should include the extent to which it has developed a coherent plan and established necessary policies in order to facilitate the implementation of the organization's strategy. It should consider the extent to which there is an appropriate organizational infrastructure and architecture in place to facilitate the implementation of the plan, and it should consider the extent to which required roles and responsibilities have been assigned and delegated.

*Operational governance*: Consideration of the organization's operational governance efforts should include the extent to which it has developed appropriate operational objectives that are in alignment with its strategic objectives. It should consider the extent to which it has developed appropriate practices to help achieve these objectives and it should consider the extent to which appropriate procedures have been developed to help instruct its staff on how to consistently execute these practices on a day-to-day basis.

### 14.2.2.2 Example: Organizational Level—Assurance

Due consideration should be given to how the assurance initiative (see Chapters 10 and 13 for more detail) is addressed through the different levels of the organization. The following include examples of issues that require due consideration:

*Strategic assurance*: Consideration of the organization's strategic assurance efforts should include the extent to which the organization has taken measures to ensure that it is provided with an appropriate level of assurance on matters of a strategic nature. It should consider the extent to which appropriate assurance is provided to stakeholders surrounding the execution of strategy and the performance of the board, and it should consider the nature of the board's relationship with the organization's external auditors.

*Tactical assurance*: Consideration of the organization's tactical assurance efforts should include the extent to which the board is provided with appropriate assurance regarding the performance of the broader organization. It should consider the extent to which it has established committees or subcommittees of the board to provide assurance to the board and it should consider the nature of assurance provided by executive management to the board.

*Operational assurance*: Consideration of the organization's operational assurance efforts should include the extent to which it has established an internal audit function to provide assurance on the effectiveness and efficiency of its operations. It should consider the extent to which line management provides assurance regarding its operations, and it should consider the nature of the line management's assessment of its operations.

## 14.3  BUSINESS ACTIVITY-LEVEL APPLICATION

The CDM mind-set needs to be applied at a business activity level in order to help ensure the adequacy and consistency of corporate defense efforts across all business activities. At this level, the organization needs to consider how it is currently addressing the principles of each of the critical components across each of its business activities including its front, middle, and back-office activities. While a degree of flexibility and adaptability may be required, it is important that each business activity at least meets with minimum standards or benchmark requirements.

### 14.3.1  BUSINESS ACTIVITY-LEVEL PRECONDITIONS

In order to apply the CDM mind-set at a business activity level, it is important to set certain corporate defense preconditions to help facilitate this process. A primary precondition is the expectation that the organization has a responsibility to address each of the critical components across its front, middle, and back-office activities.

### 14.3.1.1 Business Activity-Level Matrix

The CDM matrix can be applied to the business activity level and can be a useful tool or checklist for an organization when considering how it is addressing each of the critical components at a front, middle, and back-office level. Table 14.3 outlines the business activity-level CDM matrix.

### 14.3.2 Business Activity-Level CDM Mind-Set

In order to apply the CDM mind-set at this level, the organization must give due thought and consideration to how it is addressing each critical component across each activity level. The business activity-level CDM matrix can help an organization to adopt a systematic and comprehensive approach when undertaking this exercise and help to quickly identify any anomalies that require specific attention. It can also help to establish which corporate defense initiatives can be classified as the leaders and laggards within the business activities and help determine where additional efforts are required.

### 14.3.2.1 Example: Business Activity Level—Risk

Due consideration should be given to how the risk initiative (see Chapters 9 and 13 for more detail) is addressed across business activity levels. The following include examples of issues that require due consideration:

*Front office risk*: Consideration of the front office risk management efforts should include the extent to which the organization has taken appropriate measures to help ensure that all front office risks are identified, measured, and managed. It should consider the extent to which front office risks are individually assessed for activities such as the sale of products and services, public relations, marketing, and advertising and promotion. It should consider the inherent and residual risk of front office risk types and their interconnectivity with other risk types.

**TABLE 14.3**
**Business Activity-Level CDM Matrix**

|  | **Front Office** | **Middle Office** | **Back-Office** |
|---|---|---|---|
| Governance | Front office governance | Middle office governance | Back-office governance |
| Risk | Front office risk | Middle office risk | Back-office risk |
| Compliance | Front office compliance | Middle office compliance | Back-office compliance |
| Intelligence | Front office intelligence | Middle office intelligence | Back-office intelligence |
| Security | Front office security | Middle office security | Back-office security |
| Resilience | Front office resilience | Middle office resilience | Back-office resilience |
| Controls | Front office controls | Middle office controls | Back-office controls |
| Assurance | Front office assurance | Middle office assurance | Back-office assurance |

*Middle office risk*: Consideration of the middle office risk management efforts should include the extent to which the organization has taken appropriate measures to help ensure that all middle office risks are identified, measured, and managed. It should consider the extent to which middle office risks are individually assessed for activities such as the transaction processing, customer service, performance reporting, and product development. It should consider the inherent and residual risk of middle office risk types and their interconnectivity with other risk types.

*Back-office risk*: Consideration of the back-office risk management efforts should include the extent to which the organization has taken appropriate measures to help ensure that all back-office risks are identified, measured, and managed. It should consider the extent to which back-office risks are individually assessed and evaluated for activities such as the supply chain management, finance, manufacturing, and human resource (HR) management. It should consider the inherent and residual risk of back-office risk types and their interconnectivity with other risk types.

### 14.3.2.2   Example: Business Activity Level—Controls

Due consideration should be given to how the controls initiative (see Chapters 10 and 13 for more detail) is addressed across business activity levels. The following include examples of issues that require due consideration:

*Front office controls*: Consideration of the front office internal control efforts should include the extent to which the organization has taken measures to ensure that appropriate front office controls are in place in order to adequately mitigate its risk exposure. It should consider the extent to which there is appropriate segregation of duties in place over activities such as the sale of products and services, public relations, marketing, and advertising and promotion. It should consider the extent to which front office controls adequately address issues such as conflicts of interest and the risk of fraud.

*Middle office controls*: Consideration of the middle office internal control efforts should include the extent to which the organization has taken measures to ensure that appropriate middle office controls are in place in order to adequately mitigate its risk exposure. It should consider the extent to which the middle office controls help achieve the business objectives of activities such as transaction processing, customer service, performance reporting, and product development. It should consider the extent to which middle office controls contain an appropriate blending of preventative and detective controls.

*Back-office controls*: Consideration of the back-office internal control efforts should include the extent to which the organization has taken measures to ensure that appropriate back-office controls are in place in order to adequately mitigate its risk exposure. It should consider the extent to which back-office controls provide an acceptable level of comfort over activities such as supply chain management, finance, manufacturing, and HR management. It should consider the extent to which back-office controls have been tested and reviewed to help ensure they are operating effectively.

## 14.4   DEPARTMENT-LEVEL APPLICATION

The CDM mind-set needs to be applied at a department level in order to help ensure the adequacy and consistency of corporate defense efforts across all departments. At this level, the organization needs to consider how it is currently addressing the principles of each of the critical components in relation to each department's people, processes, and systems. Although a degree of flexibility and adaptability may be required, it is important that each department at least meets minimum standards or benchmark requirements.

## 14.4.1 DEPARTMENT-LEVEL PRECONDITIONS

In order to apply the CDM mind-set at a department level, it is important to set certain corporate defense preconditions to help facilitate this process. A primary precondition is the expectation that each department has a responsibility to address each of the critical components in relation to its people, processes, and systems.

### 14.4.1.1 Department-Level Matrix

The CDM matrix can be applied at a department level and can be a useful tool or checklist for an organization when considering how it is addressing each of the critical components in relation to its people, processes, and systems. Table 14.4 outlines the department-level CDM matrix.

## 14.4.2 DEPARTMENT-LEVEL CDM MIND-SET

In order to apply the CDM mind-set at this level, the department must give due thought and consideration to how it is addressing each critical component in relation to its activities. The department-level CDM matrix can help an organization adopt a systematic and comprehensive approach when undertaking this exercise and quickly identify any anomalies that require specific attention. It can also help establish which corporate defense initiatives can be classified as the leaders and laggards within the department and help determine where additional efforts are required.

### 14.4.2.1 Example: Department Level—Compliance

Due consideration should be given to how the compliance initiative (see Chapters 9 and 13 for more detail) is addressed across the department's activities. The following include examples of issues that require due consideration:

*People compliance*: Consideration of the department's people compliance efforts should include the extent to which the department has taken measures to ensure that its people are in compliance with all mandatory and voluntary requirements in the performance of

**TABLE 14.4**
**Department-Level CDM Matrix**

|              | People              | Process              | Systems              |
|--------------|---------------------|----------------------|----------------------|
| Governance   | People governance   | Process governance   | Systems governance   |
| Risk         | People risk         | Process risk         | Systems risk         |
| Compliance   | People compliance   | Process compliance   | Systems compliance   |
| Intelligence | People intelligence | Process intelligence | Systems intelligence |
| Security     | People security     | Process security     | Systems security     |
| Resilience   | People resilience   | Process resilience   | Systems resilience   |
| Controls     | People controls     | Process controls     | Systems controls     |
| Assurance    | People assurance    | Process assurance    | Systems assurance    |

their duties. It should consider the extent to which the department has provided appropriate compliance education and training to all staff members and the extent to which the department has familiarized its staff with the appropriate codes of ethics and codes of conduct when conducting its daily tasks.

*Process compliance*: Consideration of the department's process compliance efforts should include the extent to which the department has taken measures to ensure that its business processes are in compliance with all mandatory and voluntary requirements. It should consider the extent to which the department is aware of all its legal and regulatory obligations. It should consider the extent to which the department can attest that its processes are in conformance with all its compliance requirements.

*Systems compliance*: Consideration of the department's systems compliance efforts should include the extent to which the department has taken measures to ensure that its systems are in compliance with all mandatory and voluntary requirements. It should consider the extent to which the department has implemented its systems in compliance with international best practices. It should consider the extent to which the department's systems are in compliance with requirements such as data retention and data privacy.

### 14.4.2.2   Example: Department Level—Security

Due consideration should be given to how the security initiative (see Chapters 10 and 13 for more detail) is addressed across the department's activities. The following include examples of issues that require due consideration:

*People security*: Consideration of the department's people security efforts should include the extent to which the department has taken measures to ensure that its people are appropriately protected and working in a safe and secure environment. It should consider the extent to which the department has implemented appropriate physical and information security measures to protect its staff members. It should consider the extent to which the department has provided its staff members with appropriate security training.

*Process security*: Consideration of the department's process security efforts should include the extent to which the department has taken measures to ensure that its business processes are adequately secured at all times. It should consider the extent to which the department has appropriate security measures in place over the processing and recording of business transactions. It should consider the extent to which the department has adequate security measures in place over cash handling processes and the storage processes of other tangible and intangible assets.

*Systems security*: Consideration of the department's systems security efforts should include the extent to which the department has taken measures to ensure that its systems are adequately secured at all times. It should consider the extent to which the department has appropriate security measures in place over the ongoing operations of its systems. It should consider the extent to which the department has tested its security measures or undergone professional penetration testing of its systems.

## 14.5   CRITICAL COMPONENT PROGRAM-LEVEL APPLICATION

The CDM mind-set needs to be applied at a critical component program level in order to help ensure the adequacy and consistency of corporate defense efforts across all of critical component programs themselves. At this level, each program champion needs to consider how it is currently addressing the principles of each of the critical components in relation to its own program. While a degree of flexibility and adaptability may be required, it is important that each program at least meets with minimum standards or benchmark requirements.

### 14.5.1 Component Program-Level Preconditions

In order to apply the CDM mind-set at a critical component program level, it is important to set certain corporate defense preconditions to help facilitate this process. A primary precondition is the expectation that each critical component program has itself a responsibility to address each of the critical components in relation to its own program.

#### 14.5.1.1 Critical Component Program-Level Matrix

The CDM matrix can be applied at a critical component program level and can be a useful tool or checklist for a program champion when considering how it is addressing each of the critical components in relation to its critical component program. Figure 14.1 outlines the critical component program-level CDM matrix.

### 14.5.2 Critical Component Level CDM Mind-Set

In order to apply the CDM mind-set at this level, each critical component program must give due thought and consideration to how it is addressing each critical component in relation to its own program. The critical component level CDM matrix can help an individual critical component program to adopt a systematic and comprehensive approach when undertaking this exercise and to quickly identify any anomalies that require specific attention. It can also help establish which corporate defense initiatives can be classified as the leaders and laggards within the program and help determine where additional efforts are required.

#### 14.5.2.1 Example: The Intelligence Program

Due consideration should be given to how the critical corporate defense components (see Chapters 9 and 10 for more detail) are addressed within the intelligence program. The following include examples of issues that require due consideration:

*Intelligence governance*: Consideration of the governance component of the intelligence program should include the extent to which a prudent approach to governance (see Chapter 9) is applied to the management of the intelligence program.

*Intelligence risk*: Consideration of the risk component of the intelligence program should include the extent to which a prudent approach to risk (see Chapter 9) is applied to the management of the intelligence program.

*Intelligence compliance*: Consideration of the compliance component of the intelligence program should include the extent to which a prudent approach to compliance (see Chapter 9) is applied to the management of the intelligence program.

*Intelligence²*: Consideration of the intelligence component of the intelligence program should include the extent to which a prudent approach to intelligence (see Chapter 9) is applied to the management of the intelligence program.[*]

*Intelligence security*: Consideration of the security component of the intelligence program should include the extent to which a prudent approach to security (see Chapter 10) is applied to the management of the intelligence program.

*Intelligence resilience*: Consideration of the resilience component of the intelligence program should include the extent to which a prudent approach to resilience (see Chapter 10) is applied to the management of the intelligence program.

*Intelligence controls*: Consideration of the controls component of the intelligence program should include the extent to which a prudent approach to controls (see Chapter 10) is applied to the management of the intelligence program.

---

[*] Intelligence² refers to the intelligence requirements of the intelligence program itself.

| | Governance program | Risk program | Compliance program | Intelligence program | Security program | Resilience program | Controls program | Assurance program |
|---|---|---|---|---|---|---|---|---|
| **Governance** | Governance[2] | Governance risk | Governance compliance | Governance intelligence | Governance security | Governance resilience | Governance controls | Governance assurance |
| **Risk** | Risk governance | Risk[2] | Risk compliance | Risk intelligence | Risk security | Risk resilience | Risk Controls | Risk assurance |
| **Compliance** | Compliance governance | Compliance risk | Compliance[2] | Compliance intelligence | Compliance security | Compliance resilience | Compliance controls | Compliance assurance |
| **Intelligence** | Intelligence governance | Intelligence risk | Intelligence compliance | Intelligence[2] | Intelligence security | Intelligence resilience | Intelligence controls | Intelligence assurance |
| **Security** | Security governance | Security risk | Security compliance | Security intelligence | Security[2] | Security resilience | Security controls | Security assurance |
| **Resilience** | Resilience governance | Resilience risk | Resilience compliance | Resilience intelligence | Resilience security | Resilience[2] | Resilience controls | Resilience assurance |
| **Controls** | Controls governance | Controls risk | Controls compliance | Controls intelligence | Controls security | Controls resilience | Controls[2] | Controls assurance |
| **Assurance** | Assurance governance | Assurance risk | Assurance compliance | Assurance intelligence | Assurance security | Assurance resilience | Assurance controls | Assurance[2] |

**FIGURE 14.1**    Critical component program-level CDM matrix.

*Intelligence assurance*: Consideration of the assurance component of the intelligence program should include the extent to which a prudent approach to assurance (see Chapter 10) is applied to the management of the intelligence program.

### 14.5.2.2　Example: The Resilience Program

Due consideration should be given to how the critical components (see Chapters 9 and 10 for more detail) are addressed within the resilience program. The following include examples of issues that require due consideration:

*Resilience governance*: Consideration of the governance component of the resilience program should include the extent to which a prudent approach to governance (see Chapter 9) is applied to the management of the resilience program.

*Resilience risk*: Consideration of the risk component of the resilience program should include the extent to which a prudent approach to risk (see Chapter 9) is applied to the management of the resilience program.

*Resilience compliance*: Consideration of the compliance component of the resilience program should include the extent to which a prudent approach to compliance (see Chapter 9) is applied to the management of the resilience program.

*Resilience intelligence*: Consideration of the intelligence component of the resilience program should include the extent to which a prudent approach to intelligence (see Chapter 9) is applied to the management of the resilience program.

*Resilience security*: Consideration of the security component of the resilience program should include the extent to which a prudent approach to security (see Chapter 10) is applied to the management of the resilience program.

*Resilience$^2$*: Consideration of the resilience component of the resilience program should include the extent to which a prudent approach to resilience (see Chapter 10) is applied to the management of the resilience program.[*]

*Resilience controls*: Consideration of the controls component of the resilience program should include the extent to which a prudent approach to controls (see Chapter 10) is applied to the management of the resilience program.

*Resilience assurance*: Consideration of the assurance component of the resilience program should include the extent to which a prudent approach to assurance (see Chapter 10) is applied to the management of the resilience program.

## 14.6　ISSUE-LEVEL APPLICATION

The CDM mind-set needs to be applied at a specific issue level in order to help ensure the adequacy and consistency of corporate defense efforts across all specific issues addressed by the organization. At this level, the organization needs to consider how it is currently addressing the principles of each of the critical components in relation to specific issues being addressed. While a degree of flexibility and adaptability may be required, it is important that each specific issue at least meets with minimum standards or benchmark requirements.

### 14.6.1　ISSUE-LEVEL PRECONDITIONS

In order to apply the CDM mind-set at a specific issue level, it is important to set certain corporate defense preconditions to help facilitate this process. A primary precondition is the expectation that those responsible for managing each specific issue have a responsibility to address each of the critical components in relation to the specific issue being managed.

---

[*] Resilience$^2$ refers to the resilience requirements of the resilience program itself.

#### 14.6.1.1 Issue-Level Matrix

The CDM matrix can be applied at an issue level and can be a useful tool or checklist for the organization when considering how the management of different issues addresses each of the critical components. Table 14.5 outlines the issue-level CDM matrix and examples of issues an organization may need to address.

### 14.6.2 ISSUE-LEVEL CDM MIND-SET

In order to apply the CDM mind-set at this level, the management of each specific issue must give due thought and consideration to how it is addressing each critical component in relation to the issue being managed. The issue-level CDM matrix can help those responsible for managing a specific issue to adopt a systematic and comprehensive approach when undertaking this exercise and to quickly identify any anomalies that require specific attention. It can also help establish which corporate defense initiatives can be classified as the leaders and laggards within the management of specific issues and help determine where additional efforts are required.

#### 14.6.2.1 Example: Reputation Management

Due consideration should be given to how the critical components (see Chapters 9 and 10 for more detail) are addressed within the reputation management process. The following include examples of issues that require due consideration:

> *Governance*: The organization should consider governance implications both to the firm's reputation and to the reputation management process itself. Consideration should include the extent to which a prudent approach to governance (see Chapter 9) is applied to reputation management. The following are examples of just three basic governance questions[*]

**TABLE 14.5**
**Issue-Level CDM Matrix**

|  | Reputation Management | Fraud Management | Cyber Defense Program | Whistle-Blowing Program |
|---|---|---|---|---|
| Governance | Reputation management governance | Fraud management governance | Cyber defense governance | Whistle-blowing governance |
| Risk | Reputation management risk | Fraud management risk | Cyber defense risk | Whistle-blowing risk |
| Compliance | Reputation management compliance | Fraud management compliance | Cyber defense compliance | Whistle-blowing compliance |
| Intelligence | Reputation management intelligence | Fraud management intelligence | Cyber defense intelligence | Whistle-blowing intelligence |
| Security | Reputation management security | Fraud management security | Cyber defense security | Whistle-blowing security |
| Resilience | Reputation management resilience | Fraud management resilience | Cyber defense resilience | Whistle-blowing resilience |
| Controls | Reputation management controls | Fraud management controls | Cyber defense controls | Whistle-blowing controls |
| Assurance | Reputation management assurance | Fraud management assurance | Cyber defense assurance | Whistle-blowing assurance |

[*] These questions represent only selected examples and should not be considered as an exhaustive list. Refer to the individual component sections in Chapters 9 and 10 for a more detailed comprehension of the types of issues that should be considered in each case.

that stakeholders might be expected to ask in relation to the organization's approach to reputation management:

- What impact could deficiencies in the organization's corporate governance practices potentially have on its reputation?
- What measures has the organization taken to help ensure that its reputation management process is effectively governed?
- Have formal roles and responsibilities been assigned for the reputation management process?

*Risk*: The organization should consider how to manage the risks to its reputation and any risks arising out of the reputation management process itself. Consideration should include the extent to which a prudent approach to risk (see Chapter 9) is applied to reputation management. The following are examples of just three basic risk questions that stakeholders might be expected to ask in relation to the organization's approach to reputation management:

- Has the organization identified the most significant risks to its reputation?
- Has the organization estimated the levels of inherent and residual risk associated with the significant risks to its reputation?
- Has the organization determined how its risk management process could actually help to promote its reputation?

*Compliance*: The organization should consider the compliance implications both to the firm's reputation and to the reputation management process. Consideration should include the extent to which a prudent approach to compliance (see Chapter 9) is applied to reputation management. The following are examples of just three basic compliance questions that stakeholders might be expected to ask in relation to the organization's approach to reputation management:

- Has the organization considered how deficiencies in its compliance practices could potentially have a negative impact on its reputation?
- Has the organization identified any specific compliance issues that may have a disproportionate negative impact on the organization's reputation?
- What action plans are in place to help minimize the potential negative impact of non-compliance events on its reputation?

*Intelligence*: The organization should consider the intelligence implications both to the firm's reputation and to the reputation management process. Consideration should include the extent to which a prudent approach to intelligence (see Chapter 9) is applied to reputation management. The following are examples of just three basic intelligence questions that stakeholders might be expected to ask in relation to the organization's approach to reputation management:

- Has the organization considered how deficiencies in its intelligence practices could potentially have a negative impact on its reputation?
- Which intelligence issues have been identified as having the greatest positive impact on the organization's reputation?
- Has the organization determined the specific intelligence requirements of the reputation management process?

*Security*: The organization should consider the security implications both to the firm's reputation and to the reputation management process. Consideration should include the extent to which a prudent approach to security (see Chapter 10) is applied to reputation management. The following are examples of just three basic security questions that stakeholders might be expected to ask in relation to the organization's approach to reputation management:

- Has the firm considered how its security practices could potentially have a positive or negative impact on its reputation?

- Has the firm identified any specific security issues that may directly or indirectly impact on its reputation?
- Does the reputation management process require any specific security measures to be put in place?

*Resilience*: The organization should consider the resilience implications both to the firm's reputation and to the reputation management process. Consideration should include the extent to which a prudent approach to resilience (see Chapter 10) is applied to reputation management. The following are examples of just three basic resilience questions that stakeholders might be expected to ask in relation to the organization's approach to reputation management:

- Has the organization considered how its resilience practices could potentially have a positive or negative impact on its reputation?
- Has the organization identified any significant resilience issues that may directly or indirectly impact on its reputation?
- Does the reputation management process have any specific resilience issues that need to be addressed?

*Controls*: The organization should consider the controls implications both to the firm's reputation and to the reputation management process. Consideration should include the extent to which a prudent approach to controls (see Chapter 10) is applied to reputation management. The following are examples of just three basic controls questions that stakeholders might be expected to ask in relation to the organization's approach to reputation management:

- Has the organization considered how its controls practices could potentially have a positive or negative impact on its reputation?
- Has the organization identified any specific controls issues that may directly or indirectly impact on its reputation?
- What actions has the organization taken to help ensure that its reputation management process is effectively controlled?

*Assurance*: The organization should consider the assurance implications both to the firm's reputation and to the reputation management process. Consideration should include the extent to which a prudent approach to assurance (see Chapter 10) is applied to reputation management. The following are examples of just three basic assurance questions that stakeholders might be expected to ask in relation to the organization's approach to reputation management:

- Has the organization considered how deficiencies in its assurance practices could potentially have a negative impact on its reputation?
- What have been identified as the critical assurance matters that have the most influence on stakeholder opinions?
- How does the organization obtain assurance over its reputation management process?

### 14.6.2.2 Example: Cyber Defense Program

Due consideration should be given to how the critical components (see Chapters 9 and 10 for more detail) are addressed within the cyber defense program. The following include examples of issues that require due consideration:

*Governance*: The organization should consider the requirement for sound governance practices in the management of its cyber defense program. Consideration should include the extent to which a prudent approach to governance (see Chapter 9) is applied to its cyber defense program. The following are examples of just three basic governance questions that stakeholders might be expected to ask in relation to the organization's approach to cyber defense:

- Does the organization have a formal cyber defense program in place?

- Has the organization established the precise roles and responsibilities of the key cyber defense program players?
- What is the role of the board in the cyber defense program?

*Risk*: The organization should consider how to manage its cyber risks and the risks to the cyber defense program itself. Consideration should include the extent to which a prudent approach to risk (see Chapter 9) is applied to its cyber defense program. The following are examples of just three basic risk questions that stakeholders might be expected to ask in relation to the organization's approach to cyber defense:

- Has the organization established a mechanism to determine its cyber risk tolerance levels?
- Has the organization formally identified, assessed, and evaluated all of its significant cyber risks?
- Has the organization established appropriate mechanisms for the monitoring and reporting of its cyber risk exposure?

*Compliance*: The organization should consider the requirement for sound compliance practices in the management of its cyber defense program. Consideration should include the extent to which a prudent approach to compliance (see Chapter 9) is applied to its cyber defense program. The following are examples of just three basic compliance questions that stakeholders might be expected to ask in relation to the organization's approach to cyber defense:

- Has the organization determined all of its required cyber defense compliance obligations and requirements?
- Has the organization specifically assessed and evaluated the compliance risk to the cyber defense program?
- How can the organization demonstrate that it is in conformance with its required cyber defense compliance obligations?

*Intelligence*: The organization should consider the requirement for sound intelligence practices in the management of its cyber defense program. Consideration should include the extent to which a prudent approach to intelligence (see Chapter 9) is applied to its cyber defense program. The following are examples of just three basic intelligence questions that stakeholders might be expected to ask in relation to the organization's approach to cyber defense:

- Has the organization adequately considered the cyber intelligence requirements of the cyber defense program?
- Has the organization specifically assessed and evaluated the intelligence risks to the cyber defense program?
- How has the organization addressed its requirement to educate and train its staff on the importance of cyber defense to the achievement of its organizational objectives?

*Security*: The organization should consider the requirement for sound security practices in the management of its cyber defense program. Consideration should include the extent to which a prudent approach to security (see Chapter 10) is applied to its cyber defense program. The following are examples of just three basic security questions that stakeholders might be expected to ask in relation to the organization's approach to cyber defense:

- Has the organization identified significant cyber threats that could negatively impact on the achievement of the organization's objectives?
- Has the organization determined the required level of cyber security that it intends to implement across the organization?
- Has the organization established a holistic layered approach to securing its different cyber security domains?

*Resilience*: The organization should consider the requirement for sound resilience practices in the management of its cyber defense program. Consideration should include the extent to which a prudent approach to resilience (see Chapter 10) is applied to its cyber defense program.

The following are examples of just three basic resilience questions that stakeholders might be expected to ask in relation to the organization's approach to cyber defense:

- Has the organization adequately considered the resilience requirements of the cyber defense program?
- Has the organization specifically assessed and evaluated the resilience risks to the cyber defense program?
- Has the organization considered the potential business impact of deficiencies in its cyber resilience practices?

*Controls*: The organization should consider the requirement for sound internal control practices in the management of its cyber defense program. Consideration should include the extent to which a prudent approach to controls (see Chapter 10) is applied to its cyber defense program. The following are examples of just three basic controls questions that stakeholders might be expected to ask in relation to the organization's approach to cyber defense:

- Has the organization considered how deficiencies in its controls practices could potentially have a negative impact on its cyber defense program?
- What control mechanisms has the organization put in place to appropriately mitigate its identified cyber risks?
- Has the organization clearly established robust primary and secondary control mechanisms relating to the management of the cyber defense program itself?

*Assurance*: The organization should consider the requirement for sound assurance practices in the management of its cyber defense program. Consideration should include the extent to which a prudent approach to assurance (see Chapter 10) is applied to its cyber defense program. The following are examples of just three basic assurance questions that stakeholders might be expected to ask in relation to the organization's approach to cyber defense:

- How has the organization satisfied itself that it can obtain at least a reasonable level of assurance regarding the operation of its cyber defense program?
- What sources and forms of cyber assurance does the organization rely on as part of its cyber defense program?
- Has the organization clearly established the required assurance criteria to be applied to the management of the cyber defense program?

## 14.7   THE APPLICATION OF CDM IN OTHER CONTEXTS

The issues addressed by CDM can be considered in terms of the past or present but perhaps of more importance is going forward, how organizations intend to prepare for the future? CDM is primarily concerned with helping organizations to address their value preservation obligations and the CDM approach can be applied in both the public and private sector, or indeed in the political, religious, legal, or banking sectors.

### 14.7.1   THE APPLICATION OF THE CDM APPROACH IN THE NATIONAL CONTEXT

It has however also been suggested that the CDM approach should also be applied at a national level in terms of how individual nations approach their value preservation obligations. In the national context, the following are examples of issues that nations should perhaps be giving due consideration:

- In relation to *governance*, nations need to consider issues such as the prevailing culture, in particular issues such as the tone at the top, their expectations in relation to issues such as ethics, integrity, and transparency, and issues related to individuals in positions of power and influence (such as probity and fitness).
- In relation to *risk,* nations need to consider issues such as their understanding of the nature of risk, the potential impact of both internal and external factors, and the actual level of

competence required in this area (including the status and authority afforded to those with responsibility for risk oversight).

- In relation to *compliance,* nations need to consider issues such as the type of laws and regulations in place (if any), findings of ongoing and future investigations, which test their laws and regulations, and the consequences for breaches of these laws and regulations.
- In relation to *intelligence,* nations need to consider issues such as the quality of available information, the level of accurate information required in order to make intelligent decisions, and the impact of and changing role of the media in this area (including social media).
- In relation to *security,* nations need to consider issues such as the protection of the most vulnerable in society, privacy, and data protection issues, the growing impact of cyber crime, and their strategies relating to cyber defense going forward.
- In relation to *resilience,* nations need to consider issues such as the threat of global issues (such as the economic downturn and global warming), initiatives in relation to long term sustainability (such as alternative energy supplies), and issues such as the degree of preparedness required going forward (such a the level of scenario analysis and stress testing required).
- In relation to *controls,* nations need to consider issues such as the prevailing control dynamics in place (such as how the principle of segregation of duties is applied), the importance of reacting to red flags when these are raised, and the extent to which whistle-blower protection is required. Also, the value placed on dissenting voices that attempt to challenge the prevailing wisdom or herd mentality.
- In relation to *assurance,* nations need to consider issues such as the current assurance frameworks in place, the resulting level of stakeholder comfort received, and the degree of confidence required from assurance providers (e.g., regulators, rating agencies, and external auditors) going forward.

Based on past experiences all over the world, weaknesses and deficiencies in each of these individual component areas when taken together can exponentially compound the extent of the problems experienced in different nations. These problems are generally followed by demands for reform and government promises to reform existing structures. If individual nations are genuinely serious about cleaning up their act and getting their house in order, a CDM-type approach represents an opportunity to create a more robust system of checks and balances to help ensure that stakeholder interests are better safeguarded going forward.

Perhaps the next wave of governments or some future governments will fully appreciate the requirement for such reform, and a CDM-type approach will become a high priority in the weeks, months, and years ahead. Who knows, perhaps one day there will even be laws and regulations that demand such an approach!

# 15 Delivering the Corporate Defense Program

In theory there is no difference between theory and practice, in practice there is.*

**Yogi Berra**

## 15.1 CORPORATE DEFENSE ESSENTIALS

Implementing an effective corporate defense program means overcoming many different challenges over the short, medium, and long terms. There are many issues that may arise, which could undermine the effectiveness of the program, some of which are predictable, while others are less so. In order to ensure its effective implementation, it is perhaps more important to focus on managing *what needs to go right* than focusing on *what could go wrong*. A formal structured approach can help in this regard.

### 15.1.1 CORPORATE DEFENSE STANDARDS

Given the responsibility of its station, there should be an expectation that the corporate defense program should involve adherence to the highest possible professional standards. This should include adherence to the existing professional standards of the critical corporate defense components (e.g., corporate governance, risk management, and internal audit). Adherence to such standards will contribute to the program building a reputation for competence and the standards will facilitate the application of international best practices. The field of corporate defense has already many

---

* Per *Research Methodology in Strategy and Management*, Vol.3, 2006, D.J.Ketchen Jr. and D.D.Bergh, JAI Press, Oxford, UK.

disciplines, ranging across all of the critical corporate defense components and it is unreasonable to expect any one individual to be considered *an expert* in more than one such discipline. This needs to be recognized, particularly with the body of knowledge required to be mastered by any one person. The constant changes occurring within each of these disciplines together with the dynamic development of new disciplines in corporate defense means that the standards themselves should be continuously developed, and individuals should anticipate lifelong learning in these areas.

Corporate defense is by its very nature a management discipline that requires its own specific managerial skills and expertise. The breadth of experience, the depth of knowledge, and the precise level of detail required by particular individuals within the corporate defense program will ultimately be dependent on the organization and the business activities in which that organization engages. Therefore, each organization must determine its own unique staffing requirements; however, the application of professional standards can help provide a helpful level of guidance in times of uncertainty.

### 15.1.1.1  Application of Professional Standards

Professional standards are clear statements that reflect the minimum qualifications for mastery and knowledge of processes, skills and practices, which professionals should have before undertaking work, which may put their organization at risk, either physically or financially. Professional standards should at a minimum address the following matters:

| | |
|---|---|
| • Ethics of professional practice | • Professional experience |
| • Established body of knowledge | • Best practice and proven methodologies |
| • Education and training | • Maintenance of competence |

The benefits of applying professional standards in practice include a reasonable level of assurance that critical work is performed by competent individuals regardless of where qualifications and experience were obtained. It includes assurance that the person who meets such standards is competent to perform tasks regardless of where work is performed or where the output of the work is used. Also, there is the assurance that individuals who have gained the necessary qualifications and experience will be recognized internationally.

### 15.1.2  ETHICS, INTEGRITY, AND CONDUCT

Each organization should ensure that it has clear, unambiguous, and appropriate codes and policies in place to address ethical behavior, professional and personal integrity, and standards in relation to the conduct considered to be appropriate by its staff members. It is advisable that at a minimum, recognized external codes should be applied to ensure compliance with best practice. The corporate defense program should strictly comply with all codes and policies relating to ethics, integrity, and conduct. Such codes and policies are considered necessary and appropriate for the corporate defense profession, as they provide instruction to those operating within the program. The purpose of such codes and policies is to promote an ethical culture within the corporate defense program and within the organization itself.

### 15.1.2.1  Guiding Principles

Guiding principles represent prudent practices and their purpose is to provide education and guidance for those engaging in corporate defense. As organizations operate in different ways and because of their varying levels of sophistication, the application of different methodologies and the evolving nature of these methodologies, guidelines cannot offer specific guidance to be followed in all cases. Each organization should therefore develop, adapt, or adopt corporate defense methodologies that best suit its own business needs and capabilities, in addition to the needs and interests of its stakeholders. Consequently, the application of these principles, the approach taken, the structure implemented, and day-to-day operations will vary by organization. Although these variations are considered to be appropriate and proper, the core principles do fundamentally address what the management of corporate defense should aim to achieve. Accordingly, each organization should retain the flexibility and right to tailor the program where it sees fit and ultimately to prudently design a program that meets its own needs and capabilities within the spirit of these core principles.

When considering the approach and structure to be pursued in relation to corporate defense within your organization, a number of issues must be clarified in advance. In order to be in a position to accurately determine the appropriate course of action, adequate advance consideration should be given in the initial planning phase. Due advance consideration should therefore be given to the expected role of corporate defense, and its expected position within the organization. Equally important however is the consideration of the organization having realistic expectations of what the corporate defense program can achieve within its remit. The setting of unrealistic or impractical expectations can only result in eventual failure and ultimately a feeling of disillusionment among all parties concerned.

Prior to the establishment of a corporate defense program, the following principles should be adequately considered in advance:

*Independence*: Due consideration should be given to the level of independence expected of the corporate defense program. This includes determining the expected status of the corporate defense program, its position within the organization, the nomination of the chief corporate defense officer, addressing potential conflicts of interest, and any restrictions on access to information and personnel.

*Resources*: Due consideration should be given to the level of resources to be made available to the corporate defense program. This includes the adequacy of the resources required, the competency of the resources required, and the level of quality assurance required.

*Scope*: Due consideration should be given to the intended scope and feasibility of the corporate defense program. This includes determining the scope of the organization's activities to be covered, the scope of its entities, the scope of its systems, and the legal and geographic jurisdictions.

*Responsibilities*: Due consideration should be given to the intended responsibilities of the corporate defense program. This includes the identification of, assessment of, and response to corporate defense threats. It also includes considering issues such as its purpose and authority, the degree of advice and direction to be provided, the guidance and education expectations, its reporting requirements, and the format of the corporate defense program.

*Relationship with other parties*: Due consideration should be given to the intended relationships between the corporate defense parties and other parties both internal and external to the organization, including the board and subcommittees of the board. It also includes the type of framework to be implemented, the roles and responsibilities of the different parties, and the proposed mechanisms for delegating and communicating.

*Other matters*: Due consideration should also be given to a number of other matters that will impact on the corporate defense program. This includes the monitoring of the corporate defense program, the possibility of outsourcing corporate defense activities, liaison with regulatory bodies, and international jurisdiction issues.

## 15.1.2.2 Characteristics and Attributes

Taking responsibility for defending people, property, and other assets (e.g., information) requires that corporate defense employees respect and support the ethical philosophy of the organization. The overriding concern should be to continuously improve the service by employing appropriate individuals, and developing their competence and level of professionalism in order to build trust and confidence in the corporate defense program throughout the organization.

Attribute standards address the characteristics of both the organization itself and the personnel performing the corporate defense activities. In order to operate in an effective manner, members of the corporate defense program should possess certain personal characteristics and professional attributes that are considered essential to the performance of their duties and responsibilities.

There are certain core attributes that every organization should look for in its corporate defense personnel and these include the following:

*Integrity*: Integrity is required in order to create a culture of honesty, high ethics, and transparency. It is a prerequisite within the corporate defense program and is also a necessary ingredient in order to help promote trust with fellow partners.

*Objectivity*: Objectivity is required in order to ensure that individuals make balanced decisions based on strictly professional judgment and should not be unduly influenced by personal interests.

*Impartiality*: Impartiality is required in order to ensure that the parties engaged in corporate defense activities are sufficiently independent to remain unbiased, and avoid any possible conflicts of interest.

*Confidentiality*: Confidentiality is required in order to ensure that there is an expectation that sensitive information obtained by corporate defense staff is only disclosed in a prudent manner.

*Discretion*: Discretion is required in order to ensure that corporate defense staff exercise due consideration in decision making and in the application or exercise of authority in the performance of their duties.

*Competency*: Professional competence is required in order to ensure that individuals entrusted with responsibility for corporate defense activities possess the appropriate qualifications, skills, and experience in order to proficiently perform their duties on an ongoing basis.

*Professionalism*: Professionalism is required in order to ensure that all corporate defense activities are performed adeptly and with due professional care in accordance with professional standards.

*Diligence*: Diligence is required in order to ensure that individuals develop the discipline and responsibility to work unsupervised and on their own initiative in an honest and professional manner.

*Vigilance*: Vigilance is required in order to ensure that individuals involved in corporate defense activities are constantly attentive in their communication, observation, and evaluation, thus fostering the development of a higher level of intuition and perceptual awareness.

*Helpfulness*: Corporate defense staff should respect the role of other disciplines and when required, individuals must be prepared to lend help and assistance as part of ongoing efforts to defend the organization and its stakeholders.

The existence of the aforementioned attributes in staff participating in the work and activities of the corporate defense program is considered essential for the required and expected functioning of the program. The precise attribute requirements should be assessed on a case-by-case basis taking into account the exact nature and role of the individual position, the staff member, and the organization requirement. Individual organizations should take all necessary measures to ensure that these required attributes are fostered, nurtured, and maintained at all times, through periodic, systematic, and continuous evaluation and education.

### 15.1.3 Purpose of Corporate Defense

The purpose and vision of the corporate defense program should be sufficiently determined in order to adequately justify the necessity for such a program within the organization. This vision should clearly outline the organization's belief in the importance of safeguarding stakeholder value, in defending the interests of the stakeholders, and in the process helping the organization achieve its objectives. Defending the interests of the stakeholders means placing due regard on the welfare and well-being of these stakeholders, and ensuring that an appropriate duty of care is exercised concerning the health and safety of all of the stakeholders in the long term, and not just focusing on short-term interests. What is required is a long-term commitment to stakeholders as valued partners. There must be a concentrated effort to protect and safeguard the stakeholders as human beings, and not purely their financial impact on the bottom line. Such a partnership fosters a reciprocal relationship of mutual trust and commitment.

To achieve this objective, corporate defense must project its own ideology, an ethos which espouses certain core beliefs that are considered fundamental to it as a discipline. This ethos must advocate a value system that regards moral fiber above the search for short-term profit at all costs. Its philosophy must promote not only the aspiration of the highest ethical standards, but the practical implementation of these standards. There must be a strong emphasis on the appropriate application of duty and responsibility, and above all, integrity must be at its essence, both individually and collectively. Corporate defense represents an opportunity to fortify the lower-level motivational needs of the organization (e.g., safety, shelter, and security) and balance these long-term needs against the relentless pressure to maximize short-term profits.

The culture of an organization can be positively influenced by corporate defense as it aligns itself to organizational strategy, and helps ensure long-term success through the prudent application of the corporate defense strategy. Corporate defense can help ensure that the necessary system of checks and balances are operating effectively throughout the organization, despite possible pressures to focus on short-term gains.

### 15.1.3.1  Role of Corporate Defense

The role of the corporate defense program is to help ensure that all defense-related disciplines are operating in unison toward the attainment of a common set of goals and objectives. This management, coordination, and supervisory role relates to a diverse group of disciplines, and people as individuals, with a diverse set of knowledge and skills. It also relates to diverse processes, systems, and technologies. This difficult challenge requires a flexible strategic approach and a strategic agility, which will allow the organization to quickly adapt to an evolving environment and enable it to react in a speedy and integrated manner to incidents that occur in an ever-changing set of circumstances. Each organization will determine the precise model that best suits its needs, addressing issues such as structure, duties, and responsibilities of the corporate defense program. Whether it should be resourced in a centralized or decentralized manner needs to be determined. The degree of participation by corporate defense staff in the organization's operations can potentially include policy decisions, education, advice, ratification, approval, collaboration, and even certain task implementation.

### 15.1.3.2  High-Level Purpose

At a high level the corporate defense program serves to adequately defend the organization from a multitude of potential hazards. In so doing, the organization needs to address the corporate defense cycle throughout the enterprise. It needs to ensure that appropriate mechanisms are in place to anticipate potential threats and vulnerabilities in advance of occurrence. It needs to ensure that appropriate measures are in place to prevent the occurrence of identified threats and vulnerabilities. It needs to ensure that appropriate measures are in place to detect the occurrence of activities that indicate potential threats. Finally, it needs to ensure that appropriate measures are in place to react in a timely, effective, and efficient manner to activities identified as potential threats.

### 15.1.3.3  Lower-Level Purpose

At a lower level the corporate defense program should strive to address the following operational issues:

*Education*: To help ensure that appropriate measures are in place so that all members of the organization are appropriately educated in their ethical and professional responsibilities in relation to corporate defense.

*Recognition*: To help ensure that there is an appropriate recognition within the organization of the dangers that can result from the existence of threats and vulnerabilities, and the organization's resulting obligation to comply with corporate defense protocols.

*Identification*: To help ensure that there is an appropriate system in place to make certain that all significant risks, threats, and vulnerabilities facing the organization are identified and documented in a timely manner.

*Evaluation*: To help ensure that the inherent and residual risks represented by the identified risks, threats, and vulnerabilities are appropriately assessed and evaluated in terms of issues such as impact and probability.

*Deterrence*: To help ensure that appropriate deterrent measures are put in place to effectively mitigate those risks, threats, and vulnerabilities that have been determined to be of a low risk nature.

*Protection*: To help ensure that appropriate physical and technological protective measures have been taken to secure the organization and prevent the occurrence of any risks, threats and vulnerabilities that have been determined to be medium to high risk.

*Interceptions*: To help ensure that appropriate measures are in place to intercept in an effective and timely manner any activities that are deemed to be of a threatening nature or a breach of corporate defense protocol.

*Robustness*: To help ensure that appropriately robust measures are in place to address threats to the health and safety of staff, destruction of facilities, or disruption to the business operations.

*Capture*: To help ensure that appropriate processes and systems are in place to capture and collect all required information in relation to potentially threatening activities or breaches of corporate defense protocol.

*Monitor*: To help ensure that appropriate processes are in place for the effective and timely monitoring of information, which indicates evidence of the occurrence of potentially threatening activities or breaches of corporate defense protocol.

*Investigate*: To help ensure that appropriate procedures are in place to adequately investigate the occurrence of any possible threatening activities or breaches of corporate defense protocol in a timely and comprehensive manner.

*Communicate*: To help ensure that appropriate mechanisms are in place to effectively communicate potentially threatening activities or breaches of corporate defense protocol to all the relevant parties in a timely manner.

*Identify options*: To help ensure that appropriate measures are in place in order to identify the best available response options in the event that potentially threatening activities have been identified.

*Make decisions*: To help ensure that appropriate measures are in place in order to allow for timely and informed decisions (i.e., tolerate, treat, transfer, or terminate) in relation to the most appropriate response to an identified threat.

*Take action*: To help ensure that appropriate measures are in place to allow appropriate mitigating action to be taken in a timely response to an identified threat or breach of corporate defense protocol.

*Correct*: To help ensure that appropriate procedures are in place to obtain assurance that the root cause has been identified and appropriate corrective measures put in place to prevent these events reoccurring in the future.

Ultimately, the most robust organizations will have the highest preemptive capabilities in place. It is the reaction times to potentially devastating events that will determine the magnitude of the initial impact and the subsequent collateral damage.

## 15.2   BUILDING AN EFFECTIVE CORPORATE DEFENSE PROGRAM

The smooth implementation of a corporate defense program is no easy feat and one that will be subject to many challenges over time. In order to ensure that the corporate defense program stands the best chance of operating in an effective manner, certain important issues first need to be addressed.

### 15.2.1   APPROPRIATE ENVIRONMENT

An appropriate working environment within the organization is essential for effective corporate defense. A number of key elements are required in order to create an appropriate working environment in which to establish an effective integrated corporate defense program.

#### 15.2.1.1   Setting the Tone at the Top

For corporate defense to operate in an effective manner, it must first be understood and supported by those at the very top of the organization. Top-down endorsement and support is essential and this understanding and support must in turn filter and cascade its way down throughout the organization so that it begins to be reflected in the culture of the organization. Once corporate defense has become embedded into the organization's culture, then meaningful integration can become a reality.

The board of directors should set the tone at the top by approving the establishment of the corporate defense program and the associated framework, and should also provide their senior management with clear guidance and direction regarding the principles underlying the framework. The program's strategic objectives should be represented in the organization's corporate strategy and supported by the executive management team.

#### 15.2.1.2   Tone at the Middle and the Bottom

It is not enough to simply set the tone at the top in relation to the corporate defense program; each organization must also foster an appropriate tone at the middle of the organization. Communications received from the top of the organization will have very little impact if the frontline staff see and/or hear a different message every day from their middle management team. The more the management layers are present, the greater the risk of the original message being altered, distorted, or lost. Without middle management's buy-in and support, many organizational initiatives lose momentum and simply fizzle out.

Bottom-up support and commitment is essential for effective corporate defense and this requires active engagement and participation from the frontline staff. An effective program requires bottom-up interaction, buy-in, and feedback as without support for the program in the frontline of defense the entire corporate defense initiative can be undermined. Organizations need to be particularly aware that the message being communicated can very often become distorted as it moves down the organization from the top, to the middle, and to the bottom, and equally as it moves up the organization from the bottom, to the middle, and to the top. Where information is distorted as it travels through the communication chain, this can lead to a serious disconnect between what the board is aware of and what is actually happening in the frontlines.

#### 15.2.1.3   Establishing Oversight

The board is ultimately responsible for corporate defense oversight; however, both senior and middle management are also key elements of effective corporate defense, as they have the responsibility for implementing the corporate defense program in practice. They should in turn assume appropriate corporate defense oversight roles with respect to their line management responsibilities and their fulfillment of their corporate defense assurance duties. The quality of the oversight and assurance provided is dependent on the delegated chain of command and the establishment of clear lines of responsibility and accountability from top to bottom. Oversight is concerned with monitoring and supervising and should flow down the organization from the top, to the middle, and to the bottom. Assurance is concerned with providing comfort, and should flow up the organization from the bottom, to the middle, and from the middle to the top.

Corporate defense oversight responsibilities and accountabilities need to be clearly understood from the outset and the adoption of the five lines of corporate defense model (see Chapter 7) can help an organization to deliver comprehensive oversight from top to bottom. This model provides a structured accountability hierarchy based on the delegation of authority, the assignment of responsibilities, and the allocation of corporate defense duties. Corporate defense roles, responsibilities, and reporting lines should be clearly and transparently addressed via organization charts, workflow programs, and job descriptions. The fulfillment of these corporate defense responsibilities needs to be monitored and assessed in order to provide a reasonable level of accountability. The quality of their performance, both quantitative and qualitative, needs to be fully appraised on an ongoing basis. This can include appraisals such as annual performance reviews, periodic assurance assignments, and continuous assessments in real time. Performance appraisal mechanisms should be in place at strategic, tactical, and operational levels.

### 15.2.2   The Corporate Defense Mandate

An important starting point for any corporate defense program is to clearly establish a robust corporate defense mandate. Such a mandate needs to be determined by the board in order to send out a clear and transparent message regarding the purpose and authority of the corporate defense program within the organization. The clearer and more forthright the mandate, the more straightforward the mission for all concerned. Clarity and transparency greatly reduce the risk of confusion and help to eliminate unnecessary complications.

#### 15.2.2.1   A Necessary Degree of Clout

To operate effectively, those engaged in the corporate defense program must have the necessary level of clout to be in a position to effectively perform their corporate defense duties. The apparent degree of clout associated with the program may well determine how the program is perceived to be prioritized and how seriously it is to be taken. Without a sufficient degree of clout, the program is unlikely to operate successfully. Clout requires a clear mandate that confers sufficient status, influence, and authority so that those involved in the program are in a position to contribute to the organization in an optimum manner. This applies to those involved in the corporate defense program at strategic, tactical, and operational levels.

#### 15.2.2.2   Status, Position, and Authority

Ideally, those individuals with leadership roles within the corporate defense program should have sufficient status within the organization to ensure that they are respected and that their views and opinions are taken seriously. Status within the organization can often be a perception based on an individual's grade, rank, or position. It can also be based on their reputation and standing among their peers, and their profile within the organization. Influence within an organization is often based on the personal networks and relationships developed with other individuals. A person of influence can very often be instrumental in persuading others to accept (or reject) proposed changes to the status quo. Authority within an organization is generally associated with a level of power that has been delegated to an individual. The authority to make the final decision on a particular issue confers a certain degree of power on the decision maker.

Unfortunately, in the realm of corporate defense there are too many examples where critical positions are not always filled by the best people in the organization, but rather by those whose careers are perceived to have stalled and are being *moved sideways*, or those nearing the end of their careers that are simply perceived as being *put out to pasture*. This quite often results in situations where on paper, and to external audiences, the appointment would appear to tick all the correct boxes; however, internally it is regarded as weak appointment or a nonappointment. Such appointments can seriously undermine the entire corporate defense program. Therefore, the importance of selecting and appointing the right individuals to key corporate defense roles should not be underestimated.

### 15.2.2.3 Utilization and Integration of Corporate Defense Disciplines

A successful and effective integration program should involve an understanding of the complex interdependences and interconnections that exist among the various corporate defense-related disciplines in order to avoid unnecessary duplication, omission, or conflict. Effective enterprise-wide corporate defense will require cooperation from all of these areas. The precise nature of the relationship among these corporate defense-related disciplines will need to be determined so that they are not at variance with one other. What is needed is a mechanism for leveraging and maximizing their potential added value to the organization. The seamless integration of these disciplines is critical to establishing an effective integrated program. Such integration requires the design of a corporate defense alliance network that facilitates the creation of a partnership alliance among all corporate defense-related activities. Such an alliance will involve identifying and engaging with all of the key corporate defense players across the organization. This includes various corporate defense champions and cheerleaders within the business who are considered to be valuable partners within the corporate defense program. It involves determining their roles as valued partners and fostering multidimensional (vertical and horizontal) engagement, participation, and collaboration among these partners.

### 15.2.3 Providing Structure to the Program

An effective corporate defense program needs to be built around a clear structure from the very beginning. A clear structure is required to help provide guidance to all those involved in the program and to help ensure that they have a clear understanding of what is required of them.

### 15.2.3.1 Corporate Defense Vision and Mission Statement

A clear corporate defense vision and mission statement should be determined outlining the purpose of the corporate defense program within the organization and clearly stating the requirement for its introduction (for more details, refer to Chapter 4). It is important that the program's long-term contribution to the organization is fully appreciated from the beginning.

### 15.2.3.2 Corporate Defense Strategy

A corporate defense strategy, which clearly gives direction on how ongoing activities should be conducted, should be established in order to achieve its strategic corporate objectives (for more details, refer to Chapter 4). In determining its concise strategic objectives, care must be taken to ensure that these are aligned to the strategic objectives of the organization, and its strategy and policies must clearly set out in broader terms how the organization is hoping to achieve these high-level objectives.

### 15.2.3.3 Corporate Defense Framework

An appropriate corporate defense framework should be selected in order to provide an infrastructure that can help the organization achieve its strategic corporate defense objectives (for more details, refer to Chapter 4). The organization should select a framework that is deemed as the best fit for its own unique circumstances (for details on the corporate defense management [CDM] framework, refer to Chapter 12).

### 15.2.3.4 Corporate Defense Charter

The appropriate status, position, and authority of the corporate defense program should be guaranteed by a documented charter that ideally should be required to be approved by the executive committee and confirmed by the board of directors (for more details, refer to Chapter 6).

The charter should state the terms and conditions under which the corporate defense program should operate within the organization. This charter will act as a continuous reference point and will help enhance the standing and authority of the corporate defense program within the organization.

### 15.2.3.5   Creation of a Corporate Defense Committee

An important step is the establishment of a corporate defense board committee or subcommittee that clearly indicates a direct reporting line to the board (for more details, refer to Chapter 6). A permanent corporate defense committee should be created in line with the procedure for creating other board committees such as the audit committee or a similar roundtable. The composition, powers, and functioning of this committee should be determined in advance and should be documented. It should be approved by the board of directors.

### 15.2.3.6   Corporate Defense Function

In order to effectively integrate and coordinate all of the critical corporate defense components, it is advisable to set up a centralized corporate defense function with the responsibility for the tactical management of all corporate defense-related activities (for more details, refer to Chapter 6). This centralized function should report to the corporate defense committee and have the responsibility for liaising with executive management and the business on a day-to-day basis.

### 15.2.3.7   Corporate Defense Plan

A comprehensive corporate defense plan should outline all of the work to be performed by the function, taking into consideration current activities and expected developments and innovations (for more details, refer to Chapter 4). This plan should include the nature, timing, frequency, and required resources for planned work. The plan should be prepared by the corporate defense function and approved by the corporate defense committee.

## 15.3   THE PROGRAM IN PRACTICE

Once an appropriate infrastructure has been decided upon and addressed, the next challenge to be addressed is the challenge of putting the theory into practice. This phase involves the execution of the corporate defense strategy and the implementation of the corporate defense plan.

### 15.3.1   Pulling It All Together

Getting the program up and running is no easy task and requires skillful management at different levels within the organization. It also requires the management of multiple different issues simultaneously and this is particularly important in the initial stages of the program. Once it is up and running, the next challenge is to ensure that the momentum is maintained and that the initial enthusiasm is not lost along the way. This requires both human resource (HR) skills and leadership skills in order to continuously motivate and inspire individuals to continue to perform their duties at the highest levels. Certain practical steps are therefore required to be addressed during the roll-out of the corporate defense program.

#### 15.3.1.1   Policies, Procedures, and Work Programs

The establishment of appropriate policies and procedures requires sufficient determination, development, documentation, and approval, before being effectively communicated to all personnel involved in the corporate defense program (for more details, refer to Chapter 5). Professional work programs should also be prepared in advance for all work to be undertaken by those involved in the corporate defense program. Corporate defense policies and procedures should reflect the seamless integration of the corporate defense-related disciplines with the operations of the business.

### 15.3.1.2 Education and Communication

The corporate defense function should assist and support senior management in educating staff on corporate defense matters. An education program should be introduced to ensure that all staff members have a clear understanding of the purpose of corporate defense, and their own key role in corporate defense as it relates to their area. Maintenance and development of professional competence and skills should be facilitated by regular and systematic education and training. It is also important that the ownership of corporate defense is seen to rest with all the members of the organization, as the role of each of its members cannot be underestimated in order to ensure a successful corporate defense program. Interactive communication is required on an ongoing basis to help ensure that all relevant parties are kept abreast of developments in the corporate defense realm.

### 15.3.1.3 Corporate Defense Resources

The corporate defense program requires the approval of sufficient investment in order to deliver the required resources. The resources to be provided to the corporate defense program and function should be both sufficient and appropriate to perform the required duties and responsibilities effectively. Corporate defense resources need to have the capability and capacity to execute the corporate defense strategy and to implement the corporate defense plan. Capability refers to recruiting and retaining appropriately talented and competent individuals who possess the relevant qualifications, expertise, and experience required to perform the required duties. It can also refer to the capability of technology and systems to perform required tasks. Capacity refers to the actual or potential ability to perform the required amount of work within specified periods. It refers to the maximum capacity of people, processes, and systems to deliver on schedule. Where constraints on capability or capacity are identified, these need to be addressed in a timely manner so that the desired levels of capability and capacity are in place. Corporate defense resources include people, processes, and systems.

### 15.3.1.4 Program Operations and Administration

Managing the program's operational issues means addressing many issues that are common to many different types of organizational initiatives and are regarded as being part of normal business management, rather than being considered specific to the corporate defense program. Therefore, rather than attempting to reinvent the wheel specifically for corporate defense, the organization should incorporate the adoption of proven professional methodologies, management tools, and management systems to help progress the program through the various stages of its program cycle. Examples of some of these management approaches include the following:

*Project management*: The adoption of a project management approach during the initial program start-up stage of the corporate defense program can get the program off the ground and up and running. Project management is concerned with initiating, planning, and executing projects by organizing, motivating, and controlling resources to achieve specific goals. The use of recognized project management tools and techniques can assist in the short term in order to help launch the program and to progress it to the next stage. An initial project management focus can help ensure that the early milestones are delivered on time, within budget, and to specification.

*Program management*: Implementing a corporate defense program requires addressing a large number of related projects across the entire organization. Program management is concerned with selecting the right projects and executing the projects correctly. Typically, these projects involve several parallel initiatives or activities that need to be managed and coordinated in an integrated manner. The use of recognized program management tools and techniques can help an organization to optimize economies of scale and consistently deliver across a number of different related components over the medium to long term.

*Process management*: The use of recognized process management tools and techniques can help an organization to focus on managing and optimizing the organization's corporate defense processes. The corporate defense process cycle should include designing, modeling, executing, monitoring, optimizing, and reengineering corporate defense processes in order to ensure that they are effective and efficient, and flexible and adaptable.

*Performance management*: The use of recognized performance management tools and techniques can help the organization to ensure that goals are consistently being met in an effective and efficient manner. This includes the use of mechanisms to monitor, measure, and improve corporate defense performance and productivity, and to monitor costs incurred and the timely achievement of goals and objectives in line with targets and deadlines. Performance management can be applied to people, processes, and systems.

*Change management*: The use of recognized change management tools and techniques can help an organization to address the requirement for change in order to continuously transform the program and arrive at the desired future state. Change management is important in addressing employee resistance to different change initiatives and in aligning employees with the strategic direction of the program.

*Continuous improvement*: The use of recognized continuous improvement tools and techniques can help an organization to continuously improve people, processes, and systems by monitoring maturity levels and learning from ongoing events. Continuous improvement involves improving knowledge, awareness, capability, and performance.

In addition to the above, there are also certain ongoing day-to-day operational matters that need to be addressed in collaboration with departments and functions that provide shared support services throughout the organization. These include

*Human resources*: The program needs to leverage from the potential support provided from the HR function. This includes support in addressing personnel issues such as the recruitment, development, and retention of corporate defense staff. The HR function can help in not only dealing with succession planning, talent management, personnel appraisals, and compensation issues, but also in the provision of educational and training support necessary for talent development.

*Finance*: The program needs to leverage from the potential support provided from the finance function. This includes support in addressing finance-related matters such as budget submission, approval, and adherence. The finance function can also provide assistance in relation to assessing the return on corporate defense investment and ongoing cost–benefit analysis and value for money evaluations.

*Operations*: The program needs to leverage from the potential support provided from the operations function. This includes support in the selection of fixtures and fittings, and in the procurement of office furniture and other supplies. The operations function can also provide assistance in relation to other ongoing logistical issues.

*Information technology (IT)*: The program needs to leverage from the potential support provided from the IT function. This includes the support in addressing the program's requirements in relation to its technology infrastructure and architecture, and in the procurement, installation, and maintenance of the required IT equipment.

### 15.3.2 PROGRAM MONITORING AND SUPERVISION

Once the corporate defense program is up and running, it is essential that its ongoing operation is appropriately monitored and adequately supervised in order to ensure the ongoing accomplishment of corporate defense objectives. It is equally important to identify deviations from the corporate defense plan in order to take appropriate remedial action. Corporate defense oversight and ongoing supervision should be in line with the agreed corporate defense oversight framework and follow the agreed direct reporting lines.

### 15.3.2.1 Monitoring and Assurance

A number of parties should be actively engaged in monitoring the operation of the corporate defense program; this specifically includes the corporate defense committee, the corporate defense function, and business management. On an ongoing basis, monitoring can involve day-to-day internal controls, continuous monitoring systems, and quality control management. Periodic monitoring can include periodic management controls (i.e., weekly, monthly, quarterly, or annually) and periodic audits and reviews performed by the different critical corporate defense units. In addition, the operation of the corporate defense committee and the corporate defense function should be subject to periodic independent reviews by the internal audit function. Other forms of assurance on the operations of the corporate defense program can also be obtained from different available assurance providers both internal and external to the organization (for more details, refer to the assurance section in Chapter 10).

### 15.3.2.2 Corporate Defense Reporting

In order to assess the progress of the execution of the corporate defense strategy and the implementation of the corporate defense plan, a clear reporting structure should be put in place. Such reporting can help provide a clear indication of whether or not the corporate defense strategy is on schedule and on its intended course, and it can also provide a status update on the implementation of the corporate defense plan. Corporate defense reporting is also required to provide information in relation to a variety of different matters including the impact of material corporate defense-related events and experiences, the results of corporate defense reviews or root cause explanation of issues of concern, and focusing on emerging corporate defense issues or the future corporate defense outlook.

In Chapter 9, the intelligence component was described as *how an organization ensures that it gets the right information, for the right purpose, in the right format, to the right person, in the right place, and at the right time.* This maxim specifically applies to reporting. Table 15.1 outlines the important basic reporting questions that need to be addressed when considering the corporate defense reporting requirements:

The answers to the above questions should help determine the specific corporate defense reporting requirements at different levels within the organization, including at strategic, tactical, and operational levels. For example, strategic level reports may contain summary information and take the form of corporate defense heat-maps or dashboards. Tactical level reports may be broader in focus and take the form of a corporate defense balanced scorecard or corporate defense analytics. Operational level reports may specifically address individual critical corporate defense components or other specific operational issues that require a deeper level of technical detail.

Key corporate defense indicators may include the reporting of various quantitative metrics, for example, the number of occurrences of hazard events or potential near misses, and the financial

---

**TABLE 15.1**

**Reporting Questions**

| | | |
|---|---|---|
| *Right information* | What? | What reports are required and what information needs to be contained in these reports? |
| *Right purpose* | Why? | Why are these reports required? What is their purpose and what do they hope to achieve? |
| *Right format* | How? | How can the required information be best presented in these reports? |
| *Right person* | Who? | Who are the intended recipients of the reports? Who are the target audience in each case? |
| *Right place* | Where? | Where should these reports be located? Where should they be delivered to? |
| *Right time* | When? | When should the reports be produced and when should they be delivered? |

impact of losses resulting from operational errors. They may also include reporting on qualitative information such as stakeholder feedback on corporate defense-related matters and analysis of the organization's success or failure to anticipate, prevent, detect, and react to the various corporate defense events experienced by the organization itself or within the industry. In any event, each organization must determine its own precise corporate defense reporting requirements, but this should be driven by those with responsibility for corporate defense oversight.

### 15.3.3 THE KEY TO SUCCESS

The key to success in implementing an effective corporate defense program is to identify those aspects of the program that need to go right and ensuring that sufficient focus, time, and effort is devoted to ensuring that this occurs. In the normal course of business, it is highly likely that there will be certain surprises and setbacks; however, these can be overcome if the organization is sufficiently prepared for potential knock-backs and these events can actually act as learning experiences from which to learn and improve.

#### 15.3.3.1 Critical Success Factors

The important point is to identify what are considered to be the critical success factors for the corporate defense program to operate effectively. There are different techniques available in order to not only identify the critical issues that can have the greatest impact on the success of the program but also to determine how these issues might arise and what can be done to anticipate, prevent, detect, or react to these events occurring. Techniques such as critical path analysis, scenario analysis, root-cause analysis, and bow tie analysis can prove helpful in this process, as can various other group exercises such as brainstorming or mind-mapping. Whatever approach is chosen by the organization, it is important that the organization is fully aware of its critical success factors in order to meet its targets, achieve its milestones, implement its plan, execute its strategy, and fulfill its vision.

#### 15.3.3.2 The Seven Deadly "C"s

The degree to which certain specific factors are present can have a strong bearing on the ongoing success or failure of a corporate defense program (Lyons 2006c). The following key factors are considered critical to the successful implementation of any corporate defense program:

*Commitment*: It is critical that there is a sincere level of commitment to succeed right from the very top of the organization. This commitment must begin with the board of directors and must also include executive management.

*Confidence*: It is critical that the nomination of responsibility and accountability for corporate defense must be of a suitable level of authority, seniority, and status to inspire confidence in the above level of commitment.

*Competence*: It is critical that the corporate defense program must include individuals who possess the appropriate qualifications, experience, skills, attributes, and knowledge necessary to fulfill the obligations of the program.

*Comprehensiveness*: It is critical that the scope of the corporate defense program must be comprehensive and complete. It must include all aspects of the organization including head office, branches, subsidiaries, business units, divisions, and departments.

*Coordination*: It is critical that the coordination of corporate defense program must be from a centralized source whose role is to integrate, align, and unite the business and the various corporate defense-related disciplines.

*Collaboration*: It is critical that there is adequate collaboration between all defense-related disciplines to optimize the experience and expertise possessed within the organization and help form a partnership to ensure that all partners are operating in unison.

*Continuation*: It is critical that those involved in the corporate defense program are continuously vigilant to ensure that the program is operating effectively on an ongoing basis, while at the same time continuously evolving and improving.

## 15.3.4  PROGRAM CHECKS AND BALANCES

In order for most initiatives to operate effectively over time, there needs to be an appropriate system of checks and balances in place throughout. This applies as much to the corporate defense program itself as it would to any other program. Similar to an enterprise risk management (ERM) or internal audit program, in order to determine the extent to which the corporate defense program is fit for purpose, assurance is required over different elements. This includes an evaluation of the design and implementation of the program as a management system, and an evaluation of the operational practices of the program (Swanson 2010).

### 15.3.4.1  Assessing the Corporate Defense Program

Any assessment of the corporate defense program should begin with considering the extent to which it is successfully contributing to value preservation and also its contribution to the achievement of the organization's business objectives. The value proposition of the corporate defense program (see Chapter 17) is dependent on a close strategic alignment with the organization's business objectives. Without such a focus, the potential of the program is unlikely to be realized.

A traditional review of the corporate defense program can include assessments at strategic, tactical, and operational levels as follows:

*Strategic assessment*: An assessment at a strategic level should include an evaluation of the existence of a formally approved corporate defense program, including a corporate defense vision, a corporate defense mission, and a corporate defense strategy (see Chapter 4). The existence of a formal corporate defense program charter may address many of these issues. This evaluation should also include the extent to which the above are in close alignment with the vision, mission, and strategy of the business, and an examination of the measures in place to ensure that the strategic corporate defense objectives are continuously in alignment with business objectives.

*Tactical assessment*: An assessment at a tactical level should include an evaluation of the existence of a formal corporate defense framework, a corporate defense plan (see Chapter 4), and formal corporate defense policies (see Chapter 5). This evaluation should include the maturity of the corporate defense initiative and the level of available resources. It should include the existence and workings of the identified groups and individuals with responsibility for corporate defense, and extent to which these are helping to successfully implement the corporate defense plan. This evaluation should also include the extent to which all of the critical corporate defense components are individually addressed within the above, and an examination of the measures in place to ensure that their objectives are in continuous alignment.

*Operational assessment*: An assessment at an operational level should include an evaluation of the existence of formal corporate defense systems, processes, and procedures. This evaluation should include the operational execution of the corporate defense plan, the identified corporate defense-related key performance indicators (KPIs), and the mechanisms in place for monitoring and reporting on these. This evaluation should also include the operational performance of corporate defense-related activities on a day-to-day basis and the extent to which these activities have become integrated into business practices.

**TABLE 15.2**

**Corporate Defense Program's CDM Approach**

| | |
|---|---|
| Governance | How is the corporate defense program addressing its own governance requirements? Has a prudent approach to governance been adopted in relation to the program's people, processes, and systems and to its activities at strategic, tactical, and operational levels? (See Chapter 9.) |
| Risk | How is the corporate defense program addressing its own risk requirements? Has a prudent approach to risk been adopted in relation to the program's people, processes, and systems and to its activities at strategic, tactical, and operational levels? (See Chapter 9.) |
| Compliance | How is the corporate defense program addressing its own compliance requirements? Has a prudent approach to compliance been adopted in relation to the program's people, processes, and systems and to its activities at strategic, tactical, and operational levels? (See Chapter 9.) |
| Intelligence | How is the corporate defense program addressing its own intelligence requirements? Has a prudent approach to intelligence been adopted in relation to the program's people, processes, and systems and to its activities at strategic, tactical, and operational levels? (See Chapter 9.) |
| Security | How is the corporate defense program addressing its own security requirements? Has a prudent approach to security been adopted in relation to the program's people, processes, and systems and to its activities at strategic, tactical, and operational levels? (See Chapter 10.) |
| Resilience | How is the corporate defense program addressing its own resilience requirements? Has a prudent approach to resilience been adopted in relation to the program's people, processes, and systems and to its activities at strategic, tactical, and operational levels? (See Chapter 10.) |
| Controls | How is the corporate defense program addressing its own controls requirements? Has a prudent approach to controls been adopted in relation to the program's people, processes, and systems and to its activities at strategic, tactical, and operational levels? (See Chapter 10.) |
| Assurance | How is the corporate defense program addressing its own assurance requirements? Has a prudent approach to assurance been adopted in relation to the program's people, processes, and systems and to its activities at strategic, tactical, and operational levels? (See Chapter 10.) |

### 15.3.4.2  Application of the CDM Diagnostic

Alternatively, the robustness of the corporate defense program can be determined by applying the CDM methodology to the program itself. Such interdisciplinary scrutiny can help to quickly identify weaknesses and deficiencies in the program so that they can be rectified in a timely manner. The CDM matrix can therefore be applied to the management of the corporate defense program and can be a useful diagnostic tool for an organization when considering how it is addressing this program. Table 15.2 outlines the corporate defense program's CDM approach.

In relation to the above, a review of the assurance component in particular should include evaluating the mechanisms in place to provide the organization with at least reasonable assurance that the corporate defense program is operating in an effective and efficient manner. This should include the provision of strategic assurance, tactical assurance, and operational assurance.

The application of the CDM diagnostic is important to ensure that the corporate defense program is in fact applying the same corporate defense standards and protocols to its own corporate defense initiative as it would expect other aspects of the business to apply to their initiatives. It can also be helpful in understanding and empathizing with the difficulties faced by other parts of the business when faced with similar corporate defense expectations.

# 16 Organizational, Technological, and Future Challenges

It is not the strongest of the species that survives, nor the most intelligent that survives. It is the one that is most adaptable to change.*

**Charles Darwin**

## 16.1 ORGANIZATIONAL CHALLENGES FACING CORPORATE DEFENSE

Corporate defense by its very nature requires a cross-functional approach as it seeks to unite the activities of a number of discrete functions within the organization. This means that it can face unique challenges in an attempt to address the diverse points of view and expectations of several partners, each of which may have their own independent strategies and objectives. The overriding challenge will be to develop a mechanism to ensure that these diverse perspectives can be facilitated by forming a durable coalition with a common set of objectives and expectations.

### 16.1.1 BOARD AND EXECUTIVE COMMITMENT

A primary challenge for any corporate defense program is in securing an appropriate level of support and commitment for the program from the very top of the organization. The board and executive management need to be sold on the requirement for a robust corporate defense program, as any lack of the required commitment from these parties can completely undermine the entire program and thereby limit its potential effectiveness. Where an organization fails to secure the required top level

---

* Per *The New Science of Sustainability: Building a Foundation for Great Change*, 2008, S.J. Goerner, R.G. Dyck and D. Lagerroos, Triangle Center for Complex Systems, Chapel Hill, NC.

buy-in, typically these corporate defense initiatives tend to be regarded as mere window dressing for the benefit of external stakeholders. Such circumstances unfortunately are far too common in the corporate world as revealed time and again by postmortem reviews of corporate scandals.

### 16.1.1.1 Top-Down Endorsement

To be effective, the corporate defense program needs to be firmly placed on the board of directors' agenda and openly endorsed by the board. It requires that an appropriate *tone at the top* is set by the board in relation to the organization's commitment to corporate defense. The board, as the ultimate guardians of the organization and its last line of defense, needs to take ownership of the corporate defense program and needs to be seen as its driving force. This can most clearly be demonstrated by the corporate defense champion(s) having a direct reporting line to the board. Ownership by the board may be achieved more easily if the board composition includes at least certain members who already have some form of corporate defense experience. It is however still advisable that the entire board receives an appropriate level of education and training in relation to its corporate defense oversight obligations.

A particular challenge arises where board members lack the required expertise or a firm appreciation and understanding of the organization's value preservation imperative. This can potentially result in a complacent board and its associated committees or subcommittees, and can reflect a general lack of interest in and commitment to corporate defense activities. Under such circumstances, the general attitude to corporate defense in the organization is likely to follow suit, thereby potentially undermining the entire corporate defense program and its related corporate defense activities.

### 16.1.1.2 Executive Buy-In

Executive management has an important role to play in helping to shape the culture of the organization and in the process its attitude to corporate defense. In reality, executive management needs to be fully convinced of the business case[*] for a corporate defense program before such an initiative will receive their full support. A clear and compelling cost–benefit analysis is therefore of crucial importance in order to gain the genuine support of executive management. The executive in turn has an important role to play in helping to ensure that the business buys into the need for a corporate defense program, and in helping to ensure that corporate defense activities are regarded as adding positive value to the organization. It is essential that executive management is truly convinced that a corporate defense program can genuinely help to enable the business in its efforts and actually add value in the process.

This challenge becomes even more difficult where executive management remains unconvinced of the added value of the corporate defense program and does not have a genuine appreciation of the merits of such a program. In such circumstances, corporate defense activities can be viewed as a hindrance to the business and in some cases as business disablers. Such an attitude can result in distrust and even in conflict between the business and the different corporate defense activities. In such a climate, the corporate defense program can lack the required support, and the effectiveness of the program can be greatly diminished.

### 16.1.1.3 Guarding against Overselling and Distraction

Unfortunately in many organizations, while boards and executive management intuitively associate the primary role of corporate defense-related activities with value preservation, they rarely associate these roles with the pursuit of opportunities and the creation of stakeholder value. This has resulted in a general feeling among many corporate defense practitioners that their contribution to the organization is undervalued. In ongoing efforts to convince boards and executive management of the potential for corporate defense-related activities to contribute toward value creation, certain practitioners and groups are quite rightly now promoting a more positive image of this potential contribution.

---

[*] Refer to Chapter 17.

This stretching outside traditional comfort zones can no doubt be of benefit; however, caution also needs to be exercised. Examples of this include promoting internal audit as internal consultants,[*] replacing the traditional duality of risk and reward with downside and upside risk,[†] and renaming the lines of defense approach as the lines of offense.[‡] Any attempt to paint corporate defense activities in a more proactive light must also respect certain competence boundaries. It is important that in the ongoing quest for greater business acceptance that overenthusiasm or exuberance does not lead to overselling or overstating what can actually be delivered in practice. With this in mind, corporate defense practitioners need to guard against the creation of overly optimistic expectations or unrealistic promises. While it is no doubt important that corporate defense-related activities adopt a *strategy-centric* focus in order to ensure that they are contributing to the execution of the organization's strategy and the achievement of its objectives, it is also important that their focus is not deflected or distracted away from their primary responsibility, that of value preservation.

## 16.1.2  BUSINESS ALIGNMENT AND SUPPORT

The support of the business for any corporate defense initiative is essential if corporate defense is to be effective, is to positively contribute to business activities, and is to become embedded into the organization's culture. Any successful alliance with the business however means that the corporate defense objectives must be in alignment with the overall business objectives in order to help foster an environment of cooperation and collaboration. For corporate defense to be in alignment with the business, there is a requirement for corporate defense practitioners to have a certain degree of empathy with the business and an understanding of the needs of the business. This means that there needs to be knowledge of the business processes, a comprehension of what actually motivates the business, and how its individuals are incentivized. It means that there needs to be an awareness of the expectations and goals of the business, and a clear understanding of the underlying business assumptions. Successful partnership and alignment with the business requires mutual trust and mutual respect. Where such a partnership is in place, it becomes far easier for both parties to demonstrate the requirement for a mutually beneficial relationship.

### 16.1.2.1  Business Acceptance

The extent of the challenge of encouraging the business to accept the need for a robust corporate defense program should however not be underestimated. Where the business is compensated for short-term results, there is a strong incentive to focus on short-term gain even if such behavior could lead to longer-term pain. Hence, the board and executive management need to carefully consider the value preservation imperative when formulating incentive schemes for the business. Where corporate defense activities are seen to be in conflict with the organization's incentive schemes, the business may consider such activities as being a business disabler. Where this occurs, the business is unlikely to support such measures and is more likely to resist any effort that it feels may restrict business performance. At best, the business will only pay glib attention to such corporate defense measures; at worst, the business will strongly oppose such measures and may result in the creation of a working environment full of distrust, antagonism, and hostility. Such a reaction can result in a highly dysfunctional organization. Business acceptance of the need for a robust corporate defense program is therefore fundamental to the effective working of such a program.

---

[*] Certain commentators argue that in acting as an internal consultant, the independence of the internal auditor(s) can be undermined or compromised.

[†] The concept of upside risk is a somewhat controversial matter, given the mainstream business understanding of risk being associated with a negative impact. It can therefore be difficult for some to comprehend the notion of upside risk as being the risk associated with something working out for the best.

[‡] Business strategy commentators may suggest that any *lines of offense* approach should logically focus on the role of the organization's core offense activities. It should therefore primarily address the important roles of business activities such as sales, marketing, advertising, promotion, public relations, customer service, and product development.

#### 16.1.2.2  Business Integration

To operate effectively, corporate defense activities need to become integrated and embedded into the day-to-day business activities of the organization until they form part of the organization's DNA. For this to occur, the business must first be educated on the advantages for the organization of adopting such practices, and how it will benefit the business to incorporate such activities into their daily practices. Corporate defense activities must then be tailored to best suit the business and help ensure the minimum disruption to business activities. Therefore, appropriate attention to detail needs to be given to the actual design, configuration, and engineering of corporate defense activities if they are to be seamlessly integrated into the business. The initial integration exercise is crucial as over time these corporate defense activities will become accepted as being part of normal business activities. By being aligned to the needs of the business, the organization's corporate defense activities can more easily be streamlined, and synchronized with business activities, thereby removing possible triggers for resistance or opposition. Ideally, once corporate defense activities become integrated into normal business activities, from that point onward corporate defense should then form part of normal business decision making going forward.

### 16.1.3  Cross-Functional Integration

The integration of various existing corporate defense functions in itself can represent a formidable challenge to the smooth operation of the corporate defense program. Although aligning, coordinating, and integrating these activities under one corporate defense umbrella makes a great deal of rational sense, such an exercise may not prove to be all smooth sailing and is not without its difficulties, which will need to be navigated around.

#### 16.1.3.1  Functional Silos

In circumstances where individual corporate defense functions previously operated in isolation of one another, very often this may result in functional silos, whereby each function was only concerned with the achievement of their own functional objectives rather than taking a broader corporate defense perspective. In many cases, these functional silos may have developed their own subcultures that may prove to be a potential barrier or source of resistance to a smooth integration with other corporate defense-related functions. There may be difficulties experienced by the use of a different vocabulary and taxonomy in each of these functions that can present unexpected communication challenges. These types of language issues, sometimes referred to as a *Tower of Babel* syndrome, can result in communication among these functions often being at cross purposes, leading to a degree of confusion, frustration, and miscommunication. The integration of existing stand-alone legacy systems in each function can also prove a distinct challenge at least in the short term, whereby certain systems may require a degree of reengineering or may not in fact be compatible with other systems. Organizations with prior experience of addressing such issues from previous mergers or acquisitions may find such challenges easier to overcome. In any event, effective cross-functional integration will require an appropriate level of education and cross-training in order to help all sides appreciate their individual and collective roles in the corporate defense program. Generally speaking, in order to encourage and facilitate greater cooperation and collaboration among existing corporate defense functions, it is necessary to unite them under a common vision and align them with common strategic objectives.

#### 16.1.3.2  Power Struggles and Turf Wars

Uniting all corporate defense functions under one umbrella may sound good in theory; however, it requires enlightened and determined management to implement successfully in practice. For example, the heads of risk, compliance, and assurance are rarely considered to be easy pushovers and a unified corporate defense program can therefore be considered a threat to their personal fiefdoms, and can therefore be the source of potential conflict. The determination of *who will be responsible for what* requires a certain degree of diplomacy and can easily result in power struggles among different corporate defense functions, as each function head wishes to exert their influence for personal gain. An environment where there is already a residue of distrust and rivalry present among these functions as a result of previous personality clashes can quickly develop into full-scale turf wars as each function attempts to expand their sphere of influence and further their own functional agenda. Circumstances that result in corporate defense functions being at loggerheads and actually viewing one another as rivals rather than allies can result in a toxic environment and in dysfunctional behavior, which can be detrimental to the organization and the achievement of its objectives. So while there is a very strong case for implementing a unified corporate defense program, each organization should be aware that it may not be easy to achieve in practice and should be approached with caution and care. Ultimately, any such personality clashes require diplomacy and strong leadership if they are to be successfully resolved.

### 16.1.3.3  Resistance to Change

Organizations will always be faced with a certain level of resistance to any proposed changes to the status quo, no matter what form of change is being proposed. Whether what is being proposed is a change in work practices, a change in technology, or a change in personnel there is always potential for resistance to change if not dealt with sensitively and in a professional manner. Experts in human behavior and people management have developed various approaches to introducing change to the status quo and change management has developed as a discipline all of its own. Many organizations therefore recognize that change to the status quo needs to be managed in a professional manner and that there are certain change management practices and techniques that need to be adopted in order to help ensure that the change being proposed is tailored to the organization's circumstances and therefore meets with minimum resistance. There are far too many examples of organization's poorly handling changes, which in theory could have been beneficial to the organization; however, in practice they were not considered to be a good fit with the organization's culture and expectations. Proposed changes to the corporate defense status quo require the adoption of appropriate change management practices and techniques in order to help ensure that these changes are addressed in a manner that is considered to be acceptable and in line with the organization's culture.

### 16.1.4  Proactive Engagement Required

In order to address many of these organizational challenges, there has to be proactive engagement by all parties at all levels within the organization. An environment of mutual respect and mutual trust needs to be created, whereby the respective roles of all parties are recognized and appreciated. This requires open and continuous communication and engagement among all parties in order to help foster the required level of cooperation and collaboration. There needs to be a recognition of the rights of each party to agree, disagree, or even agree to disagree. Such engagement should however be conducted in a professional manner where differences of opinion are welcomed and discussed among colleagues who are regarded as being on the same team rather than in an adversarial manner. On points of fundamental disagreement there should be an appropriate arbitration mechanism available in order to resolve these issues in a professional manner.

### 16.1.4.1  A Coalition of the Willing

A unified approach to corporate defense incorporating all corporate defense-related activities needs to be viewed in the context of being similar to a confederation or a coalition of partners and willing collaborators. Such an approach recognizes that all parties are committed to a common objective that will serve the greater good, while also recognizing their need to protect their own constituency in the process. Although most organizations are not run as democracies when attempting to arrive at a consensus, there should still be scope for input and challenge from all parties in the search for unanimous agreement. Under such circumstances, dissenting voices should be regarded as providing a healthy scrutiny of the issue under discussion rather than adopting a herd mentality, whereby the necessary scrutiny may be absent.

### 16.1.4.2   A Valued Partnership

Organizations need to focus on creating a valued partnership among all corporate defense-related parties, whereby each party understands its expected value input into the corporate defense program and also understands the associated output to expect in return. Each party not only feels valued within this partnership, but also values the existence of the other parties within the relationship. A valued partnership is where all parties understand and appreciate that the existence of the partnership is a mutually beneficial arrangement. Such a partnership can help to reinforce the shared value that each of the parties adds to the organization and how value preservation is essential to the sustainability of the organization. A valued partnership includes an arrangement involving mutual trust and respect for the dignity of others. It involves an appreciation that collectively far more can be achieved than when operating individually in isolation.

### 16.1.4.3   Focus on Collective Requirements

By focusing on the collective requirements of the different parties concerned, it becomes possible to move beyond any differences of opinion that might exist and allows the larger extended group to focus on what is best for the organization rather than what is right for any one individual function. Collective requirements are closely linked to the alignment of objectives so that all parties are clearly *on the same page* and *singing from the same hymn sheet* so that they can move forward together in unison in the same direction. All parties need to be clearly on the same side and all pulling in the same direction as a team. Working together in teams can achieve far more than individuals in the short, medium, and long term, and this equally applies to the corporate defense team.

## 16.2   ONGOING TECHNOLOGY CHALLENGES

The twenty-first century presents organizations with many different challenges and many believe that the most daunting challenges will be those presented by developments in technology. As organizations all over the world now enter into the technological age, how they address the challenges posed by technology may well determine their future success or failure. How organizations address the technology challenge therefore has a major role to play in achieving long-term sustainability. From a corporate defense perspective it is important to appreciate that technology presents its own unique corporate defense challenges in terms of safeguarding the organization and in terms of how corporate defense operates in practice.

### 16.2.1   Business in a Technological Age

Organizations need to appreciate that doing business in a technological age is similar to dealing with a double-edged sword. The technological age can no doubt present incredible opportunities for a business to flourish, but it can also present sometimes unimaginable threats that can prove to be devastating to the business. The role of a corporate defense program is to help the organization take full advantage of the opportunities that present themselves, although at the same time providing the organization with safeguards against possible threats.

### 16.2.1.1   Technology as an Opportunity

Technological developments present opportunities for organizations to gain a competitive advantage over their rivals by using this technology to offer new or improved products and services. Technological development can present organizations with opportunities to enhance the effectiveness and efficiency of their operations by reducing costs, improving performance, and increasing productivity. It can also present organizations with the option of expanding into new markets previously beyond their reach as the corporate world increasingly becomes a global village. Industries and business sectors are constantly being revolutionized by disruptive technology, and for those organizations that are capable of harnessing value from this game-changing technology to address their own specific needs, the sky appears to be the limit. Intellectual property (IP) is emerging as the dominant corporate asset and the emergence of giant multinational organizations such as Google, Microsoft, Intel, and Apple serve as examples of how quickly new technology-driven organizations can overtake more traditional but historically successfully organizations in terms of market value and profitability. An effective corporate defense program needs to focus on helping its organization to leverage from technological development in order to take full advantage of the opportunities it presents.

### 16.2.1.2  Technology as a Threat

Developments in technology also present an organization's rivals and competitors with opportunities to gain a competitive advantage by offering new and improved products and services. The technological age creates competition and not all organizations can be winners. Corporate history is the story of technological innovation, where new technology regularly kills off and replaces older technology, and where over time the winners are those who react quickly and the losers are those who are slower to react. For every example of an organization that has taken advantage of the technological opportunities that has presented itself, there are many more examples of organizations that have suffered from failing to adapt quickly enough to the changing circumstances that resulted from technological advances. Over the years market leaders in many different industry sectors (e.g., music, entertainment, and telecoms) have failed to recognize the impact that advances in technology would have on their industries and markets, and have subsequently paid a heavy price for such complacency. For example, in the camera manufacturing sector, the arrival of the digital age meant that former market leaders such as Polaroid and Kodak would fall victim to disruptive technology. In other areas, as IP and critical infrastructure become more important to organizations, introducing effective measures to help safeguard them has also become an emerging challenge that is continuous and unending in its nature. Revelations from whistle-blowers such as Julian Assange and Edward Snowden have raised many sensitive issues into the public consciousness, and this in turn has had a knock-on effect on the business world. What has become apparent is that as technology advances so too do the threats posed by technology, and these threats are constantly evolving, morphing, and mutating, which means that there is no place for complacency or smugness in the technological age. The corporate defense program must help the organization to best anticipate, prevent, detect, and react to the general and specific issues that arise out of the technological challenges facing organizations in the twenty-first century.

### 16.2.2  TECHNOLOGICAL ADVANCES

Significant technological advances have been occurring throughout the twentieth century; however, it is the pace of these advances that is of most concern given that these advances are occurring at what appear to be exponential rates when compared to the previous century and even previous decades. The sheer speed, scale, and impact of these advances have already fundamentally changed how our world operates and how human beings interact with each other on a daily basis. The only thing certain is that ongoing technological advances will continue to change how we interact and behave; however, what is less certain is the impact that such a change will have on business the world over.

### 16.2.2.1  Communication and Information Sharing

Technological advances have seen incredible changes to how human beings and organizations communicate with one another in the twenty-first century. Traditional forms of communication such as direct face-to-face contact, letter writing, and even telephone calls have been replaced by online websites and social media, e-mails, texting, and messaging, and of course video calls. Successful companies such as Facebook, Twitter, and Skype have been influential in shaping many of these changes and have reaped the rewards. More and more organizations are now appreciating the importance of developing a strong social media presence and are experiencing first hand both the upside and the downside of social media and the speed at which an individual issue (positive or negative) can go viral.

The manner in which organizations share information was drastically altered in the 1980s and 1990s with the roll-out of the World Wide Web and the use of website content and email. Search engines such as Yahoo and Google mean that information once obscure was now readily available at our fingertips. The use of multimedia to share information has continued and traditional forms of media such as television, newspapers, and magazines have had to adapt accordingly. The modern tech savvy business person now expects and demands state-of-the-art technology and this has led to a growth in the *bring your own device* (BYOD) concept in the workplace, simply in order to help facilitate the individual's specific requirements. Such devices, while value adding in their own right can also prove to be problematic and bring fresh challenges that need to be addressed.

### 16.2.2.2  Advances in Automation

Technological advances have resulted in an increasing number of organizations globally adopting automated equipment to perform work previously done by human beings, and to enhance work currently being done by human beings. Examples include the use of robotics in the production lines in the manufacturing industry, the emerging use of drones in commercial and military activity, and the use of 3D printing in areas such as production and more recently construction. There is even an example of a Hong Kong-based venture capital firm, Deep Knowledge Ventures, appointing a computer algorithm called *Vital* to its board of directors. Consumer behavior has also changed by the use of mobile apps in everyday life, and as an increasing percentage of retail sales are now being transacted over the Internet as online shopping is gradually being accepted by consumers. Early adopters such as Amazon have reaped the benefits. The use of automation is having a considerable impact in many different industries and how they now operate. While there is no doubt that advances in automation have the capacity for positive impact, there is always the potential for a counterbalancing negative impact. For example, the ability to automatically download material online has had a dramatic impact on the entertainment industry and how it operates. It has also resulted in the development of an extensive black market and an upsurge in illegal downloading online.

All of these technological advances and many more besides present organizations with lucrative upsides; however, they also bring with them the potential for devastating downsides. The corporate defense program should be designed to be able to help the organization achieve a balance between maximizing the upside of technology and minimizing its downside.

### 16.2.3  Business Technology

The use of business technology is increasingly becoming essential in supporting an organization in the achievement of its objectives, as an increasing number of organizations are now dependent on technology for their survival. The twenty-first century has certainly seen important advances in business technology many of which have been enabled by broadband access to the Internet, constantly improving software development tools, and the scalability and reliability of data centers. What technology an organization uses, and how it uses it, is fast becoming a differentiator in the business world.

### 16.2.3.1  Business Technology Developments

More and more businesses are now adopting ever-changing business technology to enable them to interact with their customers and other business partners. Developments in *e-commerce* has seen a move away from high-street shopping and toward online shopping with traditional retail shops being replaced by corporate websites that in turn are being replaced by other open source content management systems. Organizations are now using *social networks* such as Twitter and Facebook, video and audio hosting such as YouTube and iTunes, and community-based web conferencing and webinar applications such as BrightTALK to communicate with their stakeholders. They are also using IP telephony such as Viber and Skype for direct contact with stakeholders internationally, and mobile apps to enable stakeholders to access their systems and to share information.

The scale of business information technology (IT) infrastructure has changed dramatically in the last two decades alone, not only in the front end but also in the back end. This has resulted in increased investment in IT resources such as hardware, software, data networks, and data centers. It has been accompanied by significant changes within the IT architecture, and the design and use of IT hardware platforms, software applications, and IT technical support services. During this period, organizations have moved from stand-alone servers in computer rooms in their basements, to more sophisticated data centers with hundreds of servers, and to state-of-the-art cloud computing with thousands of servers. The sheer challenge and cost associated with IT management has seen a migration of IT systems and data storage from in-house servers to the use of *the Cloud* and a dramatic uptake in the use of outsourced IT services such as *software as a service* (SaaS) and the outsourcing of IT staff. The use of the cloud and other outsourcing facilities can certainly assist organizations in optimizing their application hosting, network, and end-user environments to operate at scale through shared, virtualized, and highly bundled infrastructure platforms. It may also help ensure that the organization's infrastructure capabilities are effective and efficient by identifying opportunities to reduce costs and improve performance. It does however significantly increase third-party risk that cannot always be mitigated in contractual terms.

### 16.2.3.2   Third-Party IT Solutions

The use of third-party IT solutions can enable an organization to take full advantage of next generation products and services developed by specialists in their respective fields. In addition to outsourcing, this also includes the provision of products and services in-house that form part of the organization's infrastructure. In some instances this may involve one vendor or supplier providing a complete package of products and services while in other instances it may involve a multitude of vendors and suppliers. Where a complete package is provided by a single product or service provider, issues of compatibility, scalability, and integration may be more easily addressed; however, there is increased exposure to the third party in question. Where multiple product or service providers are engaged, this reduces the exposure to a single third party; however, it may complicate issues relating to compatibility, scalability, and integration. Whether an organization chooses a single or multiple provider(s) of products and services, it must however be diligent in selecting the right partner mix, in managing the third-party relationship, and in maintaining its client satisfaction. Issues such as responsibility and accountability can however become more complex and confusing when dealing with multiple product or service providers. In all cases although the organization may relinquish a certain degree of control by entering into arrangements with third parties, this does not absolve the organization from its own responsibility to its stakeholders. Ultimately, the organization is still responsible for the performance of its products and services, and problems encountered with third parties will reflect poorly on the organization and its reputation.

## 16.3   ANTICIPATION OF FUTURE CHALLENGES

Chapter 5 referred to how the four stages of the corporate defense cycle represented an organization's unifying defense objectives. The corporate defense cycle begins with the concept of anticipation, being able to adequately anticipate the future challenges that the organization is likely to be faced with. In the final analysis it is those organizations that are best at anticipating future challenges, which will be the best prepared and best equipped to deal with them, and this represents a significant source of competitive advantage.

The science and art of being able to anticipate future trends means ensuring that those who are in the know are best placed, to not only identify future threats, but also to be in a position to take full advantage of future opportunities in a manner their competitors may not be. The ability to anticipate and adapt to future challenges is central to Darwin's *Theory of Evolution* and has been at the very heart of the story of human survival. It is likely to continue to play an equally important role in the story of corporate survival into the next century and beyond.

### 16.3.1  FORETELLING THE FUTURE

Since the beginning of time, human beings have been fascinated with the concept of being able to predict the future. The ancient art of divination was closely associated with the mystical, supernatural, and occult, and history has seen many individuals elevated to the role of oracle, soothsayer, or prophet. The ability to prophesize future events under divine guidance could ensure exalted status within the local community, and for some, much further a field. There are numerous examples of famous religious prophets across many religions including Christianity, Judaism, and Islam. The ancient Chinese divination text the *I Ching*, also known as the *Book of Changes,* is based on the production of seemingly random numbers to determine divine intent. The French seer Michel de Nostredame, better known as *Nostradamus,* whose legacy has continued right up until this very day, established himself as a household name with his book *Les Propheties,* which was first published in 1555 and is still in print today.

The art of *fortune telling* has also developed over the centuries across all of the Earth's continents and still remains in popular culture. It involves predicting information about a person's life; however, the methods used can vary from astrology and horoscopes, to reading palms and tea leaves, to tarot cards and crystal balls, and even in the throwing of bones. The paranormal is also a source of prediction and there is no shortage of parapsychologists, clairvoyants, and psychics providing services in this field. Another form of forecasting in popular culture is the activity of gambling, whether it is betting on the outcome of a toss of coin, roll of a dice, spin of a wheel, or indeed the outcome of a sporting event.

Some may say that many activities in life that are based on future outcomes are nothing more than subtle forms of gambling. With this in mind, the worlds of politics, finance, and economics and many others strive to foretell the outcome of future events and have their own versions of sages, futurists, and visionaries. These range from political forecasters, to financial gurus, and economic weathermen. In every field of business, huge amounts of money are invested in attempts to get one step ahead of the competition, the sector, and the market. Organizations all over the world employ the services of intelligence agencies, advisory firms, and market analysts in an attempt to gain an advantage that they can exploit ahead of their rivals.

#### 16.3.1.1  Impossible to See the Future Is—Yoda[*]

Despite centuries of research, development, and refining of the above techniques, the ability to accurately predict the future remains somewhat illusive as either a science or art. However, the ability to accurately forecast the outcome of certain events, in the short term at least, is showing signs of improvement in many areas. A prime example of this is the increased confidence in modern short-term weather forecasting in comparison to say 20 years ago. It is however important to appreciate that although the occurrence of standard events is somewhat predictable under normal or expected circumstances, difficulties begin to arise when an unexpected set of circumstances materialize. (Refer to Chapter 2 where the concepts of predictability and randomness were previously addressed.)

#### 16.3.1.2  Learning from the Past

In business, the future by its very nature is uncertain and unpredictable and if history has taught us anything, it is that in general businesses are not very good at predicting the outcome of future events. There are of course exceptions but these tend to be less and less the longer the time horizon under consideration. In business as in economics, events tend to follow somewhat predictable

---

[*] Reference to a statement by Jedi Master Yoda in the movie, *Star Wars: Episode II—The Empire Strikes Back* (1980).

cycles, such as boom and bust, and these cycles are generally driven by greed and fear. Greed tends to overheat the economy during the good times, while fear tends to stifle the economy during the bad times. What is less predictable however are the precise variables that cause these boom and bust cycles as these tend to fluctuate depending on the prevailing circumstances. History teaches us that there are important lessons to be learned from the past but although such lessons can provide valuable insight, they are not a guarantee of future outcomes. Common failures in decision making do however appear to be repeated over and over, time and again.

### 16.3.1.3　Avoid Repeating Past Mistakes

The financial crisis highlighted a collective arrogance regarding the perceived level of control in place over the economy, and a general overconfidence in the underlying economic assumptions at that time. This unfortunately was also accompanied by a lack of desire to listen to contrary points of view, and dissenting voices who warned of historical red flags were met with claims that everything was different this time around. This regrettably has been a recurring feature in boom times. The study of historical cycles and trends includes not only comparing past and present conditions and other parameters but also comparing past and present behavior. Learning from the past involves learning from the mistakes of others so that they are not repeated, and it also involves recognizing that due consideration needs to be given to a diverse range of perspectives in order to adequately scrutinize prevailing assumptions.

### 16.3.2　Managing Expectations of the Future

An important by-product of foretelling, predicting, or forecasting future events is that an expectation is created among stakeholders that certain events could occur that could potentially present both threats and opportunities for the organization in question. Lessons learned from the past can help an organization to recognize the importance of being well prepared in advance for such occurrences in order to be in the best position to deal with the resulting threats and opportunities. A key aspect of learning involves learning to successfully manage stakeholder expectations so that the requirement for being well prepared is fully appreciated in advance of any predicted events. As previously mentioned, organizations that are best prepared to deal with emerging challenges have a distinct advantage over their competition.

### 16.3.2.1　Technological Forecasting

Without doubt, there has been significant technological development in the area of providing assistance in both prediction and forecasting. The final decisions however invariably need to be made by individuals with the delegated authority to make such decisions. In the past, such decisions may have been largely dependent on the guess, opinion, or intuition of the decision maker based on their information, knowledge, and experience. There is now however considerable technological support and assistance available to help the decision maker in arriving at more informed decisions than was possible in the past. Decision makers are no longer expected to rely on projecting their own imagination into the future in order to try and visualize future outcomes. Developments in science and technology now means that forecasting techniques using mathematical models and computer-generated algorithms can now interpret all available data and forecast a range of possible outcomes from general to specific with an individual confidence level assigned to each one. Formal systematic predictions are now possible using statistical analysis, regression analysis, and time series analysis. In business, predictive models and predictive analytics can now be used to analyze data in order to make future predictions and to help identify patterns that indicate potential opportunities and threats. Any use of the results of such forecasting however comes with a health warning, as the quality of the output is subject to the quality of the input, and projected results are dependent on the stated assumptions, on the awareness of all relevant parameters, and are based on the completeness, accuracy, and validity of the available data. So although the conditions for informed decision making are constantly improving, the ability to forecast accurately is still considered to be a unique talent that requires a certain skill set not necessarily possessed by all decision makers. Continuous practice and an awareness and understanding of the constraints of the available technological tools can help improve the decision-making process.

### 16.3.2.2 Proactive Preparedness

In order to ensure that an organization is in the best possible position to take advantage of opportunities and to avoid threats, an adequate level of preparation is required. In business, the concept of preparedness is by its very nature proactive and involves taking proactive steps to ensure that the organization is prepared for both the expected and, as much as possible, the unexpected. The higher the level of preparedness present, the higher the probability of a positive outcome. Although it may not be realistic or indeed practical to expect the organization to be fully prepared for all possible eventualities, an organization can however take certain steps to ensure that it achieves at least a reasonable level of preparedness for certain identified future scenarios.

Once certain scenarios have been anticipated, predicted, or forecasted, the organization needs to ensure that it is in a position to react and respond to the occurrence of such events in as speedy a manner as possible. This requires identifying required decisions to be made, resources required, and action steps to be performed in the event of a particular scenario presenting itself. In order to ensure that the organization is fully informed and aware of the possible outcomes of its proposed decisions and actions, many organizations are now turning to computer-aided techniques, such as scenario planning and analysis, computer-simulated modeling, and the use of business gaming technology in order to help gain firsthand experience of expected conditions in a virtually simulated environment. These techniques and exercises can allow an organization to manipulate various business parameters in order to test its operations under conditions of potential stress, and allow it to analyze the sensitivity of its operations under various crisis scenarios. The more dynamic the organization's business environment, the more complex its set of parameters and the greater the organization's requirement to develop agile, flexible, and adaptable responses. The more comprehensive these simulated exercises, the greater the potential for insight into the organization's required resources, actions, and behaviors in relation to the identified future scenarios. The use of computer-assisted exercises and training enables an organization to proactively prepare for changing conditions. This applies as much to exploiting possible opportunities as it does to safeguarding against potential threats. Such an approach can also facilitate interdisciplinary cooperation and collaboration in the search for the best possible solutions to the problems and challenges presented.

### 16.3.3 Medium- and Long-Term Predictions

Typically, it is much easier to accurately forecast the occurrence of events over a short-term time horizon than over a medium- to long-term time horizon. This is generally due to the accelerating rate of change, which is a feature of the twenty-first century and the potential impact that such changes can have on the outcome of future events. Because of this, medium to long-term forecasting can seem less like a science and more like an art given the lack of up-to-date relevant information over longer time frames. Although it may be less likely to accurately forecast precise outcomes in the longer-term future, this does not diminish the organization's requirement to anticipate to the best of its abilities the challenges it may face going forward. The impact of a future event on a given organization is likely to be determined, to a certain extent at least, by the organization's level of preparedness to deal with the occurrence of such an event.

### 16.3.3.1 Horizon Scanning

Anticipation of, and preparation for, future events is an ongoing process that is required to cover many different time horizons. The occurrence of events today, tomorrow, or next week is naturally of more immediate concern than the occurrence of an event in six months' time or five years' time.

An organization's ability to deal with the occurrence of an event today however will be dependent on how it has prepared for such an event in the past. In theory at least, the more time available to prepare, the better the preparation should be. The degree of preparation for an event is however dependent on the time lag between when such an event first appeared on the organization's radar and the occurrence of the event in question. In order to maximize the available time lag, organizations need to continuously scan short, medium, and long-term time horizons with the intention of anticipating, forecasting, or predicting events, series of events, or trends, which could impact on the organization in a positive or negative manner. Horizon scanning involves a systematic examination of information to identify potential threats and opportunities in the short, medium, and long-term time horizons. Traditionally, organizations tend to consider the short term as being out to a one-year time horizon, the medium term as being out to two to five years, and the long term as out to ten years and beyond. In terms of long-term sustainability however due consideration should also be given to longer time horizons and the anticipation of issues and trends that are likely to present the greatest threats and opportunities in the longer term future. For this reason, organizations need to consider horizon scanning in terms of 10, 20, 50, and 100-year time horizons. Logically, it is the organizations that are best prepared to address future matters that are the most likely to maximize the opportunities and minimize the threats.

### 16.3.3.2   Predicting Future Impact

Going forward, corporate defense programs need to not only focus on improving how they are anticipating major issues and trends over longer time horizons, but must also consider the possible implications of such events both from the potential opportunities they present and the potential threats they present to the organizations concerned. In an increasingly globally interconnected world, this will involve focusing on developments and changes occurring in a number of different areas any of which could either directly or indirectly impact on the organization and the achievement of its objectives. Addressing many of these larger issues will require organizations contributing their fair share by coming together with other interested parties to cooperate, collaborate, and lobby in order to help bring about the necessary changes required.

In order for stakeholders to determine the extent to which their organization is truly committed to focusing on long-term sustainability, they may be interested to know the extent to which their organization has considered different issues, the likelihood of the occurrence of these issues over different time horizons, and the potential impact of these issues on the organization and its stakeholders over these time horizons. For example:

*Economics*: Economic developments and changes that could positively or negatively impact on the organization and its stakeholders.

Examples of economic issues could range from the following:

- The continuation of stagnant economic conditions over prolonged periods of time leading to economic trade wars among major economic zones.
- The occurrence of extreme global stock market fluctuations between boom and bust over extended periods leading to ever increasing and deeper economic depressions.
- The development of global economic and currency union in an attempt to stabilize global markets and economic conditions.
- The collapse of international currencies and confidence in financial systems leading to a return to some form of the barter system in some or all geographic regions.
- Mankind's potential to reboost economic development by being able to harness the energy resources of other planets before our own energy resources run out.

*Environment*: Environmental developments and changes that could positively or negatively impact on the organization and its stakeholders.

Examples of environmental issues could range from the following:

- The gradual collapse of regional ecosystems leading to a chain reaction of events that results in regional environmental disasters.
- Unexpectedly high rates of ozone depletion in certain geographic regions resulting in increased UV exposure and much higher risks to humans, plants, and ocean life.
- The discovery of a powerful new sustainable source of clean power and energy that is environmentally friendly.
- The acceleration of climate change leading to a massive increase in the number of natural disasters as a result of extreme climatic conditions.
- The occurrence of a long-term global environmental catastrophe as a result of a seismic shift in temperatures over a short period of time.

*Politics*: Political developments and changes that could positively or negatively impact on the organization and its stakeholders.

Examples of political issues could range from the following:

- Continued increases in income and wealth disparity between rich and poor leading to a significant rise in anti-capitalist left-wing extremism.
- Increasing crime levels used as a justification to promote the development of *Big Brother* police states that greatly encroach on civil liberties.
- Increasing polarization based on sex and gender leading to a restructuring of mainstream politics into gender-specific political parties.
- The extension of the concept of democracy to include the wisdom of crowds, whereby all political decisions are decided via regular online voting by the electorate.
- An energy crisis as a result of diminishing fossil fuel resources resulting in a third world war.

*Society*: Social developments and changes that could positively or negatively impact on the organization and its stakeholders.

Examples of social issues could range from the following:

- Severe shortages of food and water leading to widespread famine across not only the developing worlds, but also impacting on the developed world.
- Continued population explosion leading to uncontrolled urbanization and resulting in the growth of unmanageable and uncontrollable supercities in certain regions.
- A massive increase in migration from developing nations and the third world to the developed nations leading to social chaos and a significant rise in xenophobia.
- A rise in the level of social unrest directed against global multinational corporations in reaction to their perceived contribution to continued social inequality.
- An inability to redress levels of social inequality resulting in wide-scale social unrest and eventually leading to anarchy and/or widespread social rebellion.

*Technology*: Technological developments and changes that could positively or negatively impact on the organization and its stakeholders.

Examples of technological issues could range from the following:

- Further development in automation leading to mainstream acceptance of driverless forms of transport such as cars, buses, trains, and airplanes.
- The use of biotechnology and genetically modified crops to turn previously uninhabitable regions into fertile productive agricultural land.
- Advances in neuroscience and biometrics leading to the ability to implant technologies into the human body in order to supplement physical and mental activity.
- The development of humanoid robots and cyborgs that help eliminate many of the physical challenges associated with human old age.
- The capacity to download the humanoid brain into a virtual matrix, resulting in the creation of a digital world controlled by technology.

*Science*: Scientific developments and changes that could positively or negatively impact on the organization and its stakeholders. Issues could range from the following:

Examples of scientific issues could range from the following:

- The potential damage and fall-out of a large meteorite or comet colliding with the planet Earth and affecting densely populated areas.
- Significant breakthroughs in human communication with other life forms such as animals, plants, and insects.
- Developments in human genetic engineering leading to genetic modification and resulting in widespread human cloning and/or human-animal hybrids.
- Significant breakthroughs in the ability to travel such as developments in teleportation and/or in time machines that enable time travel.
- The discovery of a planet(s) inhabited by other life-forms and/or the repercussions of an alien invasion of the planet Earth.

### 16.3.3.3  A Word of Caution

At this point in time in the twenty-first century, some or many of the above examples may seem somewhat far-fetched and unlikely to occur; however, it is important that organizations try to keep an open mind and try as best as they can to avoid the pitfalls of tunnel vision and unconscious bias. Although the above are only random examples, it is also worth considering how many individuals at the beginning of the twentieth century would have anticipated the outbreak of two world wars in less than 30 years, the development of atomic energy, and a man setting foot on the moon. Indeed how many would have anticipated the developments in technology that have resulted in the use of mobile telecommunications or having a virtual world available at our fingertips via the Internet. Many unforeseen events have occurred in the last 100 years and this is likely to continue.

Long-term forecasting is difficult because there can be so many different variables to process; however, it is important to remember that what can appear improbable today because of the prevailing set of circumstances can very much become a reality further down the line as circumstances continue to change. Over time, constraints can significantly diminish as things tend to change and become better, smaller, faster, stronger, cheaper, lighter, bigger, tougher, and simpler. It is therefore important to remember that although all the parameters, ingredients, or conditions may not be right today, they may well be right some day in the not-too-distant future. Those involved in corporate defense have a responsibility to ensure that their organization is taking reasonable steps to anticipate possible future scenarios that could positively or negatively impact on the organization and its stakeholders and help ensure that their organization is best prepared to deal with such eventualities.

# Section IV

## An Integrated Perspective

# 17 The Corporate Defense Value Proposition

Not everything that can be counted counts, and not everything that counts can be counted.[*]

**Albert Einstein**

## 17.1  PRESENTING THE BUSINESS CASE FOR CORPORATE DEFENSE

In most organizations in order to get the necessary buy-in on the requirement for any business initiative, it is crucial that a sound business case can be made to justify the required investment in both time and money. The corporate defense initiative is of course no different in this regard. Fundamentally, a sound business case should clearly outline how the corporate defense initiative can help the organization in the achievement of its objectives. The extent to which a clear and convincing case can be presented on behalf of corporate defense will help determine the organization's attitude to corporate defense and will help to set the corporate defense agenda within the organization. This in turn will determine the structure of the organization's approach to corporate defense and the extent to which it is held in high regard.

The basic business case for corporate defense should clarify the role of corporate defense, the organization's corporate defense obligations, and the benefits to be derived from an effective corporate defense program. At a minimum, it should encompass the business cases being made for each of the individual corporate defense components and include an amalgamation of the organization's obligations and benefits associated with each of these components. A more

---

[*] Per *The Intuitive Compass: Why the Best Decisions Balance Reason and Instinct*, 2012, Francis P. Cholle, Jossey-Bass, Hoboken, NJ.

sophisticated business case for a corporate defense program should also include addressing the additional obligations and benefits associated with adopting a more formal structured approach to managing corporate defense activities in an integrated manner. The remainder of this chapter is designed to help organizations understand, prepare, and present the business case for such a corporate defense program.

### 17.1.1  EFFECTIVE CORPORATE DEFENSE CAN ADD SIGNIFICANT VALUE

An effective corporate defense program should be in alignment with the objectives of the business and therefore should not hinder the business, but rather it should facilitate it and help enhance business performance wherever possible. In so doing, corporate defense can add significant value to the organization and its stakeholders. Ideally the effective implementation of a corporate defense program can result in an organization putting itself in the best possible position to not only take full advantage of business opportunities as they present themselves, but also to safeguard its interests and help minimize both uncertainty and the resulting hazards in the process.

#### 17.1.1.1  Contribution to the Bigger Picture

The overarching objective of the corporate defense program should be to help the organization achieve its objectives and this requires a sound understanding and appreciation of the organization's big picture. The corporate defense program has, however, a certain obligation to help ensure that the organization's objectives are in the best long-term interests of its stakeholders, rather than in the short-term interests of certain individuals within the organization. Where healthy, balanced objectives are in place, the efforts of the corporate defense program should be geared toward supporting the business in the achievement of their unified objectives. This means contributing in a positive manner to help enable the business deliver long-term sustainable success to its stakeholders. In this regard, corporate defense should not be seen in vacuum, but rather as an essential element in the achievement of business success. Individuals with specific corporate defense responsibilities need to be regarded as essential members of a team who are all working together for the greater good of the organization as a whole.

#### 17.1.1.2  A Dual Role with Dual Responsibilities

The organization as a whole has a dual role with dual responsibilities. Old sporting aphorisms state that *offense wins games, defense wins championships* or that *defense decides who wins, offense decides by how much.* In the corporate context, this refers to the requirement for a dual focus whereby each organization is required to focus on bringing the dollar in through the front door (offense) while also focusing on preventing the dollar from leaving through the back door (defense). In business as in sport, for best results, these dual roles should be part of an integrated strategy that facilitates offense supporting defense, and defense supporting offense in as seamless a manner as possible. The corporate defense program therefore ideally should support and enable the organization's offense activities in order to help exploit opportunities such as developing new products and services, breaking into new markets, or expanding market share while at the same time delivering on its own essential defense activities that help protect against hazards which could have a negative impact over the longer term.

### 17.1.2  AN APPRECIATION OF THE CORPORATE DEFENSE CONTRIBUTION

The business case for the corporate defense program needs to ensure that the organization has a firm appreciation and solid understanding of the potential overall contribution which an effective corporate defense program can offer to the organization in the pursuit of its objectives. It needs to highlight how corporate defense should not be considered a restriction on business activities, but rather a mechanism for establishing a reliable basis for decision making that has the potential to create new opportunities and reap higher rewards by making better and more informed decisions. The positive contribution of corporate defense therefore can perhaps be best understood by the fact that it can help enable an organization to exploit the possible upsides of a given situation, while at the same time helping to mitigate the possible downsides.

### 17.1.2.1 Transformation of Attitudes

To achieve this appreciation, first there must be a transformation in how organizations view corporate defense activities. The traditional attitude toward corporate defense involves a negative stereotype that needs to be overcome and eradicated. This stereotyping involves viewing corporate defense activities as a necessary evil which adds little value to the organization and is therefore regarded as an overhead whose associated costs need to be kept to a minimum. For this reason corporate defense issues tend to only appear on the radar as a knee-jerk reaction and direct response to the occurrence of an individual incident. Often only short-term fixes are put in place to address the symptoms, rather than implementing a long-term cure, and as memories fade the reasons behind these fixes are often forgotten.

The contemporary attitude toward corporate defense needs to be one where corporate defense is seen in a much more positive and proactive light, one which views corporate defense as an essential safety initiative which is necessary to ensure the ongoing corporate health of the organization. All stakeholders need to regard corporate defense as a mandatory safeguard required to protect their long-term interests. The board needs to regard the corporate defense program as a fundamental ingredient necessary to produce a successful outcome. The CEO needs to consider the chief corporate defense officer as being similar to the *Left Tackle* in American football whose job it is to protect the *Quarterback* so that he or she can focus on the important task of running the organization. Organizations as a whole need to consider the corporate defense program as an investment in a strategic asset that needs to be nurtured and cared for, an intangible asset that can add considerable value to the organization's overall worth.

### 17.1.2.2 Recognition of the Value of Corporate Defense

Corporate defense could be considered an asymmetric challenge as something only needs to go wrong once in order for a loss to be incurred. While this is a difficult challenge, it is however a manageable one if approached in a responsible manner. Just because an organization may consider the corporate defense program as too difficult to manage certainly does not remove its corporate defense obligation as it is still expected to make every effort to address it.

Corporate defense activities are traditionally concerned with safeguarding against hazards; therefore, their core value lies in preventing and mitigating losses, which at times is difficult to measure in straightforward quantitative terms. For example, the direct cost of an effective corporate defense program in "Organization A" may be quantifiable in terms of direct expenditure on people, processes, and systems. The direct expenditure by "Organization B" may be much less; however, it results in an ineffective program and leads to devastating losses to the organization. The real cost to "Organization B" is therefore reflected in its losses, while the real value to "Organization A" is in its loss prevention, although this is more difficult to prove conclusively at "Organization A" as these potential losses have been avoided. It is clear, however, from this example that the implementation of an effective corporate defense program can help an organization achieve considerable payback in terms of long-term sustainability.

Short-term gain through direct cost savings can prove to be very expensive indeed in the longer term and conjures up the phrase *penny-wise and pound-foolish*, as cost savings can pale into insignificance against the eventual losses incurred. Recognizing that *prevention is cheaper than the cure* is an important first step in appreciating the real value of corporate defense. At the end of the day, good corporate defense can indeed cost money, but poor corporate defense can end up costing a fortune.

Calculating the direct value created and the indirect contribution to business value can also be difficult as organizations tend to quantify what went wrong rather than quantifying what went right. The selection of appropriate corporate defense KPIs is therefore of great importance in this regard. Organizations need to understand the requirement to positively report on corporate defense activities in order to appreciate the value contribution. This can be achieved by reporting on issues such as near misses avoided, reductions on loss events, and accelerated response times to incidents. Organizations also need to appreciate the corporate defense contribution to the business as an intangible asset and learn to quantify its contribution in value terms in relation to such issues as better decision making, increased stakeholder trust, and improved market confidence. Organizations need to be able to quantify corporate defense as a valuable intangible asset, and the value of providing the board of directors, the CEO, and senior management with higher levels of comfort so that they are able to sleep better at night.

### 17.1.3   THE BENEFITS OF ADOPTING A CDM APPROACH

Given the increasing levels of uncertainty in the business world, the implementation of a structured corporate defense framework is by no means a guaranteed recipe for success or a certainty that all potential losses will be avoided or mitigated. It could, however, be argued that ignoring corporate defense and not having a framework in place is a guaranteed recipe for disaster. Given that more traditional approaches to corporate defense have consistently failed to deliver, there is absolutely no reason to be satisfied with this status quo. Applying the CDM approach can provide the organization with its best chance of achieving its objectives and succeeding over the long term. The CDM approach presents an opportunity to develop a coherent corporate defense program. If implemented effectively, it can help organizations to improve performance, increase productivity, and reduce overheads while at the same time helping the organization to create a more robust corporate defense structure.

#### 17.1.3.1   Adoption of a Unified Methodology

The CDM approach facilitates the implementation of a consistent methodology across the entire organization. The CDM framework introduces a systematic approach to the strategic, tactical, and operational management of what have been identified as the critical components that constitute an organization's program for self-defense. Its holistic approach helps to enable the organization to unify, align, and integrate these critical components so that they are strategically aligned, tactically integrated, and operating in unison toward common objectives. By managing corporate defense activities in a coordinated and unified manner, an organization can ensure that there are similar performance expectations across all corporate defense activities and help ensure that they are all working together to collectively safeguard stakeholder value.

Through the vertical and horizontal integration of the organization's people, processes, and systems, CDM can help an organization to embed an integrated methodology into all levels of the organization's business activities. Such an approach can help achieve a healthy balance between offense and defense by ensuring that due consideration is given to the potential upside and downside of every situation and circumstance. Such consideration can help improve the decision-making process throughout the organization. Improved decision making can in turn help in the achievement of the organization's objectives and help reduce the occurrence of unexpected and unwanted losses.

#### 17.1.3.2   Provide Defense-in-Breadth and Defense-in-Depth

The CDM framework can help integrate the management of the organization's corporate defense activities and provides the toolkit to orchestrate a more progressive and proactive approach to the defense of the organization. Effective implementation of the CDM approach can help to provide the organization with an adequately robust corporate defense structure going forward. CDM's holistic approach examines the corporate defense program as a complete functioning unit and therefore helps provide the organization with both *defense-in-breadth* and *defense-in-depth* in the process. *Defense-in-breadth* is provided by the cross-functional integration of the critical corporate defense components across the organization whereby the interaction of these components provides a robust system of checks and balances for strategic, tactical, and operational issues. *Defense-in-depth* is provided by the five lines of defense oversight structure that helps the organization to ensure that corporate defense duties are adequately supervised and that adequate assurance is provided regarding their execution in practice. These two attributes taken together means that the CDM framework can provide an organization with a comprehensive corporate defense structure and a solid foundation from which to build the future success of the organization. Ultimately the CDM approach provides a holistic framework that helps to integrate the organization's strategic, tactical, and operational perspectives on corporate defense.

## 17.2   THE VALUE PROPOSITION—A STRATEGIC PERSPECTIVE

What strategic value can corporate defense add to an organization? An effective corporate defense program can present certain strategic benefits and advantages. First and foremost, effective corporate defense practices are considered to be essential mechanisms for any well-run organization in order to achieve long-term sustainable value. Organizations that put a premium on sound corporate defense practices can cope with ever-increasing business risks while at the same time being in a position to seize the opportunities that present themselves. Effective corporate defense can add value at a strategic level by supporting the achievement of the organization's strategic objectives, by helping the organization address its value preservation obligations, and by helping to protect the organization's reputation on an ongoing basis. Sound corporate defense practices can help to proactively defend the organization against potential hazards while at the same time helping it to optimize its return on corporate defense investment.

### 17.2.1   Support the Achievement of the Organization's Objectives

As an important part of the trusted guardianship of the organization, the corporate defense program needs to take a holistic portfolio view. A sound corporate program requires a strategic outlook so that it can adequately support the organization in the achievement of its strategic objectives. A strategic outlook enables corporate defense to be well-positioned to help lay a solid foundation from which the organization can then build for the future and to contribute to the development of solutions to the strategic challenges facing the business.

#### 17.2.1.1   Help Accomplish the Organization's Vision and Mission Statement

To be in a position to optimize its support of the business, the vision and mission statement of the corporate defense program should mirror that of the organization itself. This however is a two-way process as corporate defense must also have a positive influence on the organization's vision and mission statement. In this way, corporate defense can also have a positive influence on the organization's culture. Where, in the interests of its stakeholders, the organization's vision or mission statements require amendment, the corporate defense program should facilitate this process. Where no amendments are required, the corporate defense program should focus on wholeheartedly supporting the organization in accomplishing its vision and mission statement.

Ideally, corporate defense should be considered as an essential element of the organization's strategy and the corporate defense input should influence the setting of this strategy (and the business model) in a positive way. This makes it easier to ensure that the corporate defense strategy itself and related objectives and goals are in alignment with the organization's strategy and its strategic objectives and goals. The more closely aligned, the more the corporate defense program can have a positive contribution toward the achievement of the business strategy and business objectives. Such alignment also facilitates the alignment of all individual corporate defense activities with the business, which should result in a smoother relationship between the business and various corporate defense activities. Once the objectives of all parties are in close alignment, there can be a synchronization of efforts in order to produce maximum returns.

### 17.2.1.2  Help Deliver Long-Term Sustainability

In the majority of cases, one would expect the common overarching goal to be the delivery of long-term sustainable value to its stakeholders. As previously stated, such a goal requires the organization to be able to both create value and preserve value on a sustainable basis. The value chain involves an iterative cycle of value creation and value preservation in order to provide a growth in value over time and in order to build a sustainable future. The corporate defense program must therefore safeguard the value chain and support both of these efforts, although clearly its influence in the creation of value is more indirect than its influence on value preservation. The existence of a corporate defense program can help an organization appreciate the requirement to achieve a healthy balance between these two efforts and clearly understand the long-term implications of any imbalance that might arise. It can have a positive influence on the value creation process by working with the business in order to deliver smooth business processes which enable, rather than disable, the value creation process. The robustness of the organization's long-term sustainability efforts is very much the responsibility of the corporate defense program and its primary focus is on the development of a healthy organization capable of delivering long-term sustainable value to its stakeholders.

### 17.2.1.3  Help to Optimize Stakeholder Value

An effective corporate defense program can help an organization to optimize its stakeholder value by not only protecting its value chain but by supporting the organization in maximizing its return on investment. Once an appropriate corporate defense framework is in place, management's time can be freed up to focus its attention on increasing revenues and successfully growing the business. By helping to protect current and future profitability and by focusing on the prudent balancing of risks and rewards, the corporate defense program can help improve stakeholder value via increased profits, improved share price, and higher market value. It can enable the organization to better manage and rationalize its capital requirements by helping to improve its capital adequacy allocations. By focusing on efficiency, it can help ensure that there is an effective allocation of the organization's limited resources and help the organization strive to optimize the return on these resources. By collaborating with the business, it can help improve business processes and thereby contribute to increasing sales, turnover, and revenues. An effective corporate defense program should demand a positive return on the organization's corporate defense investment and ensure that corporate defense activities are managed in an effective and efficient manner. By adopting a business focus, the corporate defense program can become a valuable mechanism to help the organization enhance stakeholder value through the optimization of its resources.

### 17.2.2  ADDRESS THE VALUE PRESERVATION IMPERATIVE

Every organization has a certain obligation to its stakeholders to take reasonable measures to preserve the value that is being created in order to help prevent a corporate meltdown and to help deliver long-term sustainability. In that sense, an effective corporate defense program is seen as a precondition to effective value preservation as corporate defense activities are directly responsible for ensuring that stakeholder value is adequately preserved. The corporate defense program helps to ensure that the value preservation obligation is appropriately incorporated into the organization's vision, mission statement, and strategy. It is responsible for ensuring that value preservation obligation is appropriately prioritized at the board and senior management level. The corporate defense program is also responsible for ensuring that the organization as a whole clearly appreciates and understands the nature of the value preservation imperative. It is responsible for safeguarding the assets of the organization (both tangible and intangible) from internal and external risks, threats, and vulnerabilities. It is responsible for ensuring that the organization's risk exposures are at levels which the organization considered to be acceptable in order to continue to run its business. In essence, the corporate defense program and the organization's value preservation obligation are forever intertwined.

### 17.2.2.1  Better Safeguard Stakeholder Interests

Value preservation is concerned with safeguarding the interests of stakeholders and in preserving that which is valued by stakeholders, be it financial, economic, social, or environmental. It is, therefore, not solely concerned with shareholder issues such as earnings, dividends, and share price but extends beyond that to issues such as corporate social responsibility and the environment. In recent years, stakeholder groups have become much more active in expressing their expectations of their organizations in this regard. Corporate defense is concerned with how best to achieve this objective and this involves safeguarding, shielding, and protecting the interests of multiple stakeholders and their varied interests from hazards. It is concerned with helping to build a sustainable business and building long-term stakeholder value. By adequately safeguarding the interests of the multiple stakeholders, the business value of the organization is also being protected in the process. Corporate defense is therefore concerned with engaging with stakeholders using a taxonomy and language which they understand, and educating them about the potential risks, threats, and vulnerabilities faced by the organization. It is concerned with helping stakeholders to form realistic expectations of the organization and establishing the desired competence levels throughout the organization. An effective corporate defense program does all of these things far better than an ineffective one.

### 17.2.2.2  Help Create a More Resilient Organization

Achieving long-term sustainability is all about survival over time, and organizations do not survive without being sufficiently robust and developing a high level of resiliency. The aim of corporate defense is to help the organization to increase its robustness and improve its resiliency therefore creating a more robust and resilient organization. By building a more robust corporate defense framework, the more robust the organization becomes and the less vulnerable it is to hazard events. By hardening its corporate defense activities, dangers are reduced and there is greater stability in times of stress, emergency, crisis, or disaster scenarios. The better an organization can anticipate risk, prevent threats, detect breaches, and react to incidents, the more robust and resilient it becomes. Effective corporate defense can help deliver these attributes through continuous learning and constant improvement. The value preservation imperative demands the creation of a robust and resilient organization; however, this also means that it is in a position to take the greater risks in order to reap greater rewards and create greater value in the process.

### 17.2.2.3  Help to Nurture and Maintain Organizational Health

It has been said that organizational health is similar to human health as it improves when it is taken good care of and deteriorates when neglected. Therefore, an organization's health plan needs to include value preservation in order to demonstrate a defensible standard of care. There are many aspects to organizational health and it is more than just financial and economic performance, although they are obviously very important. It also includes the health and safety, and the welfare and well-being, of its management, staff, and other stakeholders. An organization must achieve a certain level of health and remain healthy over time in order to achieve long-term sustainability, as an unhealthy organization is limited in its potential to grow and develop over an expanded period of time. Corporate defense has a vital role to play in nurturing organizational health and in helping to ensure the organization remains healthy over time. For example, organizational health also encompasses issues such as ethics and integrity and the extent to which these values are ingrained in the organization's culture so that healthy behavior is encouraged at all levels. Healthy behavior can include avoiding high-risk activities and dysfunctional behavior. It requires discipline and involves restraint in the short term in order to reap the benefits over the longer term. An obsession with instant gratification and short-term performance can be unhealthy and can be detrimental to the organization in the long term.

Corporate defense can provide periodic health screening and ongoing fitness checks to the organization. It can help the organization to introduce a healthier lifestyle by ensuring that it maintains a healthy diet, has an appropriate exercise program, and has factored in sufficient recovery periods. In organizational terms, dietary issues reflect its people, core values, strategy, objectives, and policies. The exercise program involves attaining the appropriate weight level and fitness conditioning required in order to achieve its objectives. To transform an organization into lean operating machine, it must reduce fat by increasing efficiency and turn fat into muscle by improving performance and productivity. The cardio requirements involve focusing on constantly improving the speed at which the organization can perform its required tasks in a safe and secure manner. It also involves focusing on its stamina and endurance in order to be able to repeat its required level of performance over a sustained period of time. The recovery capability is addressed by ensuring that there is sufficient redundancy and resilience built into the organization's activities, be it economic, financial or operational. A healthy robust organization is capable of working harder over longer periods in order to achieve higher levels of performance and is more resistant to shocks and disruptions.

### 17.2.3  PROTECT THE ORGANIZATION'S REPUTATION

An organization's reputation is increasingly regarded as one of its most valuable intangible assets; therefore, protecting its reputation needs to be considered a high priority for every organization. A reputation therefore has value in itself and this value needs to be preserved. Damage to the organization's reputation can have a significant negative impact on the achievement of its objectives as it can take considerable period of time to restore a reputation and in some cases it may never be restored to its former status. All assets need to be adequately protected; however, due to its intangible nature, protecting a reputation presents a complex challenge. An organization's reputation can be indirectly impacted by many variables and it is impacted by its public image, its brand, its products, its services and above all the behavior of its workforce, any one of which can result in damage to its reputation. Corporate defense therefore can add considerable value by helping ensure that the organization's reputation is adequately protected at all times.

#### 17.2.3.1  Help Foster Stakeholder Trust

An organization's reputation has an impact on stakeholder trust and the power of stakeholder trust should never be underestimated. Stakeholders place a certain level of trust in their organizations and require their organizations to live up to their expectations of them. Once this trust is broken, it is not easily restored and there can be significant fallout as a result. For example, where there is distrust between management and staff, this can lead to a culture of cynicism, suspicion, and disbelief, all of which can have a negative impact on performance and productivity. In extreme cases, there can be a downward spiral which can lead to the creation of a toxic environment and a dysfunctional organization. In a broader context, the loss of stakeholder trust can diminish stakeholder support, loyalty, and faith in the organization, thereby making it difficult to attract talent, and creating stakeholder attrition and turnover issues. Effective corporate defense can address stakeholder retention through a stakeholder focus, and help to foster stakeholder trust through the knowledge that appropriate measures are being taken to safeguard the interests of the multiple stakeholders. A formal corporate defense program can give additional comfort to stakeholders and provide a tangible indication that the board is taking proactive steps to safeguard their interests. In this sense it could be said that from a stakeholder perspective corporate defense represents a very important challenge, one which may have significant stakeholder implications. In fact it could well be argued that an indication of an organization's true valuation of its stakeholders is reflected in its approach to corporate defense.

#### 17.2.3.2  Help Inspire Market Confidence

Market confidence is intrinsically linked to an organization's reputation. The level of confidence that the market has in a particular organization will in most cases determine its access to and cost of capital, its share price, and its market value. The greater the level of market confidence, the easier it becomes to access capital at lower rates, the higher the share price, and the higher the market value.

The existence of an effective corporate defense program is increasingly being reviewed by parties undertaking due diligence exercises of organizations of interest. Therefore, it can help inspire market confidence by demonstrating that the organization is taking proactive measures to safeguard against potential hazards, and by helping to demonstrate that the organization is well run and protecting itself against instability. By helping to smooth earnings and avoid profit volatility, corporate defense can play its part in inspiring market confidence. Increased market confidence can result in a number of positive outcomes as the following examples highlight:

*Increased shareholder demand*: It can result in an increased shareholder demand for shares in the organization. An increased demand for equities can result in a higher share price.

*Investor premium*: It can result in investors such as venture capitalist firms and institutional investors being prepared to pay a premium to invest in the organization.

*Regulator comfort*: It can result in regulators taking additional comfort from the fact that the organization is taking reasonable steps to safeguard against the occurrence of hazards and is showing a firm commitment to the long haul.

*Higher ratings*: It can result in rating agencies being more likely to consider the organization to be a well-run institution and give higher ratings such as credit ratings and corporate governance ratings.

*Positive market outlooks*: It can result in market analysts being more likely to predict a positive future outlook for the organization given its higher level of confidence.

*Lower borrowing rates*: It can result in lending institutions being more likely to be prepared to lend the organization larger amounts and at lower rates of interest.

*Reduced insurance costs*: It can result in insurance companies being more likely to improve their insurance rating and lower their premiums given their confidence in the effectiveness of the corporate defense program.

*Attraction of suitors*: It can result in attracting additional corporate suitors. Organizations that are actively seeking to engage in M&A activities are more likely to be impressed by the existence of a formal corporate defense program during their due diligence exercise.

### 17.2.3.3 Help Develop Competitive Advantage

A solid reputation can in itself be a significant source of competitive advantage. Success in the marketplace requires being able to successfully compete against your rivals and successful organizations develop unique selling points (USPs) that set them apart from their rivals. Organizations continually strive to achieve competitive advantages in order to give them an edge over their competition. Innovation is important but also important is the ability to react faster than your competitors, as failure to do so can actually put the organization at a competitive disadvantage. An effective corporate defense program can also be a source of sustainable competitive advantage for an organization as its collaborative approach can help to not only safeguard against threats but also provide the potential to turn threats into opportunities. The most successful organizations differentiate themselves from their competition by being able to stay ahead of the curve, and this can also be an important feature in relation to corporate defense. The organizations that can become leaders in this aspect of business and implement a seamlessly integrated and optimized corporate defense program can expect to utilize this competitive advantage to their benefit in terms of outperforming their rivals and exploiting opportunities which their rivals simply cannot. As previously stated, corporate defense, as an intangible asset, has the potential to positively impact on the achievement of business objectives and help set the organization apart for its competition.

## 17.3 THE VALUE PROPOSITION—A TACTICAL PERSPECTIVE

What tactical value can corporate defense add to an organization? An effective corporate defense program can present certain tactical benefits and advantages to an organization that are an additional source of value. By adopting the CDM approach to corporate defense, an organization can successfully tackle the challenge of breaking down operational silos. Typically, a silo-type environment means that the organization's corporate defense functions tend to be compartmentalized so that they operate in isolation of one another with little or no interaction, sharing of information, cooperation, or collaboration. This can typically result in a lack of cross-functional support, power struggles, and certain dysfunctional behavior that can all have a negative impact on the health of the organization. By integrating and aligning all the organization's corporate defense activities under one framework, it can help to remove the silo mentality and unlock latent potential that can add significant value to the organization. A proactive approach to the tactical management of corporate-defense-related activities can help the organization to optimize the return it receives on its existing investment in this area. Such an approach can help to take advantage of corporate defense synergies through partnership, collaboration, and cooperation thereby facilitating creativity, encouraging innovation, and driving positive change. A common alignment with business objectives can lead to a better understanding of the goals of the business and an opportunity to reengineer and streamline business processes in order to help improve business performance.

### 17.3.1 IMPROVE CORPORATE DEFENSE EFFECTIVENESS

A CDM approach to corporate defense can help an organization to be more effective in its corporate defense activities and thereby contribute more to the overall effectiveness of the organization in its efforts to achieve its objectives. Through cross-functional collaboration, effectiveness can be considerably improved by identifying and appropriately addressing potential weaknesses and deficiencies that are likely to render the organization vulnerable to hazard events. Such an exercise is most effective when there is a multidisciplined assessment of practices and processes as it can help the organization to avoid any blind spots that may otherwise occur. A CDM approach facilitates the timely communication of critical decision-making information and can help ensure that good news and bad news are speedily communicated both vertically and horizontally. In a competitive environment it is essential that both good and bad news is communicated upward without delay. Improvements in critical decision making in turn should lead to a more effective organization.

#### 17.3.1.1 Help to Minimize Losses

The identification of corporate defense weaknesses and deficiencies provides the organization with an opportunity to take proactive steps to address these issues and in the process reduce the organization's level of vulnerability to hazard events. This reduction in vulnerability in turn should help to reduce the number of occurrences of events which can have a negative impact on the organization. Where these events do occur, it should also help to reduce the initial impact of such events and help to mitigate any subsequent collateral damage which may otherwise arise. Such a cycle of events can therefore help the organization to significantly reduce any potential negative impact on the achievement of its objectives and exposure to losses. Corporate defense therefore has an important role to play in helping the organization to realize its value preservation obligation to minimize losses.

#### 17.3.1.2 Help to Increase Profitability

Corporate defense can contribute to increased profitability in a number of ways. Improved relations and communication between the business and the corporate defense functions through the use of a common language can help to free up business management to focus more time on business issues and seek out and exploit new opportunities. Collaborating and working with the business can help to accelerate the development of new products and services by removing unnecessary obstacles and barriers, and in the process contribute to helping increase revenues and improve cash flows. Corporate defense by eliminating an organization's potential liability is in that same process also helping to protect profitability. By decreasing potential liability, corporate defense is helping the organization to minimize losses which also contributes to improving profitability.

### 17.3.1.3 Help to Reduce Shocks and Surprises

The more healthy, robust, and resilient the organization, the better equipped it is to deal with any unexpected shocks or unpleasant surprises. Effective corporate defense helps ensure that the organization is also appropriately prepared to handle emergency incidents and crisis situations should they arise. By helping to reduce an organization's vulnerability to hazard events, corporate defense is also helping to minimize the number of negative incidents and therefore is also helping to reduce the occurrence of shocks and surprises. This has a stabilizing affect on the organization and means that there is greater certainty in relation to its operations. This creates an environment in which the organization can be more confident about smooth earnings, more predictable profitability, and greater certainty over its future cash flows, all of which help to improve market confidence.

### 17.3.2 INCREASE CORPORATE DEFENSE EFFICIENCY

By breaking down silo structures, an organization can expect to increase the efficiency of its corporate defense operations as silos typically result in a series of inefficiencies that need to be eliminated. Corporate defense processes need to be streamlined in order to be efficient and should be subject to the same level of scrutiny and review as any other business processes. Any efficiency review of its corporate defense activities needs to consider whether the organization wishes to achieve the same levels of performance and productivity by investing fewer resources, or, whether it wishes to increase the levels of performance and productivity while continuing to invest the same level of resources. Either way, the objective is to achieve a higher rate of return on its considerable corporate defense investment. An optimum level of efficiency is achieved through process streamlining, continuous improvement, and constant learning, and by incorporating proven lean manufacturing and quality management techniques into corporate defense processes in order to help achieve this end.

### 17.3.2.1 Help Ensure Resource Optimization

All organizations have finite resources at their disposal and there are always restraints on the level of resources that can be allocated to any part of the business, normally subject to some form of cost–benefit analysis. Resource management and the optimization of the return on allocated resources is therefore an essential element of any well-run business. The efficient management of corporate defense resources can directly impact on improving the organization's return on its corporate defense investment. In addition, an effective corporate defense program can also contribute by helping to ensure that the organization's resources are managed in an efficient manner. A holistic approach to corporate defense can help an organization obtain a clearer big picture of its resource management constraints and thereby help to reduce the complexity of the related processes. By considering resource management from multiple perspectives such as a risk perspective, a compliance perspective, and a resilience perspective, organizations can better estimate required reserves and buffers. Such an approach can also help in the setting of required limits and in determining the resources available for allocation. This approach can be of particular benefit with considering the organization's capital requirements. For example, financial institutions by improving their risk weighted optimization processes can help ensure the more accurate calculation of its risk weighted assets, help to boost its capital efficiency, and in the process improve its financial ratios. By adopting risk adjusted performance measurement systems, organizations help improve their overall resource efficiency and effectiveness through real-time monitoring. Such a holistic focus can help an organization develop a resource-focused business model with a greater emphasis on the optimization of resources.

### 17.3.2.2  Help to Reduce Bureaucracy

Many organizations find themselves burdened by excessive bureaucracy that can very often be a result of a general lack of clarity of purpose and a lack of alignment between business units and functions. Excessive bureaucracy can lead to increasing levels of frustration and unnecessary delays in business processing timescales that can negatively impact on performance and productivity. A holistic approach to corporate defense by focusing on aligning and integrating corporate defense activities can help an organization to efficiently streamline critical business processes and controls. A purpose-driven, *strategy-centric* focus can help an organization to more clearly identify its critical path requirements and in the process remove unnecessary bureaucracy. Such an approach can assist in process reengineering by scrutinizing the purpose and necessity of the individual tasks performed in the business process, thereby helping to remove any unnecessary formalities and red tape inherited by legacy systems and processes. The elimination of a silo-type culture can help facilitate a smoother more efficient business process while still insuring that all necessary safety features are still present in the process. By focusing on ongoing process streamlining and reengineering, an organization can continuously improve efficiency and safeguard against bureaucracy leading to enhanced performance and increased productivity.

### 17.3.3  Promote Greater Transparency and Accountability

A lack of transparency and accountability can be a challenge for organizations and can present considerable difficulties that need to be overcome. A lack of transparency can result in an unhealthy organizational culture and environment that encourages heightened levels of internal politics which can result in dysfunctional behavior due to inaccurate assumptions, dispersed loyalties, and organizational jealousy. A lack of transparency can typically result in confusion be it in relation to the delegation of authority, individual responsibility, and individual accountability. Such confusion can result in fragmented or ambiguous responsibilities, and diluted or nonexistent accountability. An effective corporate defense program can have an important role to play in helping to promote greater transparency and improved accountability at all levels of the organization. The corporate defense program can be used as a mechanism for promoting being transparent in all aspects of the business and at all levels. It can help enhance visibility and communicate clarity about all of the activities of the business and how they knit together in a sound manner. It can help promote more open disclosure and information sharing between different functions and help break down any silo structures and *Chinese walls* that may exist.

### 17.3.3.1  Help to Reinforce Oversight

On occasions where the responsibility for performing a given task is delegated to a subordinate, it is very important to clearly establish who exactly is responsible for what, in order to entrust ownership for the tasks, and to avoid any possible confusion which may arise. Typically, delegation flows downward; however, responsibility for delegation flows upward. There is, therefore, an additional responsibility on the delegator to oversee the performance of the delegated tasks and to hold individuals to account for the performance of their responsibilities. While the corporate defense program helps to foster a culture of collective responsibility for corporate defense, it also helps ensure that there is transparent oversight of the corporate defense process so that individuals and groups can be held accountable for fulfilling their responsibilities. The five lines of defense as a comprehensive oversight model can help an organization ensure that all concerned individuals are aware of their responsibilities and provide a vigilance mechanism throughout the organization to ensure that these individuals are held accountable for those activities within their remit and within their line of sight. A healthy defense culture, which is nurtured from the very top, can help an organization improve its oversight, supervision, and assurance, via improved monitoring and reporting at all levels of the organization.

### 17.3.3.2   Help to Improve Corporate Defense Activities

Greater transparency and accountability can help the organization to improve its corporate defense activities. Greater transparency and accountability can help facilitate efficiency and remove unnecessary bureaucracy while also ensuring conformance with all mandatory obligations and requirements. Greater transparency and accountability can enable an organization to successfully demonstrate that it has taken all reasonable steps to help ensure that there is an appropriate program in place to adequately defend its stakeholder interests. At a functional level, greater transparency and accountability can help remove obstacles to change, and unlock latent potential which the organization may previously have lost out on due to silo type structures. It can help with the integration of corporate defense activities and facilitate the leveraging of these functions through collaboration, cooperation, and information sharing. Such behavior can deliver a more efficient corporate defense activity mix and help deliver a higher level of performance and increased productivity in each of the critical corporate defense components (i.e., governance, risk, compliance, intelligence, security, controls, and assurance).

## 17.4   THE VALUE PROPOSITION—AN OPERATIONAL PERSPECTIVE

What operational value can corporate defense add to an organization? A lack of operational alignment with the strategic objectives of the organization can result in a narrow operational focus which in turn can actually hinder the achievement of broader business objectives and can fail to deliver many additional operational benefits to the organization. This lack of alignment can result in operational ineffectiveness and wastefulness leading to increased costs, inadequate productivity, and a suboptimal return on investment. An effective corporate defense program can help to rectify this situation and present certain operational benefits and advantages to an organization which in themselves represent an additional source of value. The CDM approach can help to provide sustainable value by enhancing operational effectiveness through improved performance and increased productivity, and it can help enhance operational efficiency by reducing overheads and operating costs.

### 17.4.1   Improve Performance

Effective corporate defense can contribute to operational efficiency by helping the organization to operationally align with strategic and tactical objectives thereby helping to ensure that operational effectiveness is positively contributing to the overall effectiveness of the organization. The more the organization's people, processes, and systems are closely aligned at an operational level, the greater clarity of purpose and the clearer the focus is on operational activities in terms of its overall contribution to the organization. Clarity of purpose can also generate a tremendous source of creativity and innovation necessary for the development of new ideas. An effective corporate defense program can help the organization to ensure that operationally it is doing all *the rights things* and that it is doing them all *in the right way* in line with the organization's policies and supporting the achievement of its objectives. Corporate defense can help the organization ensure that it is selecting the most appropriate metrics in terms of its KPIs and that these metrics are being monitored and evaluated in the appropriate manner.

### 17.4.1.1   Help to Accelerate Operations

Corporate defense needs to be concerned with improving organizational performance. By helping to streamline the operational workflow and reengineer the business process, the corporate defense program can help the organization accelerate its operational processes. By helping to remove obstacles, barriers, and bottlenecks that can cause time delays, corporate defense can make the business process easier, and thereby contribute to the smooth running of the organization. More efficient workflows can result in a speeding up of the business process, in reduced time frames, and in faster turnaround times. Being able to provide products and services more quickly in turn helps contribute to an organization's competitive advantage. By helping to ensure that the organization has anticipated and is best prepared to deal with different eventualities, its reaction times can be accelerated thereby reducing vulnerability and avoiding or minimizing the impact of negative events. At the same time, this also allows the organization to be able take advantage of opportunities as they present themselves and ideally more quickly than the competition.

### 17.4.1.2   Help to Improve on Quality

A work ethic of continuous learning and constant improvement lies at the heart of delivering improved quality on an ongoing basis and is an important source of competitive advantage for any organization. By promoting a proactive rather than reactive approach to corporate defense, this can help to facilitate the development of integrated, superior, and innovative performance. By embracing innovation and creativity in the workplace, an organization can reap the benefits through a positive contribution to the development of new products and services. By helping to improve business processes, corporate defense adds value by helping the organization to constantly deliver better products and services. A collaborative approach supports leveraging from technology wherever possible and facilitates continuous improvement in how the business is run, including how plans are implemented and how tasks are executed. Corporate defense by demanding increased levels of vigilance and alertness at all times can help the organization to improve on the quality of its preemptive capabilities in order to help prevent the occurrence of hazard events that can have a negative impact on its performance.

### 17.4.2   INCREASE PRODUCTIVITY

The creation of a more stable business environment can help to smooth the business process and facilitate a more productive environment. Better synchronization of operational activities and the optimization of synergies through integration and partnerships can also contribute to increasing the organization's productivity. Streamlining of the business process through aligning corporate defense activities with the business objectives can lead to improved performance which in turn can lead to increased productivity. Effective corporate defense can contribute to increasing productivity by helping ensure that operational activities are being performed in an effective and efficient manner. Scrutiny of work practices can help differentiate between what is considered to be productive and nonproductive efforts, thereby providing an opportunity to increase the amount of time spent on productive efforts and help to maximize return on investment.

### 17.4.2.1   Help to Boost Output

An organization's productivity is typically measured in terms of its output, the quality and quantity of output, and the value associated with this output. At an operational level, there are important differences between being idle and being productive, between being busy and being productive, and between nonproductive output and productive output. Organization's need to be fully focused on maximizing their productive output and these subtle differences can very well be the difference between a successful organization that maximizes its potential value and a less successful organization that fails to maximize its potential value. Effective corporate defense by aligning objectives at strategic, tactical, and operational levels can help an organization to eliminate idle operational time, ensure that busy operational time is also productive time, and help reduce nonproductive operational output and increase productive operational output and its associated value to the organization. Corporate defense can help improve business processes through process streamlining that can improve the speed of operational productivity thereby improving the organization's health by helping to turn fat into muscle, whereby the organization can increase its operational output without a corresponding increase in its operational investment. By analyzing, assessing, and evaluating its operational value drivers, it can help ensure that operational KIPs are appropriately measured and closely monitored. Effective corporate defense safeguards the organization's critical assets from damage and impairment, thereby helping to minimize downtime and maximize productive time.

### 17.4.2.2 Help to Empower the Workforce

A fully mature corporate defense program that has finally arrived at the optimized maturity phase is focused on optimizing the use of the organization's resources. Optimizing resources requires operational processes to be flexible, adaptable, and innovative, and is dependent on the participation of an empowered workforce. An organization's workforce is empowered through trust, partnership, and education, and by aligning incentives with the business values and objectives of the organization. An empowered and incentivized workforce takes full ownership of its duties and responsibilities and is motivated to shepherd its operational activities in a positive and proactive manner in order to continually strive for improvement. An empowered and motivated workforce is dynamic, flexible, and adaptable, and constantly seeking to unlock latent potential through innovation and creativity in a search for excellence. An empowered workforce can be a driver for changing work practices for the better and be a springboard for continuously evolving business processes. It can be a driver for the adoption of accelerated learning techniques in order to continuously strive to achieve higher standards of performance and productivity, thereby helping to maximize the organization's return on investment. An empowered workforce is focused on knowledge sharing, continuous learning, and avoiding a repeat of past mistakes. An empowered workforce is a productive and reliable workforce, and an incredibly powerful source of competitive advantage for any organization.

### 17.4.3 Reduce Overheads and Operating Costs

An important aspect of achieving operational efficiency is having strict controls over its levels of overheads and operating costs in order to help maximize operating margins. Overheads can be reduced by more efficient management of operational resources, and operating costs can be reduced by eliminating operational inefficiencies. Operational inefficiencies include bureaucracy, overlaps, duplication of effort, and costs associated with unnecessary redundancy. Costs can also be kept to a minimum by avoiding or mitigating potential liability that can result in the organization incurring losses. Effective corporate defense can contribute to the health of the organization by helping it avoid potential liability and by helping to reduce operational fat through the elimination of duplication and by minimizing unnecessary redundancy so that the organization can achieve the same level of output at a reduced level of investment.

In order to manage operational costs in an efficient manner, an organization must first be aware of the associated costs involved. For example, in the case of corporate defense, most organizations may only recognize overheads and costs directly associated with corporate-defense-related functions (e.g., salaries, equipment, fixtures, and fittings). An organization's corporate defense costs, however, also include costs associated with the various corporate defense training received by the business workforce (e.g., compliance and security), in addition to the time spent by the business workforce on corporate defense related tasks (e.g., risk management and controls) in the performance of their day-to-day practices and procedures. By taking these figures into account, the overall cost of the corporate defense program can be significant and therefore requires close scrutiny. Once overall costs are established, efforts can then be made to manage these costs in as efficient a manner as possible. A low overhead and operating cost base can provide the organization with another source of competitive advantage.

### 17.4.3.1 Help in the Avoidance of Potential Liability

Failure to avoid potential liability gives rise to the incurrence of operational losses which reduce the organization's bottom line contribution. Potential liability typically arises from weaknesses and deficiencies in an organization's corporate defense framework. Corporate defense therefore has an important role in helping the organization to avoid potential liability that could be detrimental to the achievement of its objectives. An effective corporate defense program can therefore help an organization ensure that potential liabilities are avoided or at least mitigated where possible. For example, an effective corporate defense program can help an organization ensure it is in compliance with all legal and regulatory requirements thereby avoiding issues such as fines and penalties, legal fees, litigation expenses, license revocation, prosecutions, and even jail sentences. By adequately safeguarding the organization's assets, it can help to avoid or at least reduce the incurrence of losses relating to fraud, theft, or sabotage of assets. Robust risk management processes can help minimize the profit seepage that occurs as a result of everyday low impact high probability events, as well as minimizing the initial impact and subsequent collateral damage associated with rare high impact low probability events should they occur. Effective business processing controls can help reduce the incurrence of losses due to human error and assist in improving reaction times to incidents in order to help mitigate losses.

### 17.4.3.2  Help to Minimize Duplication and Redundancy

In many instances, overheads and operating costs can be dramatically reduced by the efficiencies that can be derived from integrating certain operational activities. This particularly applies to organizations that are intent on abolishing their corporate defense silo functions. In such silos, there is very often considerable intersection, overlap, and duplication of activities and responsibilities between different silo groups, which can be considerably inefficient, nonproductive, and costly to the organization. By reviewing and assessing the operational activities of these functions, the organization can identify unnecessary bureaucracy and the duplications of operational activities.

The alignment, integration, and convergence of corporate defense activities also provides an opportunity to pool its resources in terms of people, processes, and systems. It is prudent to ensure a certain level of redundancy is built into each of these areas in order to help deal with occasions where there may be additional stress applied on the organization's people, processes, or systems. The pooling of cross-functional resources, however, can provide unexpected additional capacity which may not be required and will therefore remain unnecessarily redundant. Such unnecessary redundancy can therefore result in unnecessary expenditure and cost. The minimization of redundancy can present organizations with additional cost savings. The extent and cost of this wastage can then be reduced by the elimination of identified unnecessary duplication and redundancy which also serves to improve the efficiency and effectiveness of the corporate defense program itself and the return on the corporate defense investment.

## 17.5  THE VALUE PROPOSITION—AN INTEGRATED PERSPECTIVE

Before making any final decision on the business case for corporate defense, it is important to incorporate the value proposition from strategic, tactical, and operational perspectives in order to finally consider it from an integrated perspective. Viewing the value proposition from an integrated perspective can help the organization and its stakeholders to appreciate the crucial role that effective corporate defense can play in relation to the bigger picture. The ability to view the value proposition from an integrated perspective is essential in appreciating that the value proposition in its totality is far greater than simply adding the sum of its parts.

### 17.5.1  The Requirement for Integrated Thinking

An integrated perspective requires integrated thinking, which involves the ability to comprehend the value proposition in its entirety, as a complete package. In an increasingly complex business world, the capacity for integrated thinking is fundamental to how an organization conducts its business and is considered the essence of the twenty-first century organization. Integrated thinking can be contrasted with *silo thinking* by taking into account the connectivity and interdependences between the range of factors that have a material effect on the organization's ability to create and preserve value over time. It requires a holistic view and the ability to think critically about these interconnections and interdependences.

### 17.5.1.1 A Holistic Comprehension of the Organization

A holistic view of the organization demands a comprehensive understanding of the breadth and depth of its activities in order to be in a position to form as complete a picture as possible. Integrated thinking therefore needs to be wide ranging in order to form a multilevel view which addresses issues both internal and external to the organization. This process must consider macro issues which may impact on the organization's achievement of its objectives such as the global economy and international markets' fluctuations. It should consider issues relating to the organization's culture, the business sectors, and the geographic regions in which it operates. It should consider the parent company, its subsidiaries, its branches, and its supply chain. Within the organization, it should consider issues relating to the business units, divisions, departments, and functions, in addition to portfolios, products, and transactions. This process should therefore begin with a high-level strategic view of the organization in question, by considering its vision, mission statement, and strategy. This should be followed by gradually drilling down into a tactical view of its planning, infrastructure, and architecture. Finally it should end by considering an operational view of the organization and the execution of ongoing activities.

### 17.5.1.2 An Appreciation of the Corporate Defense Ecosystem

Integrated thinking involves an appreciation of the corporate defense ecosystem and the ability to consider the interactions, linkages, interconnections, interdependences, and potential cascade of consequences that exist throughout this ecosystem. It involves considering the alignment of the organization's interconnectivities both vertically (top-down, bottom-up) and horizontally (across, cross-functionally), at strategic, tactical, and operational levels. It involves an appreciation of the evolution of this ecosystem, past and present, and projecting it into the future (short, medium, and long term). Such an appreciation does indeed represent a complex challenge that organizations cannot afford to underestimate. Ongoing developments in emerging fields such as *complexity science*, *network science*, and *systems thinking* can provide organizations with useful guidance, skills, and tools. These can enable an organization to better appreciate and understand universal principles, common properties, and the complex workings of interconnected environments, and the potential hazards resulting from risks, threats, and vulnerabilities, which are inherently present as a result of such complex relationships. In reality, however, many organizations are unlikely to have a clear appreciation and understanding of the complex workings of their own ecosystem and are also unlikely to have a clear understanding of how they should go about forming such an all-encompassing view. For this reason, the totality of the corporate defense value proposition may often be underestimated.

### 17.5.2 Consideration of the Corporate Defense Business Case

Generally speaking, every organization is different from another organization as each is likely to have a different culture, different objectives, different structures, different people, etc. As such, every organization is likely have its own rationale for, and stakeholder expectations of, its corporate defense responsibilities. The business case for each organization will therefore be different and will need to be tailored to the requirements of that organization and considered on its own merits. Ideally any consideration of the corporate defense business case should be viewed from an integrated perspective so that due consideration is given to its overall value proposition and not just its potential impact at different levels within the organization. When assessing the value of the corporate defense business case, each organization should consider its current situation (as is) and its preferred situation going forward (to be). This may involve a diagnostic of its current corporate defense profile and an analysis of what level of effort and investment is required in order to arrive at its preferred profile. This will help the organization to more clearly evaluate the perceived strengths and weaknesses associated with an integrated corporate defense proposal.

### 17.5.2.1 Perception of Strengths and Weaknesses

In assessing the strengths and weaknesses of the business case for an integrated corporate defense program, the organization should consider not only the direct benefits and costs, but also other potential indirect positives and negatives and these may vary by organization. Different types of tradeoffs are commonplace as what may be considered a positive in one organization may be considered a negative in another organization. For example, an organization with a hands-off board may prefer that the board only have oversight for the integrated corporate defense program, while an organization with a more hands-on board may prefer that the board have direct responsibility for individual corporate defense *hot topics* such as risk oversight, reputation oversight, and cyber-security oversight. Also the appetite for change may be based on the organization's perceived current level of corporate defense maturity, both functionally and cross-functionally. For example, one organization that has been diagnosed as having a very low level of corporate defense maturity may feel that this is a sufficient reason to address perceived deficiencies and weaknesses, before it is too late, by implementing an integrated corporate defense program. Another similar organization may feel that it may not be able to successfully manage such a degree of change in one fell swoop and may prefer to adopt a more gradual phased approach.

### 17.5.2.2 Perception of Opportunities and Threats

In assessing the opportunities and threats presented by the corporate defense business case, the organization should consider this not only in the direct context of value preservation but also in the potential indirect value creation advantages and disadvantages. Here again what may be perceived as an opportunity in one organization may be perceived as a threat in another. For example, an organization with a hands-off CEO may prefer that the CEO only regularly interact with the corporate defense champion who is responsible for coordinating the corporate defense initiative in the organization, while an organization with a more a hands-on CEO may prefer that the CEO also regularly interact with the heads of the individual corporate defense functions on a regular basis. For one organization, there is a perceived opportunity to free up the CEO's time to focus on business issues while for the other there is a perceived danger that the CEO could become too removed from individual corporate defense issues. The corporate culture and attitudes to corporate defense activities may also influence the extent to which the corporate defense business case is viewed in terms of opportunities and threats. For example, in a more traditional organization, there may be a perception that the objective of corporate defense activities is strictly to address threats facing the organization, while in a more progressive organization, there may be a perception that the objective of corporate defense activities is to help the organization achieve its objectives which includes helping it to take advantage of opportunities that present themselves.

## 17.6  CONCLUSION

In summary, the corporate defense value proposition is concerned with employing an effective corporate defense program to support the organization in the realization of its vision, in the accomplishment of its mission, and in successfully executing its strategy. It is concerned with helping the organization to attain long-term sustainability, and in assisting it in the achievement of its strategic, tactical, and operational objectives.

### 17.6.1  A SUMMARY OVERVIEW

At a strategic level, it is concerned with the adoption of a holistic view in order to promote a healthy culture and help ensure that the organization's strategy incorporates a healthy balance between its focus on value creation and its focus on value preservation. It is concerned with ensuring that the organization's value preservation obligations to its stakeholders are addressed via a formal structured corporate defense program, and that the related corporate defense strategy is in close alignment with the organization's business strategy. It is concerned with adding value and ensuring that the organization challenges itself to optimize the potential benefits to be derived from its corporate defense efforts and to maximize the return on its corporate defense investment.

At a tactical level, it is concerned with joining the dots and implementing an integrated framework which helps to unify all of the critical corporate components under one umbrella so that they are all strategically aligned, tactically integrated, and operating in unison toward common objectives. It is concerned with ensuring that an integrated approach to corporate defense can help improve decision making at all levels within the organization and therefore lead to enhanced profitability. It is concerned with ensuring the effective and efficient use of resources in order to unlock latent potential and to help create a source of competitive advantage for the organization.

At an operational level, it is concerned with facilitating the closer interaction, cooperation, and sharing of information across all corporate defense functions. It is concerned with the establishment of a mutually beneficial and respectful relationship between corporate defense functions and the business through improved communication and by the adoption of a collaborative process aimed at helping to achieve common objectives. It is concerned with improving operational performance, increasing productivity, and reducing costs thereby contributing to the organization's competitiveness.

Ultimately the difference between successful and unsuccessful organizations is the ability to consistently create and preserve value over time. Shortcomings in either or both can eventually result in the failure of the business. An effective corporate defense program represents a prudent, logical, and commonsense approach to determining how corporate defense can best help address this challenge and develop a robust and resilient organization. The corporate defense value proposition is concerned with supporting the organization in creating value over time for its stakeholders, and in helping to ensure that adequate measures are taken by the organization so that this value is appropriately preserved in the short, medium, and long term. To this end, an integrated corporate defense program helps the organization to reap the full rewards of the opportunities that present themselves while at the same time helping to provide the organization with *defense-in-breadth* and *defense-in-depth* against the occurrence of hazard events which could be detrimental to the achievement of its objectives. Finally, organizations often publicly state that it is their stakeholders who set them apart, make them unique, and help to differentiate them from their competition. Such statements are normally accompanied with comments about how much the organization dearly values its stakeholders, and how it is committed to looking out for its stakeholder best interests. It could, however, be reasonably argued that the true measure of an organization's commitment to protecting its stakeholders interests is reflected in its approach to corporate defense.

### 17.6.1.1 The Elevator Pitch

An elevator pitch represents a brief opportunity to make a short sales pitch to introduce the merits of a formal corporate defense program. It is an opportunity to deliver a preprepared speech that explains the USPs of a corporate defense program in a clear and succinct manner. A typical corporate defense elevator pitch would consist of the following:

- Increasing stakeholder demands for long-term sustainability requires that organizations have a clear focus on their value creation and value preservation imperatives over the short, medium, and long term. As such, value preservation involves safeguarding and defending stakeholder value on an ongoing basis. Corporate defense as a discipline focuses on value preservation measures that help an organization to achieve its strategic objectives.
- An effective corporate defense program successfully manages and coordinates all corporate-defense-related activities so that they are strategically aligned, tactically

integrated, and operating in unison toward common objectives. Such an approach can help an organization to adequately safeguard stakeholder interests while optimizing stakeholder value. It also provides demonstratable evidence of a systematic approach to safeguarding stakeholder value at strategic, tactical, and operational levels.

- Does your organization currently have a formal corporate defense program in place?

### 17.6.2   FINALLY—FAST CARS AND SAFETY

In many respects, the CEO of an organization has similar responsibilities to that of a *Formula One* driver, in so much as the CEO is at the wheel and responsible for driving the organization forward.

---

#### THE FASTEST CARS REQUIRE THE BEST SAFETY FEATURES

It is said that the fastest cars require the best safety features. In order for a Formula One driver to be confident enough to fully utilize his or her car's acceleration features and to be able to drive at the maximum speeds, the driver needs to have confidence in the car's safety features. They must be happy not only with the car's design and racing performance capabilities, but also that the car is fitted with the best tires, the best shocks, the best brakes, and that it is equipped with the best anticrash protection features. The driver inherently understands that seemingly small operational control weaknesses can significantly impair his or her performance. The driver must have confidence that the car's features have been appropriately tested and maintained (e.g., oil and water) so that he or she can rely on its dashboard to provide accurate information in relation to issues such as speed, fuel, and distance. He or she must have confidence that all the other team members (e.g., pit-stop mechanics) are also at the top of their game and are well drilled and prepared for all eventualities. This includes the selection of tires that are best suited to deal with prevailing conditions and the actual tire pressure. It is only then that the driver can completely focus on his or her own objective, which is to drive that car as fast as it can possibly go. He or she knows that in the end he or she will be held personally responsible for the performance.

---

Similar issues also apply to the CEO and others (including the board) who are responsible for driving an organization forward. Ultimately an effective corporate defense program can help provide these individuals with the required level of comfort to drive the organization forward with sufficient confidence to enable them to focus on delivering value in short, medium, and long term.

# References

AASB. June 2014. *Framework for Assurance Engagements*. Auditing and Assurance Standards Board, Australian Government. http://www.auasb.gov.au/admin/file/content102/c3/Jun14_Framework_for_Assurance_Engagements.pdf.

ACCA. February 2014. *Creating Value through Governance—Towards a New Accountability: A Consultation*. The Association of Chartered Certified Accountants. http://www.accaglobal.com/content/dam/acca/global/PDF-technical/corporate-governance/tech-tp-cvtg.pdf.

AESRM. 2007. *The Convergence of Physical and Information Security in the Context of Enterprise Risk Management*. The Alliance of Enterprise Security Risk Management. http://ddata.over-blog.com/xxxyyy/0/32/13/25/aesrm-convergence-in-erm.pdf.

AIRMIC et al. 2002. *A Risk Management Standard*. Association of Insurance and Risk Managers, National Forum for Risk Management in the Public Sector, Institute of Risk Management. http://www.ferma.eu/app/uploads/2011/11/a-risk-management-standard-english-version.pdf.

Allen J. June 2005. *Governing for Enterprise Security*. Software Engineering Institute, Carnegie Mellon University. http://www.sei.cmu.edu/reports/05tn023.pdf.

The American Presidency Project. 1957. Dwight D. Eishenhower, 235 - Remarks at the National Defense Executive Reserve Conference, November 4, 1957. http://www.presidency.ucsb.edu.

Apgar D. 2006. *Risk Intelligence: Learning to Manage What We Don't Know*. HBS Press, Boston, MA.

ASIS. 2009a. *Facilities Physical Security Measures Guideline*. ASIS International. https://www.asisonline.org/Standards-Guidelines/Guidelines/published/Pages/Facilities-Physical-Security-Measures-Guideline.aspx?cart=ec08d3b0623d400caf9fe59103094127.

ASIS. March 2009b. *ASIS SPC.1-2009 Organizational Resilience: Security, Preparedness, and Continuity Management Systems—Requirements with Guidance for Use*. ASIS International. http://webstore.ansi.org/RecordDetail.aspx?sku=ASIS+SPC.1–2009.

AS/NZS. 2004. *Australian/New Zealand Standard Risk Management: AS/NZS 4360*. Standards Australia/Standards New Zealand. http://shop.standards.co.nz/catalog/4360%3A2004%28AS%7CNZS%29/view.

AS/NZS. June 2010. *AS/NZS 5050:2010 Business Continuity—Managing Disruption-Related Risk*. Standards Australia, Standards New Zealand. http://shop.standards.co.nz/catalog/5050%3A2010(AS%7CNZ)/view.

BAH. 2004. *Redefining the Corporate Governance Agenda: From Risk Management to Enterprise Resilience*. Booz Allen Hamilton, and Weil, Gotshal & Manges. http://www.boozallen.com/media/file/138022.pdf.

BCBS. January 1998. *Framework for the Evaluation of Internal Control Systems*. Basle Committee on Banking Supervision, Bank for International Settlements. http://www.bis.org/publ/bcbs33.pdf.

BCBS. August 2001. *Internal Audit in Banks and the Supervisor's Relationship with Auditors*. Basle Committee on Banking Supervision, Bank for International Settlements. http://www.bis.org/publ/bcbs84.pdf.

BCBS. April 2005. *Compliance and the Compliance Function in Banks*. Basel Committee on Banking Supervision, Bank for International Settlements. http://www.bis.org/publ/bcbs113.pdf.

BCBS. October 2010. *Principles for Enhancing Corporate Governance*. Basel Committee on Banking Supervision, Bank for International Settlements. http://www.bis.org/publ/bcbs176.pdf.

BCBS. June 2011. *Principles for the Sound Management of Operational Risk*. Basel Committee on Banking Supervision, Bank for International Settlements. http://www.bis.org/publ/bcbs195.pdf.

Booz & Co. 2008. *Bringing Back Best Practice in Risk Management: Banks' Three Lines of Defense*. Booz & Co. http://www.strategyand.pwc.com/media/file/Bringing-Back-Best-Practices-in-Risk-Management.pdf.

Booz & Co. 2009. *First and Last Line of Defense: How Business Assurance Makes Organizations Resilient to Risk*. Booz & Co. http://www.strategyand.pwc.com/media/file/First_and_Last_Line_of_Defense.pdf.

Booz & Co. 2012. *The Root Causes of Value Destruction: How Strategic Resiliency Can Help*. Booz & Co. http://static1.squarespace.com/static/5481bc79e4b01c4bf3ceed80/t/54e5009de4b0f2941442ff1a/1424294045993/BoozCo_The-Root-Causes-of-Value-Destruction.pdf.

BSI. July 2001. *PAS 2001 Knowledge Management: A Guide to Good Practice*. British Standards Institution. http://shop.bsigroup.com/ProductDetail/?pid=000000000030042924.

BSI. November 2014. *BS 65000:2014 Guidance on Organizational Resilience*. British Standards Institution. http://shop.bsigroup.com/ProductDetail/?pid=000000000030258792.

Burden P. February 2008. Three lines of defence model. *ACCA IA Bulletin*. http://newsweaver.co.uk/accaiabulletin/e_article001026154.cfm?x=b11,0,w.

Business Roundtable. 2012. *Principles of Corporate Governance 2012*. Business Roundtable. http://businessroundtable.org/sites/default/files/BRT_Principles_of_Corporate_Governance_-2012_Formatted_Final.pdf.

CEN. 2004. *European Guide to Good Practice in Knowledge Management (Parts 1–5)*. European Committee for Standardization. http://shop.bsigroup.com/ProductDetail/?pid=000000000030110856.

CERT. May 2007. *Podcast: Adapting to Changing Risk Environments: Operational Resilience*. Computer Emergency Response Team Division, Software Engineering Institute, Carnegie Mellon University. https://resources.sei.cmu.edu/asset_files/Podcast/2007_016_102_67229.pdf.

CERT. November 2010. *CERT Resilience Management Model: A Maturity Model for Managing Operational Resilience*. Computer Emergency Response Team Division, Software Engineering Institute, Carnegie Mellon University. http://resources.sei.cmu.edu/library/asset-view.cfm?assetid=30375.

CICA. 1995. *The Criteria of Control (CoCo) Framework*. Canadian Institute of Chartered Accountants. http://www.castore.ca/product/guidance-on-control/11.

COP. June 2010. *June Oversight Report: The AIG Rescue, Its Impact on Markets, and the Government's Exit Strategy*. Congressional Oversight Panel. http://www.gpo.gov/fdsys/pkg/CPRT-111JPRT56698/pdf/CPRT-111JPRT56698.pdf.

COSO. 1992. *Internal Control—Integrated Framework*. The Committee of Sponsoring Organisations of the Treadway Commission. http://www.coso.org/ic.htm.

COSO. September 2004. *Enterprise Risk Management—Integrated Framework*. The Committee of Sponsoring Organisations of the Treadway Commission. http://www.coso.org/erm-integratedframework.htm.

COSO. September 2009. *Effective Enterprise Risk Oversight: The Role of the Board of Directors*. The Committee of Sponsoring Organizations of the Treadway Commission. http://www.coso.org/documents/cosoboardserm4pager-finalreleaseversion82409_001.pdf.

COSO. 2013. *Internal Control—Integrated Framework*. The Committee of Sponsoring Organizations of the Treadway Commission. http://www.coso.org/ic.htm.

CSIS. December 2008. *Transitioning Defense Organizational Initiatives: An Assessment of Key 2001–2008 Defense Reforms*. Center for Strategic and International Studies. http://csis.org/files/media/csis/pubs/081209_hicks_transdeforg_web.pdf.

Dobbs R. et al. August 2005. Building the healthy corporation. *The McKinsey Quarterly*. http://www.mckinsey.com/insights/organization/building_the_healthy_corporation.

Drucker P.F. 1993. *Post-Capitalist Society*. Harper Business, New York.

ENISA. January 2011. *Enabling and Managing End to End Resilience*. European Network and Information Security Agency. https://www.enisa.europa.eu/activities/identity-and-trust/library/deliverables/e2eres.

FCIC. January 2011. *The Financial Crisis Inquiry Report: Final Report of the National Commission on the Causes of the Financial and Economic Crisis in the United States*. The Financial Crisis Inquiry Commission, Official Government Edition. http://www.gpo.gov/fdsys/pkg/GPO-FCIC/pdf/GPO-FCIC.pdf.

FERMA & ECIIA. September 2010. *Guidance on the 8th EU Company Law Directive Article 41*. Federation of European Risk Management Associations, European Confederations of Institutes of Internal Auditing. http://www.eciia.eu/wp-content/uploads/2013/09/Blog-4.4-Avoid-reg-part-1.pdf.

FRC. October 2005. *Internal Control: Revised Guidance for Directors on the Combined Code*. Financial Reporting Council. https://www.frc.org.uk/getattachment/5e4d12e4-a94f-4186-9d6f-19e17aeb5351/Turnbull-guidance-October-2005.aspx.

FRC. September 2014. *UK Corporate Governance Code*. Financial Reporting Council. https://www.frc.org.uk/Our-Work/Publications/Corporate-Governance/UK-Corporate-Governance-Code-2014.pdf.

FSA. April 2007. *Principles-Based Regulation: Focusing on the Outcomes That Matter*. The Financial Services Authority. http://www.fsa.gov.uk/pubs/other/principles.pdf.

Funston F. and Wagner S. April 2010. *Surviving and Thriving in Uncertainty: Creating the Risk Intelligent Enterprise*. John Wiley & Sons, Hoboken, NJ.

GAO. September 2014. *Standards for Internal Control in the Federal Government*. Comptroller General of the United States, US General Accounting Office. http://www.gao.gov/assets/670/665712.pdf.

Halal W.E. October 1997. *Organizational Intelligence: What Is It, and How Can Managers Use It?*. Strategy + Business. http://www.strategy-business.com/article/12644?gko=4a546.

Harner M. June 2013. *Corporate Culture and ERM*. Director Notes, The Conference Board. https://www.conference-board.org/topics/publicationdetail.cfm?publicationid=2527.

Hindle T. September 2008. *Guide to Management Ideas and Gurus*. The Economist in Association with Profile Books, London.

HM Treasury. December 2012. *Assurance Frameworks*. HM Treasury. https://www.gov.uk/government/uploads/system/uploads/attachment_data/file/270485/assurance_frameworks_191212.pdf.

Humphrey W.S. January 1989. *Managing the Software Process*. Addison-Wesley, Reading, MA.

IAASB. January 2005. *International Framework for Assurance Engagements*. International Auditing and Assurance Standards Board. http://www.ifac.org/system/files/downloads/b003-2010-iaasb-handbook-framework.pdf.

IAASB. December 2013. *International Standards for Assurance Engagements*. International Auditing and Assurance Standards Board. https://www.ifac.org/publications-resources/international-standard-assurance-engagements-isae-3000-revised-assurance-enga.

IBM. 2004. *Business Resilience: Proactive Measures for Forward-Looking Enterprises*. IBM Corporation. https://www-935.ibm.com/services/us/bcrs/pdf/br_business-resilience.pdf.

IBM. January 2009. *Business Resilience: The Best Defense Is a Good Offense*. IBM Corporation. https://www.ibm.com/smarterplanet/global/files/us__en_us__security_resiliency__buw03008usen.pdf.

ICGN. 2014. *ICGN Global Governance Principles*. International Corporate Governance Network. https://www.icgn.org/policy/guidance.

ICOR. 2010. *Resiliency Framework*. International Consortium for Organizational Resilience. http://theicor.org/university.html.

IFAC. June 2012. *Evaluating and Improving Internal Control in Organizations*. International Federation of Accountants. https://www.ifac.org/publications-resources/evaluating-and-improving-internal-control-organizations-0.

IIA. January 2013a. *The Three Lines of Defense in Effective Risk Management and Control*. The Institute of Internal Auditors. https://na.theiia.org/standards-guidance/Public%20Documents/PP%20The%20Three%20Lines%20of%20Defense%20in%20Effective%20Risk%20Management%20and%20Control.pdf.

IIA. January 2013b. *Standards & Guidance—International Professional Practices Framework*. Institute of Internal Auditors, The IIA Research Foundation. https://global.theiia.org/standards-guidance/Pages/Standards-and-Guidance-IPPF.aspx.

IIRC. July 2013a. *Value Creation: Background Paper for <IR>*. The International Integrated Reporting Council. http://integratedreporting.org/wp-content/uploads/2013/08/Background-Paper-Value-Creation.pdf.

IIRC. December 2013b. *International Integrated Reporting <IR> Framework*. International Integrated Reporting Council. http://integratedreporting.org/wp-content/uploads/2013/12/13-12-08-THE-INTERNATIONAL-IR-FRAMEWORK-2-1.pdf.

IIRC. July 2015. *Assurance on <IR>: Overview of Feedback and Call to Action*. International Integrated Reporting Council. http://integratedreporting.org/wp-content/uploads/2015/07/IIRC-Assurance-Overview-July-2015.pdf.

IMA. 2006. *Enterprise Risk Management: Frameworks, Elements, and Integration*. The Institute of Management Accountants. http://www.imanet.org/docs/default-source/research/sma/erm_frameworks-elements-and-integration.pdf?sfvrsn=2.

IOD SA. September 2009. *King Code of Governance for South Africa 2009*. Institute of Directors South Africa. http://www.iodsa.co.za/?kingIII.

ISACA. 2009. *An Introduction to the Business Model for Information Security*. The Information Systems Audit and Control Association. http://www.isaca.org/Knowledge-Center/BMIS/Documents/IntrotoBMIS.pdf.

ISACA. 2013. *ITAFTM—Professional Practices Framework for IS Audit/Assurance*, 3rd Edition. The Information Systems Audit and Control Association. http://www.isaca.org/Knowledge-Center/Research/Documents/ITAF-3rd-Edition_fmk_Eng_1014.pdf.

ISF. June 2014. *The Standard of Good Practice for Information Security*. Information Security Forum. https://www.securityforum.org/tool/the-standard-of-good-practice-for-information-security/.

ISO. 2009. *ISO 31000:2009: Risk Management—Principles and Guidelines*. International Standards Organization. http://www.iso.org/iso/catalogue_detail?csnumber=43170.

ISO. 2012. *ISO 22301:2012 Societal Security—Business Continuity Management Systems—Requirements*. International Standards Organization. http://www.iso.org/iso/catalogue_detail?csnumber=50038.

ISO. 2013. *ISO/IEC 27001:2013 Information Technology—Security Techniques—Information Security Management Systems—Requirements*. International Standards Organization. http://www.iso.org/iso/catalogue_detail?csnumber=54534.

ITIL. 2011. *ITIL Lifecycle Publication Suite*. Information Technology Infrastructure Library. http://www.itgovernance.co.uk/shop/p-824-itil-lifecycle-publication-suite.aspx.

Kovacich G.L. and Halibozek E.P. March 2003. *The Manager's Handbook for Corporate Security: Establishing and Managing a Successful Assets Protection Program*. Butterworth-Heinemann, Boston, MA.

KPMG. October 2009. *Enterprise Risk Management: The 3 Lines of Defense*, Audit Committee Forum Volume 1. KPMG, Thailand. http://www.acithailand.org/aci/event/AC_forum/vol01/ACIWebsite-Vol1_20Oct.pdf.

Lyons S. 2006a. Corporate defence: Are stakeholders interests adequately defended? *The Journal of Operational Risk*, Vol. 1, Issue 2, Summer 2006: 67–73.

Lyons S. October 16, 2006b. *Corporate Defence Management: A Strategic Imperative*. The Bank Director (www.bankdirector.com). http://papers.ssrn.com/sol3/papers.cfm?abstract_id=1032576.

Lyons S. November 16, 2006c. *An Executive Guide to Corporate Defence Management*. The RiskCenter (www.riskcenter.com). http://www.riscinternational.ie/CDMGuide.pdf.

Lyons S. May 2009a. *The Requirement for a Director of Corporate Defence in UK Banking Institutions*. Submission to the Walker Review of Corporate Governance of UK Banking Industry. https://www.frc.org.uk/Our-Work/Publications/Corporate-Governance/Review-of-the-effectiveness-of-the-Combined-Code-C/Responses-to-March-consultation-on-the-2009-Review/RISC-International-(Ireland).aspx.

Lyons S. 2009b. Optimized corporate defense programs: A 5 step roadmap. *EDPACS: The EDP Audit, Control, and Security Newsletter*, Vol. XL, Issue 1: 1–15. Taylor & Francis Group.

Lyons S. March 2009c. *Corporate Defense Insights: Dispatches from the Front Line*. Continuity Central. http://www.continuitycentral.com/seanlyons.pdf.

Lyons S. July 2010. *Security as a Critical Component of Corporate Defense*. The Conference Board Executive Action Report, No. 330. http://www.conferenceboard.ca/e-library/abstract.aspx?did=3649.

Lyons S. October 2011. *Corporate Oversight and Stakeholder Lines of Defense*. The Conference Board Executive Action Report, No. 365. https://www.conference-board.org/topics/publicationdetail.cfm?publicationid=2021.

Lyons S. April 2012a. *Achieving a Healthy Balance Between Offense and Defense in 21st Century Capitalism*. Submission to the Management Innovation Exchange (MIX) HBR/McKinsey M-Prize for Management Innovation—The Long-Term Capitalism Challenge. http://www.managementexchange.com/hack/achieving-healthy-balance-between-offense-and-defense-21st-century-capitalism.

Lyons S. 2012b. Defending our stakeholders: Corporate defence management explored. *The Business Continuity and Resilience Journal*, Vol. 1, Issue 3, Q3 2012: 34–48.

Lyons S. 2012c. *Corporate Defense Management (CDM): A Multi-Dimensional Framework*. Riscinternational YouTube Video. http://www.youtube.com/watch?v=vLoA8U0GZHI.

Lyons S. May 9, 2013. *Enterprise Defense Management: Internal Auditors to the Fore*. Keynote address to the Asian Confederation of Institutes of Internal Auditors Chief Audit Executives Leadership Forum, Mumbai, India. http://papers.ssrn.com/sol3/papers.cfm?abstract_id=2304665.

Lyons S. 2014. Striking a balance: Offence v defence. *The Ethical Boardroom Magazine*, Winter 2014 Edition: 138–140.

Lyons S. 2015. Enterprise risk management and the five lines of corporate defense. *The Journal of Enterprise Risk Management*, Vol. 1, Issue 1: 72–97.

Martin A.P. October 2008. *The Advanced Shotokan Karate Bible: Black Belt and Beyond*. Firefly Books, Richmond Hill, Ontario, Canada.

McCrie R.D. October 2002. *Readings in Security Management: Principles and Practices*. American Society for Industrial Security International, Alexandria, VA.

McKinsey & Co. December 2012. *Enterprise Risk Management: What's Different in the Corporate World and Why*. McKinsey & Company. http://www.mckinsey.com/search.aspx?q=%22enterprise+risk+management+what%27s+different+in+the+corporate+world+and+why%22.

MOD. December 2010. *How Defence Works: Defence Framework*. Ministry of Defence. https://www.gov.uk/government/uploads/system/uploads/attachment_data/file/27372/defenceframework_dec10.pdf.

NACD. October 2009. *Report of the NACD Blue Ribbon Commission—Risk Governance: Balancing Risk and Reward*. National Association of Corporate Directors. https://www.nacdonline.org/Store/ProductDetail.cfm?ItemNumber=675.

NICE. May 2014. *National Cybersecurity Workforce Framework*. National Initiative for Cybersecurity Education. http://csrc.nist.gov/nice/framework/.

NIST. March 2011. *Managing Information Security Risk: Organization, Mission, and Information System View*. National Institute of Standards and Technology. http://www.nist.gov/customcf/get_pdf.cfm?pub_id=908030.

NIST. February 2014. *Framework for Improving Critical Infrastructure Cybersecurity*. National Institute of Standards and Technology. http://www.nist.gov/cyberframework/upload/cybersecurity-framework-021214.pdf.

NYSE. December 2014. *NYSE: Corporate Governance Guide*. New York Stock Exchange. https://www.nyse.com/publicdocs/nyse/listing/NYSE_Corporate_Governance_Guide.pdf.

OCEG. December 2006. *Red Book: Foundation Guidelines*. The Open Compliance and Ethics Group. http://www.oceg.org.

OCEG. August 2007. *Internal Audit Guide: Assessing Governance, Risk, Compliance and Ethics Capabilities*. Open Compliance and Ethics Group. http://www.oceg.org.

OCEG. April 2009. *GRC Capability Model "Red Book" 2.0*. Open Compliance and Ethics Group. http://www.oceg.org.

OECD. 2004. *OECD Principles of Corporate Governance*. Organization for Economic Co-Operation and Development. http://www.oecd.org/daf/ca/corporategovernanceprinciples/31557724.pdf.

OECD. February 2009. *The Corporate Governance Lessons Learned from the Financial Crisis*. Organization for Economic Co-operation and Development. http://www.oecd.org/finance/financial-markets/42229620.pdf.

OECD. September 2015. *G20/OECD Principles of Corporate Governance: OECD Report to G20 Finance Ministers and Central Bank Governors*. Organization for Economic Co-operation and Development. http://www.oecd.org/daf/ca/Corporate-Governance-Principles-ENG.pdf.

PRMIA. 2015. *Professional Risk Managers' Handbook—2015 Edition: A Comprehensive Guide to Current Theory and Best Practices*. The Professional Risk Managers International Association, PRMIA Publications, Wilmington, DE.

PWC. April 2008. *Three Lines of Defence: How to Take the Burden Out of Compliance*. PricewaterhouseCoopers, Insurance Digest, European Edition. http://www.pwc.com/gx/en/insurance/pdf/three_lines_of_defence.pdf.

Scandizzo S. April 2013. *Risk and Governance: A Framework for Banking Organisations*. Risk Books, London, UK.

SCCE. August 2010. *A Compliance & Ethics Program on a Dollar a Day: How Small Companies Can Have Effective Programs*. The Society of Corporate Compliance and Ethics. http://www.corporatecompliance.org/Portals/1/PDF/Resources/CEProgramDollarADay-Murphy.pdf.

SCCE. 2015. *The Complete Compliance and Ethics Manual*. The Society of Corporate Compliance and Ethics, Minneapolis, MN.

SEI. May 2007. *Introducing the CERT Resiliency Engineering Framework: Improving the Security and Sustainability Processes*. Software Engineering Institute, Carnegie Mellon University. https://resources.sei.cmu.edu/asset_files/TechnicalReport/2007_005_001_14876.pdf.

Standards Australia. 2005. *AS 5037-2005 Knowledge Management—A Guide*. Standards Australia. http://infostore.saiglobal.com/EMEA/Details.aspx?ProductID=320622.

Swanson D. 2010. *Swanson on Internal Auditing: Raising the Bar*. IT Governance Publishing, Cambridgeshire, UK.

Taleb N.N. May 2007. *The Black Swan: The Impact of the Highly Improbable*. Penguin Books Ltd, London, UK.

Taleb N.N. November 2012. *Antifragile: Things That Gain from Disorder*. Random House Publishing Group, New York.

UNCTAD. October 2010. *Corporate Governance in the Wake of the Financial Crisis*. The United Nations Conference on Trade and Development. http://www.unctad-docs.org/files/CG-in-Wake-of-Fin-Crisis-Full-Report.pdf.

US Government. 1964. Public Papers of the Presidents of the United States: John F. Kennedy, 1963. US Government Printing Office, Washington, DC.

USSC. November 1991. *United States Sentencing Commission Guidelines Manual*. United States Sentencing Commission. http://www.ussc.gov/sites/default/files/pdf/guidelines-manual/1991/manual-pdf/1991_Guidelines_Manual_Full.pdf.

WEF. January 2011. *Global Risks Report 2011*, 6th Edition. World Economic Forum. http://www.weforum.org/reports/global-risks-report-2011.

WEF. January 2013. *Global Risks 2013*, 8th Edition. World Economic Forum. http://www.weforum.org/reports/global-risks-2013-eighth-edition.

WEF. January 2015. *Global Risks 2015*, 10th Edition. World Economic Forum. http://www.weforum.org/reports/global-risks-report-2015.

# Index

For Product Safety Concerns and Information please contact our EU
representative GPSR@taylorandfrancis.com Taylor & Francis Verlag GmbH,
Kaufingerstraße 24, 80331 München, Germany

Printed and bound by CPI Group (UK) Ltd, Croydon, CR0 4YY

01/05/2025

01858442-0002